THE CINDERELLA SERVICE

COASTAL COMMAND 1939–1945

THE CINDERELLA SERVICE

COASTAL COMMAND 1939–1945

by

Andrew W. A. Hendrie

Pen & Sword
AVIATION

First published in Great Britain in 2006 by
Pen & Sword Aviation
An imprint of
Pen & Sword Books Ltd
47 Church Street
Barnsley
South Yorkshire
S70 2AS

ISBN 1 84415 346 0

ISBN 978 1 84415 346 6

A CIP catalogue record for this book is
available from the British Library

Printed and bound in England
By CPI UK

Pen & Sword Books Ltd incorporates the Imprints of Pen & Sword Aviation,
Pen & Sword Maritime, Pen & Sword Military, Wharncliffe Local history,
Pen & Sword Select, Pen & Sword Military Classics and Leo Cooper.

For a complete list of Pen & Sword titles please contact
PEN & SWORD BOOKS LIMITED
47 Church Street, Barnsley, South Yorkshire, S70 2AS, England
E-mail: enquiries@pen-and-sword.co.uk
Website: www.pen-and-sword.co.uk

Contents

DEDICATED TO MY WIFE AND MY FAMILY,
WHO HAVE BEEN EVER SUPPORTIVE

Illustrations

Charts

Preface

In this book I have attempted to show the part played by Coastal Command in the Second World War. I have given emphasis to the two main roles of Coastal Command, namely its work in anti-submarine warfare in the Battle of the Atlantic, and the Command's anti-shipping operations against both warships and merchant vessels. Coastal's other roles, including meteorological flights, air-sea rescue, minelaying and photo-reconnaissance, have also been considered.

By the nature of such work, Coastal Command did not gain the recognition it deserved, and was overshadowed by Fighter and Bomber Commands, which generally were given priority in respect of aircraft and equipment.

As the prime needs of an air force in war were aircraft and armament, I devoted two chapters to those subjects, taking the view that some understanding of such technical aspects are essential for a proper appreciation of Coastal Command's work.

The book is based on the following primary sources: operational records of squadrons, the Command's records, and some Cabinet files. Additionally, I have corresponded with many Coastal Command veterans and interviewed others. The retrospective views of some of those former aircrew have been included.

My 'research' really began on 3 April 1939, when I joined the RAF for training as aircrew, but my wartime operational flying with Coastal Command began in February 1942 and ended in May 1945. I therefore consider that this book, which I can claim was written from the inside, presents the subject by one who was actively involved.

The theme is that although Coastal Command was the 'Cinderella' in respect of aircraft, equipment and publicity, it surmounted those limitations and made a considerable contribution to the Allies' war effort.

Andrew W.A. Hendrie, BA, ARHistS, ARAes, PhD

Acknowledgements

I am indebted to members of the Aircrew Association and the Coastal Command and Maritime Association who were prepared to write to me and offer assistance. They included veterans, not only from the United Kingdom, but also from Australia and Canada. Additionally, I was put in touch with other Australians who had served with Coastal Command, due to the help of Flt Lt Ray Kelly, BEM, RAAF. A considerable number of Canadians operated with Coastal Command, and many made contact with me.

Wing Commander Geoffrey Bartlett, who was my flight commander on No. 224 Squadron, has aided me throughout, in all my Coastal Command endeavours. Dr David Cheaney has given constant encouragement and help. My supervisor, Dr Mark Connelly at the University of Kent, has been ever patient in his endeavour to keep me on a true course, and I have greatly appreciated his guidance. My wife, Evelyn, above all, has been ever supportive, and of help, throughout the course of this project.

I am aware that my writing is bound to have been influenced by those whom I met in the RAF from April 1939 and in the following years. They included instructors such as my flight commander at No. 6 (Coastal) OTU RAF Thornaby, the late Sir Denis Spotswood, the late Sir Robert Craven and the late Wing Commander 'Bertie' Leach. I have quoted directly or indirectly from their letters, as also from many others who are now listed, including four former enemy submariners.

May I now acknowledge help from all of the following:

Angell, Wg Cdr M., No. 580 Squadron; Bartlett, Wg Cdr G.C.C., AFC, Nos 224, 59 Squadrons; Baveystock, Flt Lt L., DSO, DFC, DFM, No. 201 Squadron; Bednall, Wg Cdr D., No. 230 Squadron; Bevan-John, Gp Capt D., No. 228 Squadron; Brock, D; Busbridge, Capt D., No. 224 Squadron; Campbell, Flg Off G., DFC, RCAF, No. 162 Squadron RCAF; Campbell, Wg Cdr R.I.; Cook, Gp Capt. D., OBE; Craven, AM Sir Robert, KBE, CB, OBE, DFC, Nos 201, 210, 228 Squadrons; Cremer, *K/Kapt* P., U-333; De Liefde, *Lt* T., RNethNAS; Edwards, Flt Lt Gron, No. 233 Squadron; FitzGerald,Gp Capt. J.B., No. 500 Squadron RAAF; Flynn, Flt Lt P., DFC, RCAF, No. 404 RCAF Squadron; Giese, O. U-405; Green, Flg Off J., No. 179 Squadron; Greswell, Air Cdre J., No. 172 Squadron; Hodgkinson, ACM Sir Derek, KCB, CBE, CB, DFC, AFC, No. 220 Squadron; Hodgkinson, Capt V., DFC, RAAF, No. 10 Squadron RAAF; Jones, Flt Lt J., RAAF, No. 608 Squadron; Johnson, C., MSc, FRAeS; Lynham, Gp Capt. P., DSO, No. 279 Squadron; McGill, R.; Marrows, Flt Lt D., DSO, DFC, RAAF, No. 461 Squadron; Martin, Wg Cdr D., OBE, BSc, No. 201 Squadron; Page, Flt Lt C., DFC, RCAF, No. 404 Squadron; Quinlan, B., RCAF; Rackcliff, P., No. 580 Squadron; Romanes, Wg Cdr J., DFC, No. 206 Squadron; Shuleman, Sqn Ldr S. DSO, DFC, RCAF, No. 404 Squadron; Simmons, R. No. 143 Squadron; Skaugstad, Per; Smith, Sqn Ldr A. MRAeS, No. 206 Squadron; Smith, M; Spooner, Sqn Ldr T., DSO, DFC, Nos 53, 221 Squadrons; Spotswood, MRAF Sir Denis, GCB, CBE, DSO, DFC, No. 500 Squadron; Stiebler, *K/Kapt* W., U-461; Taylor, Sqn Ldr C., DFC, RCAF, No. 407 Squadron; Tomkins, Air Cdre M.; Troughton, F., HMS *Brocklesby*; Warren, L., Nos 459, 38 Squadrons; Whittaker, D., No. 279 Squadron; Willis, D.; Winfield, E., No. 1404 Flt; Womersley, Wg Cdr L., DFC, No. 224 Squadron; Wood, Capt E., DFC, USN, VP84; Yorston, Dr R., No. 269 Squadron; Zesterman, G., U-533, U-155.

Abbreviations and Glossary

AA	Anti-Aircraft
AAC	Army Air Corps
AAF	Army Air Force
ACHQ	Area Combined Headquarters
Air Cdre	Air Commodore
ACM	Air Chief Marshal
A/Flt Lt	Acting Flight Lieutenant
AHQ	Area Headquarters
Aldis Lamp	A lamp used to transmit messages in Morse code by operating a mirror and sighting through a telescopic sight
AM	Air Marshal
AM	Air Ministry
Amatol	A chemical explosive used in such as DCs
AOC	Air Officer Commanding
A/S	Anti-Submarine
ASR	Air-Sea Rescue
ASV	Aircraft-to-Surface Vessel; equipment which transmitted electro-magnetic waves that would be reflected back by vessels, producing a 'blip' on a cathode ray tube
BEF	British Expeditionary Force
Canso	The Canadian version of the Catalina amphibian
CFI	Chief Flying Instructor
C-in-C	Commander-in-Chief
CLA	Creeping Line Ahead; a navigational search method
CO	Commanding Officer
CRT	Cathode Ray Tube (as used in radar and ASV)
Cross-Over Patrol	A navigational patrol method
DC	Depth Charge
Depth bomb	A bomb designed to be dropped from medium height against U-boats
D/F	Direction Finding
DFC	Distinguished Flying Cross
DR	Dead Reckoning (navigation)
E/A	Enemy Aircraft
ETA	Estimated Time of Arrival

FAA	Fleet Air Arm
Flt Cdr	Flight Commander
Flt Lt	Flight Lieutenant
Flg Off	Flying Officer
Flt Sgt	Flight Sergeant
FTR	Failed to Return (from operations)
Gp Capt	Group Captain
GEE	Code name for a radar type of navigation but used in conjunction with a specialised chart; it was suitable for North Sea operations
GOC-in-C	General Officer Commanding-in-Chief
HE	High Explosive
'High Tea'	Code for sonobuoys used by Coastal Command to detect submerged U-boats
HMS	His Majesty's Ship
HQCC	Headquarters Coastal Command
HSL	High-Speed Launch as used for ASR
IFF	Identification Friend or Foe. An automatic transmitter in aircraft for its identification, but which could be used to home in other aircraft
KIA	Killed in Action
MAD	Magnetic Anomaly Detection
Mae West	An RAF term for a lifejacket that could be inflated by mouth or by a CO_2 bottle
MC bomb	Medium Case bomb
MID	Mentioned in Dispatches
ML	Motor Launch
MRAF	Marshal of the Royal Air Force
MTB	Motor Torpedo-Boat
MU	Maintenance Unit
MV	Merchant Vessel
Ops	Operational flying
OTU	Operational Training Unit
PBY	USN code for Catalina aircraft
Plt Off	Pilot Officer
PRU	Photo-Reconnaissance Unit
RAAF	Royal Australian Air Force
Radar	An American term applied to equipment such as the British ASV
RAF	Royal Air Force
RCAF	Royal Canadian Air Force
Retro bombs	Used in conjunction with MAD gear against submerged U-boats
RNethNAS	Royal Netherlands Naval Air Service
RNZAF	Royal New Zealand Air Force
RP	Rocket Projectile

R/T	Radio Telephony
Schnorchel	Tube fitted to U-boats to enable them to use diesel engines when submerged
Sgt	Sergeant
Sqn Ldr	Squadron Leader
SNO	Senior Naval Officer
Sperrbrecher	A heavily armed merchant ship used by Germany to protect its convoys
Sqn	Squadron
SS	Steamship
Torpex	An explosive filling for the later type of DCs
U/S	Unserviceable
USN	United States Navy
VP	USN code for a squadron with heavier-than-air patrol planes.
Wg Cdr	Wing Commander
W/op	Wireless Operator
Wop/AG	Wireless Operator/Air Gunner
W/T	Wireless Telephony

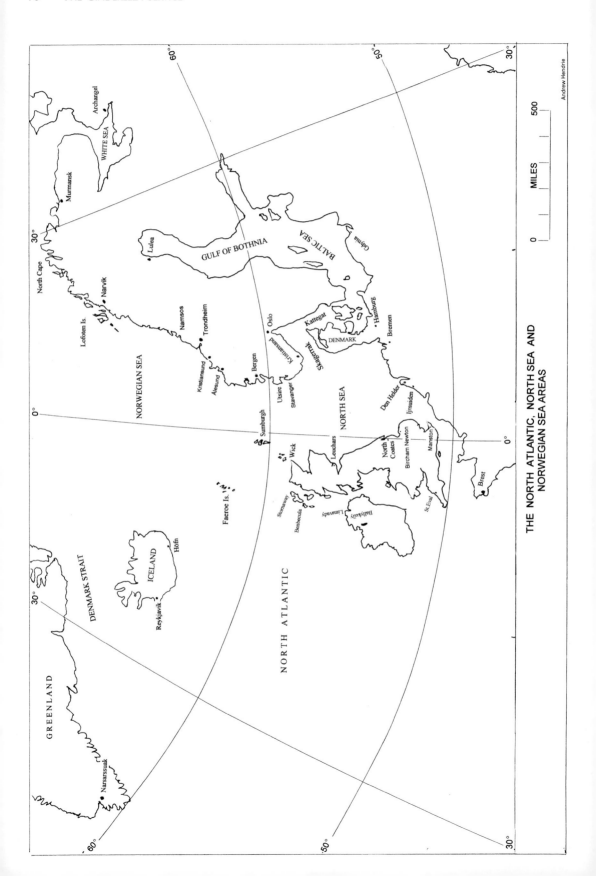

THE NORTH ATLANTIC, NORTH SEA AND
NORWEGIAN SEA AREAS

0   500

MILES

Andrew Hendrie

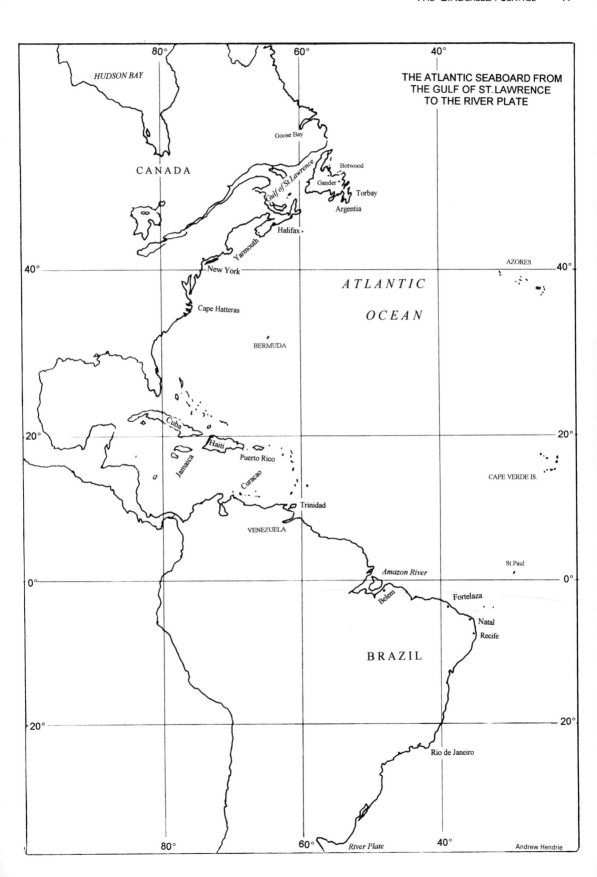

THE ATLANTIC SEABOARD FROM
THE GULF OF ST.LAWRENCE
TO THE RIVER PLATE

HUDSON BAY

CANADA

Goose Bay

Gulf of St.Lawrence

Botwood

Gander

Torbay

Argentia

Halifax

Yarmouth

New York

AZORES

ATLANTIC

Cape Hatteras

OCEAN

BERMUDA

Cuba

Haiti

Jamaica

Puerto Rico

CAPE VERDE IS.

Curacao

Trinidad

VENEZUELA

St.Paul

Amazon River

Belem

Fortelaza

Natal

Recife

BRAZIL

Rio de Janeiro

River Plate

Andrew Hendrie

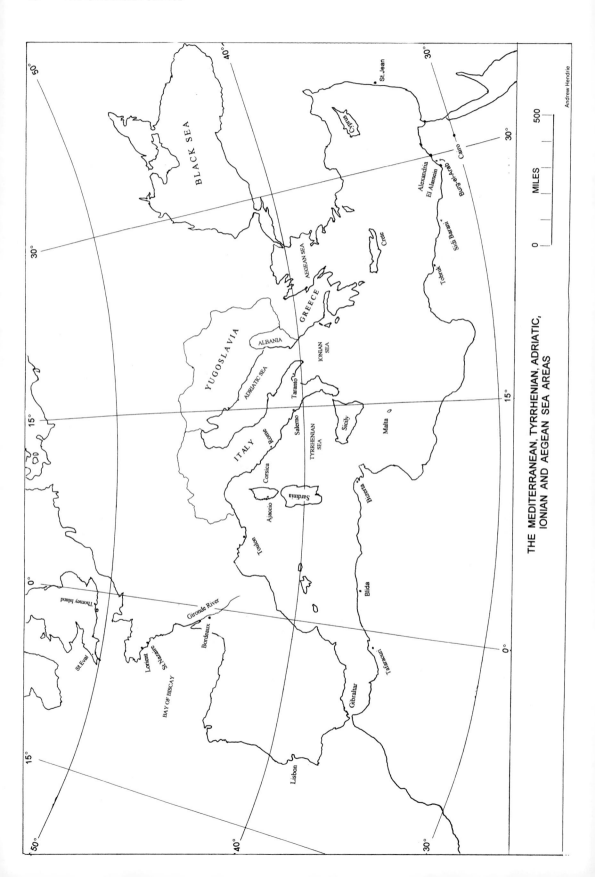

THE MEDITERRANEAN, TYRRHENIAN, ADRIATIC,
IONIAN AND AEGEAN SEA AREAS

Introduction

No official history has been devoted to the part played by Coastal Command in the Second World War, although the three small volumes *Royal Air Force 1939–1945* by Denis Richards and Hilary St.G. Saunders give references to Coastal Command throughout.

In their preface Richards and Saunders state a reason for that limitation: 'To have given ... subjects the consideration they deserve would have involved writing a history, not in three volumes but in thirty.' They continue: 'The authors of the full length official military history of the war, ... will have more space at their disposal'.[1]

The full-length official work, *History of the Second World War*, as its general editor, Professor J.R.M. Butler, states, was 'to provide a broad survey of events from an inter-service point of view'.[2]

One section of the major British official history of the Second World War where one might hope for Coastal Command to have gained more coverage, was in *The War at Sea*. Its three volumes were, however, written by a naval officer, Captain S.W. Roskill, who obviously considered Coastal Command as an adjunct to the Royal Navy, rather than as a service in its own right. As Professor Butler states in his preface: 'Captain Roskill is concerned with events as they influenced the decisions at the Admiralty.'[3]

Roskill, in his 'Conclusion and Inquiry', does give a reason for the lack of priority to Coastal Command: 'Because our air strategy was concentrated mainly on the bombing of Germany ...'.[4] Roskill also, in his conclusions, refers to the lack of 'an effective weapon' in 1939 for Coastal's Sunderlands and Hudsons.[5]

The one British official publication devoted to Coastal Command was a booklet entitled *Coastal Command*; published in 1942 and thus limited to Coastal's operations up to that time. It was written by Hilary St.G. Saunders (although not so stated), and due to wartime security, lacks the details that one would expect in an official history.

Coastal Command was almost certainly intended as wartime propaganda, but, nevertheless, was written from the 'inside', and is authentic.[6]

America has published official histories for both its Navy and its Air Force, and both refer to Coastal Command, as units of the United States Navy and United States Army Air Corps operated within Coastal Command, albeit to a limited extent.

The author of the United States Navy's Second World War history, Professor S.E. Morison, devotes two of his fifteen volumes to the Battle of the Atlantic. In the first of those, he states that the RAF 'Was not equipped to fight submarines.' He adds that Coastal Command was set up with '19 squadrons and about 220 planes, practically a separate air force'. This, for Morison, was a 'typical British compromise' It nevertheless 'succeeded in driving submarines out of the Western Approaches ...'.[7] In his introduction to Volume X, Professor Morison states that Coastal Command 'had few aircraft suitable for antisubmarine operations'.[8] Thus, Morison supports the view, in his two volumes devoted to the Battle of the Atlantic, that in that battle, Coastal Command remained the Cinderella.

One of the standard American histories is *The Army Air Forces in World War II*, which was prepared under W.F. Craven and J.L. Cate. Three of its seven volumes make reference to Coastal Command. They make the same points about the Command as other official historians: of its deficiencies in the Battle of the Bay: 'The effort suffered from lack of enough long-range aircraft, lack of a "balanced" anti-submarine force ... and lack of adequate radar equipment and special weapons'.[9] They rightly state that 'the Admiralty's control over the RAF Coastal Command [was] a jurisdiction principally concerned with the mission to be performed'.[10]

Italy's *Ufficio Storico Della Marina Militare* has published a series on maritime operations in the Second World War: *La Marina Italiana Nella Seconda Guerra Mondiale*.[11] The volumes on Italy's submarine operations in the Mediterranean are in the form of the operational logs of its submarines. They demonstrate, although that could not have been the intention, the valuable part played by just a few Sunderlands from Coastal Command in countering a submarine menace.[12]

The official Italian history of her submarines operating in the Atlantic from the French Gironde to as far west as the Brazilian coast is notable in giving a detailed account of the first successful use of the Leigh Light by Coastal Command. It covers, also, their voyages round to East Africa and to Singapore.[13] Volume IV covers the Italian naval surface operations in the Mediterranean from June 1940 to March 1941, and thus includes the crucial Battle of Cape Matapan, in which a Sunderland from Coastal Command played a key role.

The Italian historians do not refer to the deficiencies of Coastal Command, rather do they report on the attacks and sightings made by Sunderlands, and it is notable that the only aircraft illustrated within four volumes of their official history is a Sunderland.[14]

Admiral of the Fleet Viscount Cunningham in his *A Sailor's Odyssey* states, as do other writers: 'Coastal Command was woefully short of aircraft, particularly aircraft of very long range.'[15] Of Coastal Command during

Operation Torch, Cunningham states: 'The demands upon Coastal Command of the RAF were heavy ...',[16] and comments on the 'persistent good work' in attacks on U-boats in that operation.[17] Admiral Cunningham, in his summing-up of Operation Overlord, says: 'Our comparative immunity to submarine attack was principally due to the enthusiastic efficiency of Coastal Command.'[18]

Four of Coastal Command's Commanders-in-Chief have published books that are autobiographical; the exception is Air Chief Marshal Sir Philip Joubert's *Birds and Fishes*. He gives as a sub-title, *The Story of Coastal Command*, which, for Joubert, begins in 1908. During the 1939–1945 war, Sir Philip was in command from June 1941 until February 1943, the period when the maximum effort was expected of the Command, but with very limited resources.[19] Some of Joubert's chapter headings reflect the Command's standing as he saw it, with 'Make do and Mend', 'The Dark Days' and 'A Rough Road'. 'Make do and Mend' outlines the limited resources of the Command in 1939.

In his final chapter, Sir Philip states, 'The Cinderella Command once again sits forlorn in the ashes ... and ... the cold hand of the Treasury ... had fallen on Coastal Command more heavily than elsewhere.'[20] In a chapter on anti-submarine warfare (ASW), Joubert adds, 'For Churchill ... Bomber Command was the favourite child. Fighter Command had done its job in the Battle of Britain. Coastal Command was merely an adjunct to a defensively minded Navy.'[21] The index to his *Story of Coastal Command* appears almost as a list of the Command's personnel, whether sergeant, flight lieutenant or air marshal. History for Sir Philip was truly a humanity, and from records it is obvious that he made every attempt to meet men who were in the front line.

Marshal of the RAF Sir John Slessor's *The Central Blue*, in chapters on Coastal

Command, states, 'I ... tried to introduce an impression of the human side of history.'[22] That, Slessor has achieved. He refers to 'my Coastal crews', and adds, 'The crews of Coastal Command certainly did not get their mead of public recognition at the time, nor have they since.'[23]

Lord Douglas, who succeeded Slessor as Commander-in-Chief, in his autobiography, *Years of Command*, devotes a chapter to Coastal Command, 'Constant Endeavour' (the Command's motto). In another chapter, however, Lord Douglas makes the same point as other writers: 'During the early part of the war, Coastal Command had to make do with aircraft which were both outdated and insufficient on numbers ....'[24]

That aspect is reiterated by A.J.P. Taylor in his *English History 1914–1945*, with: 'The Air Ministry, set on bombing Germany, grudged supplying aeroplanes for Coastal Command .... Every now and then, during the worst moments of the shipping war, the War Cabinet intervened on the naval side; in no time at all, the Air Ministry pulled things back to their standing obsession of the strategic bombing offensive.'[25]

The only thesis, so far as is known, concerning Coastal Command, is Dr C. Goulter's *A Forgotten Offensive*, with the sub-title *Royal Air Force Coastal Command's Anti-Shipping Campaign, 1940–1945*.

Dr Goulter rightly states in her preface, 'The closest Coastal Command came to having its own official history was the coverage it received in naval historian Stephen Roskill's *The War at Sea*'.[26] Goulter's editor, Sebastian Cox, states, of Goulter's thesis, that 'The work is based on primary sources.' Regretfully, the bibliography, in listing primary sources, lacks detail, and gives such as 'Air 15 Coastal Command 1936–1965', of which there are hundreds of 'pieces'; and 'Air 27 Squadron Operations Record Books', of which there are thousands of pieces.

Nevertheless, Mr Cox advises that it 'is an important contribution to the history of economic warfare'.[27] Certainly, Dr Goulter has given much attention to the economics of Coastal's anti-shipping operations, and some emphasis towards the Beaufighter strike wings.

The prolific author Chaz Bowyer, in two of his books that were devoted to Coastal Command, makes the same point as Goulter; thus: 'No full academic history of the vital part played ... by RAF Coastal Command has ever been published to date.'[28] Again: 'The full history of RAF Coastal Command has still to be written.'[29]

John Terraine, in his *Right of the Line*, subtitled *The RAF in the European War 1939–1945*, rightly refers to Coastal Command as the Cinderella; in fact, he gives that description three times. Thus: 'The true position in September 1939 ... of the three operational Commands, one (Coastal) was an acknowledged Cinderella, weak in numbers and almost entirely equipped with obsolescent aircraft ...', which Terraine bases on its stated forces.[30] On the positive side, Terraine gives some of Coastal Command's achievements, which, 'unaided, included 169 German U-boats out of 326 destroyed by shore-based aircraft alone'.[31] On that same page, Terraine quotes Slessor, that Coastal crews did not get their mead of public recognition. Terraine again quotes Slessor, who considered that this lack of recognition of Coastal Command was due to Churchill.[32]

Probably the most useful publication devoted to Coastal Command's anti-submarine operations is Norman Franks' *Search, Find and Kill*. It is based on official operational records but includes accounts from former aircrew. Franks' invaluable introduction includes the same point made by other authors: 'Its aircraft were few and the Command was at least third on the list of any priorities of aircraft.'[33]

Professor Richard Overy, in his *The Air War 1939–1945*, states that it is a 'general history' and 'to show two things': 'Why the Allies won the air war' and 'how important air power was to the achievement of overall victory'.[34] He acknowledges that of defence tasks 'the most vital was the Battle of the Atlantic ...',[35] and that although 'the land-based bomber was seen to be the key to sea-power ... they ... became so many Cinderellas'.[36]

A conflicting view of Coastal Command is that given in *Bomber Offensive* by Marshal of the Royal Air Force Sir Arthur Harris. He rightly refers to some priority being given to Coastal Command in respect of radar; and also that some squadrons were transferred to Coastal Command.[37]

A German view of Coastal Command in the U-boat war is perhaps best given by *Fregattenkapitän* Günter Hessler, who gained help from Professor Jürgen Rohwer, a former *Leutnant-zur-See* in preparing *The U-boat War in the Atlantic*.[38]

While obviously written with the bias of a U-boat commander, it indirectly displays the positive aspects of Coastal Command, such as driving the U-boats westwards, and the obvious respect the enemy had for the Sunderlands and Beaufighters with their aircrew.

From the foregoing, it is apparent why no official history of the Coastal Command has been published: the Air Ministry gave precedence to Bomber Command, the Admiralty to the Royal Navy, and there was indifference on the part of Churchill. HM Treasury cut short even the official naval historians' work.[39]

The Research

I obtained microfilm copies of records from the National Archives of documents stemming from the Command's headquarters, copies of Cabinet files and operational records of many squadrons.[40] These were, however, supplied at exorbitant cost, and of 956 'pieces' devoted to Coastal Command under 'Air 15', I received a list of about two dozen pieces that were directly available on microfilm.[41] Coastal Command is the obvious Cinderella in respect of its official records. Regrettably, copies of some records are now unobtainable, with the advice given on some microfilm that the NA was unable to copy the originals due to their bad condition.

I was able to obtain copies of records from Canada on free loan, and from the USN and AAF in America at nominal cost; likewise for RAAF records from Canberra.

Squadron intelligence officers and adjutants in Canadian units were responsible for keeping records, and only Canadian records appear to have been checked at the time. With Coastal Command having a series of detachments, away from responsible officers, some of those records were written in retrospect, and possibly by an office orderly. They vary in detail from barely one line to one or two pages, and may not always identify the crew of an aircraft.

In contrast, all Coastal Command's aircrew were required to keep a log that was countersigned on the squadrons every month. Many aircrew correspondents sent me photocopies of pages from their logbooks. Additionally, some sent photographs of attacks on ships and U-boats, or gave an analysis of some operations in conjunction with advice from former enemies.

Some aircrew veterans also sent copies of wartime letters and diaries. Such material was provided in addition to covering letters, written in retrospect. It is apparent from the latter that many aircrew had visual memories, and recalled scenes as they wrote, even after a lapse of fifty years. To check details of a sortie, such as names, date, time, serial number of aircraft, etc., aircrew may refer to their logbooks. I find, therefore, that aircrew correspondents are a more reliable source than official records; and generally, if there was any doubt, correspondents advised me accordingly. Some former aircrew visited me; I, in turn, visited others.

Additional sources have been squadron histories written by one or more squadron associations, which may or may not have been published, such as those for Nos 14 (RAF) and 10 (RAAF).[42] As these could be based on aircrew logbooks, or diaries of both groundcrew and aircrew, in addition to official records, I have found them one of the most reliable sources, albeit published post war. I have referred to a number of other publications, and they are listed in the bibliography.

The four wartime Commanders-in-Chief of Coastal Command, although generally remote from the front line, had direct reports from Groups and liaison officers such as Captain Peyton-Ward, RN, who debriefed aircrew who attacked U-boats. In the case of Sir Philip Joubert, he made a point, on occasions, of making direct contact with individual aircrew and squadron commanders. The official records of the Commanders-in-Chiefs' conferences therefore closely reflect operations and the general situation, but obviously from their points of view. Their dispatches and memoranda from their conferences represent an important primary source.

I have given emphasis to the two major roles of Coastal Command, namely anti-submarine operations (ASW) and anti-shipping operations. As the Command's operations were highly technical, I have written chapters on aircraft and armaments that were relevant to the Command. Coastal Command had a number of other roles; including air-sea rescue (ASR), Photographic Reconnaissance, and Meteorological Flights. I have therefore included a chapter on those aspects. Veterans of the Command are conscious of their 'Cinderella' status, and their views are given in retrospect.

My theme has been twofold; although the Cinderella Command came third in priority after its two 'sisters' (Bomber and Fighter Commands), it nevertheless achieved much, as is confirmed by its record.

Andrew W.A. Hendrie
Storrington, January 2004

CHAPTER ONE

Aircraft

INTRODUCTION

In this chapter I have considered the various aspects of aircraft that feature in the Command's records emanating from the four Commanders-in-Chief. Aspects that prevailed throughout the war were the role of Coastal Command, the aircraft available, their speed, range and endurance, production, procurement and engines. For that reason, I have depended to a considerable degree on the memoranda stemming from the meetings of Coastal Command's commanders. Armament and equipment are given in Chapter 2.

Secondary sources that refer to aircraft are seldom concerned specifically with Coastal Command's needs, but rather of the RAF as a whole. Thus A.J.P. Taylor refers specifically to aircraft production and the 'innovation' of Churchill appointing Beaverbrook as Minister of Aircraft Production, and the 'battle' that prevailed with Ernest Bevin, the Minister for Labour. As Taylor states, 'Beaverbrook could produce the goods. Only Bevin could produce the labour.' A.J.P. Taylor refers to the Air Ministry being set on bombing Germany and thus grudging the supply of aircraft to Coastal Command.[1]

Dr Goulter in her thesis on the strike wings deals with those aircraft applicable to Coastal Command anti-shipping campaign, and rightly gives most attention to the Beaufighter and Mosquito with which the strike wings were armed. Dr Goulter dismisses, however, the Anson and Hudson that initiated attacks by Coastal Command on enemy shipping with: 'Neither aircraft was particularly suited to a maritime function.'[2] The operational records demonstrate otherwise.

Richard Overy in his *The Air War 1939–1945* refers briefly to eight types of British aircraft, but they were bombers and fighters. Under 'Aircraft and Sea Power', however, Overy acknowledges that land-based aircraft were the key to sea power and that naval demands for purpose-built aircraft became the Cinderellas.[3]

Owen Thetford's comprehensive *Aircraft of the RAF Since 1918* gives technical details of most types of aircraft used by the RAF, and may be considered a standard work of reference.[4]

Denis Richards in the official RAF history states that Coastal Command was initially badly equipped due to priority being given to a 'fighter force … and a bomber force', and because the Allies had 'superiority in naval resources' Coastal Command came third in priority.[5]

The official naval historian, Captain Roskill, likewise refers to the deficiencies in Coastal Command's aircraft and touches upon the availability, speed and range of its aircraft.[6]

It is left to Sir Arthur Harris to complain, later in the war, that he was losing aircraft from Bomber Command in favour of Coastal Command, although he had no wish to use the American aircraft that went to Coastal Command.[7]

Despite such an unfavourable beginning in respect of aircraft, it will be seen that there was a progressive improvement throughout the war, but never to be completely resolved in the operational range of aircraft.

THE ROLE OF COASTAL COMMAND

As early as October 1937, the Senior Air Staff Officer (SASO) at Coastal Command's headquarters, Air Commodore G. Bromet, in a memo to the Air Officer Commander-in-Chief, Air Marshal Sir Frederick Bowhill, suggested that it was essential to create a modern defence organisation in cooperation with the Admiralty behind which Coastal Command could function, adding that both Fighter and Bomber Commands had clear roles.

Bromet gave the role of the Command in war against Germany as being to give warning of air raids approaching the coast; the prevention, if possible, of raiders approaching; and to assist in the protection of shipping by escorting convoys, anti-submarine patrols and reconnaissances for surface vessels.[8]

On 1 December 1937 the Air Ministry issued a directive that the primary role for Coastal Command would be reconnaissance in Home Waters, and cooperation with the Royal Navy in convoy protection. Additionally, in defence of British trade, offensive operations would be undertaken against surface vessels, submarines and enemy aircraft, as part of British trade protection, but the primary role was to remain reconnaissance. Earlier in 1937, the Commander-in-Chief of Coastal Command, Air Marshal Sir Frederick Bowhill, had obviously considered such requirements, and had suggested that a paper be submitted to the Air Ministry 'on the characteristics we require for our aircraft in General Reconnaissance squadrons'.[9]

The characteristics that Sir Frederick specified were speed, range, good armament and good navigational facilities. Additionally he proposed that aircraft might be constructed entirely of wood, and with engines that could be jettisoned. This was so that the aircraft would float if ditched.[10]

Throughout 1938 the availability of aircraft, their serviceability, their location and the provision of suitable bases were considered. The Admiralty had overall responsibility for maritime operations, and a discussion was held at the Admiralty on 15 December 1938 covering the Coastal Command and Naval plans. During that discussion an embryo convoy system was considered and the lack of the Navy's escort vessels emphasised. Because of this lack of vessels, the C-in-C Home Fleet was concerned about protecting his minelayers in the Dover Straits, and two squadrons, Nos 500 and 42, were specified for that duty.

Although no convoy system had been organised in December 1938, it was considered that protection would be required for Norwegian convoys, in the Minch Channel, and the east-coast and Dutch convoys. For the Western Approaches convoys, protection would be required in the English, Bristol, and St George's Channels. It was considered that the east-coast and Dutch convoys would require protection against air attack, and the Air Ministry was to consult Fighter Command for that purpose.[11]

By the end of June 1939 a memorandum was issued by the Air Officer Commanding-in-Chief Coastal Command, outlining its command structure and its duties.

At that time there were three operational Groups in the Command, with headquarters to coincide with those of the Naval Commanders-in-Chief at Plymouth, Rosyth and Nore, and Coastal Command would be formed that year. The role of the Command was then specified as:

(i)   To assist the Home Fleet in the detection and prevention of enemy vessels escaping from the North Sea to the Atlantic.

(ii) The provision of air patrols in cooperation with anti-submarine surface craft, or air escorts to convoys.

(iii) Air searches, when required, over Home Waters.

(iv) Provision of an air striking force for duty, mainly on the east-coast.

The AOC-in-C would order any readjustment of his forces according to conditions. Of the routine North Sea patrols, there was to be a continuous patrol from Montrose to the nearest point on the Norwegian coast (Obrestadt) every 45 minutes during daylight hours.

As the only aircraft available in sufficient numbers, the Avro Anson, lacked the range, submarine patrols would be established at the Norwegian end of the line. The submarines would be withdrawn when the Anson squadrons were re-equipped with the longer-range American Lockheed Hudson.[12]

In April 1940, at a conference held at the Air Ministry, the operational roles of the aircraft then available were given thus:

(i) General Reconnaissance – the flying-boats Sunderland, PBY4 (Catalina), Saro Lerwick and Singapore Mark IIIs.

Reconnaissance was to be by day or night over the sea and coasts of enemy territory to assist Naval, Land and Air Force in the protection of sea communications against sea-borne attack. Convoy escort by day and anti-submarine cooperation generally.

(ii) Bombing: high, low and shallow dive-bombing by day or night of both stationary and moving targets.

Hudsons, Beauforts and Bothas were to be used for reconnaissance by day or night in addition to bombing requirements. Nos 22 and 42 Squadrons with Beauforts were to be trained for torpedo attacks.

Ansons were to be used for reconnaissance, especially for convoy and anti-submarine patrols, but additionally for bombing.

These extreme measures indicate how desperate the situation was considered. They were made just a week after the invasion of Norway. At home, the obsolescent Singapore flying-boat must have been included of necessity; the Anson was certainly no bomber aircraft; and the Botha was to be proved unsuitable for operations.[13]

Prior to the invasion of Norway it had been decided that Sunderlands and PBYs (Catalinas) would be mainly employed in the Atlantic and the Arctic, 'where particularly long endurance is required'.[14] Air Chief Marshal Sir Philip Joubert succeeded Sir Frederick as Commander-in-Chief Coastal Command in June 1941, and was to express the role of the Command thus:

Recent experience shows conclusively that there are two main tasks which have to be carried out by this Command ... close escort of convoys up to the limit of endurance of present day aircraft and the sweeping an area ... for sighting, attacking or neutralising enemy submarines by forcing them to submerge. These two are complementary ... carried out only if Coastal Command possesses sufficient aircraft to do the jobs.

Thus the role of the Command was redefined. Joubert added that additional tasks were shipping reconnaissance, attacks on warships and merchant vessels and reconnaissance against possible invasion forces, and further that there was 'at present a tendency to force on to Coastal Command commitments which more properly belong to the Navy and to ship-borne aircraft'.[15]

AIRCRAFT AVAILABLE

At the outbreak of war in September 1939 Air Marshal Sir Frederick Bowhill, the Air Officer-in-Chief of Coastal Command, had forces of ten Anson squadrons, including four Auxiliaries, one Hudson squadron, and two strike squadrons of Vildebeests. The flying-boat units were two squadrons of Sunderlands, three with Saro Londons, and one equipped with Supermarine Stranraers. The Vildebeest strike-aircraft and the London and Stranraer flying-boats were all obsolescent.

The Ansons represented the equipment for more than half his total force, but with insufficient range to undertake the reconnaissance required, and four out of the six flying-boat squadrons were equipped with obsolescent aircraft. Sir Frederick was thus left with just three squadrons with modern aircraft, namely Hudsons and Sunderlands, that were considered able to operate effectively.[16]

In the early months of 1939 supplies of engines for the Avro Anson aircraft were limited, and there was a need to restrict the flying of Ansons on that account. It was necessary also to conserve even the outdated Vildebeests, as there were only six in store to supply both home and abroad. At that time the Command had ten Stranraers, seventeen Londons, four Short Singapore flying-boats, and two Sunderlands. Deliveries of the latter to the Command were given as only two per month.

The Director of Organisation at the Air Ministry, then Charles Portal, following the Munich crisis, foresaw what was to be a problem in respect of the availability of aircraft throughout the war. That was that aircraft could be weather-bound for days at various places round the coast. Coastal Command was required to operate throughout the twenty-four hours, and to do that bases were required for both take-off and landing with some degree of safety. This applied particularly to flying-boats. The new twin-engined flying-boat, the Saro Lerwick, had not been expected to be delivered before April 1939, and therefore was unlikely to be operational before the end of the year, but then it was to be found unsuitable for operations.[17]

There was a need, therefore, for land-based aircraft to cover the South-Western Approaches, and significantly, in the same memo of 25 October 1938, Portal refers to having Newquay (St Eval) laid out to take two squadrons.[18]

Between December 1939 and August 1940 the following reinforcements were received by Coastal Command: No. 10 Squadron RAAF Sunderlands in December 1939, four Blenheim squadrons on loan from Fighter Command in February 1940 (Nos 235, 236, 248 and 254); in June 1940 Nos 53 and 59 Squadrons with Blenheims on loan from Bomber Command, and in August 1940, No. 98 Squadron's Fairey Battles, also on loan from Bomber Command, the latter to be based in Iceland.

These additions had followed an agreement by the Air Ministry with the Admiralty for Coastal Command to have an additional fifteen squadrons by June 1941. By 15 June, that had only been achieved by the loan of seven squadrons from other Commands, with aircraft unsuited to the maritime role, and with a daily average availability of 298 aircraft.[19]

Just a month later, the Command had 612 aircraft with thirty-nine squadrons, but by then it was estimated that future requirements would be sixty-three and a half squadrons with 838 aircraft.[20] The 612 aircraft then available included eleven types, and that would have produced problems in training for aircrew when they converted to a different type of aircraft. At Air Chief Marshal Sir Philip Joubert de la Ferté's first staff meeting on 30 June as Air Officer Commanding-in-Chief Coastal Command, the number of aircraft available was not stated, but rather that there were only four strike squadrons.[21]

By 1 December 1941 reconnaissance aircraft available to Coastal Command included eighteen Catalina flying-boats, nine Sunderlands, twenty Whitleys and 170 Hudsons. The Command's strike aircraft comprised sixty Beaufort torpedo-bombers, twenty Beaufort bombers and forty Beaufighters. Additionally, Coastal had sixty of the Blenheim fighter version. The total of 397 aircraft was available to equip eighteen squadrons.[22]

The total number of aircraft available to Coastal Command in June 1942 was 496, and would have included aircraft of four squadrons on loan from Bomber Command, but for Sir Philip, there was a shortage of three landplane squadrons, and ten flying-boat squadrons; and in his report to the Air Ministry he added: 'I therefore cannot accept your view that we are comparatively well off, nor do I feel that we have sufficient strength to carry out our job.'[23]

Although, in November 1942, Coastal had 259 Hudsons, Sir Philip was concerned about their availability, due to ten squadrons plus other units still operating them, and stated that with the 'present Hudson commitment ... continuance of the present numbers of squadrons is impossible'.[24]

Sir Philip was still concerned about the two types from Bomber Command, such as the Whitley, '... on the whole, given unsatisfactory service' and the Hampden, which was 'incapable of operating in daylight ... off the enemy coast ... without a very strong escort of long-range fighters'.[25]

There were no Beaufort-equipped squadrons left with Coastal Command (they were posted overseas), and no trained Beaufighter squadron, and it was known that German Fw190 fighters were 50 mph faster than the Beaufighter, which was therefore hardly suitable as escort to the Hampdens even if available.[26] De Havilland Mosquitoes had been made available for Photo-Reconnaissance in 1942, but for the Mosquito Mark VI fighter-bomber priority was given to Fighter Command.[27]

When Air Marshal John Slessor assumed command of Coastal Command in February 1943, the strength was sixty squadrons with 'some 850 aircraft'.[28] Although he appeared largely content with the aircraft available to him, in respect of both quantity and quality, he wrote to the Air Ministry in September stating, 'I now find that there are 120 first line Mosquitoes going into photo-reconnaissance in this country, and over 200 first line Mosquitoes going to the Army support in the Tactical Air Force'.[29]

Thus, despite the need for reconnaissance, priority was given to the TAF. He refers, however, to the 'unforeseen requirement for modification of certain four-engined types to Very Long Range [VLR]' coinciding with the introduction of a system of 'planned flying and maintenance ... in what was a "difficult period of availability" '.[30]

Air Chief Marshal Sir Sholto Douglas succeeded Air Marshal Slessor in January 1944, when, in respect of numbers of aircraft, equilibrium had obviously been reached. The Command's records written during his tenure refer to equipment of aircraft such as ASV, and modifications to aircraft rather than the need for more aircraft. Forces for Sholto Douglas included (again, as was the case for Slessor) 430 aircraft for anti-submarine operations.

The 430 aircraft, however, were the equipment for ten squadrons of Liberators, including three of the United States Navy; five Leigh-Light Wellington squadrons, and two squadrons each equipped with Halifaxes,

Hudsons and Fortresses. There were also seven Sunderland and two Catalina squadrons.[31] The heavy four-engined aircraft that Sir Sholto then had available did, however, raise another requirement – the need for runways of sufficient length to take such as the Liberator, Fortress and Halifax.

Thus, on 7 February 1944, the Air Ministry was asked to approve the lengthening of the runways at Brawdy, Chivenor, Aldergrove and Leuchars.[32] Although Sholto Douglas expressed no need for more aircraft, he referred to the 'Bomber Baron's decision finding the Liberator unsuitable for night operations', such that Coastal Command's near starvation came to an end'. He added, 'By the time that I became C-in-C of Coastal we were using twelve squadrons of them.'[33]

However, by 27 April the Command was obviously preparing for Operation Overlord – the invasion of Europe, and a signal was sent to No. 19 Group regarding the necessity for 'reducing wastage to conserve aircraft for forthcoming operations'. Specifically mentioned were Mosquitoes and Liberators.[34]

In November the re-equipment of Halifax squadrons with Liberators was again mooted, although these were all bombers that had to be modified for Coastal Command.[35]

In 1945 the Air Ministry agreed to thirty Mark V Sunderlands (those with Pratt & Whitney Wasp engines), which had been intended for overseas service, to be allocated to Coastal Command. This was in sharp contrast to Sir Philip Joubert's experience three years earlier, when he was losing both aircraft and crews to overseas. During Sir Sholto's final meetings, a whole spectrum of aircraft types had to be considered. Thus, during the 4 May meeting he asked the Senior Air Staff Officer to find from the Air Ministry what the Command's commitments might be for modifying fifty Gloster Meteor jet aircraft for photo-reconnaissance, and those required for the Supermarine Sea Otter.[36]

AIRCRAFT REQUIREMENTS

Until the outbreak of the Second World War the number of aircraft considered necessary for Coastal Command to provide trade protection in Home Waters was 281. This number assumed a war by Britain alone against Germany.[37] The prime duty was then to cover the exits from the North Sea.[38]

The capitulation of France, the over-running of the Low Countries and the occupation of Norway and Denmark resulted in a vast coastline from the French Biscay ports to North Cape to be covered. The entry of Italy into the war in addition to a possible hostile French fleet made further demands on Coastal Command. Thus, in addition to covering the North Sea exits, three additional flying-boat squadrons were considered to be immediate requirements to cover the Irish Sea, Faeroes areas, and Western Approaches, plus an additional general reconnaissance landplane squadron and two long-range fighter squadrons – say, another 100 aircraft.

For overseas, an additional five flying-boat squadrons and one landplane squadron were specified; thus, for additional home and overseas commitments, possibly 200 aircraft above the 281 already stated were needed. This assumed that other forces would cover the Caribbean and Newfoundland areas.[39] In December 1939, however, the Command was concerned with close escort of coastal convoys and the chain of patrols to the Norwegian coast.

For those duties reference was made specifically to two types of aircraft, the Avro Anson and the Lockheed Hudson, the reconnaissance landplanes then available. With those two types, a total of 273 aircraft was anticipated, following an agreement to increase the requirements of each squadron to twenty-one aircraft.[40] Other landplanes for reconnaissance then being considered about that time were the Blackburn Botha, the Bristol Blenheim and Bristol Beaufort, with the comments that the Botha was 'specially designed for reconnaissance', but that the Blenheim was 'adversely reported'.[41] It was hoped that twenty Bothas would be delivered to the Command by the end of 1939, and twelve Beauforts were expected in October/November.

The Bothas, however, were found unsuitable for operations, and no more of the Mark IV Blenheims were being allocated to Coastal Command.[42]

In October 1941 the Prime Minister became aware of U-boats operating further afield, and suggested to the First Lord of the Admiralty that it was probably due to our air operations. Following this, Coastal Command's requirement programme was considered to be 150 Catalinas and seventy-two Sunderlands for twenty-six flying-boat squadrons; thirty-two Liberators and thirty-two Wellingtons or Whitleys to equip four long-range GR squadrons; sixty-four Mosquitoes and 180 GR Hudsons for fifteen and a half medium- and short-range squadrons; 128 Beauforts for eight torpedo-bomber squadrons; and 160 Beaufighters for ten long-range fighter squadrons. However, four flying-boat and two GR short-range squadrons were to be earmarked for West Africa, and three flying-boat squadrons for Gibraltar.[43]

By December 1941 the types of aircraft required were stated as a long-range flying-boat, a long-range landplane, a medium-range landplane, a high-speed reconnaissance landplane, a long-range fighter, and a torpedo-bomber. Changes had been made to requirements following the previous three months' experience and an analysis of U-boat attacks.[44] At that time it was considered that extra-long-range aircraft should have a range of 2,000 miles because some U-boat attacks had been 700 miles from British bases, and if air patrols were deployed 350–600 miles, the enemy would move to the 600–700-mile area

(600 miles from a United Kingdom base would be up to 20'E 15'W; from Iceland, up to 40'E 12'W).[45]

Reconnaissance aircraft were then expected to have ASV (Aircraft-to-Surface Vessel) radar for homing; long-range planes were to be able to operate in all weathers and have a short take-off and landing distance. For high-speed reconnaissance aircraft the Air Ministry suggested the Mosquito, but other services were given priority in their supply.[46]

Three types were suggested to undertake the task of a torpedo bomber: the Handley-Page Hampden, the Bristol Beaufort and the Vickers Wellington III.

All three were to operate as such, despite the lack of forward armament in the Hampden and Beaufort, and the Wellington and Hampden had not been designed for maritime work.[47]

In early 1942 the functions of the Command's operational aircraft were clearly stated in six categories. Anti-submarine warfare was first in order of importance, covering reconnaissance, depth-charging and bombing. Second and fifth were torpedo warfare (reconnaissance and the attack on large merchant vessels and enemy naval forces) and anti-shipping warfare (reconnaissance and bombing). Third, fourth and sixth in order of importance were photo-reconnaissance, meteorological reconnaissance and coastal fighter warfare.

Coastal fighter and anti-shipping warfare were rated former RAF peacetime functions; anti-submarine warfare had become a highly specialised category, as also torpedo warfare.[48] Little consideration had been given to the latter, as it was 'uneconomical to have torpedo squadrons locked up for a target which may never materialise so may find ourselves making more use of the GR/TB squadrons for GR work', as was the case with Beauforts.[49]

At the time of Air Marshal John Slessor

assuming command of Coastal in February 1943, the trend (which is reflected in the Command's records) was concerned about the equipment then being added to aircraft, rather than the aircraft itself. This was resulting in an effect on the aircraft's range due to the additional loads – a matter of concern throughout the war. Slessor addressed this matter in a letter to all his Group's headquarters in May 1943.[50]

RANGE

Range of aircraft for a given design is affected by many factors, such as the all-up weight, the quantity of fuel carried and the type of engine(s). When airborne, other factors include the height at which the aircraft is flown (this because the engines would be designed for an optimum height for greatest efficiency).

Other factors for Coastal Command's aircrew to consider were whether they should deploy side guns in, for example, Wellingtons or Hudsons; and in the case of the Sunderland flying-boats, whether they should run out their depth charges onto the wings from the bomb-bay.

These were continuing tactical problems in addition to the reduction of speed and range. All four of Coastal Command's Air Officers Commanding-in-Chief show their awareness of the importance of range for aircraft in the Second World War– notably Sir Philip Joubert – who imposed a limit on the endurance for crews of eighteen hours; and even that figure was to be under exceptional circumstances. At RAF Waddington in April 1998, it was understood that the endurance of aircrew is still the deciding factor in maritime operations, albeit due to toilet facilities.

Although given as having an endurance of 5½ hours at 103 knots, the Anson represented the operational equipment for Coastal Command's land-based reconnaissance squadrons at the outbreak of war, excluding

No. 224, which had just rearmed with Hudsons. The Anson's lack of range precluded it being effectively used, even for the Command's prime task on the outset of war, reconnaissance from Britain to Norway. As Capt T. Dorling, RN, stated: 'Ansons were unable to reach Norway and blockade the North Sea. Only flying-boats and Hudson squadrons were able to do so.'[51]

The Air Ministry, when writing to the C-in-C of Coastal Command in September 1941, stated that a limit should not be set on the range of reconnaissance aircraft, but that the matter would be pursued with the Admiralty with a view to limiting the maximum operating distance from base of 600 miles, as convoy escorts beyond that would be uneconomical.[52] Range was necessary to cover, in particular, convoy routes, notably out into the North Atlantic as far as the 'prudent limit of endurance', or 'PLE'.

If on a 'sweep', that would have sufficed; but if a convoy was to be escorted, say, at 12°W, it was essential also to have some hours in that area circling the convoy; endurance was therefore also required. Opinions vary in what was considered a useful time with a convoy, but typically two to three hours. In a letter dated 28 July 1941, however, from Air Commodore Lloyd, the Deputy SASO, it was recommended that at least one-third of sorties should be with the convoy.[53]

In Coastal Command, it was decided that the limit of long-range aircraft should be the endurance of the crew rather than the fuel supply. This was decided at a Command meeting on 7 January 1942, when Catalinas were considered able to have a radius of 600 nautical miles, 'on the fringe of the U-boat area', with a sortie of eighteen hours' duration.[54]

Sir Philip Joubert decided that routine patrols should not exceed fourteen hours, but in cases of emergency could be extended up to eighteen hours due to 'conditions of cold and cramp in which the crews are called upon to operate, and the need for sparing their endurance and not stretching it to the limit unless an emergency arises'.[55]

As an economy measure in Coastal Command's use of Catalinas in respect of long-range work, it was suggested by the Deputy Senior Air Staff Officer (D/SASO) that Sunderlands could be used for sorties between 250 and 440 nautical miles along convoy routes. It is not clear, however, if that idea was followed.[56]

Range was considered so important that the question of Liberators with or without self-sealing fuel tanks was raised, as without them there would be a reduction of unladen weight but an increase in fuel capacity.[57] In January 1942, however, the Mark I Liberator's maximum range is stated as 2,720 miles, but with the crew's endurance limiting it to 2,240 miles.[58]

When the Liberator was just coming into service with Coastal in June 1941 for anti-submarine warfare, the C-in-C wrote to the Air Ministry:

> For duties of this nature, which involve flying for long periods by day and night, out of sight of land in all conditions of weather, the Long Range bombers do not provide the same amenities and freedom of movement to the crew as a flying-boat. The Liberator, which is being provided for one squadron, meets these requirements to a greater extent than any existing British bomber ....

He added, however, that more attention should be given to their layout for reconnaissance rather than bomb load.[59]

The long range of 2,240 miles enabled the Liberator in Coastal Command to help close the 'Mid-Atlantic Gap' south of Cape Farewell with such as a shuttle service between Newfoundland and Iceland.[60]

Sir Philip Joubert stated that his first problem when he succeeded Sir Frederick Bowhill in 1941 was 'the need to fill the Gap', and here the only land-based aircraft that could do the job was the American B24, the Liberator.[61] The C-in-C Coastal Command in a review of the Command's expansion and re-equipment programme dated 12 June 1941 wrote: 'The extension of unrestricted U-boat warfare against shipping in the Atlantic to areas outside the range of MR [medium-range] aircraft has necessitated the use of LR [sic] bombers such as the Whitley and Wellington as anti-submarine aircraft.'[62]

The twin-engined medium bombers that came from Bomber Command, the Wellington 1C and Whitley V, were both serving in Coastal by late 1940. Although they helped to fill a gap in the Command's general reconnaissance requirements, Air Commodore I.T. Lloyd, the D/SASO, wrote to the C-in-C Coastal Command on 28 July 1941: 'Whitleys and Wellingtons are uneconomical at their speed and with only nine-hour sorties; we require a replacement for these types to give range up to 600 miles ... or at least 440 miles.'[63]

Four-engined bombers that were loaned or allocated to Coastal Command included the British Handley-Page Halifax and the Avro Lancaster, but the Halifax when used for meteorological flights was provided with drop tanks to increase the range.

By 30 November 1944 Coastal Command was due to receive Pathfinder-type Mk III Halifaxes from Bomber Command's production, but it was considered necessary for the first one to be examined and modified at Gosport to bring it up to the Command's standard.[64] When No. 502 Squadron was due to re-equip with Halifaxes they were to be fitted with long-range tanks, compensated, apparently, in respect of all-up weight, by having the front turret removed.[65]

This was despite the fact that when considering the provision of Halifaxes for No.

58 Squadron, it was stated that for operations in the Bay of Biscay front turrets were needed, largely against enemy fighters.[66]

These essentially bomber aircraft were nevertheless operated by Coastal Command in anti-submarine warfare, and for meteorological flights and anti-shipping sorties.[67] The Avro Lancaster, another four-engined bomber, was only on brief loan to Coastal Command during the war, and does not feature in the RAF's official history as a Coastal Command aircraft. With a range of 2,350 miles it could have been invaluable,[68] but the Chief of Air Staff was strongly opposed to Lancasters being transferred to Coastal Command, as it was the only aircraft able to take an 8,000 lb bomb to Berlin.[69]

The American-built B17 Flying Fortress was rated a long-range aircraft, but was selected for Coastal Command because it was considered unfit for Bomber Command's night operations.[70] The Fortress served as a useful reconnaissance aircraft with such as Nos 59, 206 and 220 Squadrons; fortunately it was not required by Bomber Command, and it was reported on 27 January 1942 that all Fortress aircraft from America would go to Coastal Command.[71]

The C-in-C Coastal Command, Air Chief Marshal Sir Philip Joubert, wrote to the Air Ministry on 7 January 1942 of his concern that his long-range aircraft, 'except the Liberator, fall far short of Coastal Command's needs ... when U-boat attacks on shipping were about 700 miles westwards with Catalinas at 600 miles only on the fringe of the U-boats' area'. In that same letter, Sir Philip referred to the medium-range Hudson as a 'stop gap' with the Ventura [a development of the Hudson] of lesser range; that a medium-range aircraft should have a range of 1,200 nautical miles, while the Wellington and Whitley 'more nearly meet requirements'.[72] The Air Ministry's ultimate response was in a letter dated 7 March 1942,

which stated:

> It would be uneconomical to divert a successful heavy bomber type to a Coastal Command role particularly if ... a less successful type of heavy bomber is available ... the Fortress ... is unfit for night bomber operations and weather conditions strictly limit its employment ... in high altitude bombing ... for these reasons it was selected for ... Coastal Command.

The Air Ministry did show some appreciation of Coastal Command's requirements, but indicated the priority given to Bomber Command with:

> We should hamper the normal evolution of GR [general reconnaissance] aircraft by setting a limit to their range. It is now apparent that our requirements for heavy bomber types are unlikely to be realised in full for a very long time. It will therefore be impracticable to provide many squadrons equipped with this type for general reconnaissance work. Consequently this role will have to be fulfilled by normal GR landplanes for some time to come.

The Air Ministry added that the matter would be pursued with the Admiralty, with Coastal Command aircraft limited to a radius of 600 miles; greater distances 'should be the responsibility of surface forces'.[73]

At Sir Philip Joubert's fifth staff meeting, photo-reconnaissance aircraft were said to be Coastal's 'weak point', and he stated, 'We must have long-range Spitfires.'[74] For both the Beaufighter, and later the Mosquito, attempts were made to increase their endurance and range by the addition of drop tanks. For the Mosquito, modifications are recorded from November 1941 until towards the end of the war.[75]

ENGINES

British engines fitted to aircraft operated by Coastal Command included those designed by the Bristol Aeroplane Company, Rolls-Royce, and Armstrong-Siddeley. Predominating in the Command's aircraft were Bristol engines, which were in five groups – Mercury, Taurus, Pegasus, Hercules and Centaurus (all air-cooled radials) – but for much of the front-line aircraft in the Second World War the Pegasus and Hercules were perhaps the most important. The Pegasus served to power the Wellingtons and Sunderlands; and the more powerful Hercules the Beaufighters and later marks of Wellington, increasing the latter's power by as much as fifty per cent (from 1,000 hp to 1,500 hp per engine).

This increase in power for the Wellington was important, as the early marks were apt to lose height if one engine failed.[76] The Pegasus engines on both the Wellington and the Sunderland were rather overstretched, and they ran dry of lubrication, resulting in the propellers shearing off, with or without the reduction gear.[77] Problems with Pegasus engines persisted throughout the war. Thus on 4 November 1944 the question of engine failures with Sunderlands at Operational Training Units (OTUs) was raised. It resulted in a conference by the Commander-in-Chief Coastal Command with the AOC of No. 17 Group on 6 December. Sunderlands at the OTU at that time were unlikely to have had Pratt & Whitney Wasps.[78]

Two American-designed and -built engines that were used to power many Coastal Command aircraft were the Pratt & Whitney Wasp and the Wright Cyclone. The Wright Cyclone was installed in the first three marks of Hudson, and also in some marks of the Boeing Flying Fortress. An advantage of the Cyclone over the Wasp was that no gills were necessary. This reduced the possibility of an aircraft being u/s through lack of a gill motor; and in flying, less need to watch the cylinder-head temperatures.

Despite the improvement by having Wasp engines in the Sunderland, it was not until 12 March 1944 that trials were undertaken at Shorts. They were obviously successful, as No. 10 Squadron RAAF was apparently to be fully equipped with them by the end of that month. That would have been by No. 10's Sunderlands having the engines installed retrospectively.[79] It was to be in September that Coastal Command asked the Air Ministry for the first Mark V Sunderland coming off the production line with Pratt & Whitney engines to be provided for familiarisation.

The same type of engine on different types of aircraft might well be run very differently, so that the Pratt & Whitney Wasp on a Liberator could have cruising revolutions of 1,400 rpm, but on a Mark VI Hudson 1,800 rpm.[80]

With most of the aircraft allotted to Coastal Command being designed either as bombers or fighters, by implication, the engines fitted to them would have been intended to operate from say 10,000 ft to 24,000 ft altitude, rather than, typically for Coastal Command, 50 ft to 3,000 ft altitude.

The height to fly could well be 50 ft when approaching the Norwegian coast; while over the Atlantic it would normally be just below cloud. Problems were experienced with some engines when used in the maritime role, such as the Rolls-Royce engines on Halifax aircraft used by the meteorological squadrons, when they might well be expected to operate from sea level up to the maximum heights obtainable.[81]

In my experience, for day-to-day operations the first indication of trouble with any type of aero-engine was likely to be a 'mag-drop'. When magnetos were switched there was likely to be a small drop in revolutions, and that was a routine test before any take-off, although I can recall only one occasion when a take-off was aborted on that account. It was with a Sunderland at OTU, with three out of four engines considered unserviceable – all were Bristol Pegasus engines. In contrast, No. 48 Squadron was able to operate for a fortnight its Mark VI Hudsons equipped with Pratt & Whitney Wasps without any maintenance by ground staff, who had not arrived.[82]

Apart from a mag-drop, another possible fault was with lubrication: either low oil pressure or excessive oil consumption. It could be such that some Wellington squadrons operating in North Africa carried extra cans of lubricating oil. With a good aircrew which was allocated a specific aircraft, and certainly for such as a Sunderland, which would have had its own engineer, problems with engines were less likely to occur.[83]

Applicable to all aircraft engines were extreme operating conditions, ranging between the volcanic ash at Höfn in Iceland, the sand at Gibraltar and in North Africa, and the tropical heat of West Africa. Engines were modified with special air filters for overseas, but the hazards remained.[84]

PRODUCTION AND PROCUREMENT

At a conference of Chiefs of Staff in May 1937, Sir Edward Ellington, Chief of the Air Staff, outlined the procedure for obtaining aircraft for the service, although at that time he was responding to remarks made by the First Lord of the Admiralty. The procedure was for a general specification of the kind of machine required. The specification would be examined by technical officers to see how far the requirements could be met.

After discussions, detailed specifications would be drawn up for approval by the service (either the Admiralty or the Royal Air Force). Selected manufacturers would then be invited to tender designs and quote prices. Experimental machines would be tested, after which the service would decide which particular machine was to be adopted for production. Sir Edward added that the service 'got whatever type they wanted within the limits of practicability of design and production'.[85]

For British aircraft, manufacturers included Short & Harland, Vickers Armstrong, The Bristol Aeroplane Co., Blackburns, Supermarine, Gloucestershire Aircraft Co., A.V. Roe, de Havilland, Handley-Page, Fairey Aviation, Hawker-Siddeley and Saunders-Roe (Saro); while for American aircraft, manufacturers were Lockheed, Consolidated, Boeing and Glen L. Martin Co.

Outstanding in numbers and usefulness was the Lockheed Hudson, and Lockheed from the outset literally demonstrated its commitment not only in design, production

1. The production line of Hudsons at the Lockheed Corporation's Works at Burbank. They fulfilled their contracts on time, and maintained liaison with No.224 Squadron.

2. The first Hudson (N7210) to be received by No.224 Squadron at Leuchars, May 1940.

and delivery but in its personal attitude on receiving the British Purchasing Commission, its liaison with the first squadron to be equipped with Hudsons (No. 224 Squadron), and even post war. Unlike most of the aircraft assigned to Coastal Command, the Hudson was not designed for Bomber or Fighter Commands but as an airliner, the Lockheed 14, and modified specifically for a maritime role, with the drawings prepared in London by the late Clarence 'Kelly' Johnson in eighty days.[86]

Prior to the British Purchasing Commission visiting the Lockheed factory, Ken Smith, Lockheed's sales representative, obtained a photograph of the commission members and memorised their titles, names and faces.

Sketches of a Lockheed Model 14 were prepared for use as a reconnaissance bomber, and in ten days Lockheed produced a wooden mock-up of a medium-range reconnaissance bomber, a task that normally would have taken three months.

When modifications were suggested by the Purchasing Commission, it was surprised to find the changes were made and painted-in within the space of a lunch break. The Director of Contracts, Sir Henry Self, later invited representatives of Lockheed to London, including R.A. von Hake, their manufacturing manager; Bob Proctor, who was concerned with contracts, and the aeronautical engineer, Clarence 'Kelly' Johnson, MSc, FRAeS. An initial order for 200 aircraft was placed in early 1938, and a contract was signed on 23 June 1938 for Lockheed to supply 175 Hudsons plus as many more as could be delivered up to 250 by December 1939. The order was completed in November 1939, seven weeks ahead of schedule. The *London Evening News* reported on 10 June 1938 that the Hudsons cost £17,000 each (or $90,000), and the first Hudson arrived at Liverpool by sea on 15 February 1939.[87]

The late 'Kelly' Johnson, writing to the author, stated:

The Hudson was actually redesigned in England from the initial proposal that was shown to your purchasing group who came to Burbank. They turned down our proposal design the first day it was shown to your technical people in England. In a period of 80 hours, working alone, I was required to revise our proposal to incorporate English armament such as turrets, torpedoes, mines, bombs and forward-firing guns. Data on your military equipment was sent to Burbank in a diplomatic pouch so that when I returned we had proper data to carry on the production engineering.

When the first three airplanes were delivered to Martlesham Heath, our test pilot Milo Bursham and I spent a number of months checking out your pilots and crew, particularly Squadron Leader Red Collings. When it became time to prove our guaranteed range and dive speed, I was given an RAF uniform so that I could be considered an official member of the crew during our long flights over England, Scotland and Wales.[88]

MRAF Sir Arthur Harris, who was a member of the British Purchasing Commission in 1938 at Lockheed, stated:

The result of this visit was the purchase of the first batch of Hudsons and Harvards. The Hudson beyond doubt pulled us out of the

3. HM King George VI inspecting the pilots who converted the Anson squadrons to Hudsons, RAF Thornaby, November 1939.

4. HM King George VI viewing a No.220 Squadron Hudson which lacked a turret.

soup when we used them for anti-submarine patrols ... I was much impressed with the American business efficiency ... my reason for giving the order for Lockheed Hudsons was that I was much impressed by the aircraft itself ... and was immensely struck by the ability and energy of the comparative youngsters who were running this

5. The wireless operator's view on the Hudson flight deck that had about 100 instruments and controls to be considered. Both the wireless operator and navigator could be expected to help the pilot in landing at such places as Gibraltar in respect of flaps and undercarriage.

factory ... only twenty-four hours later I saw a mock-up of all our requirements [for the Hudson] in plywood fitted complete in every detail ... at home we were never able to get a mock-up in less than a month.'[89]

At a Coastal Command meeting in July 1941 it was reported that production of Hudsons was then 100 per month until September, when it would then be 90 per month until April 1942. The production was then in the proportion of 2:1 for Mark IIIs (with Wright Cyclone engines) to Mark Vs (with Pratt & Whitney Wasps).

This was in contrast to the British Bristol Beaufort, as, due to lack of these aircraft, two new squadrons could not be formed.[90] There was a further lack of Beauforts due to trouble with the tailwheel, and Blenheims had to serve as replacements.[91] By the end of the month, however, the Bristol Beaufort and Beaufighter were said to be 'coming on slowly'.[92] Coastal Command's experience with Short & Harland in the production of the Sunderland was very different. The Shorts factory at Rochester was then delivering four Sunderlands per month, with the probability of five per month in the new year. The new factory at Windermere was 'only scheduled to produce two boats a month', the first expected about March 1942. At Dumbarton, the programme 'calls for a peak production of three boats per month only'.

The Ministry of Aircraft Production (MAP) felt that:

The limiting factor is undoubtedly lack of interest brought about by the contract position which is too small to warrant Short & Harland stretching themselves. ... At present they hold contracts for a total of 55 boats (15 Mark II and 40 Mk III), while up to 16 August last they had only 25 ordered! You will readily appreciate in these circumstances why the Sunderland is showing so little progress here, especially when compared to the Stirling for which they hold contracts for some 600-odd machines.[93]

The Ministry of Aircraft Production wrote again to the Admiralty on 13 October 1941, suggesting that the action of Wg Cdr G. Shaw should help to 'drag the Sunderland from the limbo into which it has fallen'. It referred to labour in Belfast being a political issue, with some 11,000 unskilled registered as unemployed but who could not be engaged by Short & Harland as all its employees belonged to unions which refused to admit them. Boy labour would be admitted, but only as apprentices. The Northern Ireland Minister for Labour was 'unhelpful, or possibly unable to help'. The letter refers to a:

continuous succession of strikes and threats of strikes in Belfast, [and] I am not satisfied in my own mind that Short & Harland are even attempting to put their backs into Sunderland production ... some 2,000 operatives

6. A Sunderland of No.330 (Norsk) squadron armed with front, rear and dorsal turrets. Sunderlands of No.10 squadron RAAF became armed with 18 machine gunes for operating over the Bay of Biscay.

(on Stirling fuselage production) are temporarily redundant ... am trying to get them switched over onto Sunderlands until back on Stirlings in about 2–3 months' time.[94]

These letters were followed by Sir Philip Joubert writing to the Chief of Air Staff on 20 October, remarking that unless Coastal Command was prepared constantly to push its own case forward, 'an approved Air Ministry programme is allowed to fall behind performance because another Command has in a bigger order for aircraft and is therefore financially more interesting to the Company concerned'.[95]

Sir Charles Portal replied:

A memo on behalf of the Director of Aircraft Production stated: 'I agree ... that Short & Harland were making little effort to increase production .... The production of Sunderlands in recent months has been most disappointing and has only just met the wastage of the existing five squadrons. The programme provides for a peak of fifteen per month by March 1942.'[96] Reviewing Sunderland production generally, I feel that this aircraft is suffering, and has long been suffering from complete lack of interest on the part of all concerned and is badly in need of publicity and drive. If the Service really needs Sunderlands this need should be emphasised.[97]

My experience in writing to manufacturers post war reflected this difference in attitude; it was only the Lockheed Corporation that responded positively to my requests.

Long-range Liberators, because of their range, were much required by Coastal; but it was not until 11 August 1941 that specific numbers were mentioned, with seven 'on the line', one in Northern Ireland 'and the prototype'.[98] At the next meeting of the Command it was stated: 'Efforts to get more of these aircraft [Liberators] have been in vain',[99] and on 23 August the Commander-in-Chief called for a report concerning the position for forming a Liberator squadron.[100] Although twenty Liberators had been allocated to Coastal Command, it was to get only thirteen, and they were not forthcoming even by the end of August.[101] Of the few Liberators apparently then with Coastal Command in October, three were taken from the Command; and on 10 October it was stated that Coastal Command had a 'call on ten altogether', instead of the twenty-four it was supposed to have received.[102]

The position regarding the first Catalina (P9630) to be received by the Marine Aircraft Experimental Establishment at Felixstowe in June 1939 was, as Consolidated's representative, Mr J.H. Millar, recalls:

When the war broke out, the PBY4 was still at Felixstowe and was the only long-range aircraft England had. Air Marshal Sir Roderick Hill asked me to go to Harrogate to see him and told me that they were going to order 40 more. Eventually they took over the French contracts. I had to go back with drawings of brackets the Air Ministry wanted mounted on the leading edge of the wings for ASV ... much more important was the need to order beaching gear to arrive ahead of the boats so there would be no delay in bringing that Catalina ashore to have guns fitted, etc., but the Ministry of Aircraft Production [MAP] refused to do so.[103]

Air Commodore G. Bromet had two flights in this Catalina, possibly to give his approval in its acceptance for the RAF. After a flight on 14 November 1939 Bromet recorded: 'The Pratt & Whitney engines are about 1,050 hp each, fuel 1,460 gallons and a range of some 4,000 miles at economical height. Speed 120 knots cruising.' This PBY4 appears as the only one of that mark to be received by the RAF.[104]

In 1940 Boeing in Canada was licensed to build PBYs in Vancouver, and in 1941 Canadian Vickers Ltd agreed to construct in Carierville, Quebec, a Canadian version of the Catalina, the Canso. By 17 May 1945 Canadian Vickers Ltd had delivered 369 of these to the RCAF and USAAF. Boeing at Vancouver produced 240 Catalinas, but their first PBYs were fifty-five Canso As (similar to PBY5As). The total Catalina production was 3,272, including 1,418 amphibians. The latter had a tricycle undercarriage of 3,300 lb that reduced the range of the aircraft by 640 miles.[105] Both the Catalina (PBY5) and the amphibian version (PBY5A) served with success in the Command, but the amphibians were flown by the United States Navy and the RCAF (No. 162 Squadron), the latter using the Canso.[106] Up to 14 August 1941, sixty-seven Catalinas were delivered to Coastal Command, but seven of them were written off.

To gain more Catalinas, the Vice-Chief of Air Staff informed Coastal Command that there was agreement with the Canadians to obtain part of the Canadian allotment of aircraft, and for the nine that the Command had apparently loaned to Canada to be returned.[107] Near the end of the month, however, the C-in-C was promised fifty-four more Catalinas, and felt that there was a reasonable chance of them being received.[108]

The supply of Catalinas, none the less, in addition to that of Sunderlands, was considered 'poor' in the following month.[109] By February 1942 the Command was expecting deliveries of the Catalinas at the rate of three per week, with a final six to complete a batch of thirty before May. Those deliveries were to be offset, however, by three Catalina squadrons being posted overseas (Nos 209, 240 and 413).[110]

Wellingtons used for combating magnetic

7. A Wellington fitted with coils through which a current of electricity was passed providing a magnetic field that was used to detonate German-laid magnetic mines. This was one of the tasks allocated to Coastal Command.

mines had been placed under Coastal Command's control, and at the Command's meeting on 27 August 1941 the Senior Air Staff Officer suggested that Coastal Command might form a new squadron of these aircraft after hearing that the manufacturers – Vickers – had an order for one hundred and that they would be coming off the line at two per week, fully fitted for Coastal Command. This 'was in direct contradiction with the Air Ministry's statement that there were no Wellingtons available'.[111]

At the following meeting on 28 August it was reported that the Deputy Chief of Air Staff could only have three Wellingtons per month: that is, enough to back one squadron; the remainder of the production would go to Bomber Command. At that time Coastal Command was short of 176 aircraft.[112] By December, however, Coastal Command was expecting four Wellingtons per month modified for general reconnaissance and also six GR Whitleys per month.[113]

At Coastal Command's fortieth meeting, held on 5 September 1941, when a review of the aircraft position was given, only that for the Hudsons was given as 'very satisfactory'.

The few Liberators were non-operational; both the Bristol aircraft, Beauforts and Beaufighters, were 'unsatisfactory', particularly in respect of the tailwheel 'shimmy'. The Sunderland production was 'behind schedule', and the Catalinas were shortly due for overhaul. Following recent intensive operations, many aircraft were due for servicing, with the risk of there not being enough to escort convoys.[114]

When the aircraft position was being reviewed near the end of October 1941, the supply of Sunderlands was considered bad due to 'poor workshop management'; but Beaufighter supplies were 'at last fairly satisfactory'. Of the other aircraft produced by the Bristol company, the Beaufort, there was a need for 100 replacements per month, but it was stated that production of these was being 'cut across' due to another 'high-speed fighter' designed by Bristol.[115]

The one type of aircraft for which there never appears to have been a shortage for Coastal Command was the Hudson; and in December 1941 there were still '240 Mark III Hudsons and 65 Mark Vs to hand', besides another forty still on the way.

When the aircraft situation was reviewed at the final Coastal Command meeting for 1941, the Liberator supply was restricted apparently due to modifications required for maritime operations, but the C-in-C was prepared to have the modifications reduced to a minimum. The Ministry of Aircraft Production was able to produce twenty-four Hampdens within three months, but there was still a shortage of flying-boats, Sunderlands and Catalinas, for the OTUs.

The Commander-in-Chief of Coastal Command, Sir Philip Joubert, in the 150 meetings that he held with his staff, almost invariably considered the 'Aircraft Position'. Thus, on 15 January 1942, one-fifth were given as operationally serviceable; of Hampdens, only three were available. Hudson

8. A Handley-Page Hampden. A successful bomber aircraft that was used by Coastal Comamnd as a torpedo aircraft.

reinforcements were required for overseas, expected Swordfish had not materialised, and the two fighter squadrons, Nos 235 and 236, had only seventeen Beaufighters and six Blenheims.[116] No. 236 Squadron was then disbanded, with the statement that there was then no fighter squadron on the west coast. Of Beauforts, twenty to twenty-five should have been available, but only seven were expected.[117]

In February, Sunderlands were reported to be coming off the line at five per month, while Catalina deliveries were expected at a rate of three per week. These were being offset by losses at moorings in bad weather. There was the hope that Coastal would have two each of Liberators and Fortresses 'before long'.[118] The allocation to Coastal Command at that time included 280 Fortress aircraft, and Sir Philip stated that if there was doubt about their full delivery then the Command should be granted a part of Bomber Command's Lancaster allotment.[119] Sir Philip was informed about that time that the whole of the Hudson output for February and March was to go overseas.[120]

This was confirmed later when forty-two Hudsons were assembled at Kemble for the Far East. Another twenty-eight Hudsons that had been allocated to Coastal Command had parts removed and were thus not usable. Four

Liberators, also intended for the Command, had not materialised.[121] In a memo to the ACAS in February, Sir Philip stated: 'So far in this war we have had to scrape along ... it's clearly useless to devote all our resources to maintaining and increasing a Bomber offensive to win the war while neglecting the Coastal resources which will prevent us losing it.'[122]

When the aircraft situation was reviewed at the end of the March, the reliance on North America for supplies was made obvious, as forty-one Hudsons, five Venturas, three Liberators, two Fortresses and eight Catalinas were held up in Canada due to weather conditions.

Of the three British-made aircraft, only the position in Beaufort supplies had improved; of Beaufighters the situation was 'bad'; and only four Sunderlands had been received.[123] During the period of Sir Philip Joubert's wartime command (June 1941 to February 1943), the concern was primarily quantities of aircraft of whatever types were available. This is shown throughout 150 conferences that he held from July 1941 to April 1942.[124] Sir Philip, however, in his review of the period September 1939 to June 1942, but given in retrospect, states: 'More important than numbers, the range and hitting power of the aircraft had doubled.'[125]

Air Marshal John Slessor succeeded Sir Philip Joubert in February 1943, and gives the following in retrospect:

> The sixty squadrons of Coastal Command in February 1943 had a strength of some 850 aircraft plus three USN squadrons. There were thirty-four anti-submarine squadrons with 430 aircraft; twelve squadrons of flying-boats including eight Sunderland squadrons and four Catalina squadrons which included VP84's PBYs Catalinas were: ... lacking in performance and hence rather too vulnerable to the U-boats'

flak, but had the great asset of tremendous endurance. Of the landplanes, the prima donnas were the VLR Liberators with their range of 2,300 sea miles. In February we still had only two squadrons of these aircraft ... in the first two months of the year we had only a daily average of about fourteen in all available for operations. The remainder were the shorter-range Liberators, a few Fortresses and Halifaxes and the still shorter-range Hudsons and Wellingtons. ...[126] There were torpedo strike aircraft, totalling 127, and a hundred Beaufighters – long-range fighters and anti-flak escorts for the strike squadrons.[127]

Slessor added that the rest of the Command comprised five photo-reconnaissance squadrons, three FAA Swordfish squadrons, two air-sea rescue squadrons, and about fifty meteorological aircraft.

From November 1943 onwards, there is a noticeable change in the Command's records in respect of aircraft. The Commander-in-Chief's conferences, then under Air Marshal John Slessor, give more reference to the equipment and armament, although always with concern for the range and endurance of aircraft.

Thus the minutes of the 16 December meeting include mention of more recent equipment and armament, such as the 'Mark 24 mine', sonobuoys, cannon and radar.[128]

When the supply of Liberator aircraft was reviewed on 31 December, again there was reference to armament such as rocket projectiles being fitted rather than the number of aircraft forthcoming.[129] In that same month, however, the Command began additional meetings devoted to the aircraft situation in Coastal Command under the chairmanship of Air Vice-Marshal Maynard, or his deputy, Air Commodore Lloyd. Nevertheless, overall, the meetings to discuss the Command's aircraft situation from November 1943 to March 1945 were largely concerned with the various allocations to squadrons taking account of the equipment of ASV/Radar.[130]

Air Chief Marshal Sir Sholto Douglas succeeded Air Marshal John Slessor as C-in-C in January 1944, and found little cause to worry about aircraft deliveries. Rather was it a matter of ensuring that aircraft were modified satisfactorily for Coastal Command's requirements. At that time there was a need for building up aircraft and equipment as a prelude to Operation Overlord, and both his staff meetings and those of the committee dealing with the aircraft situation reflect those requirements.[131]

Additionally, the increasing use of heavy aircraft resulted in the need for extending runways, but only to find that the Command was limited on how much it was allowed to spend for such work.[132] Sholto Douglas's summing up of the Command's aircraft situation is, however, given in his autobiography:

> In 1940 ... Coastal Command had to make do with aircraft that were both outdated and insufficient in numbers, and when new aircraft were produced for them – the Lerwick flying-boat and the Botha – they turned out to be failures. But eventually they began to receive American Catalinas and Hudsons in sufficient numbers to be able to operate more effectively; and when Bomber Command decided that the Liberator – the American B24 – was not suitable for their night ops, Coastal Command's near starvation came to an end ... it was unquestionably the addition of large numbers of these fine aircraft that helped to bring about what Jack Slessor has described as 'the enormous advance in the lethal

efficiency of Coastal Command'.

> By the time that I became C-in-C of Coastal we were using twelve squadrons of them. In the strongest contrast to the work by our long-range heavy aircraft – the Liberators, the Sunderlands and the Catalinas and, to a lesser degree, the Wellingtons – we continued with and increased the activities of our strike wings. At first we had used Beaufighters in the Strike Wings, but later were able to add Mosquitos.[133]

CONCLUSIONS

The tasks for Coastal Command began with reconnaissance, but came to include shipping strikes, anti-submarine warfare, photo-reconnaissance, air-sea rescue and meteorological flights. Throughout the war, some of its aircraft, throughout every twenty-four hours, would be flying. For three and a half years of the war, the numbers of aircraft available to the Command were inadequate for those tasks. Numbers had to be made up by the loan of aircraft from Fighter and Bomber Commands. When some squadrons were formed and equipped, they were posted overseas, creating a deficiency.

Aircraft were required, not only in terms of numbers, but also of suitable types. Only one type had been specifically designed for Coastal Command's main task of maritime reconnaissance, namely the Catalina. The Beaufort had been designed as a torpedo-bomber, but had engine and armament problems, and many were posted overseas.

Two aircraft that had been designed specifically for maritime work were the under-powered Blackburn Botha and the Saro Lerwick; both proved to be unsatisfactory for operations. All the other types of the Command's front-line aircraft were modified civil, bomber or fighter aircraft. In modifying some types, the safety of the aircrew was

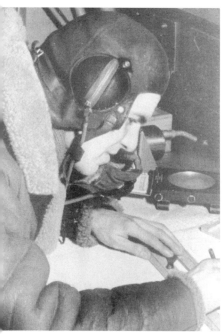

10. The circular slide rule on the Navigation computer.
I.C.A.N = International Convention of Air Navigation.

The
K.B.B.-Kollsma
Sensitive
Altimeter.

9. A navigator using the basic instruments for DR navigation in Coastal Command; a Mercator's chart, parallel rulers, Douglas protractor, dividers, pencil and a computer.

11. Altimeters could be set in millibars or altitude in feet but due to changes in air pressure, altitude displays could be false.

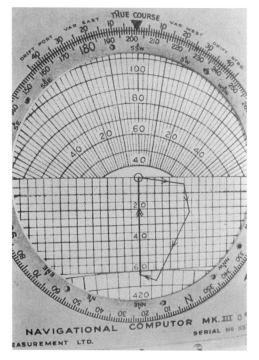

12. A Course Setting Calculator (CSC) as was still being used in April 1939 as an aid in Dead Reckoning (DR) navigation.

13. A navigational computer that succeeded the CSC in DR navigation.

jeopardised by replacing self-sealing tanks (Liberators), or reducing armament by removing turrets (Halifaxes). The prime need for most types was range, and coupled with that was endurance, for such tasks as convoy escorts. Only one type available to the Command with the range to close the 'Mid-Atlantic-Gap', and with effective armament, was the Liberator, although the Catalina had greater endurance. The deficiency in range for some, such as the Halifaxes and Mosquitoes, had to be compensated by the addition of drop tanks. As most aircraft engines were designed for fighters or bombers, there were some problems for Coastal Command's crews, who had to operate from sea level to say 24,000ft.

Substituting some engines with the Bristol Hercules or Pratt & Whitney Wasps overcame some engine difficulties. In production and procurement Coastal Command became third in priority, most notably by production of the successful Sunderland being reduced in favour of the unsuccessful Stirling bomber. It was fortunate, and literally a life-saver, that Hudsons and Liberators were not required by Bomber Command. The Lockheed Corporation was the most helpful at both Command and squadron level to Coastal Command.

Coastal Command's tasks, such as reconnaissance and convoy escorts, lacked the glamour of other Commands, and due to what was considered a 'defensive' role, it found that precedence was given to its two 'offensive' sisters, Fighter and Bomber Commands. Coastal Command was truly the Cinderella in respect of aircraft.

CHAPTER TWO

Armament

At the outbreak of war in September 1939 no clear plan for the armament of Coastal Command's aircraft was evident. The Command's duties, however, had been decided: they were to patrol the northern exits to the North Atlantic against enemy surface warships attempting to break out.[1] This task was covered by flying-boats patrolling a more northerly line from Britain to Norway, while the more southerly patrols to Norway were flown by Hudsons. Of the nineteen squadrons listed in Coastal Command's Order of Battle for 1 September 1939 only those equipped with Sunderland or Hudson aircraft were considered suitable to undertake these sorties, but at that time, only No. 224 Squadron had converted to Hudsons. Both the Hudson and Sunderland flying-boat were aircraft that operated in the front line throughout the war, and may serve as examples in respect of much of the armament used in Coastal Command.[2]

Overall control of Coastal Command was given to the Admiralty, which allocated tasks that were to undertake reconnaissance from Great Britain to Norway, covering the exit routes from German ports to the North Atlantic for surface vessels. No provision had been made for covering the whole of the European coastline from the Spanish frontier to North Cape, and no allowance had been made for enemy fighters being based in Norway; only the prospect of the Low Countries being occupied had been considered.

The armament for aircraft considered suitable to cover the exit routes in 1939, the Hudson and the Sunderland, was hardly enough, as in combat both types were outranged by the enemy's cannon.[3] No adequate provision had been made to combat U-boats, against which the British had quite useless bombs available. The Air Ministry considered Coastal third in order of priority, after Fighter and Bomber Commands, and had lacked any effective assessment of Coastal Command's needs.

The Admiralty had pinned its faith in Asdic being able to counter any U-boat activity, and as Air Vice-Marshal W.E. Oulton stated, Coastal Command's tasks reflected the Admiralty's view: 'With great confidence in the effectiveness of Asdic, they at first regarded the U-boat as a relatively minor problem; their chief concern was with the activities of the enemy's surface ships.' Lt Cdr W.J.R. Gardner expressed a similar view, with the Admiralty having 'an almost touching confidence in Asdic ...', stating also [for Coastal Command], 'There was no weapon truly suitable for engaging a submarine.'[4]

As a result of the Royal Air Force being formed in 1918 from Army and Navy services, armament available was designed more for the Army and Navy rather than for use by Coastal Command. Of essentially attack weapons such as bombs, after the First World War, 'the RAF was left with stocks of aircraft bombs which were a mixed collection of shapes and sizes, with many different methods of construction and fusing'.[5] This was possibly due to the wish to economise, but more likely, that no order had been issued to dispose of them; thus the situation prevailed by default rather than due to a definite policy.

Between the wars, 'Prevailing conditions dictated a policy in which weapon efficiency was second to aircraft design, ... restricted money available for research and development, caused proposals to be curtailed and was largely responsible for the state of affairs in which we found ourselves in 1939.'[6]

Although the Air Staff had discussions between 1921 and 1922 regarding a policy for bombs and future developments, the range of bombs considered was geared more to land targets rather than for maritime use. In 1923, however, Wg Cdr T.R. Cave-Brown-Cave, commanding the Marine and Armament Experimental Establishment, proposed a 'Buoyant Bomb'. It was intended for dropping ahead of ships under way, and therefore, unlike mines, could not be swept. They would have exploded near the unprotected bottom of the ship. These bombs were supplied to Coastal Command's bases at the outbreak of the Second World War, but no trials appear to have been undertaken by Coastal Command, and their use may be questioned due to the limited application and as a possible hazard to Allied shipping.[7]

It was not until 20 May 1935 that bombs and the necessary components for effective attacks on 'every type of target from the air' came to be considered. This was by a Bomb Sub-Committee in which there were representatives of the Air Ministry, Admiralty and the War Office.[8] The outcome was to give priority to the development of a 30–50 lb bomb intended to be used against motor transport, houses and billets. Thus was priority given to Bomber Command. However, in April 1938 there were air-drop trials for live 40 lb, 250 lb and 500 lb bombs at Martlesham Heath. For Coastal Command at the beginning of the Second World War, 'The primary weapon of all Coastal Command squadrons was the 100 lb anti-submarine bomb ...'[9]

This bomb was being developed in 1926

following a request by the Admiralty in 1925. Trials had been undertaken in 1927.[10] When the 100 lb anti-submarine bombs Marks I and II were introduced into service in 1931, no tests were made against a submarine or any investigation of their behaviour under water.[11] The Admiralty required a 100 lb bomb for the Fleet Air Arm (FAA), but the Air Council wished for 250 lb and 500 lb bombs with fillings that were unacceptable to the Admiralty because of possible corrosion, due, perhaps, to ammonium nitrate in the filling, but by May 1939 an order was given for fifty bombs of each size, almost certainly a trial order.[12]

The 100 lb anti-submarine bomb was useless; as Captain Peyton Ward, RN, a naval liaison officer at Coastal Command headquarters, stated in an appreciation of the U-boat threat:

> Aircraft alone cannot kill submarines because the majority of them can carry only two 100 lb bombs; the remainder only carry two to four bombs, neither of which are lethal to a submarine as witness the reports from our own submarines who have been bombed by them and in a Swordfish's case admit the bombs exploded right on them.[13]

DEPTH CHARGES

On 3 September 1939 No. 224 Squadron's Hudsons were armed with bombs and not depth charges (DCs).[14] At that time the only type of depth charge available to Coastal Command was the naval 450 lb DC, which then, of Coastal Command's aircraft, could only be carried by flying-boats. Its advantage over anti-submarine bombs was that it could be dropped from very low altitude, which for accuracy, with no suitable bombsight available, was essential.

Captain Ruck-Keene, RN, suggested on 16

August 1940 that DCs should be standard armament for aircraft on anti-submarine duties, and this was approved by the Admiralty. This was followed by Captain Peyton-Ward writing to the Air Officer Commanding-in-Chief of Coastal Command on 8 September 1940, proposing that aircraft deployed on convoy escorts should carry depth charges, and on 30 September 1940 he raised the matter again.[15]

The naval 450 lb DC was modified for air use with nose and tail fairings, and essentially made so that it could be dropped 'safe'. This was in case an aircrew had to ditch. As Air Vice-Marshal Oulton stated: 'Through the local initiative of a Flight Commander, the standard naval depth charge was adapted and then improved.'[16] It had a hydrostatic pistol and was considered 'a safe weapon to release from aircraft at 50 ft or less … but that the low altitude release was an advantage in comparison with a 250 lb anti-submarine bomb … which detonated instantly and was likely to porpoise',[17] that was, the bomb was likely to break surface periodically.

The 450 lb naval DC remained a standard weapon during the first two years of the war, although it would have been extremely dangerous for any aircraft that lacked an accurate means of confirming its altitude.[18] When No. 221 Squadron, equipped with Wellingtons, operated from Limavady in May 1941 over the North Atlantic, it carried three 450 lb DCs for day patrols, but for night sorties took five 250 lb bombs.

This was probably due to no suitable illumination being available to release depth charges from a low altitude; although not so stated in the squadron's records.[19] At the beginning of the war, the fuses available were unreliable and the path of the weapons underwater was unpredictable.

As the weight of 450 lb precluded many such charges being carried in FAA aircraft, the Admiralty initiated the design of a 250 lb DC.

It could be used, not only by the FAA, but also by Coastal Command's Hudsons, which had a sophisticated bomb-release gear. Initially, the DC, when just in the form of a cylinder, proved unstable, and a tail fin was fitted.

The 250 lb DC was cleared for use in the RAF on 23 January 1941, and by May 1941 tests showed that the tail fin had corrected the fall of the charge up to heights of 250 ft.[20] The efficiency of the early types of DC was to be improved by replacing the Amatol filling with Torpex. The comparative efficiencies of the Amatol and Torpex charges vary according to the source, but a figure of thirty per cent improvement with Torpex appears likely. In respect of lethal distance from the U-boat, published sources give lethal ranges from 9 ft to 33 ft, but from operational records of many attacks by Coastal's aircraft, the mean lethal range of a 250 lb depth charge appears as about 19 ft.

It was not before June 1942, however, that detonation problems with the fuse were resolved and 'the Command had a reliable and lethal weapon'.[21] A pistol that could cause detonation of the DC at 32 ft depth was available, and Torpex was coming into use. Even the relatively shallow depth of 32 ft for detonation was improved upon, and in August 1944 depths of 16–24 ft were aimed at by an Anti-Submarine Warfare Committee, but would be achieved in January 1945 with a mean depth of 19 ft.[22] These improvements stemmed, not only from practical experience in operations, but also from research and trials that were always being undertaken. Captain Peyton-Ward interviewed Coastal Command aircrew who attacked enemy submarines, and analysed those attacks. At a meeting on 29 November 1941 he had commented on the Type 13 pistol giving a setting of 26–30 ft depth for detonating a DC, and stated that an aircraft should release its whole load of charges.

The advisability of that might be

questioned, as there were some abortive actions when as many as ten DCs were released, and then later, another sighting would be made, for which there were no DCs for an attack.[23]

The development of armament and the development of tactics continued during the war; and not in isolation, but following the successes and failures in operations. A standing committee on anti-submarine warfare had reported in March 1942 that it was more efficient to release a large stick of 250 lb DCs than the equivalent weight in 500 lb DCs, as the required lethal stick was equal to four times the bombing error in range.[24] For attacks against U-boats, the Commander-in-Chief of Coastal Command, Sir Philip Joubert, wrote to the ACAS(T) on 31 March 1942: 'For the entire duration of the war, to date, we have been attempting to attack U-boats with two types of depth charge, neither of which is capable of giving satisfactory results.'[25]

Sir Philip added that Coastal Command had begun with the Admiralty's 450 lb DC, followed by the Mark VIII 250 lb DC, which was not cleared for heights above 150 ft and speeds of 150 knots. He hoped for a 500 lb DC filled with Torpex, which could be dropped from 5,000 ft at 200 knots.

Hudson aircraft that were using 250 lb DCs with success up to October 1943 were, however, unable to take 500 lb weapons. There was, none the less, a positive response to Sir Philip's letter with the Director of Operational Research, stating on 7 May 1942 that on high priority the Director of Armament Development was to develop a weapon that would satisfy Coastal Command. The outcome was the production of a 600 lb depth bomb that could be dropped from a safe height of 5,000 ft, but as the Army and Navy were given priority in respect of Torpex fillings, Coastal Command came third in that respect. Trials were undertaken under the auspices of Gp Capt D'Aeth and Professor

Williams, who reported their findings on 16 December.[26]

It had been further mooted at Sir Philip Joubert's second meeting on 17 June 1942, when the name agreed for the new 500–600 lb was decided as a 'depth bomb'. This probably followed Sir Philip's awareness of the Americans having such a weapon, which could be dropped from 500 ft, albeit using a bombsight.[27]

Coastal Command's naval liaison officer, Captain Peyton-Ward, showed his awareness of the use of such a weapon when on 1 July 1943 he stated that for the pilot to avoid being shot down when attacking U-boats he was 'to get his high level attack off before being sighted'.[28] This opinion was repeated by Capt T. Dorling, RN, when referring to new weapons, such as the 600 lb bomb, being introduced in 1943.[29]

By 5 June 1943, the 600 lb depth bomb was considered to be in service, but there were developments for fuses between August 1943 and December 1944. In tests it was found satisfactory for heights between 1,200 ft and 5,000 ft at any speed and with spacings of greater than 80 ft.[30] Although the depth bomb was successful, it came into service too late to materially affect the anti-submarine war, and the 250 lb DC remained the standard weapon.

When Air Marshal John Slessor succeeded Sir Philip Joubert as Air Officer Commanding-in-Chief Coastal Command on 6 February 1943, Coastal Command was better equipped and aircrew had gained experience in anti-submarine warfare. As Sir John Slessor commented in retrospect: 'The decisive weapon of the anti-submarine squadrons was the Mark XI Torpex-filled depth-charge, dropped in "sticks" of four to eight from point-blank altitude, fifty to a hundred and fifty feet.' But of other weapons, Slessor stated, 'The most effective was the rocket with the 25 lb solid head ... the 600 lb special anti-submarine bomb ... and the 40 mm cannon ...

none of them comparable as U-boat killers with the old Mark XI depth-charge.'[31]

GUNS

In May 1928 the Chief of the Air Staff criticised armament for aircraft, which at that time had available the Lewis and Vickers guns from the First World War. The Air Staff had also decided that there was nothing to be gained by introducing 0.5 in guns.[32]

During the 1930s there had been various trials, and by 1939 the Vickers Gas-Operated (VGO) 0.303 in machine-gun was considered suitable for service. On 22 June 1934 the Browning machine was recommended as a replacement for the Vickers gun, and by March 1936 the first British-made Brownings were delivered.[33]

The Vickers Gas-Operated 0.303 in and the Browning 0.303 in machine-guns became standard weapons for Coastal Command throughout the war. Rates of fire could be varied in the designs, but typical figures were 900 rounds per minute for the VGO and 1,030 rounds per minute for the Browning.[34]

The disadvantage of the VGO, as used in Coastal Command, was that ammunition was pan fed, with greater likelihood of jamming, and if in action, the need to change pans at a critical time. The Browning was belt fed, and despite being constructed of many parts, was almost trouble free. It could be considered of superior design, and perhaps the only problem would stem, not from the Browning, but by not aligning the rounds in the belt feed.

The all-up weight for Coastal Command aircraft was always a serious consideration, with the general aim of maximum endurance and range. This aspect had to be taken into account when the number and type of guns were being reviewed.

This was apparently left in abeyance until 21 October 1942, when an Anti-U-boat Committee considered the matter. It was then suggested that more forward-firing guns

should be fitted to Coastal Command aircraft. The weight given for an installation of two 0.303 in machine-guns with ammunition for a 15-second burst was 400 lb; for one 0.5 in machine-gun, 500 lb, and for two 0.5 in, 690 lb.[35] These factors were taken into consideration according to operational requirements, and it was always a compromise.

The enemy aircraft, using 20 mm cannon, would typically open fire at 1,000 yd, and U-boats at an even greater range. The effective range of Coastal Command's guns was considered to be 400 yd, at which they were harmonised, and so they were outranged by the enemy.[36]

Coastal Command's records show that at headquarters the Air Officers Commanding-in-Chief, firstly Sir Frederick Bowhill and then Sir Philip Joubert, were pressing for improved armament for both attack and defence. Those in the line of battle, the operational squadrons, endeavoured to improve what was in their

14. The tail of a Sunderland with a Frazer-Nash turret armed with four 0.303 inch Brownings. In air-to-air combat it was not unknown for the hydraulic leads to these turrets to be cut and then to require manual operation.

power to do, albeit often quite unofficially, that was, their forward-firing armament. For example, No. 500 Squadron was prompted by its Commanding Officer, Wg Cdr Spotswood, attacking a U-boat to become aware of the need for another in the crew to give covering fire while the pilot could concentrate on the attack. This resulted in a 0.5 in Browning from an American aircraft being fitted to a No. 500 Squadron Hudson.[37] And the United States Navy squadron in Iceland – VP84 – attempted to fit 20 mm cannon in the nose of its PBYs.[38]

In the Sunderland squadrons, particularly those operating over the Bay of Biscay, there was the obvious need for more than the initial seven machine-guns, with four of those confined to the tail turret. It was certainly on the initiative of the RAAF No. 10 Squadron that its armament was increased to eighteen machine-guns, some of 0.5 in calibre.[39]

These were not only to counter anti-aircraft fire from U-boats, but when engaged in air-to-air combat with as many as half a squadron of enemy fighters. Wg Cdr Dundas Bednall, however, commanding a Sunderland squadron, was ordered to cease modifications to his aircraft.[40] Generally, nevertheless, Coastal Command was prepared to agree modifications as exemplified in other fields such as equipment for air-sea rescue, and most notably the Leigh Light.[41]

GUN TURRETS

Although some RAF aircraft had gun-turrets at the outbreak of the Second World War, they did not satisfy the needs of Bomber Command. Bomber Command aircraft were being lost in fighter attacks, largely from below. Thus it was Bomber Command rather than Coastal that established the criteria.

Types included the Bristol, such as on the Blenheim aircraft, the Frazer-Nash and the Boulton & Paul. The Frazer-Nash and the Boulton & Paul turrets became standard

15. The nose of a Wellington which is fitted with a Frazer-Nash hydraulic turret armed with two 0.303 inch Brownings.

equipment for Coastal Command. They were certainly improvements compared with the Anson's cupola and the turrets in Bristol Blenheims. What also became a standard was the installation of Browning 0.303 in, belt-fed guns to both the Frazer-Nash and the Boulton & Paul turrets.[42]

These types were not fool-proof: the Frazer-Nash had doors for entrance and exit that had to open outwards, and could foul the fuselage unless the turret was suitably orientated; the Boulton & Paul had a table that was clamped down after the gunner was seated. This could all too easily have snagged the CO_2 bottle on the gunner's Mae West. The long hydraulic leads to turrets on Sunderlands were not infrequently cut by enemy fire in combat, although they could be operated manually.[43] While guns such as the manually operated VGO had a fixed sight. There was also a reflector gunsight to serve with twin or quadruple Brownings in turrets, it was electrically illuminated and could be varied in intensity, but on very dark nights the gunner might see only the illumination of the gunsight.

CANNON

In 1937 the War Office undertook trials with

20 mm cannon that were produced in France, and by 1939 Air Ministry draughtsmen were working on 20 mm cannon with the BSA company in England. The 20 mm cannon became a standard weapon for Fighter Command, while in Coastal Command, attempts were made to install a 20 mm cannon in a Hudson, firing aft, but without success. Also, 40 mm cannon were to be produced, and trials were undertaken in 1939.[44]

The Command's records give frequent reference to both the 20 mm and 40 mm cannon. Aspects considered were availability, weight of both the weapon and ammunition, and installation. A serious disadvantage was the limited number of shells that could be fired before the cannon components were worn out. As the 40 mm cannon could be used as an anti-tank weapon by the Army, should it not therefore be given priority where weight was of less consideration? The weight of 20 mm and 40 mm cannon was obviously greater than 0.303 in machine-guns, and there was much to be said for having 0.303 in machine-guns with the likelihood that out of, say, a total of seven guns, most would be able to fire, compared with one cannon that might fail. The weight, also, of a cannon's ammunition would preclude many rounds being taken.

Trials were attempted with the 40 mm cannon in Sunderlands, but proved unsatisfactory. The 20 mm cannon, although fitted to aircraft such as the Liberator, proved to be most suited to the Beaufighters of the strike wings. Not only were the Beaufighters then equal to enemy fighters in terms of armament (if not more so), but they were to be proved valuable in anti-shipping operations.

As pilots who operated with No. 404 (RCAF) Squadron have indicated, they could not only give covering fire for Torbeaus (Beaufighters adapted to carry torpedoes), but they could damage enemy shipping in their own right. For Coastal Command, Mosquitoes came rather late in service as strike aircraft, but some were equipped with 6-pounder cannon, and one U-boat, U-976, was claimed as sunk using this weapon on 25 March 1944.[45] Nevertheless, their greater weight and limited number of shells were not conducive to their use as an aircraft weapon.

TORPEDOES

The policy in the use of torpedoes was that they were 'always considered to be the most effective weapon against shipping at sea …', but lack of a suitable aircraft and a shortage of torpedoes resulted in this method of attack by Coastal Command being 'severely handicapped'.[46] They were nevertheless used by Coastal Command in shipping strikes on occasions.

Of torpedo supply, at a meeting on 10 December 1941 the Admiralty gave priority to the Fleet Air Arm, which was to receive 75 per cent of aircraft types, but Coastal Command would get only 25 per cent.[47]

Disadvantages of torpedoes were their high cost, they were sensitive weapons and they were restricted in use for Coastal Command due to the limited areas in which they could be dropped because of the depth of water and geographical conditions off the enemy-controlled coastline. It was also uneconomic to use them against the low-tonnage shipping

16. A Wellington of No 221 Squadron which has just released a torpedo. Torpedoes were to be of limited use in shipping strikes when most of the targets were less than 6,000 tons.

that formed most of Coastal Command's targets[48] Furthermore, Coastal Command's torpedo-bomber, the Beaufort, was being posted overseas from August 1941.[49]

Following the setting up of a joint Admiralty/Air Ministry Committee meeting on 11 June 1942, a report from the Operational Research Section (ORS) stated that attacks on merchant vessels could be more effective if bombs rather than torpedoes were used, particularly so if the Mark XIV bombsight could be available.

A similar conclusion was reached in respect of the buoyant bomb, but that it would be of no value without the use of the Mark XIV bombsight.[50] The need for intensive training, a lack of aircraft, priority being given to the Navy and production limitations for the low-level bombsight; all these factors must have influenced those who decided the policy concerning torpedoes.

Torpedo trials were undertaken with Mark I and II Catalinas during the months of July, August and September 1941, and at a Coastal Command headquarter's meeting on 3 September it was stated that a Mark XII torpedo could be used if one was prepared to accept the limitations of releasing from 35 ft altitude at an airspeed of 90 knots.

Without a radio altimeter to give an accurate altitude reading, that would be far too dangerous, and a Catalina with a 104 ft wingspan, flying steadily at 90 knots, would be an easy target for anti-aircraft fire.[51] At a further meeting chaired by the Commander-in-Chief Coastal Command on 1 November 1941, the Deputy AOA confirmed that a radio altimeter was needed for these torpedoes to be used.[52]

It was stated at a later meeting when a torpedo policy was being considered, that the Admiralty was prepared for Coastal Command to use torpedoes 'whenever a favourable opportunity ...' occurred.[53] A 'favourable opportunity' was extremely

unlikely, due not only to the limited areas, but also to the need for either suitable cloud or night cover, escorts to be available for strike aircraft, ample warning for the strike aircraft to reach the target, for the forces to be effectively on 'standby' and for a worthwhile target to justify all the forces required and to suffer the risks involved.

BOMBSIGHTS

Following the production of the 600 lb depth bomb, a Mark III angular-velocity, low-level bombsight was developed. At the eighth meeting of the Command's Anti-Submarine Committee, chaired by Sir Philip Joubert on 16 December 1942, reports on trials were submitted by two squadrons. One of those squadrons was No. 59, commanded by Wg Cdr G.C.C. Bartlett, when the squadron was operating Liberator aircraft. Bartlett gave the results of his trials thus: Thirty-four bombs were dropped by three aimers at a stationary target, and later on at a target towed at 8 knots. For forty-two bombs the average range error was 18 yd but it was considered that the low-level sight's chief advantages would be demonstrated under operational conditions. Wg Cdr Bartlett, with his navigator, Plt Off Longmuir, considered also that the sight was a great advance on any previous method of low-level bombing, either by eye or with a bombsight.

The best figures achieved in No. 59 Squadron's trials were 6 yd range error with a release from 800 ft, and 5 yd flying straight and level from 800 ft, and 5 yd error when approaching at 100 ft but releasing from 400 ft with the aircraft's nose up.

In contrast, at the same meeting, Professor Blackett gave 20 yd range error for the Low Level Mark II and Mark XIV bombsights.[54] He considered the Mark III 'promising', and that the use of the Mark II could be improved if radio altimeters were available. Air Vice-Marshal Oulton, referring to the adoption of

17. A bomb-sight as fitted to a Lockheed Hudson in the navigator's compartment.

the Mark XIV bombsight in 1943, 'never trusted that device'.[55]

It was a characteristic of many pilots that they were wary of trusting equipment with which they might lack experience. They were aware, however, of how accurately, or otherwise, they could judge with their own eyes, on which they all so frequently had to rely. Furthermore, they would not need to take directions from the bomb aimer.

Sir Philip Joubert, however, decided that the Mark III low-level bombsight should be an operational requirement and that it should be used over the Atlantic, and the Mark XV over the Bay of Biscay.[56] Although not so stated, this could have been for two reasons: only a limited number of low-level bombsights were likely to be available, and over the Bay of Biscay one was more likely to have favourable visibility compared with operating over the Atlantic.

Despite the low-level sight being an operational requirement, a pilot who must have completed two tours of operations with Coastal Command wrote of the lack of a low-level sight.[57] Here again, such a plea would have stemmed from the lack of availability, and related to what priority was given to specific units. One of the first pieces of apparatus I used in an aircraft in April 1939 was a bombsight, and yet the Command never appeared to solve the need for bombsights to cover all the operational requirements for aircrew.

This was due to changes in policy, and the development of new weapons and changes in tactics. In attacks on either ships or U-boats, there was the need to act with the minimum delay, and many pilots opted to use their own judgement by direct sighting, often with considerable success.

MAD GEAR AND THE MARK 24 'MINE'

Two further anti-submarine weapons which came into use during the Second World War were named the 'Mark 24 Mine' and 'MAD'. Both the Mark 24 Mine and MAD (Magnetic Anomaly Detection) were to be used by the United States Navy's PBYs (Catalinas) with success and when under Coastal Command control. The Mark 24 'mine' was really an acoustic homing torpedo, and was to be used by first dropping depth charges prior to releasing the 'mine'; this was to cause the U-boat to submerge and thus be unaware of any torpedo. The first success with the homing torpedo was claimed by Lt Wood when operating from Iceland on 20 June 1943 against U-388.

Lt Wood saw the U-boat split open, with 10 to 15 ft of its interior visible. Four days later, VP84 sank another U-boat, again using the Mark 24 'mine'.[58] Publicity was lacking in respect of such armament, and on RAF squadrons even the Commanding Officers were not expected to see the 'mine'. The Mark 24 'mine' does, however, gain some brief reference in the minutes of the Command's meetings on 16 December 1943, when it was stated that the Admiralty was endeavouring to obtain a relaxation in the 'conditions of extreme secrecy'.[59]

After some experience using a parachute attachment with the 'mine', the policy for carrying the 'mine' was being reviewed.[60]

'MAD' was a system for detecting submerged U-boats. It comprised a sensitive magnetometer installed in a cone within the tail of a Catalina that could detect anomalies in the earth's magnetic field within a range of 400 ft, and was sensitive enough to detect a target within a few feet.

This was used in conjunction with retro-bombs of 65.5 lb filled with 25 lb Torpex. The bombs were rocket propelled at a speed coinciding with the aircraft's forward motion, and released rearwards from rails on the wings of the aircraft. Thus the bombs fell directly onto the target detected. MAD gear therefore possessed two advantages over depth charges: no presetting was required for depth, and the enemy would be unaware of attacks if no hits were scored.

VP63 Catalinas (PBYs) of the United States Navy carried 24–30 such retro-bombs, which were released in groups of eight or ten each. The first kill by VP63 of the USN was of U-761 on 24 February 1944.[61] This was in the Straits of Gibraltar, which proved particularly suitable for operating MAD gear because, although the Straits represented a 'gate' to the Mediterranean of thirty-five miles, the gap was effectively reduced to 7 or 8 miles for submarines attempting to negotiate them due to water-depth limitations.

It was therefore comparatively easy for both aircraft and surface vessels working in conjunction with each other to form a 'barrier' to U-boats. MAD gear was also tried in other areas, such as the English Channel, but

conditions proved less suitable and no successes were recorded.[62]

ROCKET PROJECTILES

A weapon that was developed during the Second World War was the rocket projectile. Rockets had been used in the First World War fired from the ground against balloons, and before 1939 were again being considered by the War Office. In 1941 rockets were also considered by the Air Staff as an air weapon against armoured vehicles, but in Coastal Command they came to serve in both the anti-submarine war and in shipping strikes.

For use by aircraft, there were two types of head – a 60 lb one with high explosive, and a 25 lb armour-piercing head of steel. Groups of four rockets were arranged on racks under each wing of an aircraft and were to be fired

18. Beaufighters of No 404 Squadron RCAF armed with eight 60lb head rocket projectiles as used in shipping strikes. Alternatives were 25lb solid head projectiles.

electrically by the pilot.

There were trials in November 1942 at Pendine Sands, with final trials in respect of anti-submarine attacks in February 1943. Against U-boats the range was considered to be less than 1,000 yards, and the rocket projectiles (RPs) could be fired in pairs or as a salvo.[63]

One of the first successful attacks using rocket projectiles was by Flg Off H.C. Bailey of No. 48 Squadron, who sank U-594 on 4 June 1943. It was with 25 lb armour-piercing heads, and as Flg Off Bailey commented at the time, one had to be careful to avoid some heads that followed an upward trajectory.

The rockets tended to follow the line of flight of the aircraft rather than the line of sight. Although in tests one could expect to achieve 30 per cent hits, one hit was lethal to a U-boat.[64]

Against U-boats a definite procedure needed to be followed, as an ex-608 Squadron pilot stated:

We commenced rocket-firing training by doing twenty-degree dives from 2,000 ft at 200 knots and pulling out at 400 ft, hence wing ripples, etc. Next a hand-held camera was used in the nose by the navigator to photograph the target, a painted circle in a wadi, when told, as we pulled out of the dive. From the photographs the dive angle could be calculated and we adjusted the dive next time. When the angle was good enough we practised at sea with a full rocket load of eight. We would drop a sea marker and then dive at it firing single rockets and later salvoes taking photographs of the strike.

We formed a habit of making violent climbing turns after firing because the rockets were unpredictable under water and sometimes after a shallow entry would emerge from the water in front of us. As a result of using rockets under the wings the flight characteristics of the Hudson changed a great deal, our cruising speeds usually 120 knots [were increased] to 140 knots and we had to land at a higher speed of ninety-five knots to

feel safe as they were prone to high-speed flick stalls.[65]

About the same time that Hudsons were using rocket projectiles against U-boats, the Beaufighters of the strike wings were employing them against enemy shipping, but with rather different tactics and with more strongly constructed aircraft; as a survivor from No. 404 (RCAF) Squadron relates:

In August 1943 the squadron went in rotation to Tain, Scotland, to learn to fire rockets ... they were armed with armour-piercing heads and could pass straight through a ship. They were harmonised so that a pair of rockets arrived with a spread of 20 ft between each pair. When entering the water they levelled out and thereby struck a ship underwater. Aiming was relatively easy: we fired them when we reached a point in our twenty-degree dive from 1,200 ft where our cannon and machine guns harmonised. This could be determined by the splashes we observed in the water.

Early in our dive the splashes were all around the ship. As we got closer the splashes converged until they all met at 700ft, the point of harmonisation. At that point we pressed the button on the left of the control column and off went the rockets. They would then automatically straddle the ship. Only if our aim of the cannons was off or the aircraft was skidding were we likely to miss. So in our own right we did damage to the ships and we still cleared the way for the torpedo-carrying Beaufighters to sneak in under. We found that our strafing efforts almost silenced anti-aircraft fire altogether.[66]

It can be said that there was much to justify the use by Beaufighters of rocket projectiles against merchant shipping, using both high explosive (HE) and armour-piercing heads. Although they were useful against U-boats, depth charges were then the preferred weapon.

CONCLUSIONS

There was no specific armament policy for Coastal Command on the outbreak of the Second World War.

Armament available stemmed from the First World War. The Chief of Air Staff considered armament for Bomber and Fighter Commands' requirements rather than any need by Coastal in either defensive or offensive roles.

Initially, the only offensive weapons available to Coastal Command were bombs and a naval depth charge, the latter confined to use by flying-boats.

Torpedoes were 'out' due to lack of suitable aircraft; defensive armament was limited to 0.303 in machine-guns. Of necessity, naval depth charges were modified for aircraft use, and later, due to FAA requirements, a 250 lb depth charge became available for Coastal Command.

The needs of Fighter and Bomber Commands meant that there had to be improved offensive and defensive armaments, and so bombs, cannon and gun-turrets of improved design also became available for Coastal Command, albeit with priority given to other services. Likewise, for improved explosives such as Torpex, Coastal Command was last in priority.

Torpedoes proved to be limited in use, either in the conventional form such as was used with success against *Gneisenau*, or the acoustic homing torpedo (Type 24 'mine'), against U-boats. None the less, the naval historian, Capt Roskill, considered that torpedoes were the best weapons against

19. Inner view of the fuselage of a Wellington which when flying low, struck the sea, resulting in the bottom of the fuselage being torn out.

ships, but acknowledged that supplies were limited.[67]

Retro-bombs, used with MAD gear, were also shown to be of limited use, but due to geographical conditions.

The 20 mm cannon proved its worth on the specialised tasks of the Beaufighter strike wings, but the 6-pounder cannon in the Tsetse Mosquito anti-submarine role was of limited value.

Rocket projectiles were useful with either high explosive or armour-piercing heads, but best applied in the anti-shipping role rather than in anti-U-boat warfare.

Depth bombs came too late in the anti-submarine war to affect materially the outcome, as also the necessary bombsight.

The initiatives of individual officers in Coastal Command, at headquarters, on squadrons or stations, played a significant role in the use of whatever armament became available, and helped to promote the development of weapons suited to Coastal's tasks.

Despite their limited range compared with the enemy's cannon, 0.303 in Brownings proved their worth, particularly when an increased number were placed in forward-firing positions to counter AA fire during attacks on U-boats.

Overall, the three outstanding pieces of armament in Coastal Command were the 250 lb bomb, the 250 lb depth charge and the 0.303 in Browning machine-gun.

From the ultimate score of ships and U-boats sunk or damaged by Coastal Command-controlled aircraft, the most valuable weapons were the 250 lb bomb and the 250 lb depth charge.

Throughout, however, Coastal Command remained last in order of priority for armaments, even in respect of the Torpex filling for the invaluable 250 lb depth charge.

CHAPTER THREE

Anti-Submarine Warfare
1939–1941

INTRODUCTION

There are many publications that refer to anti-submarine operations in the Second World War, but few, if any, are devoted to the Battle of the Atlantic from the point of view of Coastal Command.

The standard work covering anti-submarine operations may be *The War at Sea*.[1] Parallel to that are two volumes, Nos I and X of Professor S.E. Morison's *History of United States Naval Operations in World War II*.[2] Some United States Navy squadrons of aircraft operated within Coastal Command, and Morison gives coverage of their sorties.

A work intended for the general reader is Dan Van der Vat's *The Atlantic Campaign*.[3] Van der Vat refers notably to aircraft best covering convoys by sweeps around a convoy rather than by close escort; also, the lack of Liberators provided for anti-submarine operations.

The German point of view is best given by Admiral Dönitz's *Memoirs*, which are based on his experiences and war diaries.[4] *Fregattenkapitän* Günter Hessler, in his *The U-boat War in the Atlantic 1939–1945*, gives an analysis of the U-boat diaries with emphasis on the battles between 'wolf packs' and convoys.[5] Another former U-boat commander, Peter Cremer, has published his autobiographical *U-333 The Story of a U-boat Ace*. Cremer gives an overall view of the Second World War and acknowledges help from British and American sources.[6]

From the outbreak of war in September 1939, right up to the end of hostilities in Europe, there was a progressive development in equipment used by Coastal Command in anti-submarine-warfare (ASW).

There was progressive development also in weapons specifically intended for aircraft in attacking U-boats. The role of Coastal Command changed in both emphasis and location throughout the war, responding promptly to what was required of the Command in the light of major land battles in addition to the war at sea. In 1939, Coastal Command had no ASV (Radar), no weapon lethal to U-boats, and was grossly deficient in modern aircraft, with none specifically designed for anti-submarine-warfare. The sinking of the liner *Athenia* on 3 September 1939 made it apparent that there was a threat from U-boats, and not just from surface warships.

After the Battle of Britain in 1940, Coastal Command's limited forces could be directed less to anti-invasion sorties and more to anti-submarine measures. From the outset of war, the naval liaison officer, Captain Peyton-Ward, at Coastal Command headquarters, was plotting movements of U-boats and advising the Commanders-in-Chief accordingly. The occupation of the French Biscay ports in 1940, plus the occupation of the Norwegian ports, put a greatly increased load on the Command, with German U-boats then able to use more freely a northern exit route to the Atlantic and a much shorter route from the French ports.

Mark I ASV (Aircraft-to-Surface Vessel) was coming into service in 1940, but was considered as unreliable by aircrew.

When an Admiralty memorandum on the strengthening of Coastal Command was being considered by the War Cabinet's Defence Committee on 5 November 1940, Coastal Command was referred to by the First Lord of the Admiralty, the Rt Hon. Mr A.V. Alexander, as 'the Cinderella of the RAF'.[7] This was repudiated by the Air Minister, Sir Archibald Sinclair. On 10 December 1940 Winston Churchill announced that the Command would be under operational control of the Admiralty.[8]

The year 1941 marked the entry into the war of Russia and the USA. For Coastal Command, on the debit side there was the requirement to escort convoys to Russia against U-boats; but from America, some help and cooperation was gained in respect of both aircraft and equipment, such as radar, which was still being developed.

For the development of anti-submarine warfare, however, there was Winston Churchill's directive in 1941 on the Battle of the Atlantic, followed by the first meeting of the Battle of the Atlantic Committee, which was chaired by Churchill on 19 March 1941.[9]

In 1941 there was the tentative use of a modified naval depth charge, albeit limited to one type of land aircraft in addition to flying-boats. In 1941 also there was a considerable improvement in aircraft for the Command, with Wellingtons, Catalinas and a limited number of Liberators. The German Enigma codes were broken by the Allies under what was coded Ultra, although the enemy was also able to break the Allies' codes. These sources of intelligence were considered paramount in the Battle of the Atlantic, by, for example, Professor Jürgen Rohwer.[10] In 1941 an Operational Research Unit was headed by two scientists, Professors P. Blackett and E. Williams. One of their tasks for Coastal Command was to analyse aircraft attacks on U-boats.[11]

In 1942 Coastal Command was beginning to take some offensive against U-boats, and the Leigh Light was first used with success for night attacks. During Operation Torch, the Command's aircraft undertook a successful campaign against U-boats, with the notable use of 250 lb depth charges with shallow-setting pistols.

Following the move of the German battle-cruisers from Brest, there was a definite shift of Coastal Command's effort to the Atlantic, but still using the early marks of ASV, although by then the Mark II was in service. Coastal Command's ASV, which still used 1.5 m wavelength, was countered by Metox receivers to detect it by U-boats. America was totally unprepared for countering U-boats on entering the war, and was subjected to a disastrous U-boat onslaught, *Pauchenslag*, off its eastern seaboard for the first half of the year until a limited convoy system had been organised.

Early 1943 saw the defeat of U-boats in the North Atlantic, with their withdrawal ordered by Admiral Dönitz on 24 May. In that year also, another anti-submarine weapon was used with success – the rocket projectile. About that time also, improved radar (Mark III) was coming into service, notably short wave (9.1 cm), for which, initially, the U-boats had no detecting devices.

New weapons had been used successfully, such as the Mark 24 'mine' (the acoustic homing torpedo), and the retro-bomb with MAD gear. The Allies' counter to the *Schnorchel* that enabled U-boats to operate submerged was the sonobuoy, coded 'High Tea', and able to detect submerged submarines.

An agreement had been reached in Washington with the Americans and Canadians for deployment of long-range aircraft from Newfoundland in defence of convoys. This was significant for two reasons: not only did it result in closing the Mid-Atlantic Gap south of Cape Farewell, but demonstrated also that the Americans were prepared to cooperate on an Atlantic, rather than just an American, coastline basis.[12]

With the battle in the Atlantic largely won, there was a shift from the west to the North Sea and St George's, the Bristol and the English Channels for Coastal Command in 1944. The prime duty for the Command became support for Operation Overlord – the invasion of Western Europe. Sorties for Coastal Command ranged from Norway, with the Skagerrak and Kattagat, down to the Spanish coastline. Other sorties still prevailed, however, around the shores of the British Isles. In 1944, there were then a number of *Schnorchel*-equipped U-boats, but there were some detected by sight. Another anti-submarine weapon that came into use was the 600 lb depth bomb, together with a bombsight for medium altitudes.

The anti-submarine war was not completely over in 1945, as Germany was using midget submarines, the *Seehunds*, over the North Sea, and had been developing improved U-boats, which, thankfully for the Allies, came too late to alter the course of the war. Although there was no radical change in Coastal Command's anti-submarine policy with changes in the Commanders-in-Chief, the tenures of the four wartime commanders reflect the situation during their respective periods of office.

Thus, for Sir Frederick Bowhill, from 1939 to 1941, it was a matter of holding the line with the limited forces available, but with no definite policy in respect of U-boats. The Command was still virtually ancillary to the Navy, with its prime duty being reconnaissance against surface warships.

When Sir Philip Joubert succeeded Bowhill in 1941, the Command's forces were still closely involved with the Admiralty's concern regarding the enemy's surface fleet. Although

the Command was receiving an increasing number of aircraft, whole squadrons were being posted overseas, and it was not until towards the end of his tenure that Sir Philip was able to undertake some initiative in offensive sorties against U-boats in Operation Bolero, albeit for a limited time and in a limited area.

The year 1942 might be considered a period of consolidation, when Coastal Command's policy was not only for anti-submarine warfare but also for the Command's other duties, notably anti-shipping operations. This was despite the fact that Sir Philip was losing much of his trained forces in postings, as soon as they were formed.

Air Marshal John Slessor acknowledged the 'spade work' of his two predecessors when he took command in February 1943, when the Battle of the Atlantic was not quite over. He made no appreciable change in policy but opted in anti-submarine warfare for the emphasis to be on 'the trunk of the tree'[13] that was the transit route for U-boats through the Bay of Biscay.

Air Marshal Slessor was no less mindful, however, of the need to counter any concentrations of U-boats in the area of convoys; thus his policy was to consider both areas according to operational conditions and requirements. Although the Admiralty had overall command of Coastal Command's operations, for Slessor there was no appreciable effect on Coastal Command's operations and the cooperation that prevailed between the two services.[14]

Coastal Command's records emanating from Air Chief Marshal Sir Sholto Douglas show that he continued to fight the battle against U-boats, but during his tenure it was largely in home waters, including the Channels, the Biscay ports, and, much as was the case in 1939, the northern transit route for U-boats.

Sir Sholto had succeeded Air Marshal

Slessor in January 1944, and during his tenure of office considerable effort was devoted to Operation Overlord. He showed, as was so for Sir Philip and Air Marshal Slessor, his preparedness to take the offensive in anti-submarine warfare. The minutes of his staff meetings also indicate just how much attention was given to equipment of aircraft. In his case, it was improved radar and installation of radio altimeters, and always with what he considered to be the right type of aircraft and armament.

In 1945 the Command was able to give attention to those finer points. In the anti-submarine war undertaken by Coastal Command, the connective thread virtually throughout was the naval liaison officer – Captain Peyton-Ward. There is no doubt that he played a leading role in its continuity; this was through analysis initially of U-boat transits, followed by an analysis of sightings and attacks, not only in collaboration with the Navy's tracking room, but also by debriefing of the aircrew who were involved. Peyton-Ward, therefore, provided for Coastal Command what Professor Jürgen Rohwer considers the crucial factor in the Battle of the Atlantic, that is the intelligence that he gained from those sources, which he gave as an afterword to Dönitz's *Memoirs*. Peyton-Ward conferred with the Commanders-in-Chief of Coastal Command, and they, in their dispatches and autobiographies, acknowledge his work.[15]

The anti-submarine war may be summed up in three words: ships, U-boats and aircraft. Ships were our lifeline; U-boats were to sink them; aircraft were to save them. All other factors were ancillary to those three. Throughout the following I have, therefore, given data applicable to them. Technical matters such as the wavelength of radar transmissions, lethal range of depth charges, whether or not an aircraft could reach 17° W or 27° W, were all critical factors in anti-submarine warfare. I have, therefore, stated such data in the script. Ultimately in such battles, the success or otherwise depends on the man at the controls who presses a button or trigger, and I have mentioned the names of some of those men.[16] I have also included details of some representative ASW operations of Coastal Command, such as their first and last successes in the Second World War.

1937–1939

When the role of Coastal Command was being reviewed in 1937, the Senior Air Staff Officer, Air Commodore Geoffrey Bromet, wrote to the Commander-in-Chief, Sir Frederick Bowhill, pointing out that while both Fighter and Bomber Commands had clear roles in a war against Germany, it was 'not so for Coastal Command'.[17] The primary role Bromet then considered being a part in 'keeping local sea communications open, and preventing destructive seaborne raids on our coastline and ports'.[18]

No mention was made of U-boats, but rather what was probably prompted by awareness of the surface raids made in the First World War against the east coast of England. Both Sir Frederick and Bromet considered the defence of convoys, but they were in home waters and the defence would have been against surface raiders and aircraft rather than U-boats.

They were thus following the Admiralty's belief that there would be no threat by U-boats. Sir Frederick, however, was rightly concerned, as was to be shown, that surface raiders would enter the Atlantic before war was declared, and wished his forces to be at war stations four days in advance of any declaration of war.[19]

By January 1939 the Command's primary role was considered to be reconnaissance and convoy protection, but with no mention of that protection being against U-boats.[20] Both Sir Frederick and Air Commodore Bromet appreciated the need for cooperation between the RAF Commands and the Admiralty, and both those officers made visits to the Admiralty to clarify issues.[21] As was the case within Coastal Command, so also for the Chiefs of Staff at their Imperial Defence Committee Meetings: there was no reference to a possible threat from U-boats; rather was there mention of surface raiders and the effort necessary to counter them in The First World War.

The protection of trade routes was nevertheless considered. This aspect was raised by Admiral Sir Dudley Pound; the response of the Chief of Air Staff, Sir Cyril Newall, was, 'What foundation is there for the statement that "nothing would paralyse our supply system and sea-borne trade so certainly or immediately as successful attacks by surface raiders"?'[22] Sir Dudley's answer was that '... sufficiently severe it would necessitate locking up all our traders in harbour'.[23] Sir Cyril's response was: '... there was not enough jam to go round ... it would be preferable that we should face the risk of losses on our trade routes in the Atlantic rather than accept further reduction of our Air Forces at home which we could not afford'.[24]

Thus, even as late as just one month before the outbreak of war there was no mention of a possible U-boat threat either by Coastal Command officers or any of the Chiefs of Staff, and Sir Cyril appeared indifferent to Coastal Command's requirements, and the Admiralty thought of surface raiders rather than a U-boat threat.

It had been left to an Army officer, CIGS General Viscount Gort, to appreciate what was to be the dominant factor in the Second World War – merchant-shipping tonnage, without which Britain would have starved and a war could not have been fought through lack of materials. General Gort referred to merchant shipping prophetically as our *Achilles' heel*, although for him it was in respect of movement of troops.[25]

This attitude of being prepared to suffer shipping losses resulted in attempts being made to build ships to balance the numbers being sunk; thus the additional losses of merchant crews and the ships' cargoes were to be of lesser consideration. The cost of a ten-ton aircraft such as a Hudson, that needed only a crew of four; at that time was £17,000. Those figures contrast with a ship such as the SS *Kensington Court* of 4,863 tons with a crew of 34. In this case, the ship and a valuable cargo, which in other cases could be as high as £2m, was lost; although the crew was, quite exceptionally, saved.[26]

There was some justification for both points of view. In the case of surface raiders, the forays by the battle-cruisers *Scharnhorst* and *Gneisenau*, with the cruiser *Admiral Hipper* and the pocket battleships *Admiral Graf Von Spee* and *Deutschland*, showed how serious shipping losses due to surface raiders could be,[27] but were to be far outweighed by losses due to U-boats.[28]

For the Chief of Air Staff there was always the need to consider the requirements of four Commands, when in August 1939 the effect of the U-boat menace was still to be relearned, and the maritime role for aircraft was rated of least importance, due to priority being given to the offensive requirements of Bomber Command. Germany on the outbreak of war was largely concerned with the Continent; Britain had to consider the prospect of Italy entering the war against the British, in addition to Japan.

The Imperial Defence Committee was mindful of the situation in the Middle East and Far East, with Egypt and Singapore being of particular concern.[29] At these meetings the Cabinet appeared more concerned with keeping the British Empire intact, with its line of communication through the Suez Canal, and with maintaining its presence in the Far East. As was agreed by a group at the RAF

Staff College, 'Until well into the thirties RN priorities were Imperial rather than European. Japan was the most likely enemy, which implied battle-fleet actions, not attrition campaigns in defence of trade.'[30]

Many of the War Cabinet's decisions followed conversations and discussions with the French. Matters considered concerning the French included the question: 'Could we survive if [German] aircraft and submarines were established in the Low Countries and the Channel Ports?' (perhaps the one occasion when submarines gained a mention),[31] that the French expected the British to fight in France, also that 'the French might throw their hands in' unless assured of British support.[32]

No policy appears to have been decided in the event of a French capitulation, as the fiascos concerning the French fleet and its North African bases were to demonstrate. That both the Channel and Biscay ports became lost to the Allies and that the French did 'throw their hands in' were to require a considerable additional effort on the part of Coastal Command from June 1940 until the end of hostilities. This was because an additional length of coastline from the Frisian Islands down to the northern Spanish coastline needed to be covered.

Furthermore, the Germans were likely to use the ports for both U-boats and surface craft. Additionally, former Allied airbases could prove hostile, requiring additional fighter cover for Coastal Command's reconnaissance aircraft. All this came to pass.

No attention had been given to the potential Atlantic U-boat menace, and as the naval historian, Captain Roskill, states: 'The Naval Staff was confident of the great value of the new Asdic anti-submarine device. In 1937 they reported to the Shipping Defence Advisory Committee that "the submarine should never again be able to present us with the problem we were faced with in 1917".'[33] Captain Roskill adds: 'The Naval Staff also considered that anti-aircraft fire from the escort vessels would adequately protect the convoys against air attack.'[34]

Subsequent events were to show just how wrong these statements were. Ships were attacked not only off Britain's east coast by enemy aircraft, but also over the Atlantic and the Mediterranean. Initially there were insufficient escort vessels to provide anti-aircraft fire, and initially merchant ships lacked any defensive guns. This was partly due to lack of supplies of guns, but also lack of trained men to man them.

By 31 August 1939 Germany had deployed twenty-one U-boats in the Atlantic, eighteen in the North Sea and seven in the Baltic.[35] Those U-boats intended for the North Sea had sailed on 25 August, ostensibly to be in position by 27 August. On the outbreak of war, two patrol lines of U-boats had been formed, with five west of the Skagerrak, and another five threatening the area from Flamborough Head to the River Thames.

One was on passage to Utsire, off southern Norway, two others had been detailed for mine-laying and two were off the coast of Scotland.[36] The Germans rightly assumed that on the outbreak of war Britain's 'forces and air patrols would be small and inexperienced'.[37] How true; as Captain T. Dorling, RN, recorded: 'Coastal Command was ill equipped to deal with a long campaign against U-boats ... the Command was unable to devote anything like its full strength to anti-U-boat warfare owing to the heavy commitments imposed upon it in other directions.'[38]

The forces for Sir Frederick Bowhill at that time were only nineteen squadrons, of which only three could be considered suitably equipped with modern aircraft, and they were without any adequate anti-submarine weapons.[39] Those 'other directions' were towards reconnaissance to cover the possible breakout of Germany's surface warships with which the Admiralty was preoccupied, and with some justification, as later events were to show. It was fortunate at this stage in the war that Germany lacked the French Biscay ports, and therefore the staffs at Coastal Command's headquarters were able to concentrate reconnaissance sorties to the U-boats' northern exits into the Atlantic.

The sinking of the liner *Athenia* on the first day of the war by U-30 in position 56°44'N 14°05'W, in the Rockall area, demonstrated to all that there was a need to cover rather more than the northern North Sea exits against surface raiders.[40]

This sinking must have concentrated the mind of Winston Churchill, who until then appeared more interested in a comparison of our surface warships with those of Germany,[41] but on 4 September asked the Director of Naval Intelligence for a statement of the German U-boat forces, most of which were ocean-going, and which he described as 'formidable', as they were well able to operate over the whole of the North Atlantic convoy routes.[42]

In the first seven days of the war, thirteen other ships were sunk by U-boats in addition to the *Athenia*. Those sinkings were all, apart from one, within longitudes 07°49'W and 15°34'W, and most were therefore within the range of Hudson aircraft; but the only land-based squadron, No. 224, that had been re-equipped with those modern aircraft was operating instead over the North Sea.

Even at that early stage there was one land base available in Northern Ireland that might have been used to give some coverage to ships over the North-Western Approaches, but only a short-range Anson squadron was deployed there.[43] Most ships at that time were still sailing independently, and those losses prompted the Admiralty to operate a convoy system, but it was not completed until the following month.[44]

Northern exits to the Atlantic were being used by U-boats, and on 21 September

Captain Peyton-Ward, RN, at Coastal Command's headquarters, produced plans to cover the routes used by U-boats north of Scotland. He took account of the times when the U-boats were most likely to have surfaced to recharge batteries. On his first plan he marked the locations of Rockall and the *Athenia*'s sinking. Prior to 21 October the Fleet Air Arm had undertaken recces between the Shetlands and the north coast of Scotland; but from that date Coastal Command took over that area, and also the Fair Isle Channel and anti-submarine search areas north-west of Cape Wrath and down the Minch.

Peyton-Ward advocated also covering an area bounded by 59°00'N, 57°30'N and 08°00'W and 05°00'W. Those positions effectively covered the Rockall area, which was in comfortable range of Hudsons operating from Northern Ireland, as they were later to do when based at Limavady, or Tiree in the Inner Hebrides, to undertake sweeps as far as 17°W. Unfortunately, at the beginning of the war most of the land-based squadrons were using Ansons, and when the squadrons ultimately rearmed with Hudsons, they were required to undertake reconnaissance over the North Sea against the possible sailings of surface raiders.[45]

Because of recent sightings of U-boats, Peyton-Ward provided a second plan, suggesting that U-boats might be routed northwards along the Danish and southern Norwegian coasts before heading westwards as far as Rockall. He believed that Germany would expect the British to undertake air patrols between the Scottish and Norwegian coasts. Other areas considered for patrols were a line from the Shetlands to the Faeroes, and the Fair Isle Channel, between the Orkneys and the Shetlands.[46]

In fact, the Germans assumed that Britain, to seal off the North Sea, would 'use light and heavy forces along the Shetlands–Norway line'.[47] Captain Peyton-Ward's conclusions were that while nights were short and the moon waxing, aircraft patrols should be continuous throughout the twenty-four hours; that a combination of aircraft and surface craft was essential to ensure a kill; and that hunting craft must be based near the hunting areas. He would have been aware that in moonlight a surfaced U-boat could be seen from the air, but that in 1939 Coastal Command's aircraft lacked weapons to sink a U-boat.

Thus surface craft with their naval depth charges and/or cannon were essential to achieve a kill. There was a need to work in a combination of aircraft with surface vessels, the latter equipped with Asdic to detect the U-boat after it had submerged, and also with the vessel armed with lethal 450 lb depth charges. Although the 450 lb depth charge could be carried by flying-boats, it needed to be modified for the use of aircraft, and meanwhile Coastal Command could use only 100 lb or 250 lb bombs that were useless against U-boats.

By 7 September two U-boats were deployed west of Northern Ireland, three west of the Straits of Gibraltar, and all the other nine were covering the South-Western Approaches and the Bay of Biscay.[48] At that time the U-boats were crewed by well-trained men and commanded by dedicated captains, as subsequent events were to demonstrate. Those deployments effectively covered the Allies' major shipping routes to and from the United Kingdom. By then, eight Allied ships had been sunk by U-boats.

Three ships out of the eight were sunk by the German 'ace', Lt Prien, in U-47, and the following month he sank the British battleship HMS *Royal Oak* in the Royal Navy's base at Scapa Flow.[49] By 18 September six more Allied ships had been sunk, including the aircraft-carrier HMS *Courageous*. All these sinkings were east of 16EW; the first eight sinkings were all east of 15EW.[50] Some were therefore outside the range of the Navy's escort vessels, which were then limited to 13EW. Although 16EW was safely within the range of Sunderland flying-boats, they were far too few.

The limited numbers of Hudsons were concentrated on the east coast for North Sea operations, but even if based in Northern Ireland, as they were later in the war, it would have been impracticable for them to escort ships as far as 16EW due to limited endurance.

On 13 November 1939 a directive was issued to all Coastal Command's groups from headquarters that the destruction of U-boats was to be rated as of equal importance with the location of enemy surface craft. This resulted in many patrols being flown almost entirely as anti-U-boat sorties.[51] That momentous decision almost certainly stemmed from the serious losses of ships, including HMS *Courageous*, that had been sunk by U-boats, fifty-two in September and twenty-one in October.

What was now needed by Coastal Command, however, was sufficient aircraft of the right type, with sufficient range and endurance, weapons capable of sinking a U-boat, and improved ASV/radar. There remained also the need for effective illumination to attack surfaced U-boats at night. Even when those requirements were fulfilled, there remained the desirability in anti-submarine warfare for cooperation between surface forces and Coastal Command.

The Royal Navy at that time was seriously deficient in surface escorts, and of those then in service many lacked the range and were unable to extend their patrols far enough west into the Atlantic without refuelling, although after the Allied occupation of Iceland, refuelling could be undertaken there.

The Royal Navy came to appreciate that neither aircraft alone, nor escort vessels alone, was the best means of countering U-boats, but rather that a combined force of aircraft and surface vessels was best, as exemplified at the time of sinking three U-boats (U-461, U-462, U-504) in July 1943.[52] The Navy pressed for more aircraft to be used in anti-submarine warfare on 4 November 1940, and reiterated its demand as late as 8 May 1942.[53] Thus it had taken the Admiralty over a year to change its policy.

It became the policy of Admiral Dönitz to deploy U-boats as near to the shores of the British Isles as was reasonably safe, but to operate the U-boats further and further westwards as opposition from Coastal Command aircraft improved. It was, in fact, the aircraft rather than the Navy's warships that resulted in such strategy.

Germany's success in the initial phase of U-boat operations is best illustrated by Sir Winston Churchill's chart for the period 3 September until the German invasion of Norway on 9 April 1940, with all sinkings of merchant shipping eastwards of 15EW approximately,[54] but by December 1941 all merchant vessel sinkings by U-boats were clear of the British Isles.[55] Churchill would have given 9 April as the end of the first phase of sinkings of merchant vessels by U-boats in the Atlantic because by that date the U-boats had been withdrawn to concentrate along the Norwegian coastline in Operation *Hartmut* for support in the invasion of Norway.[56]

Dönitz's overall strategy was to deploy over a wide area, thus requiring the British to spread their opposing forces thinly; he was able to hold the initiative in the first phases of the U-boat war, and it remained for the Admiralty and Coastal Command to try and counter each move by Germany as each occurred.[57]

It may be argued that this state of affairs prevailed right up to 24 May 1943, when it could be said Coastal Command had gained the initiative, with Dönitz ordering the withdrawal of U-boats from the North Atlantic.[58] By that time Coastal Command's

aircraft had been equipped with ASV/Radar and many were also equipped with the Leigh Light.

It was the policy of Admiral Dönitz throughout the war, however, to sink Allied ships wherever they could be found. He was adept in using 'soft spots' where there was a lack of air cover, as was to be shown in the 'Mid-Atlantic Gap' south of Greenland, the 'Azores Gap' and in 1942 off the American eastern seaboard, and other areas such as East Africa and West Africa.

Influencing specifically Coastal Command's modified role was the work at the Command's headquarters of Captain Peyton-Ward, who deduced with remarkable accuracy the routes followed by German U-boats, and made recommendations concerning the deployment of the Command's aircraft in what was to become anti-submarine warfare.[59] For that purpose he was assisted by the Navy's Tracking Room and reports from aircrew.

Although the Admiralty's initial assessment concerning the war at sea may not be considered 'wrong', it certainly had underestimated that the main threat to Allied shipping would be from U-boats rather than surface warships or raiders. The Admiralty had pinned its faith on Asdic, the sonic means of detecting submerged U-boats, overlooking the fact that U-boats could attack while on the surface at night, thus nullifying the use of Asdic.

CONVOYS

The Admiralty had assumed control of all British merchant shipping by 26 August 1939, and embryo outward-bound ocean convoys began on 7 September.[60] Meanwhile thousands of ships were at sea devoid of any protection, and they were to become easy targets for both U-boats and surface raiders. Nevertheless, it was not until October that a convoy system was formed.[61] Reasonable cover was provided up to 200 miles south-west of Fastnet Light,

20. The SS *Kensington Court* seen sinking from one of the Sunderlands, N9025 of No 228 Squadron, that rescued the whole of the crew on 18 September 1939 position 50°31'N 08°26'W.

although convoys to Gibraltar, which began in October, formed off the Scillies and continued as a convoy, but shortage of flying-boats resulted in limited cover after 100 miles.

Coastal Command still lacked aircraft, particularly those of suitable range and with emphasis given to its patrols over the North Sea rather than the Atlantic. The only suitable aircraft for Atlantic patrols available and deployed at that time were the few Sunderlands. According to Professor Rohwer, Coastal Command's aircraft at that time therefore posed no threat to U-boats, as most were obsolete, were lacking in range and had no suitable armament. It was not until 1941 that such deficiencies were remedied.[62]

The Navy's destroyers had limited endurance and were only able to escort convoys up to 13EW.[63] Hudsons could have operated to 17°W in sweeps, but were lacking endurance to remain there. Sir Frederick Bowhill was well aware of the shortages, and wrote to the Under-Secretary of State for Air on 12 September and again on 30 October concerning this lack of aircraft.[64]

The Inwards Ocean Convoys began on 14 September from Freetown, West Africa, on 16

September from Halifax, Nova Scotia, and on 26 September from Gibraltar. There were still many ships sailing independently, however, and the anti-submarine patrols flown by No. 15 Group's Sunderlands experienced 'a constant stream of SOS signals from sinking ships'.[65]

With all types of ships being used, it was inevitable that some compromise was necessary for masters of merchant vessels to accept. If they captained ships capable of cruising at say 15 knots, they would be reluctant to form part of a convoy confined to 11 knots. In practice, convoys came to be formed to sail at typically 11 knots or 7 knots, with some fast convoys that later prevailed for Malta at 17 knots. Such a speed would have served to reduce the likelihood of being attacked by U-boats, due to the U-boats' limited speed of about 17 knots, but not to avoid attacks by aircraft, as was to be experienced. The east-coast convoys that had been in operation from 7 September had by October 'at least one aircraft on escort from dawn to dusk'.[66]

Coastal Command endeavoured to arrange convoy escorts from 'first light' to 'last light', which resulted in a greater period of time on escort, compared with 'dawn to dusk'.

This was important, as they were likely times for U-boats to attack, as the U-boat commander could see ships silhouetted under such lighting conditions with the rising or setting sun. Not infrequently, just as a Coastal Command aircrew reached PLE (Prudent Limit of Endurance), or had reached the end of a patrol or a convoy escort, there would be a signal from the SNO (Senior Naval Officer) of the convoy escort to investigate a specific area for a possible U-boat, or perhaps the aircrew would themselves make a sighting.[67]

To compensate for the lack of suitable aircraft to escort east-coast convoys, de Havilland biplane Moth aircraft were used in providing 'scarecrow flights', so called because they could do little more than indicate their presence, as they carried no bomb load, but were to operate as far out as possible with surface craft. Nevertheless, Professor Rohwer, who was a submariner, acknowledges that just the sight of an aircraft had an important side effect, and if over the Atlantic would have forced U-boats further out. Their use followed Captain Peyton-Ward's awareness at the Command's headquarters in the early months of the war that the Command both lacked suitable aircraft and had no effective anti-submarine weapon.

There is no doubt that 'PW', as he was known, exercised considerable influence. He had a direct line from the Command's headquarters to the Admiralty, and as Sir Philip Joubert adds: '[worked] ... with an energy, an intelligence, and a courage beyond praise'.[68] For Air Chief Marshal Sir John Slessor, 'PW' was 'always ready with wise advice and willing help', and 'part of the inner circle at Coastal Command from the beginning to the end'.[69]

Flights of the DH Moths became attached to squadrons such as No. 269, although in the case of No. 269 it had a full establishment of Anson aircraft. The Command was nevertheless stretched to fulfil all its duties. Tiger Moth aircraft arrived at Abbotsinch to undertake anti-submarine patrols, although there would have been no question of them being able to make any useful attacks on U-boats. At least one of the Moth's pilots lacked operational training, although he was an experienced civil pilot, and that might well have been the case for some other DH Moth pilots. By 28 November there were nine of these biplanes serviceable, but not operational, due to them waiting for marine distress signals.[70]

The advantage of the convoy system for the Navy was that it would be covering ships rather than an area, and it was to be shown that even a few escort vessels could be enough

to deter U-boats that at that time were able to attack many ships sailing independently. Those who suggest that the east-coast convoys were pointless overlook the fact that British transport was highly specialised, and it would have been impracticable to put bulk shipping cargoes on an overstretched rail service. The Navy's destroyers, however, were limited in number and limited in endurance.[71]

Dönitz had organised trials in the Baltic during 1938/9 of 'wolf packs' against likely convoys, but then, due to lack of U-boats, he was using aircraft for reconnaissance. Later, aircraft to undertake reconnaissance on behalf of his U-boats were to become one of his requirements.

When the *Luftwaffe* was able to provide such machines they lacked the range. When ultimately he gained the use of some Fw 200 Kondors that had the range, he found that their navigation was unsatisfactory, and positions given of intended targets were unreliable.[72]

Owing to an obvious need to compensate for Coastal Command's lack of aircraft to cover the Western Approaches, the aircraft-carriers *Hermes*, *Ark Royal* and *Courageous* sailed with their own destroyer escorts in an attempt to fill this gap. HMS *Ark Royal* survived attack by U-39 on 14 September, but U-39 was itself sunk by the destroyer escort. *Courageous* was torpedoed by U-29 in position 50°10'N 14E°46'W on 17 September. This was enough for the Admiralty to withdraw the carriers from such costly operations. The loss of HMS *Courageous* demonstrated how vulnerable such a valuable target could be when deficient in its own escorts, or flying off or recovering its own aircraft. Two destroyers from the HMS *Courageous* escort had been withdrawn to help a merchant vessel that had been attacked.[73] Those carriers using tons of fuel and requiring many personnel to sail them may be contrasted with the relatively trifling cost of a few Sunderlands that could have done the job more efficiently and certainly with no risk of being torpedoed.

There was another ship that also gained the headlines out of the fifty-two that were attacked by U-boats in the North Sea–Atlantic area during September 1939.[74] This was the merchant vessel SS *Kensington Court*, which, like HMS *Courageous*, was on a regular shipping route in the South-Western Approaches.[75] On 18 September the SS *Kensington Court* was torpedoed by U-32 seventy miles west of the Scillies in position 50°31'N 08°27'W, and so well within range of both destroyers and aircraft. Signals SSS (Submarine sighted) were received from the ship by three Sunderlands of No. 228 Squadron.[76] One of those three was flown by Acting Flt Lt Thurston-Smith and Plt Off Bevan-John. Gp Capt Bevan-John's account indicates the various aspects to be considered, although they are understated:

We were returning from an A/S patrol ... when we picked up an SSS as it was then ... we soon came upon the *Kensington Court* which was well down by the bow and all her crew were in one lifeboat. Having searched for the sub without success we decided to try a landing. It was a lovely day and the sea seemed like a millpond. A/Flt Lt Smith made an excellent landing on what turned out to be quite a swell. The lifeboat which seemed very full came towards us during its passage. Another Sunderland captained by Jackie Barrett appeared overhead. He signalled by Aldis lamp asking if we wished him to land. We replied it was up to him as it was a risky business. He did. By the time we had picked up the captain and nineteen of his crew, we were prepared to take the whole lot had it been necessary. The take-off

was somewhat hairy ... we found we had landed with our bombs on ... we had to jettison them before take-off ... and two hung up and had to be pushed off with a boat-hook.[77]

Flg Off Barrett of No. 204 Squadron picked up the remaining fourteen survivors, while a third Sunderland, captained by Sqn Ldr Menzies, acted as guard overhead. (Later in the war it was not unknown for the *Luftwaffe* to attack rescue operations.) This incident, so fully reported in such as the *News Chronicle* might well have given the impression that crews of torpedoed ships were easily rescued and that flying-boats could land on any stretch of water. Neither was true.

As another pilot from No. 228 Squadron recalls: 'The Atlantic soon became a striking grave-yard of ships. Day after day we would fly over oil slicks or flotsam from sunken ships. We saw ships sink but could do nothing to help the passengers or crew ... radio silence was absolute. Landing in the open sea was strictly forbidden later because the risk of losing precious aircraft and aircrew was too great.'[78]

The intensive press reports on the SS *Kensington Court* were almost certainly intended as favourable propaganda for the British, but unfavourable to the enemy. This, however, was in contrast to the sinking of U-boats by Coastal Command, which was not given such coverage. This was apparently due to the Admiralty's wish not to disclose such information to the enemy, although the Admiralty was prepared to publish the Navy's successes.

By 19 December, when U-48 was through the Fair Isle Channel on its homeward voyage, there were no U-boats in the Atlantic.[79] Nevertheless, by the end of 1939 about 160 ships out of 5,800 at sea had been sunk by U-boats, but only thirty of those in convoy were sunk by U-boats for their loss of only nine. Aircraft sank none of those U-boats.[80] It was fortunate that Dönitz began with only fifty-seven U-boats rather than the 300 to which he aspired.

CONCLUSIONS

By the end of 1939 Britain still had France as a vacillating ally,[81] as was to be demonstrated in the following three years, when the term 'ally' could be doubted. Account had to be taken of Russia, Italy and Japan. There was an awareness of what the loss of the Low Countries to Germany could mean in respect of their ports (including notably their use by U-boats), but not the potential loss of French and Norwegian ports, which were later to prove invaluable for U-boats.

The maritime role of the RAF came last in order of priority as indicated by the Chief of Air Staff. A determined enemy could avoid detection despite reconnaissance designed to prevent any escape of surface warships. This was achieved by using dark periods and weather conditions unfavourable to aircraft that were still without radar.

Coastal Command had insufficient aircraft and trained crews to undertake the tasks expected of them, as was shown by using Tiger Moths with civil pilots to supplement even the inadequate Anson squadrons. Supplies to maintain existing aircraft were insufficient, as was demonstrated by the shortage of engines for Ansons and the lack of gun turrets for Hudsons. Armament on aircraft for both defence and attack was lacking, as shown by a Hudson being unable to respond effectively to an attack by enemy aircraft. Only 100 lb bombs could be used by Ansons, and there were no 250 lb depth charges for Hudsons. Aircrew were expected to take quite unreasonable risks due to weather conditions, lack of armament and over heavily defended areas. A convoy system was rapidly organised on the east coast and, to some extent, ocean-going convoys, but with limited cover for the latter up to 200 miles.

There were still many ships sailing independently, and fifty-two were attacked by U-boats in the first month of the war, including the liner *Athenia* on 3 September and the aircraft-carrier HMS *Courageous* on 17 September. Priorities in the role of Coastal Command changed rapidly from one of North Sea reconnaissance to include convoy escorts, and patrols in support of the Navy. Of crucial importance was the directive that anti-U-boat sorties should be of equal importance to anti-shipping reconnaissance.

Captain Peyton-Ward, RN, at Coastal's headquarters remained in the forefront by specifying areas for anti-U-boat operations for Coastal Command.

1940

By the end of January 1940 a U-boat offensive had reopened, and in that month alone forty-two ships had been sunk by U-boats.[82] At Christmas 1939 there had been no U-boats in either the North Sea or the Atlantic, but in January at least twenty-two were operating with success in the North Sea and Atlantic areas.[83]

The most alarming aspect of these U-boat successes was that they were all east of 11EW. Thus they were all in range, not only of naval escort vessels, but also Coastal Command's Sunderland and Hudson aircraft, which was indicative of our serious shortage of aircraft and also escort vessels for the Navy.[84]

At that time the Command was lacking in fully equipped Hudsons, and seriously so in respect of Sunderlands. Although the Lockheed Corporation was fulfilling its contracts, it was taking about three months for aircraft to reach operational units, due partly to them being disassembled and sent by sea. This delay was to be overcome later by flying Hudsons across the Atlantic in what came to be known as the 'Atlantic Ferry', for which much of the credit must go to Sir Frederick Bowhill and Captain Don Bennett.

Manufacture of Sunderlands was always to be limited. This was due to preference being given to Stirling bombers, for which the manufacturers had a much larger contract.[85]

Coastal Command's sorties were concentrated in the North Sea area, and the Command had a very limited number of land bases in the west, lacking also in night-flying facilities. There had been a vain hope of obtaining bases in Southern Ireland, but with negative results due to the political situation, despite the fact that Ireland was depending on Britain for some of its supplies, and therefore British convoys.

As late as July 1940, to cover the Western Approaches, the Irish Sea and Northern Ireland, there were only four flying-boat squadrons, two GR land-plane squadrons, and one long-range fighter squadron.[86] These figures take no account of overseas requirements of the Command. To detect surfaced U-boats in bad visibility, Mark I ASV had by January 1940 become available, but by the end of the month only fourteen Hudsons and one Sunderland had been equipped with it.[87]

The Command's first anti-U-boat success was in January 1940, credited to a Sunderland of No. 228 Squadron. On 21 January U-55 had sunk a ship in position 58°18'N 02°25'W, and on 30 January sank two more, both in an outward-bound convoy OA80G from the Thames through the English Channel about position 49°N 07°W. A 228 Squadron Sunderland based at Pembroke Dock was ordered out on a strike.

At the time of the attack on the convoy, only the sloop HMS *Fowey* was on escort, although two destroyers were sent to assist. The Sunderland located HMS *Fowey*, a French destroyer rescuing survivors from a torpedoed ship, and then two more destroyers. Half-an-hour later the Sunderland sighted a U-boat, which apparently was unable to submerge.

The Sunderland bombed and machine-gunned the U-boat before directing the escort vessels to the scene. The U-boat, U-55, was scuttled by its crew, who were picked up by HMS *Fowey*. In the naval historian Captain Roskill's opinion, U-55 would probably have escaped but for the Sunderland's presence.[88]

This episode is given in some detail as it demonstrates how lacking we were in anti-submarine warfare at that time. There was just one U-boat success in the month for Coastal Command, although there were at least twenty-two U-boats at sea. The Sunderland was not able to sink the U-boat as it had only the non-lethal bombs. Machine-gun fire should not be underrated, of course, for if enough of a U-boat's crew were killed or wounded it would require to return to port, but at that time the forward-firing armament of the Sunderland was very limited. Most obvious was that two ships in convoy could be sunk so close to our shores, and that only one Sunderland was sent on a strike. There was a gross lack of cover for the convoy available from the Royal Navy and Coastal Command. The shortage of aircraft was demonstrated by only one Sunderland out of all types being sent at a critical time.[89]

During the first five months of 1940 Germany progressively reduced restrictions on its U-boats in respect of what and where ships could be attacked. By 24 May in the whole of the sea areas around Britain and most of Ireland, up to as much as 100 miles from the coasts, U-boats were free to attack merchant vessels. The only exceptions were the ships of the 'friendly' neutrals, Spain, Italy, Japan and Russia. The last areas to be included were the coastal areas of France and the Netherlands.[90] This really made no difference in the anti-submarine campaign, as from the beginning of the war it had been shown that even liners with civilian passengers were targets for German U-boats, and the convention of giving warning before an attack was not followed.

There was a respite for Coastal Command

in purely anti-submarine measures during March and April, due to the U-boats' involvement in the Norwegian campaign, but Coastal Command remained fully occupied with its many other tasks of general reconnaissance and special reconnaissance.

For the Navy, there was minesweeping, mine laying, photo-reconnaissance, meteorological flights, and anti-invasion sorties.[91] The invasion of Norway, Denmark and the Low Countries, and the French campaign, resulted in an additional series of duties for the Command, such as supporting our forces that had made landings in Norway; those landings alone had required a considerable effort on the part of the Sunderland and Hudson squadrons.

Dönitz had ordered U-boat sailings to be stopped by 10 March in preparation for Germany's invasion of Norway and Denmark, and the first U-boat to sail to the Atlantic subsequently was U-37 on 15 May, which sank eight ships in ten days.[92] In June most of the U-boats were operating at the western end of the English Channel, and it was made obvious by the number of ships sunk in that area.[93] It was serious enough for the Admiralty at a meeting on 20 June to recommend the re-routeing of ocean convoys to the north of Ireland and for the mining of the Bristol Channel.

At a further meeting on 22 June it was decided that inbound convoys that had sailed from 28 June were to be routed to the north of Ireland, except those for the English Channel ports as far east as Southampton. Outward-bound convoys were to continue until necessary to meet the first re-routed inbound convoys.[94] By such means, the inward- and outward-bound convoys would effectively share the limited escort vessels then available when they were in comparatively easy range of U-boats.

Although it was obviously necessary for Coastal Command to redeploy squadrons

from the east coast to the west, there was a lack of suitable bases, notably for land aircraft. Pembroke Dock and Mount Batten in the south-west were available for flying-boats, but there were still not enough Sunderlands to cover the Western Approaches and at the same time cover the more northerly part of Norway. It was to be quite some time before the deficiency in western bases was made up, and when No. 224 Squadron was posted to Tiree in April 1942 the aerodrome was hardly complete.[95] It thus effectively resulted in an increase in the number of U-boats on operations.[96]

This change in bases for U-boats to the south did provide at least one advantage for Coastal Command. That was that over the Bay of Biscay more favourable weather was likely to prevail and therefore cancellations of Coastal Command's sorties due to bad weather were less likely. It was more favourable for the flying-boat squadrons that otherwise would have had to contend with bases on such as Islay, or the Shetlands, where strong winds prevailed.

Dönitz had become aware that the British had re-routed their convoys to the north-west and were using the Rockall latitude route. As he stated, 'I at once ordered a redistribution of my forces.' Dönitz added that improvements in his U-boat campaign were 'due primarily to our possession of the French port of Lorient on the Bay of Biscay'.[97]

That there had been thirty-one sightings of U-boats in June, and seventeen attacks by Coastal Command's aircraft with negative results, demonstrated the need for a lethal weapon to replace the 100 lb and 250 lb A/S bombs. The outcome was for A/S bombs to be rejected in anti-submarine warfare in favour of depth charges. In 1940, however, a depth charge specifically designed for use by aircraft was not available, and initially a compromise was reached with the use of a naval 450 lb depth charge modified for aircraft use. These, however, could only be carried by flying-boats.[98]

It was to be 1941 before land-based aircraft such as of No. 221 Squadron's Wellingtons were able to take three or four of these 450 lb depth charges; but then that squadron was to be lost to the Command by being posted to the Middle East.[99]

By the end of July U-boats had been sent to the North Channel, North Minch (between the Outer Hebrides and Scotland) and the Pentland Firth (between the Orkneys and mainland Scotland). From 27 August the U-boats' operational area was increased to 20°W, initially between 45°N and 57°N, but by 19 October further northwards to 62°N. Thus the U-boats were operating out of the range of most of Coastal's aircraft based in the United Kingdom.[100] This aspect was to be compensated for to some extent by the use of bases in Iceland.

They were ultimately established along the southern part of Iceland – initially at Kaldadarnes and later at Reykjavik, and with a landing strip further east at Höfn.

No. 98 Squadron, equipped with outdated Fairey Battles, was the first to be posted to Iceland, but the Fairey Battles were single-engined bombers and quite unsuitable for maritime patrols. They were to be followed notably by No. 269 Squadron Hudsons, which operated from Icelandic bases with success against U-boats up to January 1944, despite the severe conditions. Sunderlands and Liberators were to follow, however, and this was ultimately to result in the closure of the Mid-Atlantic Gap.[101]

In 1940, due to lack of forces, it was a matter of filling one gap at the expense of another, and after a Sunderland squadron was posted to Iceland, it was shortly afterwards sent to West Africa to cover convoys to Freetown, for which there was another obvious need in our defences against U-boats.

With Reykjavik at about another 14° longitude westwards of bases in Northern Ireland, the effective range westwards for Coastal Command's aircraft in Iceland was obviously increased, but the Mid-Atlantic Gap south of Cape Farewell still remained to be filled, despite Reykjavik becoming available. Lack of the required VLR Liberators to cover that gap still prevailed. There was still a need for more bases in the north-west, and the Inner and Outer Hebrides were to serve in that respect.

In August, there was another problem to engage both Coastal Command and the Admiralty. U-boats were attacking ships at night while on the surface, and against such tactics in 1940 neither the Admiralty nor Coastal Command had an effective answer. ASV was still in the development stages for Coastal Command, and likewise a means to illuminate the target was still in the embryonic stage.

Even if an aircraft located a U-boat, flares to illuminate the target could not be used at the low altitude required for the aircraft to attack. There was still no low-level bombsight. The Asdic on which the Navy had pinned its faith was useless against surfaced U-boats.[102]

The urgent need to combat the menace of night attacks on convoys by U-boats resulted in further Coastal Command/Royal Navy cooperation initiated by Sir Frederick Bowhill, who wrote to the VCAS and VCNS on 7 August concerning the U-boat effort in the Western Approaches. A discussion followed at the Admiralty on 10 August, when it was decided to have a limited programme of cooperation in the anti-submarine war under Capt B. Ruck-Keene, RN, of joint Coastal/Naval staff on HMS *Titania* at Belfast.

This was the modest beginning of what was to become a feature of the Allies' ASW, that is, close cooperation between Coastal Command and the navies. In 1940, however, it was not very obvious, due to the Royal Navy's lack of escort vessels and Coastal Command's lack of aircraft.

Later it developed into the 'hunter/killer'

groups of sloops with which Coastal Command's aircraft worked to the full, and this would be exemplified in July 1943 with Capt F.J. Walker, RN, and Flt Lt Dudley Marrows.[103]

Capt B. Ruck-Keene's work resulted in a meeting at the Admiralty on 23 September chaired by the VCNS, but with Sir Frederick Bowhill present. The conclusions were that full use was not being made of our ASW capabilities, that depth charges were the suitable weapon against U-boats and that a new Command should be based in the north-west for operational control and administration. Henceforth there were to be weekly meetings at the Admiralty to review all existing ASW methods and suggestions for new methods of trade protection.[104] No. 15 Group of Coastal Command became part of the new Area Combined Headquarters (ACHQ), which was not just the control centre for the North-Western Approaches, but effectively the 'nerve centre' of the Battle of the Atlantic, and, it is believed, had a direct line to the Prime Minister.

With about seventy ships torpedoed in September 1940, and with most of those attacked at night, and many east of 20°W, it was again demonstrated that the Command needed aircraft in sufficient numbers and suitably equipped with ASV and means of illuminating targets, plus armament that was lethal.[105]

In an attempt to improve the ASV position, No. 502 Squadron Whitleys were equipped with Mark II ASV, but they were lacking in ASV to home onto the target after it was located. Night sweeps were envisaged with these aircraft, but they could only be undertaken when there were enough aircraft available. At the end of October the Air Ministry stated that priority would be given to Fighter Command in respect of aircraft, to make up for its losses incurred during the Battle of Britain.[106]

From 1 October to 1 December, however, about a hundred Allied ships were sunk by U-boats, which must have prompted Winston Churchill to write: 'The only thing that ever frightened me during the war was the U-boat peril.'[107] He held a meeting with the Admiralty on 1 December, and ordered minefields against U-boats to cover the approaches to the Mersey and Clyde.

At that time the major Atlantic ports were Liverpool and Greenock, and Churchill decided that Coastal Command was to dominate the outlets from the Mersey and Clyde, for which 'it had supreme priority'. Churchill stated also: 'The bombing of Germany took second place.'[108] Thus there was an about-face on Churchill's part, as he subsequently acknowledged that 'the success of Coastal Command overtook ... the minelaying'.[109]

For Dönitz the first phase in the Battle of the Atlantic began in July 1940, following one U-boat sinking eleven ships totalling 43,000 tons.[110] For Professor Rohwer this was the beginning of the second phase of the U-boat war, when the use of Norwegian and French bases allowed 'wolf packs' to operate. The shorter routes they provided to the Atlantic and down to West Africa effectively made more U-boats available to form packs.[111]

Dönitz became aware from reports by his U-boats that the Rockall latitude corresponded to a convoy route and that Allied convoys had been routed from the South-Western Approaches to the North Channel between Scotland and Ireland. He deployed his U-boats accordingly.[112]

In 1940 the German High Command was able to decode the signals sent by the Allies that gave details of convoys, and Dönitz was able to use these with some limited success in the second half of 1940.[113] This was an example of the use of intelligence that Professor Rohwer rated the crucial factor in the Battle of the Atlantic.[114]

Two major changes were adopted in the second half of 1941 by the Command in its operations to counter the U-boat menace:[115]

1. To undertake sweeps along the routes followed by our convoys rather than giving close escort to the convoys by circling them. The disadvantages of providing close escort to convoys by aircraft were that only a comparatively small area of the Atlantic was covered, and furthermore, there was nothing to stop U-boats shadowing the convoy, and then, at last light, when the air escort departed, the U-boats could close in, literally, for the kill. Aircrew took this matter seriously, and although close convoy escorts were still undertaken, aircrew would endeavour to remain even after their prudent limit of endurance (PLE), and therefore at some risk of not having enough fuel to reach base.[116]

In contrast, sweeps along the convoy's route by, say, three or four aircraft flying parallel tracks (if aircraft and crews were available), were able to cover a much wider area and could effectively limit the ability of U-boats to shadow convoys. There was the further advantage that if one of the aircraft sighted a U-boat it could gain rapid support from at least one of the other aircraft on the same sweep. This aspect was not infrequently brought into practice, with the probable kill of the U-boat.

Both the Italian and German submarine logs were later to reflect the effectiveness of sweeps, with *tipo Sunderland* frequently appearing in the Italian logs, and in German U-boat logs *Durch Sunderland unter Wasser*. In the case of German U-boat logs, in later years they relate notably to the longer-range aircraft – Liberators, Catalinas and Sunderlands. Examples are U-476, April 1943; *Argo*, May 1942.[117] In practice, Coastal Command used both methods for trade protection, with sweeps along convoy routes and close escort by aircraft circling convoys. My own log confirms this, as my final six trips with No. 48 Squadron in May 1943 included three escorts, two anti-submarine sweeps and one U-boat search.

2. To institute air patrols along the route followed by U-boats from the French ports in the Bay of Biscay. This was later developed to a considerable degree; but when more aircraft and crews became available, it became a battle in its own right. 'The Battle of the Bay' was later to involve flights of fighter aircraft from both the Allies and Germany, and with many air-to-U-boat and air-to-air combats.

It perhaps reached its peak in 1943 when Air Marshal John Slessor took the view that it was better to act against U-boats while they were *en route* in the Bay of Biscay than wait until they reached the Atlantic.[118] Slessor's predecessor, Sir Philip Joubert, had also appreciated there was much to be said for attacking U-boats when *en route* through the Bay of Biscay, as, assuming that enough aircraft were available, a given area could be swamped with ASV signals from aircraft, as in Operation Gondola.

Air Marshal Slessor, nevertheless, was prepared to modify his strategy concerning the route through the Bay as the 'trunk' of the tree where attacks by aircraft should be concentrated. He acknowledged that there was a case for deploying aircraft near threatened convoys, as in such an area U-boats would be concentrated.[119] From the point of view of aircrew, there was much to be said for undertaking sweeps along the convoy routes rather than close escort of the convoys.

Apart from the obvious fact of covering a much greater area and thus having the prospect of a sighting, aircraft such as Hudsons had automatic pilots, which in straight and level flight could relieve the pilot of much strain. In contrast, during close escorts, when literally circling a convoy for two or three hours, much was expected of the man at the controls. The strain was such that three pilots were used in some Sunderland squadrons that lacked automatic pilots, and when flying up to fourteen hours.[120]

Germany had begun the war with fifty-seven U-boats, and a year later that figure had just been maintained, but with the advantage of the French Biscay ports. Nevertheless, in 1940, even with many fewer at sea than fifty-seven, Germany had been able to sink 517 ships. The Italians had claimed another six. As a result of using the French Biscay ports, the U-boats' period in transit to the Atlantic was reduced by about 450 miles. Thus, they were in effect able to have more U-boats deployed in the Atlantic at a given time.

From Rohwer's list, 252 of the ships sunk were in convoy, and many of those convoys were coded 'HX' for ships from Halifax, Nova Scotia; thus the British were losing ships

carrying vital supplies to Britain.

The American historian, Professor Samuel E. Morison, comments for that period: 'The Summer of 1940 was the U-boats' greatest harvest season of the war', and 'Obviously, if no answer could be found to the wolf-pack, Britain was doomed.'[121]

That would have been so: the British would have been starved into submission in months, certainly, if Dönitz had had available his desired 300 U-boats. Admiral Dönitz refers to the British lack of protection to our convoys in his résumé of his chapter 'The Battle of the Atlantic July–October 1940' with: 'Inadequate protection of British convoys', and that measures taken by the British Government showed 'clearly how very inadequate the measures that could be evolved against the U-boat were considered to be'.[122]

The measures that Dönitz mentions were the fifty ancient destroyers that the British acquired from America, and their occupation of Iceland. The occupation of Iceland had certainly provided bases to cover the Great Circle route in the North Atlantic, and to some extent cover for Russian convoys, as well as refuelling facilities for the Navy's escort vessels, which had limited range, but what were still needed by the Command were VLR aircraft with suitable armament to sink U-boats. For Coastal Command in 1940 its successes against U-boats are given as two sinkings shared with HM ships, one sunk unaided, and one damaged. All of those were by Sunderlands while escorting convoys.

Hudsons also damaged one, and in this case it can be said that a kill would almost certainly have resulted if they had been armed with 250 lb depth charges rather than bombs. The obvious success of the Sunderlands at this early stage, and still without depth charges designed for aircraft, indicates what was surely a major mistake in policy, which was to take men off manufacturing Sunderlands to produce the unsuccessful Stirling bomber.

Much of the Command's effort in 1940 was directed, not towards combating U-boats, but to attack enemy-controlled ships; and in that year alone it sank or damaged twenty enemy-controlled ships. There were still the other duties for Coastal Command to be undertaken, general reconnaissance and photographic reconnaissance.

1941

In 1941 the major political changes were the entry of USA and Russia into the war as allies of the British. Winston Churchill gives that as his main theme for his *The Grand Alliance* with: 'Soviet Russia and the United States were drawn into the great conflict.'[123]

America's entry into the war was tentative when in January there was a conference in Washington that included the American and British Chiefs of Staff, but with notably Air Vice-Marshal John Slessor, who was later to become Air Officer Commanding-in-Chief of Coastal Command.[124] Slessor represented the Chief of Air Staff at the Anglo-American conference, which, as he states, was to cover 'the whole range of Anglo-American strategy in the event of the United States entering the war'.[125] Britain had spent much of her assets in fighting the war, and the American President, Roosevelt, signed a 'Lease-Lend' Bill on 11 March, which provided for both military equipment and food for Britain, and as Professor Morison records, 'purposely left vague the method of repayment ...'.[126]

For the conclusion of the Anglo-American agreement on 27 March, Morison gives the American cooperation with Britain apparently quoting Roosevelt as 'short of war'.[127]

The British had been paying $90,000 (£17,000) for each Hudson aircraft; now, not only Hudsons but also the invaluable long-range aircraft such as Catalinas and Liberators were to become available to Coastal Command, and by the end of the year, Boeing Flying Fortresses.[128]

A further immediate outcome of Anglo-American liaison was that some United States Navy pilots came to serve with Coastal Command and to be crewed with RAF personnel, a figure of sixteen American pilots being quoted on 9 June.[129]

This system was obviously of mutual benefit, giving the Americans experience of wartime flying and relieving the shortage of pilots for the Command. Later also, some USN squadrons were to come under Coastal Command control in Iceland and England.

Churchill makes particular note of the supply of American aircraft with: '... we planned to increase this Command by fifteen squadrons in June 1941, and these reinforcements were to include all fifty-seven American long-range Catalinas ...', which he expected in April.[130]

There had been a meeting of the Air Ministry with the Admiralty on 27 February, and the same day there was a Chiefs-of-Staff meeting, when it was considered that six Coastal Command squadrons should be moved from North Sea operations to reinforce the North-Western Approaches by being deployed in Northern Ireland bases and also at Wick. The Hudson squadrons were each to have six of their aircraft fitted with long-range tanks. To compensate for the lack of Coastal Command's forces on the east coast and the English Channel, Bomber Command was to take over those duties. Work on the construction of new air bases in Northern Ireland and the Hebrides was to be expedited. At that time the Command was still lacking in long-range aircraft, with only ten Catalinas available.[131]

Churchill issued a directive on 6 March: 'The Battle of the Atlantic', his intention being 'to concentrate all minds and all departments concerned about the U-boat war'.[132]

The Battle of the Atlantic began in August 1939, lasted throughout the war and involved all commands of the RAF, the Royal Navy and the long-suffering Mercantile Marine.[133] The Allies had lost seventy-nine ships to enemy submarines in the first part of 1941 up to 5 March, and Churchill had been so informed by Admiral Dudley Pound; this must have concentrated Churchill's mind also, and almost certainly resulted in him issuing his Battle of the Atlantic directive.[134]

In Churchill's directive of thirteen paragraphs, the first line reads: 'We must take the offensive against the U-boat and the Focke-Wulf ...', followed in the first paragraph by: 'The U-boat must be hunted ...'.[135]

Thus, for Coastal Command, this meant that a radical change in policy had been confirmed. It was no longer to wait and then respond to enemy actions. Coastal and the Navy were to attempt the first moves.

In early 1941, however, the Command was still short of aircraft to cover all its tasks, and the Navy stilled lacked escort vessels such as were later to be used in 1943 to form 'hunter-killer groups' in cooperation with Coastal Command. Churchill had, none the less, given the go-ahead for offensive anti-submarine warfare.[136] By the beginning of June, following Churchill's directive on the Battle of the Atlantic, there was a considerable shift in the deployment of Coastal Command's forces. There was increasing emphasis towards the North-Western Approaches under No. 15 Group's control at Liverpool, and with the development of bases in Iceland, Northern Ireland and the Hebrides. As early as 10 December 1940, the Air Ministry had decided to send a flying-boat and a Hudson squadron to Iceland, and additionally to replace No. 98 Squadron, equipped with Fairey Battles, with No. 330's Northrop float-planes.

This, however, was not approved by the Chiefs of Staff until January 1941.[137] The bases in Iceland effectively extended Coastal Command's patrol area over the North Atlantic by another 14 degrees westwards compared with those in the Londonderry area

of Northern Ireland. Furthermore, they were on the Great Circle route from North America to the United Kingdom that was favoured by the convoys, being shorter, but a greater distance from U-boat bases.

Hudsons in Iceland were able to verify the extent of the icefield for the benefit of convoys, and with convoys being formed later for Russia in Iceland, aircraft based there could give more extensive cover.[138]

In July, American Marines formed part of Allied forces in Iceland, and in August aircraft of the United States Navy – six PBYs of VP73 and five PBMs (Martin Mariners) were deployed there. These American aircraft were to undertake 'neutrality patrols' over the North Atlantic convoy routes, ostensibly to protect America's neutrality.[139] For Iceland, it was really 'Hobson's choice'; if Britain and the USA had not occupied Iceland, almost certainly it would have been used by German U-boats, and no doubt, by the *Luftwaffe*. They could have cut the vital route to America and Canada, and that supply route was essential for us to continue in the war.

Following a meeting between Roosevelt and Churchill at Argentia on 10 August, the 'Atlantic Charter' was drafted. It was important enough in Churchill's view for him to include a copy of his modified draft in *The Grand Alliance*, which states eight principles. They could be summed up with the resolve to fight the aggression of dictators and to maintain the freedom of nations to live in peace. For Churchill, however, he had gained the support of the American President in the crucial Battle of the Atlantic.

On 4 September 1941, an event of great significance occurred in the Battle of the Atlantic. Until that date, captains of American ships were uncertain of what action to take on encountering a German ship or aircraft. U-652 clarified the issue by launching two torpedo attacks against the USS *Greer*, which was *en route* to Iceland. Thereafter, according to Professor Morison, America was *de facto* in the Atlantic war with Germany.[140]

On 11 September Roosevelt broadcast: 'From now on if German or Italian vessels enter these waters [between Iceland and North America], they do so at their own peril.'[141] The United States Navy would be escorting convoys that were not necessarily flying the American flag, and the Royal Canadian Navy might also escort American vessels.[142]

It was to become a feature of North Atlantic convoys that, not only would one see British destroyers, but also those remarkable Canadian corvettes, which represented a considerable Canadian contribution to the war effort. Additionally there were later the rapidly constructed American merchant vessels, the 'Liberty ships'.

With both Coastal Command and the United States Navy operating aircraft from Iceland, the senior RAF Officer, Air Commodore Primrose, suggested on 30 September that the same operations room should be used by both services. The response from Washington, however, was: 'Any departure from the principle that the Western Atlantic will be controlled from Washington and Canada must be avoided.'[143] This rebuff probably stemmed from Admiral King, who, as Sir John Slessor considered, '... never really understood the subject [i.e. the U-boat war]'.[144]

Admiral King appeared as the exception in respect of cooperation with the American forces, at both Command and squadron levels. This must have stemmed from the traditional rivalry between the USN and AAC, but also that Admiral King was more mindful of the Pacific than the Atlantic. Ultimately both the United States Navy and the RCAF demonstrated that they were quite prepared to follow Coastal Command's procedures to the full. This was to be exemplified in the RCAF by its No. 11 Squadron operating from Canada, readily adopting Coastal Command's camouflage for aircraft, and the Command's operational procedures.

Additionally, the shuttle service of Liberators from No. 10 Squadron RCAF in 1943 from Labrador to Iceland then came under Coastal Command's control. By 1943 the liaison between the USN squadrons and

21. A Wellington bomber, but modified for maritime use with aerials for detecting vessels on the beams, and Yagi ASV/radar aerials for homing.

Coastal Command was to be such that three of their 'Patrol Plane Commanders' were awarded the RAF's DFC by RAF officers in Iceland, following their success in anti-submarine operations when under Coastal Command's control.[145]

Despite both the USN and the RCAF providing cover for convoys from the western seaboard, and both the USN and Coastal Command patrolling westwards from Iceland, the notorious 'Mid-Atlantic Gap' south of Cape Farewell in Greenland prevailed in 1941, and in September, of fifty-three ships sunk, three quarters were in that gap and the area north-west Africa to the Azores.[146]

The Azores area provided another 'gap' in which U-boats could operate against British, Gibraltar and West African convoys, and so remained until bases in the Azores were granted to the Allies by Portugal. On the credit side, only three ships were sunk within 350 miles of Allied shore-based aircraft, thus again demonstrating the value of aircraft in the anti-U-boat war.[147]

In addition to land bases in Iceland, Sunderland flying-boats of No. 204 and No. 201 Squadrons were able to operate from there, but using the SS *Manela* as a base and for accommodation. SS *Manela* was one of

two such vessels controlled by Coastal Command which served to transport supplies and act as a troopship for ground staff, the other ship being the SS *Dumana*.[148]

There was much to be said for the use of those two ships that came under Coastal Command's control. They not only served as 'instant bases' for flying-boats, but could serve also as transport for personnel and the many tons of equipment necessary for each squadron (a figure of eighty tons was specified for one squadron). The two loughs in Northern Ireland, Lough Erne and Lough Foyle, could both be used by flying-boats, but Lough Erne was found to be the more suitable.

From there, squadrons such as Nos 201, 422, and 209 were able to operate with success over the Atlantic, the bases on Lough Erne serving for both Sunderlands and Catalinas. The main hazard was the weather; and it could range from dense fog to gale-force winds that could seriously disrupt flying.[149]

The C-in-C Coastal Command, Sir Frederick Bowhill, had written to the Air Ministry on 17 May, stating: 'It has been one continual struggle for aerodromes in which we have not always come off best vis-à-vis the other commands.'[150] Sir Frederick was

22. A 'first day cover' marking the Battle of the Atlantic and with the signatures of five Coastal Command pilots who all sank U-boats, namely: Flt/Lt John Cruickshank, S/Ldr Tony Bulloch, DSO, DFC; AVM W.E. Oulton, CB, CBE, DSO, DFC; S/Ldr Peter Cundy, DSO, DFC, AFC, TD, and Flt/Lt Les Baveystock, DSO, DFC, DFM.

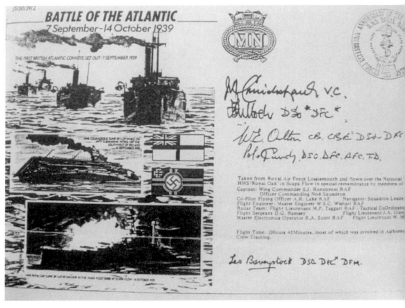

thinking specifically of aerodromes for training, but there was always to be some overlap with facilities for operations and training, such as I was to experience at both RAF Thornaby and RAF Leuchars in 1941 and 1942, and even later at Chivenor in 1944. Sir Frederick's successor, Sir Philip Joubert, also experienced the problem of bases, and found it necessary to undertake 'horse trading' for bases with other Commands. Land bases were, however, being prepared by June in Northern Ireland at Limavady, Aldergrove and Nutt's Corner.

There was a prime need for runways. With increasing use of heavy four-engined aircraft, and with a heavy war load, properly constructed runways, of considerable length, were essential. It was such that Nutt's Corner was earmarked specifically to accommodate the newly formed Liberator squadron, No. 120, in June.[151] The lack of aerodrome accommodation and adequate runways was to persist for Coastal Command, as it was to be experienced by subsequent commanders – Air Marshal John Slessor and Sir Sholto Douglas.

Further new bases were being opened at Stornoway, Benbecula and Tiree in the Hebrides, but Tiree was hardly complete in February 1942 when No. 224 Squadron was posted there.[152]

Islay had some provision for both land-planes and flying-boats, but weather conditions, particularly for flying-boats, could make it dangerous enough for the CO of No. 422 Squadron to complain.[153] The opening of these new bases reflected the emphasis then being given to the Battle of the Atlantic, and specifically the North-Western Approaches rather than the North Sea or the Bay of Biscay.

There was tacit agreement with the Irish for Coastal's aircraft flying over what was part of their neutral territory, and on those occasions when aircraft crashed there, help was provided. On the mainland, were other bases for No. 15 Group's flying-boats at Oban and Stranraer, and for land-planes at Leuchars,

and further south, Hooton Park. In the Shetlands there was Sullom Voe for flying-boats and Sumburgh for land-planes. For aircrew, all the northern bases suffered the disadvantage of strong winds, which could be serious if one suffered a change to a head wind when returning to base. Winds could be so high that the ground speed of some aircraft could be as low as 10 knots, that is less than for some convoys.[154] In contrast, aircrew might well find their base to be completely 'closed in' due to thick fog, and with the need to be diverted if possible.

To cover the South-Western Approaches in 1941, No. 19 Group had land bases at Carew Cheriton and St Eval, while Pembroke Dock and Mount Batten served for flying-boats. Both St Eval and Pembroke Dock served to cover the Atlantic, but also the Bay of Biscay.

This latter aspect became increasingly important, resulting from the U-boats using the French Biscay ports and what was to develop into the Battle of the Bay. That was to be primarily against U-boats, but also surface craft, including blockade runners. Typically, both those bases would have three operational squadrons at any one time. The two groups responsible for covering the eastern seaboard of the United Kingdom, Nos 16 and 18, were not completely bereft of forces as a result of the shift to the North-Western Approaches.

Coastal Command remained ever responsive to whatever was expected according to the changes in the war situation, and whole squadrons would be moved if necessary at twenty-four hours' notice, while flights from squadrons could be deployed almost immediately.

As an example, at the end of January 1945 I was operating off the Dutch coast from Langham, and then at the beginning of February was detached in a flight to Dallachy, ostensibly to operate to Norway. Likewise, a squadron in Iceland could be moved down to West Africa in the same month. Such a move was facilitated by using one or more of the two ships, SS *Dumana* and SS *Manela*.[155]

As prevailed in 1940, so also in 1941 Coastal Command was in a transitional stage. Overseas, Gibraltar was about to come under the Command's control, serving as a base for flying-boats such as No. 202 Squadron, and as a land base, initially for No. 233 Squadron's Hudsons. Freetown and Bathurst in West Africa were receiving No. 228 Squadron's Sunderlands, and Hudsons for No. 200 Squadron, respectively.[156]

These moves stemmed from the need to cover the Gibraltar and Freetown convoys that up to that time had been given little support. Furthermore the convoys in the Gibraltar area and further south were being reported to Admiral Dönitz, even if not attacked, by the Focke-Wulf Kondors.[157] Aircraft at Gibraltar could serve to cover the western Mediterranean and much of the Iberian coastline. With closure of the Mediterranean after the entry of Italy into the war, shipping had to use the Cape route, and the West African bases were needed to cover that route.[158]

Aircraft at Gibraltar were also to act as escorts to the convoys to Malta, and following the capitulation of the French, additionally needed to cover the western basin of the Mediterranean in support of the Navy's 'Force H' and also to counter hostile French units.

Nevertheless, the Freetown and Gibraltar convoys proved to be vulnerable even to the Italian submarines, as Admiral Dönitz confirms: 'In these southern waters, some of the Italian submarines ... achieved considerable success.'[159] This was after Dönitz had directed them to operate west of Gibraltar and off Freetown. Coastal Command's aircrew in the Gibraltar–Freetown areas found that they had to contend not only with enemy submarines but also with units of the French Navy and Air Force.

There were to be reconnaissances for the battleship *Dunkerque*, with the risk of attacks from French aircraft. It was such that Gp Capt Fergus Pearce, then the senior RAF officer in West Africa, organised a flight of Hurricanes to protect his No. 95 Squadron Sunderlands.[160]

Following Churchill's directive on the Battle of the Atlantic offensive, with the emphasis towards the Atlantic and other convoys, the North Sea areas gained less consideration. No. 16 Group at Chatham had No. 59 Squadron Blenheims at Thorney Island, and No. 500 Squadron was converting to Blenheims from Ansons at Detling, but required to move to Bircham Newton. Significantly, No. 206 Squadron had flights at both St Eval and Bircham Newton, but was required to send six of its long-range Hudsons to Bathurst.

This was indicative of how stretched Coastal Command's forces were. In this case No. 206's Hudsons were needed at St Eval for anti-submarine patrols in the South-Western Approaches, but also to protect Freetown convoys, thus depleting the east-coast forces.

Most of the attacks by U-boats in May were in the dark hours; thus there were fewer sightings made by aircraft and therefore fewer attacks. This lack of sightings was also due to fewer aircraft being available for anti-submarine operations, and of those that were used, the ASV was not considered reliable, and as Sir Philip states, 'Aircrew had little confidence in the ability of ASV to help them in their task of searching for submarines ....'[161]

In his summing up of the anti-submarine campaign as he found it in June 1941, Sir Philip confirms that while the role of his aircraft 'was to be offensive, to seek out and destroy U-boats ... rather than wait for them to come to us ... we were still fighting a defensive ... war against the U-boat and close convoy escort was still being given'. Air Chief Marshal Sir Philip Joubert succeeded Sir Frederick Bowhill as Air Officer-in-Chief Coastal Command on 13 June, to find that 'the situation in the anti-U-boat war looked bad ...'.[162] This was because the number of U-boats at sea had increased to twelve, and they were using well-organised wolf pack tactics. Joubert gives 325,492 tons of Allied shipping sunk in May, while Dönitz claimed eighty-four ships sunk by his U-boats in March and April, totalling 492,395 tons.[163]

CONCLUSIONS

In 1941 the anti-U-boat campaign was still very much trial and error. The naval liaison officer at Coastal's headquarters, Captain Peyton-Ward, was always examining reports and putting forward suggested policies, such as sweeps to harass U-boats but to be diverted to the position of any sighting report, expressing the view also that dark-night air escorts of convoys were useless, as even with an ASV contact, an air attack could not be made due to the lack of effective illumination.[164] While the British attempted to respond to any changes in the enemy's tactics, such as his use of wolf packs, the enemy, likewise, would react to changes made in the British policy and tactics. Thus, most notably, when the British were able to extend their patrols further westwards, U-boats operated even further westwards.[165] There was a comparative lack of success for the Command's aircraft in anti-submarine operations in the first half of the year, when only one U-boat had been damaged.[166] From August to December, however, three U-boats were sunk, and another three were so damaged by air attacks that they had to return to port.[167]

With about twelve U-boats at sea there was obviously a limited number of targets for Coastal Command aircraft to sight. Thus its successes are even more remarkable. They could be attributed to crews gaining experience and being more clearly aware of what was expected of them, and also the fact that in 1941 depth charges were becoming available for aircraft.[168]

The question of what weapons to use in anti-submarine war were reviewed at a new

Joint Standing Committee meeting held at the Admiralty on 26 June.

The outcome of this meeting was that Coastal Command issued Tactical Instructions on 25 July for attacks on U-boats. They stated that the approach to the U-boat should be along the shortest path and at maximum speed, but from any direction. Depth charges should be set at 50 ft depth for detonation and spaced at 60 ft, and released in one stick.

The depth of 50 ft was decided by the type of pistol then available, and the aim was to develop a pistol that would cause detonation at 25–32 ft, which was achieved later.[169] The spacing of 60 ft was later to be changed to 100 ft, but releasing all the depth charges in one stick prevailed. This decision was surely questionable. For aircraft carrying only three or four depth charges, releasing them all in one attack might have been justified, but some aircraft, such as Wellingtons, were able to carry ten 250 lb depth charges.

There was much to be said for retaining some for a second attack should the first attack fail, or in case an additional sighting was made. This was to be seen in the Polish squadron records, where a failed first attack with ten depth charges was followed by a second U-boat sighting, but then with no means to attack other than with machine-guns.[170] Just one 250 lb depth charge was enough to sink a U-boat, given that it was within 13 ft of the submarine. The altitude for release of depth charges was given as 100 ft, and to be within 30 seconds of sighting the U-boat. The limit of 30 seconds was essential as the German U-boats could crash-dive in 25 seconds. Some aircrew were prepared to attack at even lower altitude, so low that they had to 'pull up' to avoid striking the vessel. As sightings were typically made at 6 miles, or detected at that distance by ASV, it is obvious that aircraft would need to fly very fast indeed to reach the U-boat within 30 seconds.[171]

The 450 lb depth charge was being carried in 1941 by Wellingtons of No. 221 Squadron, in addition to some flying-boats. It was, however, only a naval weapon that had been modified, and it could not be released at a greater speed than 150 knots and altitude above 150 ft, otherwise it would break up.[172]

The 250 lb depth charge came into being in May, and tests showed that it could be released at 200 knots, by human eye, and was 'astonishingly accurate'; it was to become the standard anti-submarine weapon for Coastal Command.[173]

A sub-committee meeting later proved far sighted by considering alternative weapons to the depth charge, such as a small contact bomb and a heavy anti-submarine bomb.

Both these weapons were to come into being. Small bombs were later used by USN Catalinas in the Straits of Gibraltar with success, and 600 lb A/S bombs by Halifaxes of the RAF.[174]

In one analysis by the naval liaison officer at Coastal Command's headquarters for the period 1 March to 31 July, four U-boats were sighted as a result of an ASV contact, compared with sixty-one gained visually. This was considered to be due to the enemy using a receiver to detect ASV transmissions, and the use of ASV was suspended temporarily from 18 August.[175] Coastal Command was still lacking in ASV equipment for its operational aircraft, and by the end of June, out of 150 Hudsons, only eighty-seven had ASV; there were seventeen Sunderlands equipped out of twenty-seven, and twenty-three Catalinas out of thirty.

The maximum range at which an ASV contact was obtained was 15 miles, and the average for an ASV contact was 9 miles, but for sighting by the human eye, the average was 5 miles.[176] The average distance of 5 miles for visual sighting of U-boats was not to be improved very much in later years, although many operational records of the various squadrons show that, typically, the distance was about 6 miles. To counteract the detection of the ASV by the enemy, a radar officer on at least one squadron modified the squadron's ASV installations by inserting a variable capacitor in the circuit. This was to be used to reduce the strength of ASV transmissions during the approach to a suspected enemy contact. Thus the enemy might assume that the aircraft was not approaching.[177]

Although the role of the Command's aircraft became that of attacking and sinking U-boats, on 27 August in position 62°15N 18°35W, U-570 surrendered to a Hudson of No. 269 Squadron based in Iceland.[178] As the naval historian Captain Roskill records: 'This valuable prize was successfully towed to Iceland and finally entered British service as HMS *Graph*.'[179] U-570 was the first of seven successful attacks on U-boats by No. 269 Squadron Hudsons up to October 1943.

The position is of note; it was out of effective range of Hudsons operating from the United Kingdom, but obviously not from Iceland. The service of No. 269 indicated just how useful Iceland could be as a base for aircraft engaged in anti-submarine warfare. In those northern latitudes with few hours of darkness in the summer months, U-boats were more likely to be sighted on the surface to charge their batteries. This capture of U-570 became the subject for one of two wartime posters depicting the exploits of Hudson aircraft, the other one being No. 220 Squadron's shipping strike at Ålesund.[180]

Sir Philip Joubert had chaired a meeting at the Air Ministry with the Admiralty in the spring when it was agreed that the principal role of Coastal Command's aircraft was to be to seek and destroy U-boats rather than wait for them, but 'full implementation was prevented only by reason of the shortage of the right type of aircraft'.[181] The general trend was to be sweeps in the area of convoys with the object of contacting shadowing U-boats and also to attack any following U-boat packs.

As a result of this policy, in September there were forty sightings and thirty-seven attacks.[182] Nevertheless, in the author's experience, close convoy escorts were always to remain part of the Command's anti-U-boat role. There were ever the facts that a friendly aircraft in sight of the convoy was good for the morale of the merchant seamen, and a discouragement for the enemy, whether aircraft or U-boat, which might consider closing for an attack.

By July, Coastal Command's patrols had forced U-boats from the United Kingdom's shores to 300 miles out into the Atlantic; thus the enemy was in an area with a reduced density of shipping and where he would gain less help from *Luftwaffe* aircraft. British air patrols, however, were also reduced in density; thus, at 500 miles from British bases, there was only 20 per cent of aircraft density that prevailed at 300 miles. For threatened convoys, however, some air support could be given up to 700 miles. It would have been limited at that time, as only long-range aircraft such as the Catalina and Liberator could extend that far, and they were only just coming into service.

The Liberators with which it had been hoped to form a squadron, No. 120, were required for transport and ferrying purposes, and by October only ten were available to the Command. Furthermore, the Admiralty required that they should be kept in reserve in the autumn due to the prospect of a breakout of German capital ships.[183] Sir Philip Joubert, as prevailed with his predecessor, was setting a policy for the Command to function effectively by cooperation of the various authorities involved.

In the case of Coastal's operational Groups, Nos 15, 18 and 19, he stated that while the disposition of squadrons remained his responsibility, nevertheless there should be cooperation between groups sharing boundaries, such as Nos 15 and 19 Groups using their aircraft in the Western Approaches to mutual advantage.[184] Even without Winston Churchill's directive on the Battle of the Atlantic, some minds were concentrating on

the U-boat war, such as those of Captain Peyton-Ward at Coastal Command's headquarters, and the Commander-in-Chief Western Approaches at Liverpool.

Peyton-Ward gave his views in May, which included reference to the opening of new bases such as in Greenland and the Azores; aircraft sweeps to harry U-boats; D/F facilities to fix the positions of U-boats that were transmitting in W/T, and that independent ships should be in the faster convoys. He added, however, that the policy would be wrecked due to lack of long-range aircraft.[185] The policy of using sweeps certainly prevailed, but not to the exclusion of convoy escorts, as I was to experience.

The C-in-C Western Approaches effectively endorsed Peyton-Ward's policy by abolishing regular convoy escorts in favour of sweeps and abolishing night escorts by aircraft, but stipulating that protection of ships against air attacks would be made by fighters.[186] All that was required were the aircraft and the aircrew to fulfil that policy.

Later in the war, a base for Coastal Command was established in the Azores, in cooperation with Britain's oldest ally – the Portuguese. The Americans installed bases in Greenland, notably at Narsarssuak, which they coded Bluie West 1 (BW1). Its position was important, as it gave immediate cover to the 'Mid-Atlantic Gap' south of Cape Farewell.

The geographical conditions, however, rather than the weather, made it very difficult for aircraft to operate from there.[187]

At the twenty-second meeting of the Battle of the Atlantic Committee in October, the question of a base in Greenland had been discussed; and at a further meeting in November it was stated that the Americans did not intend forming an air base there until the spring of 1942; meanwhile their ships would use Greenland.[188] Nevertheless, the Greenland base of BW1 was later used to a limited extent by Coastal Command's aircraft.

The advantage of a base in the Azores was that it could help to cover the Freetown and Gibraltar convoys. It ultimately had its own headquarters control under the late Sir Geoffrey Bromet.[189]

During the second half of 1941, Coastal had on average about 200 aircraft available for anti-submarine operations. They included seventeen Sunderlands, thirty Catalinas, eighty Hudsons, forty Whitleys and twenty Wellingtons. Thus Coastal Command was relying very much on the American Hudsons and Catalinas. The Hudsons would have served to keep U-boats away from British shores, thus effectively dispersing them away from where Allied shipping was concentrated and into the wide Atlantic. The Catalinas with their long range and endurance could serve to harass the U-boats, which in June were operating as far west as 40°45′W.[190]

Despite the new policy of avoiding close escort to convoys, the Catalinas were to be used for that purpose. They were most suitable due to their endurance and low speed; the latter, particularly, was an advantage when circling convoys, say at 90 knots instead of possibly 120 knots as with the Sunderlands and Hudsons; and compared with the Sunderlands, about half as much petrol was being used. The mere presence of aircraft was enough to discourage U-boats, as their logs were to show.[191]

There was a compromise in the Command's policy, with close convoy escort being given only if it was thought that the convoy was threatened, but nevertheless with aircraft undertaking sweeps in the area of the convoy. This had the obvious advantage of covering a much greater area in a given time.

Even if such aircraft failed to make any U-boat sightings, any U-boats that sighted the aircraft would be thwarted to some extent, and might well lose track of a convoy being shadowed. This was ostensibly a defensive role, but for the U-boat's transit areas in the Bay of Biscay and between Scotland and Iceland, regular sweeps were flown with the object of attacking U-boats.[192]

By the end of 1941 Coastal Command was able to claim successes against seven German U-boats that were either sunk or damaged, and one Italian submarine that was sunk. Most notable about these successes was the fact that they were sighted by the aircrew rather than detected on ASV.

The exceptional one was U-570, which was first sighted by a Hudson, which in turn homed in a second Hudson to which the U-boat surrendered.[193] That aspect of the Command's anti-submarine sorties could be quantified; what could not be treated so was the likely effects on the crews of the U-boats and those merchant seamen in the Allied convoys. The morale of the former was likely to be lowered, but of the latter raised. Furthermore, a number of ships may well have been saved simply by keeping U-boats submerged at a critical time.

23. Korvettenkapitän Peter Cremer commanded U-333 with great success. He demonstrated his concern for former enemies having shot down a Sunderland that attacked him. As he said, 'I had no choice'.

24. Sunderland W6077 U/461 whose Captain, Flt/Lt
Dudly Marrows, RAAF, sank U-461, a unique incident
in WW2. He dropped his own dinghy and so saved
the captain of U-461.

25. Korvettenkapitän Wolf Stiebler
(U-461), was the senior officer
of three U-boats sailing in
convoy on the surface, U-504,
U-461 and U-462. All three U-
boats were sunk in a
combined Naval/Coastal
operation on 30 July 1943,
position 45°40'N 10°55'W.

26. A rubber dinghy
dropped by
Sunderland N/228
in position
45°04'N 09°14'W
on 13 July 1943
for the survivors of
U-607 who were
later taken aboard
HMS *Wren*.

CHAPTER FOUR

Anti-submarine Warfare 1942–1945

For the naval historian, Captain Roskill, 1942 was the 'Period of Balance' in the war, but in respect of anti-submarine warfare this was hardly so. From Roskill's own figures British imports were only two-thirds of those for 1939, and the Allies had lost 1,664 ships, and of that total 1,160 had been claimed by U-boats. Although the Allies had built 7,000,000 tons of shipping, the enemy had sunk almost a million tons more. There was a deficit, therefore; the British were not in balance.[1]

Winston Churchill's volume covering 1942, *The Hinge of Fate*, although it gives some emphasis to the 'hinge', i.e. the Allies' victory at El Alamein, nevertheless, on two pages, charts all the Allied ships sunk by U-boats in the Atlantic. The first of these two charts gives a total of 3,250,000 tons sunk during the period 7 December 1941 to 31 July 1942, and they are notable in being sinkings largely off the American seaboard from Newfoundland southwards to include the Caribbean. The second chart, covering the second half of 1942, but also up to 21 May 1943, gives a total of 3,760,000 tons of Allied shipping lost to U-boats. These sinkings, however, reflect the sea areas that were lacking in air cover, such as notably south of Greenland, what was referred to as the 'Mid-Atlantic Gap'.[2] All of those sinkings would have been in range of aircraft such as the Consolidated Liberator (B24), but in 1942 very few of these aircraft were provided for Coastal Command.

1942 for the Command in respect of its anti-submarine operations was, however, a year of the offensive over the Atlantic, the Bay of Biscay, and the western Mediterranean. To a limited extent also, Hudsons of No. 53 Squadron were on the offensive off the American seaboard from July. In this year, Coastal Command's squadrons were operating not only from the United Kingdom but also from Iceland, Russia, Gibraltar, North Africa and West Africa. Despite, therefore, any possible improvement in supplies of aircraft, the Command's resources was stretched to the limit.

Due to the entry of Japan into the war, some of the Command's squadrons, such as No. 413, were posted to the Far East. Additionally, Coastal Command's forces were being depleted by postings to the Middle East in support of the North African campaign, which was to be followed by Operation Torch.

On the credit side for the Command, its efficiency in anti-submarine operations was increased by new armaments becoming available, such as the Torpex-filled 250 lb depth charge, with an improved pistol for detonation at shallower depths. Against submarines also, another weapon, rocket projectiles, was being developed.

One of the most important innovations in 1942, however, was that the Leigh Light came into operation, initially with No. 172 Squadron Wellingtons, but subsequently to be fitted to other types of aircraft, such as the Liberator. This device enabled successful night attacks on U-boats to be undertaken. Additionally, improved ASV/radar was becoming available, albeit to a very limited extent, due partly to production limitations but also the demands of Bomber Command.

Captain Peyton-Ward summarised the U-boat war in early 1942 from his standing as the Command's naval liaison officer. His view was that once U-boats had sailed there were two areas within the reach of Coastal Command's aircraft – the Bay of Biscay, and the northern exit from the North Sea. There was thus the implication that the Command should concentrate its forces on the two transit areas.

At that time Gibraltar was not under the Command's control, and the Mediterranean area is omitted. On the outbreak of war, Peyton-Ward had given full attention to the northern exit, but then the French ports were not available to the U-boats, and Norway was still neutral. There was much to be said for concentrating on the U-boats' transit routes as it had been proved possible to forecast with some accuracy just where they were likely to be at a given time. Agents in both Norway and France were able to give details of sailings, and the transit routes, as Peyton-Ward indicated, were in range of Coastal Command's shorter-range aircraft. There was the additional advantage that due to the shorter range, in the event of a sighting, reinforcements could be activated more rapidly.

Despite the Command's limited number of long-range aircraft, the Atlantic was considered reasonably clear of risks from U-boats up to about 350–400 miles from the coasts of the United Kingdom. That view is endorsed by the American historian, Professor Samuel Morison.[3]

Coastal Command's sorties in the Bay of Biscay had resulted in U-boats diving by day when east of 12°W, and Peyton-Ward considered the northern exit from the North Sea impossible to guard due to Norway being under enemy control, and that U-boats could only be harried between the Shetlands and Faeroes, and the Faeroes to Iceland, but for the latter more long-range aircraft were required. It was certainly true that U-boats could be harried between the Shetlands and Faeroes, as I was to experience in 1942.

There were bases for both flying-boats and land-planes in the Shetlands, and some attempts were made at using the Faeroes as a base. As to the eastern seaboard of Canada and America, 'the present plague spot', events could only be resolved when measures similar to those applied off the United Kingdom were employed in the western Atlantic. Peyton-Ward's view at that time was: 'There is no continuity of policy or purpose and [anti-submarine warfare] has become a Cinderella branch of a Cinderella Service. Anti-U-boat matters, in the present organisation, are of necessity tacked on as an afterthought to Plans, Training, and Operations.'[4]

Germany had declared war on America on 11 December 1941, but Hitler had removed restrictions on attacking American ships on 9 December, and Admiral Dönitz asked his Command 'to release twelve U-boats for operations off the American coast'.[5] What followed from January to July 1942 under the U-boat's operation *Paukenschlag* was by Dönitz termed a 'merry massacre'. Professor Morison also refers to it as a 'massacre', and for the Americans a 'national disaster'.[6] Although Dönitz was allowed only half the U-boats he had asked for to operate off the American seaboard, they were able to select their targets at leisure with no effective opposition, and ships were clearly illuminated at night by the unrestricted lights on the mainland.

Ships were not in convoy and lacked effective cover by the American forces. The policy of Dönitz was for his U-boats to sink ships wherever they could be attacked, and he is quoted as stating in his diary for 15 April: 'The enemy merchant navies are a collective factor. It is therefore immaterial where any one ship is sunk … what counts … is sinking over new construction.'[7]

Off the American seaboard in the first half of 1942, it was a 'happy hunting ground'. Unfortunately for the Allies also, many of the ships sunk carried most valuable cargoes of oil or bauxite, the latter used in the production of aluminium required for aircraft. The U-boats had been expected to confine their attacks to ships greater than 10,000 tons;[8] in fact, from Morison's figures, the average tonnage of those sunk was 6,000 tons, which still represented serious losses to the Allies. Professor Morison sums up *Paukenschlag* with 360 ships totalling 2,250,000 tons sunk by Germany for the loss of only eight of their U-boats.[9] The Americans had expected U-boats to operate off their coast due to their experience in the First World War, but it was not until April that the beginnings of a convoy system was formed.[10]

There were each day 120 to 130 ships requiring protection, but only twenty-eight vessels available to serve as escorts.[11] This resulted in one of the positive measures made by the Americans: they were to request aid from Britain both for escort vessels from the Admiralty and for aircraft from the RAF. In respect of aircraft, that aid was rather late. However, when Coastal Command dispatched No. 53 Squadron on 5 July, equipped with Hudsons, as their Commanding Officer, Gp Capt Leggate recalls:

The move of the squadron of comparatively short-range aircraft from Cornwall to Trinidad was more than just interesting for all the pilots and aircrew, both in midsummer and midwinter on the return. Prestwick–Reykjavik–Bluie West One–Goose Bay–Montreal–Quonset Point, Rhode Island–New York–Jacksonville–Miami–Guantanamo Bay–Cuba–San Juan–Puerto Rico– and so on to Port of Spain, Trinidad.

... After a few days in the Caribbean it was agreed with our Engineer Officer that we would be able to remove the turrets from all the Marks of Hudsons in the squadron. The absence of the turret made a considerable difference – not only to the handling qualities of the aircraft, but also its speed and range. As we were operating outside the range of enemy aircraft, these improvements were vital to the efficiency of anti-submarine work.[12]

By 31 July fifteen of the squadron's aircraft were in America, and on 22 August there was a move to Trinidad. The United States Navy had provided a liaison officer, Lt Cdr Sutherland, and some USN personnel flew with No. 53 Squadron. It had come under the RAF's Delegation in Washington for administration, but for operational control, under the United States Navy. While operating off the American seaboard, No. 53 Squadron made a number of attacks on U-boats, but its greatest contribution was probably to promote the methods of Coastal Command, which both the Canadians and the Americans came to accept. This is confirmed by the official history of the RCAF.[13]

A mistake made by both adversaries in the war was to give insufficient care in respect of radio transmissions, and during the U-boat campaign off the American seaboard in the first half of 1942, transmissions to ships were intercepted by Germany to be passed on to its U-boats. This intelligence Professor Rohwer considered to be a major factor in the U-boat war.[14] At the 123rd meeting of Coastal Command's headquarters staff on 2 February it was stated that fifteen U-boats were off the American coast, six were homeward bound from the Bay of Biscay, and four U-boats were in the South-Western Approaches.[15]

It was possible to keep track of U-boat positions because of Dönitz's policy of expecting U-boats to transmit radio messages.

By such means, the first U-boat to sight a convoy would transmit to the U-boat High Command, and Dönitz was then able to control the deployment of his U-boats and maintain overall control by W/T. He was prepared to forego security on that account.[16]

Because of the U-boats' policy of attacking ships indiscriminately, regardless of the consequences, some Brazilian ships were sunk with serious loss of life. This prompted Brazil into declaring war on Germany and Italy on 22 August.[17] This resulted in considerable cooperation between the United States Navy and Brazil. Although Brazil's forces were limited, what were of great use, not only to the United States Navy, but also to the British, were invaluable bases along the Brazilian coastline, which extends out eastwards into the South Atlantic and was to provide a route to British bases in West Africa.

There was a fear at that time that the Vichy French might again cooperate with the enemy by providing a foothold in South America through its former colonies, such as had occurred in the Far East.

Three days after the Channel Dash, my squadron was posted from St Eval to Limavady in Northern Ireland. My log for the next three months reflects the shift of Coastal Command's operations from the North Sea and Bay of Biscay to the North-Western Approaches. It confirms that, by early April 1942, bases such as Limavady, Aldergrove and Nutts Corner in Northern Ireland, and Stornoway and Tiree in the Inner and Outer Hebrides to cover the North-Western Approaches were available, at least for a twin-engined aircraft such as the Hudson, but not all of those bases at that time could have been suitable for a four-engined Liberator due to the length of the runways.

The question of suitable bases for Coastal Command was of much concern to Sir Philip; thus, a runway for Stornoway needed Treasury approval, and the Air Ministry was asked to give a 'daily reminder'. For both Stornoway and St Eval, Sir Philip was 'emphatic that the runways should be first class'.[18] This was due to aircraft such as Flying Fortresses and Liberators, which were then coming into service and required a much greater length of runway than medium-sized aircraft.

For the first part of my first tour of operations, my log again reflects what was to prevail for the Command's anti-submarine operations; they were convoy escorts, anti-submarine sweeps and reconnaissance patrols. From those north-western bases sorties would have been over the North Atlantic, and typically to about 14°W or as far as 17°W. That would have been enough to cover what appeared as a favourite area for U-boats at that time, namely Rockall, the one 'landmark' to check one's position, and, incidentally, give an indication of the massive swell of the Atlantic Ocean should an aircraft have to ditch.

On 4 June 1942 Wellington ES986, captained by Sqn Ldr Jeaf H. Greswell, gained an ASV contact at 6 miles, and on homing sighted two submarines. The Leigh Light was switched on at 1 mile from the target, and Greswell attacked one of the submarines in a shallow dive beginning $3/4$-mile distant, releasing four depth charges from 50 ft altitude. Three of the depth charges exploded, one on the starboard quarter about five yards from the hull and the other two on the port side.

The second submarine was located about 12 miles from the first and was attacked from about 150 ft altitude with machine-gun fire, scoring hits on the hull and conning tower. Sqn Ldr Greswell with his crew visited Coastal Command's headquarters the following day for interrogation.[19]

This sortie marked a turning point in anti-submarine warfare. It was the first successful attack using the Leigh Light against a submarine, and Sqn Ldr Greswell was the Command's pilot who was directly involved in the Leigh Light trials. No. 172 Squadron's record of this operation is notable also in giving details of the armament used – Torpex-filled depth charges, fitted with a pistol set at 25 ft depth. Thus, at long last, Coastal Command had the necessary weapon that would be lethal to a U-boat.

According to an account by Sir Philip Joubert, the lethal radius of the Torpex depth charges were at least 30 per cent greater than the earlier Amatol-filled charges.[20] Detonation at 25 ft depth increased the chance of the U-boat being at least damaged before it could escape. The Torpex-filled depth charge was also considered lethal to a U-boat within the range 15–18 ft.[21] The use of the Leigh Light not only gave the necessary illumination for attack on U-boats, but also enabled the aircraft to achieve surprise.

The submarine, however, was an Italian one, the *Luigi Torelli*. The first German U-boat sunk by a Leigh Light aircraft was U-502, and was credited to a Wellington of No. 172 Squadron captained by Plt Off W.B. Howell on 6 July 1942. These successes were the beginnings of as many as forty German U-boats and two Italian submarines sunk or damaged by Wellington aircraft equipped with Leigh Lights. Additionally, other types of aircraft were also to have Leigh Lights. A necessary adjunct to their use, however, was suitable ASV/radar, which was being progressively improved.[22]

It was in June 1942 that Germany became certain that Coastal Command's aircraft had a detecting device such as ASV. Her response was to have the French company, Metox, produce a receiver capable of detecting the 1.5m ASV transmissions from aircraft.

On 24 June all U-boats on transit in the Bay of Biscay were ordered to remain submerged night and day except to recharge their batteries.[23] This order would of course,

have put additional strain on the U-boat crews and limited the time that they could spend on operations in the Atlantic. Additionally, but as a temporary measure, four machine guns were provided for defence against attacking aircraft. After U-71 had been damaged by aircraft on 5 June, and U-105 on 11 June, Dönitz requested fighter cover from the *Luftwaffe*, and on 2 July twenty-four JU88 C6 aircraft were promised.[24]

As was to be demonstrated later, however, Coastal Command's aircraft such as Sunderlands and Wellingtons were able to give a good account of themselves in air-to-air combat against ostensibly overwhelming numbers of German fighters.[25] A German account of what was most likely the first attack using the Leigh Light on a U-boat stated:

> In June 1942, the first dark night attack was made in the Bay of Biscay when a U-boat was caught in the beam of a searchlight which switched on suddenly 1,000 to 2,000 metres away. Before fire could be opened, an aircraft, with a powerful light in its nose, roared over the conning tower at low level, dropped bombs, and turned to renew the attack.[26]

This unsuccessful attack, from No. 172's records, must have been by Wg Cdr Russell, who would probably have had little experience with his equipment in a Leigh Light Wellington, and probably overshot the target, thus the lack of success. He had as a passenger a Royal Navy officer, Lt Cdr Brooks, who was nevertheless 'impressed'.[27] Air Commodore Greswell in a letter to me remarked:

> I think it important to include ... [the] U-boat sightings and attacks which took place between 3/6/42 and the first kill by Howell on 6 July '42. On my second patrol on 6 June '42, I made contact with a U-boat.

Unfortunately my approach to attack was too high, because of the altimeter error, and the Leigh Light overshot the target, rendering it impossible to drop the depth charges. The sub crash-dived before I could have another try.[28]

That brief statement demonstrates two aspects applicable to attacks by aircraft on submarines at that time. They were an unreliable altimeter (which effectively measured the column of air above rather than the distance to the surface below), which it would have been unwise to have attempted to check at night by going down to sea level; also, that after an abortive first attack, the element of surprise was lost. In this case, it was not human error, as Sqn Ldr Greswell was almost certainly the most experienced pilot in handling a Leigh-Light-equipped aircraft, having been directly involved in its trials. To overcome the problem of measuring altitude, particularly at night, there was the need for radio altimeters still to be satisfied.

Although the Germans were initially able to counter the Allies' use of 1.5m ASV/radar using the French-produced 'Metox' receiver, they also had production problems. It was such that they considered U-boats in transit sailing in convoy, with one of the vessels equipped with Metox, as they required the equipment for U-boats in transit from Bergen and Kiel in addition to those from the Biscay ports.[29] Metox receivers gained the U-boats some respite against Allied aircraft using the early marks of ASV, which transmitted at a wavelength of 1.5 metre, but that disadvantage for the Allies was later to be overcome by radar transmitting on a 9.1 cm wavelength.

The German fighters were intended to protect their U-boats against Allied anti-submarine aircraft, while the British fighters, such as the Beaufighters, were to protect our reconnaissance aircraft. Nevertheless, reconnaissance aircrew in such as the Sunderlands were able to give a good account of themselves, and against them the *Luftwaffe* considered it needed at least two fighters. If the *Luftwaffe* encountered Beaufighters over the Bay of Biscay, it decided to withdraw.[30] Even the Wellington anti-U-boat aircraft were able to gain an advantage against superior *Luftwaffe* odds as the Polish No. 304 Squadron demonstrated, and on one occasion,

27. Flt/Lt David Hornell, VC (second from right) here at RAF Wick in 1944. Hornell was lost with some of his crew after ditching, following his attack on U-1225.

28. Hornell's Canso No 9754 in which he sank U-1225 in position 63°00'N 00°50'W. It was due to the arrival on the scene of the sinking by a No 333 squadron Catalina, that the event became known.

successfully opposed six Junkers 88s.[31]

By July 1942 there was increasing evidence of Coastal Command gaining the initiative and with U-boats having to react accordingly. Thus, with the U-boats then attempting to resume operations against the Atlantic convoys, such as SC97 and SC99, but also OS33 and SL118, they found that they had to cease operations due to 'continuous air cover'.[32]

Coastal's naval staff considered that Sunderland flying-boats had an operational radius of 600 miles,[33] but on 17 July U-202 sighted an aircraft 800 miles out into the Atlantic from the nearest land base. This event is recorded by three writers: Dönitz in his

29. The Italian submarine *Luigi Torelli*, 1,191 tons, entering Bordeaux ex La Spezia. It was the first enemy submarine to be successfully attacked by Leigh Light. That was on 4 June 1942, position 44°43'N 06°46'W by a No 172 Squadron Wellington captained by S/Ldr Jeaff Greswell.

memoirs, Hessler in the edited U-boat diaries, and the naval historian, Captain Roskill. It was, however, an exception, due, as Roskill adds, to Coastal Command being able 'to scrape together only one squadron of American Liberators'.[34] That Liberator would have been from No. 120 Squadron, which had

been earmarked to receive Coastal Command's first few aircraft of that type.

The distance of 800 miles, from the U-boats' point of view, was an increase of 300 miles over the previous year.[35] This increase could be accounted for by the Allied use of bases in Iceland in addition to long-range aircraft such as the Liberators that were coming into service.

During the months of July and August Coastal Command's successes in the anti-U-boat war were greater than for the previous six months. A total of 114 sightings had been made with eighty-nine attacks. This was due to the return of U-boats from their forays off the American seaboard, but also because 62 per cent of Coastal Command's operations had been on the offensive rather than on convoy escorts. Aircraft based in Iceland had enabled the Command to give more attention to the northern transit area of U-boats, i.e. to and from Norwegian and German ports in addition to those using the Bay of Biscay route from French ports.[36] The U-boats had suffered losses of 15 per cent in July and 9.3 per cent in August, but only 6 per cent in September. The monthly average for the previous year had been 11.4 per cent.[37] The progressive drop in U-boat losses could be attributed to the countermeasures taken by U-boats against air attacks, such as the use of the Metox receiver to detect ASV signals from aircraft, and that the U-boats were remaining submerged except to charge their batteries.

In July 1942 the U-boats became aware of Coastal Command aircraft using another innovation – sonobuoys, which could be thought of as the air equivalent of the Navy's Asdic. A U-boat reported them on 29 July being dropped in the north transit area, and they were thought by the enemy to be devices for preventing U-boats travelling on the surface.[38]

They were, in fact, for detecting submerged U-boats, and were to be used by such squadrons as No. 201 operating Sunderlands.

In operational records they were coded 'High Tea'.[39] Although I was on anti-submarine operations in 1942, I was quite unaware of the existence of sonobuoys until I studied the operational records of the Sunderland squadrons post war, and it was 1998 before I saw these devices, which were then with an operational squadron. The RAF appeared adept at keeping details of equipment secret, even from those who could be expected to use it.

There was another factor in favour of the Allies' aircrew involved in anti-submarine warfare in 1942: that was the increasing use of aircraft with a greater speed. This was important, as typically a sighting or contact was made at about 6 miles, and with a U-boat able to crash-dive in 25 seconds slow aircraft such as the Catalina could hardly hope to attack before the U-boat had dived. Traditionally, the U-boats relied on vigilant lookouts, but with faster aircraft, as a former U-boat officer, Hessler, records: 'Greater airspeeds changed this ... that even if detected by U-boats attacking aircraft could not always be evaded.'[40]

Convoys to Russia had begun in September 1941 from Iceland,[41] and Coastal Command had been able to provide air escorts only as far as 70°N. It was at the suggestion of Sir Philip Joubert that a detachment of aircraft should be established in Russia. The Russians permitted Coastal Command's Catalinas to operate from Lake Lakhta, near Archangel, where there were facilities for six flying-boats. During the period 1–4 July, four Catalinas from No. 210 Squadron and two from No. 240 Squadron flew to Russia and were able to operate as far north as 77°N. From bases in Norway, the enemy was able to threaten the Russian convoys, not only with U-boats but also with capital ships such as the battleship *Tirpitz* and heavy cruisers.

For that reason, Coastal Command provided additional support by means of the strike squadrons, Nos 144 and 455, which

were detached to Russia.[42] My own involvement was to be on a reconnaissance of Trondheim Fjord on 10 June looking for *Tirpitz* and the heavy cruiser *Admiral Hipper*.

In September I was on a detachment to Iceland from No. 48 Squadron to escort a Russian convoy, but, perhaps due to one of our aircraft being lost, the task was aborted.[43]

Other squadrons, including Nos 422 (RCAF) and 333 (Norwegian), also provided detachments to Russia, but were more involved in transport of goods, personnel and diplomatic missions than anti-submarine warfare. Accounts from their aircrew show that the Russians gave very mixed receptions to their allies, which ranged from armed guards to an escort by young ladies!

The aircraft chosen for the Russian detachments for convoy escorts, Catalinas, were suitable in that they had the required range and endurance; they were, however, sadly lacking in not having an efficient heating system. This was to be critical when even the interior of the aircraft became frosted up, including the cockpit, thus reducing visibility to nil. Even at the much lower latitude of Trondheim, the air temperature in mid-summer was found to be -7 °C. One Catalina operating over the White Sea reported a complete 'white-out'.[44]

Sir Philip Joubert sums up the support given by his Command for one cycle of Russian convoys that involved thirteen squadrons with over a 100 aircraft. They flew 269 sorties totalling 2,320 hours, of which 184 hours were over the convoys. This was because they had to fly 1,000 miles before reaching the convoy. The detachments to Russia were to be proved justified because in the Russian area covered by those aircraft only one ship was lost.[45] Other factors justifying the detachments cannot be quantified.

They were the effect on the morale of the merchant seamen who sighted a friendly rather than hostile aircraft, and the effect on the enemy who did sight a hostile aircraft.

There was, above all, the need to ensure the 'safe and timely arrival' of Allied convoys to whatever ports they were routed. There was a particular need in the case of the Russians, not only to deliver essential supplies, but also to show that they had the support of their allies.

BREMEN

One of the most controversial uses of Coastal Command's forces took place on the night of 25/6 June 1942, when 102 of the Command's aircraft, including eighty-two Hudsons, took part in *Millennium II*, the second thousand-bomber raid on Germany. This was to Bremen, and rated part of the anti-U-boat campaign, with Coastal's forces comprising a number of squadrons plus incompletely trained crews from OTUs, the latter albeit with experienced captains. While about 900 of Bomber Command's aircraft attacked a Focke-Wulf factory, Coastal Command was to bomb the Deschimag U-boat yards. The Hudsons were armed with either four 250 lb or ten 100 lb bombs, while Bomber aircraft had such as 4,000 lb bombs. Some Bomber aircraft also had the invaluable navigation aid GEE, although that was not available to Coastal Command's Hudsons. The organisation of such a raid meant that squadrons operating over the Atlantic had to be withdrawn from western bases to the east coast and put on standby for the signal to take off. Although Bremen was covered with cloud, aircraft with GEE should at least have been able to bomb with some degree of accuracy. For others, such as all the Coastal Command aircraft, it would have meant 'finding a hole in the cloud' or bombing on fires already produced. Sir Arthur Harris claimed that 'a very important Focke-Wulf factory was largely destroyed',[46] but didn't state an opinion on the use of Coastal Command's maritime aircraft.

By the standards of Coastal Command's anti-shipping strikes, the overall losses of only 4.9 per cent were of little concern; in fact one of its squadrons, which suffered over 50 per cent losses in a shipping strike, wanted to go on further bombing raids to Germany; its aircrew who were not detailed for the raid were disappointed. All the aircraft returned safely from at least three of Coastal Command's squadrons.[47]

Professor Overy has stated: 'Bomber Command insisted that the threat from U-boats could only be met by attacking the sources of production rather than the end product at sea.'[48] That statement was to be disproved even in that year, and certainly by October 1943, by which time the Command's Hudsons alone had sunk about two dozen U-boats at sea.

They would not have just destroyed the hulls of the vessels, as in a factory, but the enemy would have lost with each U-boat at sea two or three dozen trained men, plus tons of valuable oil. Coastal Command's aircraft just flying over the sea rather than Germany would always present a potential hazard to U-boats. Captain Roskill confirms the uselessness of combating the U-boat menace by bombing building yards with: 'Not until April 1944 was a completed U-boat destroyed in a German building yard.'[49]

The 18,000 tons of bombs and incendiaries dropped on U-boat bases and building yards in the first five months of 1943, apparently without destroying a single U-boat, may be contrasted with one 25 lb rocket projectile or one 250 lb depth charge capable of sinking a U-boat at sea.

OPERATION TORCH

The invasion of the French North African colonies was agreed by Churchill and President Roosevelt in April, and on 1 August, Field Marshal Dill, the Head of British Joint Staff Mission, Washington, informed Churchill that orders had been issued for that operation.[50] The purpose was to relieve the pressure imposed on the Russian forces, which

30. U-200 seen from a PBY5A (Catalina amphibian) of VP84 USN 24 June 1943. U-200 was attached and sunk using DCs and then an acoustic homing torpedo (a 'Mark 24 mine'). This was one of the first successful uses of that 'mine'.

31. U-106 on 2 July 1943 which was sunk in co-ordinated attacks by Sunderlands N/228 and M/461.

were fully engaged by the Germans. General Auchinleck, who commanded the British forces in North Africa, had made a stand on 8 August at El Alamein, about 60 miles west of Cairo; it remained then for Generals Alexander and Montgomery to advance westwards against German forces when sufficient strength in both men and armament had been built up. This was to result in the Battle of El Alamein.

Before Operation Torch could be launched, it was essential that victory at El Alamein was achieved. It was in the Middle East, probably more than in any other area, where cooperation of the three services, Army, Navy and Air Force, was essential; all three were individually dependent on the other two. For the Army to capture the French bases, troops and supplies had to be shipped, and those ships had to be protected by both the Navy and Coastal Command. When once bases or ports were captured, they needed to be protected by the Army.

The date of 8 November 1942 was fixed for the landings near the French bases in North Africa, for which 340 ships were required to pass through the Straits of Gibraltar during 5 and 7 November in a definite sequence.

For the Army, about 70,000 troops were to be deployed to attack the areas of Casablanca, Oran and Algiers. The enemies, Italy and Germany, therefore had the means to make a

32. An attack using rocket projectiles on U-594 by F/O H.C. Bailey in Hudson F/48 on 4 June 1943 position 35°55'N 09°25'W. It was one of the first 'kills' on a U-boat using RPs.

killing by sinking many ships, with the Allies possibly losing thousands of troops.[51]

That most of the ships were unmolested was due to Germany being taken by surprise, as she had not expected an assault to be made on the North African shores, believing rather that Allied shipping movements were geared to the support of Malta and a possible attack on Dakar.[52]

About the time of the operation, there were twenty-five U-boats in the Mediterranean, while the Italians had thirty-four submarines between 02°E and 11°E off the North African coast in November. On 8 November the German U-boat group *Streitaxt* was shadowing a Sierra Leone convoy SL125, and five from the U-boat's *Delfin* group were entering the Straits of Gibraltar, while two others from that group were off the coast of Portugal. Three others were outward bound from Biscay ports, while twenty-one U-boats were in the North Atlantic but at least as far west as 23°W.

While the Allies wondered whether Germany would react by sending troops through Spain, Germany wondered if the Allies would occupy Spain. The German Naval Staff gave an appreciation on 20 October, which considered that an Allied second front was militarily impossible.[53]

The success of Operation Torch could be attributed to taking Germany completely by surprise, due to various rumours being successfully spread, and the only one to which Germany reacted was of a possible Allied attack on Dakar.[54] An additional feature was the close cooperation between the Americans and the British, from their Commanders General Eisenhower and Admiral Cunningham, who shared a tunnel within the Rock as their headquarters.[55] As Admiral Cunningham stated, 'With a number of services involved ... there reigned a spirit of comradeship which provided the vital force which brought success. ... The embodiment of

that spirit was exemplified in our Commander-in-Chief, General Dwight D. Eisenhower....'[56]

Of Gibraltar, Eisenhower stated: '[It] made possible the invasion of north-west Africa. Without it the vital air cover would not have been quickly established on the North African fields.'[57]

When the U-boat Command received a report of the North African landings, fifteen U-boats were ordered to the Mediterranean, although they were aware of the additional risks there due to the calm waters.[58] This was to be made apparent later when there were a series of attacks by Coastal Command's Hudson aircraft.

With 340 Allied ships at sea and of necessity having to concentrate in the approaches to the Straits of Gibraltar, the Command's squadrons had to be withdrawn from northern areas to operate from Gibraltar, and subsequently from former French bases in North Africa after those had been captured. Two squadrons, Nos 202 and 233, were already at Gibraltar, but No. 500 Squadron was moved from Stornoway, and No. 608 Squadron from Wick down to southern bases in August to prepare for Mediterranean operations. I was posted with No. 48 Squadron from Sumburgh in the Shetlands to Gosport in November, where the squadron re-equipped with Mark VI Hudsons, but to reach Gibraltar by Christmas. By that time the three squadrons, Nos 233, 500 and 608, had sunk or damaged seven U-boats, all within a fortnight.

Such success was not due to luck: the comparatively clear and still waters of the western Mediterranean area, with generally good visibility, favoured visual sightings, although only Mark II ASV was then being used by Hudsons. Very high morale prevailed within many of the Hudson crews, such as in No. 500 (County of Kent) Squadron, and the aircrew would have included a number of battle-hardened and experienced men, many on their second tour of operations.

Another factor was that in a comparatively confined area with many aircraft available, it was possible, and it did occur, that when once an aircraft made a sighting, other aircraft could be homed to the area. This was by using other apparatus, which gained little publicity, if any, due to the nature of the equipment, which was IFF (Identification Friend or Foe); this could be switched to give a homing signal and could result in as many as three squadrons being involved.

A further factor was that Coastal Command's aircraft were camouflaged white, and under the lighting conditions that prevailed over the Mediterranean at that time white camouflage could certainly have made a difference.

To undertake anti-submarine night operations, a detachment of No. 179 Squadron Wellingtons began operations on 19 November, but ultimately the whole squadron would be based at Gibraltar. However, it gained no successes against U-boats during Operation Torch, but claimed a number of successes the following year.[59] Sir Philip Joubert gives the Command losing ten Hudsons, four Catalinas and three Wellingtons during the campaign, some to our own forces. Four of No. 233's Hudsons were shot down by the French at Casablanca.[60]

Aircrew were warned to beware of French aircraft, even after the landings had been made. Arabs appeared rather more friendly, and aircrew from Nos 48, 500 and 221 Squadrons all experienced courtesy and help from them.[61] In an attempt to placate the French, leaflets had been dropped over French bases in North Africa, written in French but emphasising the American rather than the British involvement, by the Stars and Stripes being printed in colour – no doubt because of anti-British feelings.

The success of the Eighth Army, commanded by General Alexander, with General Montgomery, gained the publicity and rather overshadowed what was a remarkable anti-submarine campaign by Coastal Command's squadrons. They were given reasonable operating conditions (although not necessarily living conditions), and achieved much. The leadership shown by the Commanding Officers of Nos 500 and 48 Squadrons was certainly a factor in maintaining high morale, with both aircrew and ground crew. That high morale was duly acknowledged for at least one of those squadrons in a subsequent issue of 'Coastal Command Review'.[62] An official Italian view of Operation Torch was given thus: '*Il mese di novembre 1942 rappresento il "turning point" della 2 guerre mondiale nel Mediterraneo.*'[63] It was certainly a turning point for Italy, as control of North African bases enabled the Allies to harass Axis shipping and ultimately to invade Sicily and the Italian mainland. Coastal Command squadrons continued to play a part in such operations.

Dönitz acknowledged the successes against U-boats in the Mediterranean at the time of Operation Torch with: 'I received orders on November 16 to make good the heavy U-boat losses in the Mediterranean by transfers from the Atlantic …', but was permitted to reduce the number to twelve, and added: 'I myself was still most anxious to see these twelve U-boats withdrawn from the murderous area west of Gibraltar....'[64]

Those Hudsons that had operated with such success during Operation Torch carried no more than four 250 lb depth charges with, possibly, two 100 lb A/S bombs. That success may be contrasted with the same type of aircraft used to bomb the U-boat building yards at Bremen with the equivalent weight of bombs. In Operation Torch not only had some of the U-boat menace been removed, but also some of the potential French menace, aided about that time by the French scuttling their fleet at Toulon. The capture of French North African bases such as at Tafaraouri (Oran) enabled Coastal's aircraft to gain closer control over the western Mediterranean. Roskill stated, 'The greatest benefits of all lay in the additional security of Atlantic shipping, and in the prospect that the Mediterranean would soon be opened.'[65]

The Gibraltar area had obviously proved a 'happy hunting ground' for medium-range aircraft against U-boats; it was not so, however, in the Bay of Biscay and the North Atlantic in the latter part of 1942. The prime reason for this was that from August onwards, the U-boats were being equipped with Metox receivers, which could detect aircraft using the Mark II ASV transmitting on the 1 m wavelength.[66] In the Bay of Biscay, U-boats when on the surface were relying on their Metox receivers to give warning before any possible attack. Sir Philip Joubert ordered countermeasures in the inner Bay, with constant patrols by Leigh-Light Wellingtons supplemented by other aircraft dropping flares periodically.

Normal day patrols continued, with ASV to be switched on for ten seconds every fifteen minutes, except in good visibility when U-boats could well be detected visually. There was also an attempt to maintain long-range patrols up to 15°W.

These measures proved unsuccessful, and in November Sir Philip issued a further directive to the AOC of No. 19 Group. They were that aircraft with ASV, other than Liberators, should fly only at night and operate from as high an altitude as was practicable.

The higher altitude would enable the ASV in individual aircraft to cover a greater area, albeit at reduced intensity. By this means it was hoped that the area would be so flooded with ASV transmissions that U-boats could only ignore them at the risk of being attacked. It was considered that if the night patrols were able to keep the U-boats submerged, there was a greater chance of them being sighted in the

day. The emphasis was to be in the inner Bay, which was probably considered to be at about 3°W. There were, additionally, to be Beaufighters armed with bombs or depth charges when possible. It was realised that aircraft flying so near the enemy-controlled French coast were vulnerable, but that the risk was to be accepted. [67]

However, from the German account, the sight of Beaufighters would have deterred enemy fighters.[68] In December, Joubert extended the patrols over this southern transit route for U-boats another 200 miles west beyond 15°W with long-range aircraft and the few aircraft that had the experimental 10 cm wavelength radar. It was to be the following year, however, before such units as No. 224 Squadron, which had then converted to Liberators, were to receive such equipment.[69] Despite all these measures, for the latter months of 1942, No. 19 Group claimed only two U-boats sunk and two damaged. The two damaged were in November, and U-216 and U-599 were sunk in October.

Flg Off David Sleep claimed U-216 at 19°W, and it was notable that he released his depth charges from only 30 feet, with instant detonation, and his Liberator was seriously damaged by the blast from the depth charges. The recommended height for release at that time was 50–100 ft, but flying at probably at least 140 knots it would not be easy to judge height precisely with an aneroid altimeter and at the same time follow a precise track against a hostile vessel. U-599 was also sunk near the limit of effective range of medium aircraft at 17°W by another No. 224 Squadron Liberator.[70]

Sir Philip Joubert considered that the sightings and attacks on U-boats in the Bay of Biscay during this latter part of 1942 as 'dangerously low';[71] it may be said, however, that there had been success on account of some of the patrols, in that the U-boats were not sighted – that is, they had been forced to remain submerged due to the air patrols. Thus the U-boat crews would have been under additional strain and taken longer in transit.

The German Naval Staff considered that the Gibraltar area was too well defended, and on 21 November decided that only four U-boats would be sent to the Mediterranean and twelve U-boats should be deployed west of Gibraltar. The defence of that area could be attributed in no small measure to the aircraft under Coastal Command's control, such as the four Hudson squadrons, Nos 233, 48, 500 and 608. Subsequently there was a renewal in attacks on the North Atlantic convoys, all west of 20°W, and thus out of effective range of Coastal Command's medium-range aircraft operating from the United Kingdom.

As Captain Peyton-Ward records: 'By the 28th November the U-boats in the Gibraltar area had had enough ... the remnants being withdrawn to refit.'[72] Most Allied ships in the last two months of 1942 were sunk between about 20°W and 60°W.[73] Many of these were centred about the 'Mid-Atlantic Gap' south of Cape Farewell, but also in the Trinidad area. This was due to lack of air cover, as only a limited number of aircraft could have operated so far west, and Allied forces covering the American seaboard still lacked the efficiency of that which prevailed from the United Kingdom. The Allies were still 'one jump behind the U-boats as regards "soft spots"', according to Peyton-Ward.

He considered that situation would prevail until the offensive against U-boats in all parts of the world were under a single Anti-U-boat Command.[74] That opinion was reflected by John Slessor, who considered that the whole of the Atlantic should be considered as one battlefield, contrasting with the view of the United States Navy, which tended to think of the American eastern seaboard in sections to be defended individually.[75]

The most necessary requirement was to close the gap in terms of air cover south of Cape Farewell; this was so because of the need to cover the vital convoys from Halifax, Nova Scotia, to the United Kingdom (those coded HX and SC).

Other gaps in respect of air cover for convoys still prevailed in the Azores area and also near the Canary Islands.[76] Churchill was well aware of the desirability of having bases in the Azores for that purpose, and diplomatic moves towards Portugal, which controlled the Azores, were being considered.[77] Bases in the Azores could have provided air cover for the Gibraltar convoys and those routes further south to West Africa and onwards round the Cape of Good Hope.

This route was of great importance due to the Mediterranean still being closed to through-traffic of merchant vessels. It had been demonstrated very clearly in the second week of December just how effective air cover could be in the notorious Mid-Atlantic Gap. It was not until October in the following year, however, that a Coastal Command base became established in the Azores.[78]

One of the few Liberators available to the Command flew out 800 miles from Iceland and was able to escort Convoy HX217, which was bound for the United Kingdom. The Liberator remained with the convoy for six hours, and was followed by three more Liberators. Although fifteen U-boats were deployed against HX217, only two ships in the convoy were lost, plus one straggler.[79] This episode, however, was exceptional. Few aircraft were available to fly that distance and remain with a convoy for six hours; two–three hours was more likely. Furthermore, all crew positions would at least be duplicated, and for circling a convoy where the automatic pilot could not be used, three pilots would have been considered necessary. Nevertheless, it demonstrated how valuable aircraft escorts could be in protecting ships.

CONCLUSIONS

In the year 1942 there had been some improvement in the numbers of aircraft available to the Command, and the types of aircraft that were to come into service. There had been considerable improvements in the equipment available and armament – most notably the Leigh Light and the 250 lb Torpex-filled depth charge fitted with a pistol able to detonate at 25 ft depth.[80] The Leigh Light enabled the Command to attack U-boats at night.

By the end of 1942, most reconnaissance squadrons appear to have been equipped with Mark II ASV, and some, such as No. 500 Squadron, had Yagi aerials for homing. Although the initiative using Mark II ASV, which transmitted at 1.5m wavelength, had been lost due to U-boats gaining the use of the French Metox receiver, the U-boats had nevertheless been put on the defensive, as shown by their attempts to improve their anti-aircraft armament with machine-guns. They were also seen to be on the defensive by asking the *Luftwaffe* to cover them in the Bay of Biscay.[81]

In 1942 Coastal Command claimed twenty-seven enemy submarines sunk, one captured and eighteen damaged. Some of the successes had been shared with HM ships. This year marked the entry of the United States Navy squadrons operating under Coastal Command control in Iceland, and two of the sinkings were claimed by VP73 PBYs and one of the U-boats damaged by a PBY of VP84.

More operations were being undertaken by longer-range aircraft, including the Liberator, Flying Fortress and Catalina. Nonetheless, the successes of medium-range aircraft such as the Hudson operating from both Iceland and Gibraltar still served a useful purpose in anti-submarine warfare.

There was still a need for greater numbers of the long-range Liberator bases, provided with longer runways able to accept the heavier four-engined aircraft; a need also for aircraft to be equipped with Mark III radar, and for

the provision of radio altimeters and a low-level bombsight. Owing to campaigns in the Middle East and the Far East, a number of squadrons had been taken from Coastal Command for those overseas postings.

1943

POLITICAL DECISIONS

The Allied leaders arranged a number of conferences in 1943, and all had a direct or indirect bearing on Coastal Command. Those relevant to Coastal Command's anti-submarine operations took place in Casablanca in January and at Washington in March. At the Casablanca conference in January, the Combined Chiefs of Staff decided that the first charge on the combined Allied resources in 1943 should be directed towards the defeat of U-boats.

For the Air Officer Commander-in-Chief of Coastal Command at that time, Air Chief Marshal Sir Philip Joubert, 'It revealed the degree of concern with which the Battle of the Atlantic was regarded, and it held promise, if interpreted literally, of Coastal Command receiving its full requirements.'[82] At that time, as throughout his tenure with the Command, Sir Philip appreciated that fully to satisfy the requirements of Coastal Command, it would be at the expense of the resources for other forces.[83] Prior to the Washington Conference there had been no coordination of the Canadian (RCN and RCAF) forces, and likewise no coordination between the American Navy and Air Force.

The RCN and RCAF had needed to settle their differences in much the same way as had prevailed with Coastal Command and the Admiralty. They were resolved with maritime air sorties being under the operational direction of the naval commander responsible for protecting shipping, but the Air Officer Commanding was to exercise general operational control.

This agreement was considered necessary to satisfy the American Admiral King (Cominch). Portal, the CAS, appeared more interested in bombing Germany, his 'Course B' for winning the war.[84]

There had been five separate controls for the Americans' naval and air forces on their eastern seaboard, but following the conference chaired by Admiral King, a statement was issued on 11 March that:

> All ASW aviation of the Associated Powers based in this region is to be under the general operational control of the Canadian AOC EAC Halifax who, under general operational direction of the C-in-C North Western Atlantic shall be responsible for the air coverage of all shipping within range, including Greenland convoys and other shipping under US control.[85]

Decisions made at a conference at Washington in March had an immediate bearing on the Battle of the Atlantic. That was to close the 700-mile 'Mid-Atlantic Gap' by having convoys with escort carriers, which were provided by the United States Navy.

A further outcome of the conference in March was the reorganisation of the convoy system on the eastern seaboard of the Americas, with both the United States Navy and the RCAF having anti-submarine forces that included VLR (very-long-range) aircraft in Newfoundland. For the effective protection of the North Atlantic convoys it was necessary to have intelligence of U-boat movements, and this was gained largely through decoding of the enemy's signals.

The British Admiralty began the organisation by issuing a daily message prefixed 'Stipple', and categorised convoys according to whether they were under attack or threatened, needing air cover in the near future, or considered out of danger. Account was taken also of the fast liners such as the

Queen Elizabeth that sailed independently. Coastal Command prefixed its messages 'Tubular', which outlined the probable U-boat areas with the object of helping to coordinate air patrols under Eastern Air Command at Halifax and those under No. 15 Group at Liverpool.[86]

In applying this procedure, Air Marshal Slessor adopted the view that it was for the Admiralty to state what air cover was required, but for the Air Officers to decide how they could best deploy their air forces to achieve the required aim. He advised the Canadians that it could be through day-to-day discussions rather than to 'raise it as a policy issue'.[87]

The practical application of the agreement made at the Washington Conference was that there was daily telephoning between the Admiralty, Coastal Command HQ, and ACHQ Liverpool to check the dispositions of convoys and of the believed positions of U-boats, which were based largely on decoded German signals. All of Coastal Command's Groups and HQ at Iceland, Gibraltar and the Azores, plus the RCAF at St John's and Cominch in Washington, signalled each other as to what they were able to undertake the following day.[88] Britain and Canada were to become entirely responsible for convoys on the North Atlantic route, with their headquarters at Liverpool, England, and Halifax, Nova Scotia, respectively. It was to result in a shuttle service of VLR Liberators between Newfoundland and Iceland that thus covered the gap south of Greenland.

The crucial aspect that resulted from the Allies' agreement was that VLR aircraft were operated from Newfoundland in protecting the North Atlantic convoys, notably those from Halifax. The VLR aircraft that sortied from Newfoundland were in addition to Coastal's limited VLR Liberators operating from Iceland. This resulted in a shuttle service of Liberators in sorties of about 12–13 hours' duration between Newfoundland and Iceland. Thus was the notorious Mid-Atlantic Gap closed. That the United States agreed to provide VLR aircraft to operate from Newfoundland, for a total of thirty-six VLR aircraft to operate from there, and to accelerate the supply VLR Liberators for the RCAF in that area, represented a considerable concession on the part of Admiral King, whose thoughts were always directed to the Pacific rather than the North Atlantic. Sir John Slessor considered this to have 'more than any other single factor ... closed the Mid-Atlantic Gap'.[89]

Both Sir Philip Joubert and Air Marshal Slessor had wished for the Atlantic battle to be considered in its entirety by the Allies, and that aim had now been achieved.[90] Any dissension, notably from Admiral King, had effectively been removed. Appropriately, after Churchill attended a conference at Quebec in August, HMS *Renown*, in which he returned, was escorted by No. 10 Squadron RCAF Liberators operating from Gander.[91]

A decision had been made at the Casablanca conference in January to invade Sicily. This may have had no immediate effect on Coastal Command's anti-submarine operations over the Atlantic, but resulted in some of the Command's squadrons, such as Nos 500 and 608, remaining in the Middle East, which might otherwise have been deployed in the Battle of the Atlantic.[92]

By February 1943 there were a series of changes of command. Admiral Horton had been appointed C-in-C Western Approaches at Liverpool, Admiral Dönitz had succeeded Admiral Raeder as Commander-in-Chief of the *Kriegsmarine*, and Air Marshal John Slessor became AOC-in-C of Coastal Command. For Dönitz it meant that he was able to approach Hitler direct and plead more strongly for his requirements in his U-boat campaign, including not only materials for U-boats but his requirement for support from the *Luftwaffe*.[93]

Admiral Horton at ACHQ Liverpool was an ex-submariner and therefore, in fighting the Battle of the Atlantic, was well suited to the task and able to anticipate how the enemy would react to any of his decisions. As Dönitz stated:

> Under the command of Admiral Horton the British anti-submarine forces made great improvements ... particularly in tactical leadership and morale. Admiral Horton was better qualified than anyone else to read the mind of German U-boat Command and therefore to take steps which would render more difficult the prosecution of our U-boat campaign.[94]

For Coastal Command, it was apparent that the views of its naval liaison officer, Captain Peyton-Ward, also an ex-submariner, were considered by Admiral Horton in respect of his proposals in connection with the U-boat war.[95]

Air Marshal Slessor had the advantage of having attended the Casablanca Conference, and earlier in his service he had visited America as the representative of the CAS and met the American Chiefs of Staff. Therefore, he was effectively well briefed to understand the American points of view when liaison was necessary in combating U-boats and requiring supplies of American-built aircraft and equipment.[96]

At the Washington Conference in May, Winston Churchill recorded that he 'did not propose to deal with the U-boat war'; rather was he concerned with the invasion of Sicily and to 'take the weight off Russia'.[97] That Churchill was prepared not to deal with the U-boat war at that time was understandable, as Sir John Slessor stated: 'The Gap was closed in May',[98] and Dönitz withdrew U-boats from the North Atlantic on 24 May.[99]

RADAR

As late as May 1943 Mark II ASV was still being used in operations, although by then Germany had the Metox receivers to detect the 1.5m radiations. A modification undertaken on at least one squadron was to install a variable condenser in the output circuit, to act as an attenuator and thus reduce the strength of the signal after a U-boat had been located, to give the enemy the impression that the aircraft was disappearing.

Aircraft of some units, such as No. 500 Squadron, were equipped with Yagi aerials for their Mark IIs, which should have enabled them to home onto a target with greater accuracy and to obtain a much stronger return signal.

There was a radical change in 1943 with radar equipment when the Mark III was becoming available to Coastal Command. Its most important advantage was that it transmitted on a much shorter wavelength of 9.1 cm instead of 1.5m as with the Marks I and II, and could not be detected by the Metox receivers in U-boats.

Instead of fixed aerials there was a rotary scanner, and thus the return signals gave a visual trace through 360 degrees on a CRT known as the Position Plan Indicator (PPI). This was in contrast to the Mark II, which (unless beam aerials were installed) would cover only a forward arc. Near land, it would give a trace of the outline of the coast while vessels on the surface of the sea would be indicated by little more than dots on the screen. Mark III radar had another important advantage over the earlier marks, which was the lack of 'sea returns' that masked targets at short range. Some operators found that targets remained visible on the screen down to a quarter of a mile. Other forms of radar were being developed for Bomber Command, such as 'Oboe', 'H2S', and 'GEE'; there was thus a conflict of interest for components such as magnetrons and CRTs that were common to

the various forms of radar. Production of radar was being undertaken in both North America and the United Kingdom, and this was one occasion when priority was given to Coastal Command, with the supply of a limited number of Mark III ASV.

There was obvious cooperation between Britain and USA in respect of radar in development, production and availability; it

33. An attack on U-980 on 11 June 1944 by F/O Sherman of No 162 squadron RCAF, position 67°07'N 00°26'E. The U-boat was sunk using four 250lb DCs.

34. U-461, U462 and U-504 in position 45°40'N 10°55'W on 30 July 1943, seen from Sunderland JM 679. All three U-boats were sunk in a combined operation.

was such that, 'As a stop gap, fourteen 10 cm [9.1 cm] sets were built at the MIT [Massachusetts Institute of Technology] radiation laboratory and flown to the British, to be used in the RAF planes patrolling the Bay of Biscay.'[100] The VCAS had also decided in favour of Coastal receiving 9.1 cm radar; in preference to Bomber Command being supplied with H2S radar that would have needed related components, and provision had been made at a Cabinet Anti-Submarine Committee meeting for the two Wellington Leigh-Light squadrons, Nos 172 and 179, to be equipped with the new radar by February 1943.[101]

That the earlier marks of ASV could be detected by U-boats was in one respect a disadvantage to the enemy. If Coastal Command deployed enough aircraft in a transit area such as the Bay of Biscay, it could be 'swamped' with 1.5m transmissions. The U-boats would then have the option of either submerging or risking being attacked by remaining on the surface.

A series of alarms would at the very least affect the morale of the U-boats' crews by their being made aware of hostile aircraft. There would also be a limit to the number of crash dives that could be undertaken, due to reducing supplies of compressed air. The U-boats, nevertheless, were able to detect Mark II ASV signals at 30 miles, while Coastal aircraft with Mark II ASV would detect U-boats at about 6½ miles, and perhaps up to 10 miles.[102]

The German reaction was that Admiral Dönitz had ordered his U-boats to dive for thirty minutes when they became aware of radar transmissions from aircraft, but he stated that it was of 'doubtful effect'.[103] Sir Philip Joubert deployed his aircraft accordingly by so arranging patrols in the Bay of Biscay transit area in what was part of Operation 'Gondola' during late January and early February. The patrols extended from the inner Bay at about 3°W using the shorter-range aircraft, and to as far as 22°W with his limited number of Liberators during the day and Catalinas with Leigh Lights during the night. Sunderlands, Halifaxes and Wellingtons covered an area 120 miles east of 10°W, and Leigh-Light Wellingtons that same area during the night.[104]

Sir Philip was conscious of having a very limited number of Leigh-Light Wellingtons equipped with Mark III radar, and limited also in the numbers of Liberators available. Throughout his tenure as Commander-in-Chief of Coastal Command, it was to be as he said, 'Make do and Mend'.[105] He had concentrated his forces in the Bay of Biscay because in that area he could take the initiative. In contrast, in the area of the Atlantic convoys, the enemy had the initiative.[106] By deploying his forces in the Bay of Biscay rather than the Atlantic, his shorter-range aircraft, such as Wellingtons, could play a more active part and for a greater length of time. Furthermore, there was a greater likelihood of obtaining sightings of U-boats as they were in a more confined area.

Joubert would have been well aware of the risks for aircrew in flying to about 3°W, well in range of enemy aircraft, but as operational records of both Sunderlands and Wellingtons were to show, their crews could give a good account of themselves, and they were prepared to accept the risks.[107]

ARMAMENT AND TACTICS

Following the unsuccessful tactics of U-boats being ordered to dive for thirty minutes on becoming aware of aircraft using radar, further measures were attempted. They included increasing the armament of U-boats, with the addition of machine-guns, quadruple installations of 2 cm cannon, and a 3.7 cm cannon. Additionally, some U-boats were given exceptionally heavy anti-aircraft armament, with the intended object of attracting aircraft to shoot them down. The additional armament did, however, make the vessels top heavy. These measures were to prove successful only briefly, due to the surprise advantage and, it appears, against some inexperienced pilots.

Thereafter, U-boats found that aircraft would circle and call for assistance. As was to be acknowledged by the enemy in the Bay, 'It was patrolled by units of Nos 15 and 19 Groups ... which were highly trained in anti-submarine methods.'[108] It was so. As one aircraft captain, Flt Lt Baveystock, after getting a blip on his radar at 9 miles stated, 'We felt sure it was our quarry as the size of the blip was the same as we normally got from our tame sub [a Royal Navy submarine that was cooperating with Coastal Command training].'[109] After dropping a flame float to mark the position of the U-boat that had crash-dived, Baveystock started baiting tactics to give the impression of having left the area. He added, '... knowing that the U-boat would have to resurface to recharge'.[110] Baveystock correctly estimated when the U-boat would surface; and despite its improved anti-aircraft armament of quadruple cannon, it was sunk.

Because of Coastal Command's ability to detect U-boats on the surface, and following the improved anti-aircraft armament on U-boats, Dönitz ordered some to traverse the Bay of Biscay in convoys of up to five in number, remaining on the surface and being prepared to 'fight it out' against Coastal Command's aircraft.

The first outward-bound group of U-boats sailed on 12 June 1943.[111]

The failure of traversing the Bay by U-boats on the surface was clearly demonstrated by three U-boats, U-461, U-462 and U-504, although in fact they were only on the surface for one of the three to charge its batteries. Because they were in convoy, all had to be on the surface. The senior officer, Captain Wolf Stiebler, recalled: 'It wasn't long before several planes were above us ... our defence with the quadruple guns worked very well....'[112] But when two aircraft attacked from different angles the quadruple cannon could counter only one, leaving the other aircraft free to attack.

One of the aircraft captains, Flt Lt Dudley Marrows, recalled: 'When we got within attack range aircraft were circling, the U-boats manoeuvring in formation keeping bows on to aircraft, and putting up a formidable barrage of cannon and machine-gun fire.'[113] Marrows found, as did other aircraft captains, that U-boats could always outmanoeuvre aircraft. Nevertheless, in his attack with Sunderland U/461, he sank U-461. Against orders he dropped his own dinghy, which saved Captain Stiebler and some of his crew.

This episode on 30 July 1943 appears unique in Coastal Command's records, as all three U-boats were sunk, with the support of an escort group of sloops, which in turn was operating with the cooperation of a Catalina aircraft. This cooperation between the Navy and the Command had been long advocated; it was delayed, however, due to the lack of escort vessels in the Navy.[114] In addition to such as Marrow's Sunderland, and the Catalina, there were other aircraft types, including a Liberator and Halifax, which was indicative of an improvement in Coastal Command's supply of aircraft, but the question of types of aircraft with the appropriate equipment was still not completely resolved.[115]

In May and June 1943 another weapon was being used against U-boats. It was the rocket projectile, and for the RAF its first successes were gained by Hudsons of Nos 48 and 608 Squadrons in the Mediterranean. Its success as an anti-submarine weapon was confirmed by the sinkings of U-755 and U-594.[116]

Although rocket projectiles could be used with success against U-boats, there was perhaps more to be said for them to form part of the armament together with cannon of long-range fighters such as Beaufighters, which came to constitute the strike wings of

Coastal Command: particularly so, as Beaufighters were more strongly built and better able to withstand the stresses involved.

THE LAST NORTH ATLANTIC CONVOY BATTLES

In the North Atlantic the last great convoy battle was fought by three groups of U-boats, appropriately named *Stürmer, Dränger*, and *Raubgraf*. They formed a combined force of thirty-eight U-boats to attack two convoys, SC122 and HX229, from 16 March. At that time British cipher officers had been unable to decode the enemy's signals, but in sharp contrast Germany was using British signals from either the Admiralty or the C-in-C Western Approaches that gave the enemy the vital details of not only the position of convoys, but also their courses across the Atlantic. Thus the enemy was able to deploy its U-boats accordingly.[117]

It was not until air cover from Coastal Command appeared on 17 March that the U-boats were restricted, 'which allowed only five boats to make submerged attacks', and 'ever-increasing air defence caused us to lose contact with both convoys'.[118] For Admiral Dönitz there had been no air cover on the night of 16/17 March, 'and the U-boats took full advantage of the fact'. Of the signals sent by the British Admiralty and the C-in-C Western Approaches, Dönitz comments: 'These signals were most useful to U-boat Command.'[119] Of air cover then available, from the limited successes achieved by Coastal Command, Sunderlands and Fortresses of No. 18 Group were deployed, damaging three U-boats, which were not identified.[120]

Although at the Washington Conference in March it had been decided to reorganise cover for convoys from Newfoundland, this had not taken effect at the time of the sailings of HX229 and SC122. Thus the RCAF patrols at that time by No. 5 Squadron from Gander were short by 60 miles from the U-boats' first attack.

It was apparent that from both Coastal's bases in the east and from Gander in the west long-range Liberator aircraft were still lacking. As the official Canadian Air Force historian has stated: 'Even one VLR Liberator, able to extend that patrol by another 200 miles, might have made a crucial difference.'[121]

Three causes may be attributed to the serious losses in those two Atlantic convoys, therefore: the enemy's use of the Admiralty or C-in-C North Western Approaches signals giving positions and courses of the convoys, the lack of deployment of VLR aircraft on both sides of the Atlantic for convoy protection and the inability at that time of the Allies to decode the enemy's signals. Former Coastal Command aircrew, who were forbidden to transmit by W/T when near convoys, might well ask, 'Why was the Admiralty so blasé in transmitting courses and positions of our convoys?'

Various accounts differ in respect of the number of ships sunk in the U-boat attacks on Convoys SC122 and HX229, but the naval historian gives the figure of twenty-one merchant vessels for one U-boat sunk. This battle demonstrated the need for cover by aircraft rather than escort vessels, as only one ship was sunk when once air cover was maintained.[122] These serious losses did not gain the publicity given to the 'Channel Dash', although there was infinitely more need. The movement of the three warships was not life threatening to Britain, but the rate of loss of merchant vessels in March was so. Sir John Slessor gives the losses in that month alone as 620,000 GRT. As he rather understates, 'It clearly could not go on.'[123]

What followed in the following two months in the Battle of the Atlantic resulted in the defeat of the German U-boats, which was to be acknowledged by Admiral Dönitz on 24 May 1943. During the period 26 April to 23

35. Coastal Command veterans who were invited by the Flag Officer, Liverpool, to the Battle of the Atlantic Commemoration in May 1993: namely: W/Cmdr Derek Martin, OBE, BSc., F/O John Appleton, Flt/Lt John Cruikshank, VC and the author.

38. A Liberator in maritime camouflage such as was pioneered by Coastal Command, and the type flown by F/O Harper and Flt/Lt Fisher.

AIRCRAFT		PILOT, OR	2ND PILOT, PUPIL	DUTY
Type	No.	1ST PILOT	OR PASSENGER	(INCLUDING RESULTS AND
				TOTALS BROUGHT
LIBERATOR	600	SELF	F/O FORSYTHE	BOMBING
"	591	SELF	F/O FORSYTHE	CONVOY ESCORT
"	587	SELF	F/O FORSYTHE	GANDER – GOOSE
"	587	SELF	F/O FORSYTHE	GOOSE BAY – SWEEP
"	587	SELF	F/O FORSYTHE	REYKJAVIK – SWEEP
"	594	SELF	F/O FORSYTHE	CONVOY ESCORT
"	590	SELF	F/O FORSYTHE	CONVOY ESCORT
		OPERATIONAL TIME – 68.30		TOTAL FOR MONT
Commanding		OPERATIONAL SORTIES – 5		TOTAL FOR SQUAD
N. 10 (RCAF) Sqdn.		TOTAL OPERATIONAL – 727.35		GRAND TOTAL
LIBERATOR	3703	F/L INGR		

36. Part of No 10 Squadron RCAF records which corresponds to F/O Harper's log and shows that another Liberator, captained by Flt/Lt R.F.Fisher, while on the same sweep across the Atlantic, attacked U-341 which was one of three sunk, and three damaged in a major battle against convoys ON202 and ON518.

37. A page from the logbook of F/O Harper of No 10 Squadron RCAF who was one of the pilots on the shuttle service of Liberator aircraft between Reykjavik and Gander which closed the 'Mid-Atlantic Gap' south of Greenland.

M.M. (P)	Reykjavik – Sweep – Gander	0600	1910	DCO
R.G. (P)			
n, R.A. (N)			
.R. (W)			
e (W)			
H. (W)			
.R. (WMAG)			
d, W.V.			
.F. (P)	Sweep – Reykjavik – Gander	0600	1845	DCO	Sub siam 0900
.B. (P)			
J.S. (W)			
. (W)			
f, J.A. (W)			
y (WMAG)			

May fourteen groups of U-boats were involved in attacks at various times against four Atlantic convoys.[124]

The most significant fact about those convoy battles was that they were in the area south of Cape Farewell, and thus within what had been the 'Mid-Atlantic Gap', which had been a 'happy hunting ground' for U-boats. Now it was to become a grave-yard for U-boats rather than merchant ships.

Between 3 and 6 May six U-boats were sunk directly south of Cape Farewell in operations against ONS5; two in attacks against HX237; two more were sunk during attacks on SC129; four were sunk in operations between 15 and 20 May against SC130; and two between 21 and 23 May against HX239.[125] The reasons for the Allies' success were greatly improved provision of surface escorts, including aircraft-carriers, and improved air escorts.

The American surface escorts had HF/DF (high-frequency direction finding), with their aerials located higher up than was the case with the Royal Navy's escorts, and were able to detect U-boats on the surface and before the U-boats had seen such vessels.

The Royal Navy, with aerials set lower on their vessels, lost some of their advantage. Allied Intelligence had enabled the convoys to be aware of the U-boats, and air escorts were thus laid on accordingly. It was Air Marshal Slessor's policy to be fully prepared to deploy maximum effort in support of threatened convoys, and such was to prevail at this time.

Of the four U-boats sunk in attacks against SC130, three were claimed by Coastal Command's aircraft – two by Liberators, and one by a Hudson – that operated from Iceland as far west as 25°48'W. Convoy SC130 was considered by the naval staff to be the last convoy to be seriously menaced, and Roskill stated: 'This fine achievement was largely due to the almost continuous presence of air cover during the time when the convoy was being threatened.'[126]

Thus was Air Marshal Slessor's policy justified. The German Commander Hessler's view was: 'The most surprising feature of the enemy's success was that according to our radio intelligence there were never more than one or two aircraft in the air at the same time.'[127]

Admiral Dönitz's opinion was that the success of the Allies against the convoys was due to the escorts working in 'exemplary harmony' with support groups that were specially trained, but supported by 'continuous air cover' with aircraft equipped largely with the latest radar, although the Hudson, which sank U-273, had sighted it through a gap in the clouds from 8 miles. It had used baiting tactics, which appear as a feature of No. 269 Squadron's anti-U-boat successes. Aircraft equipped with radar had for Dönitz 'robbed the U-boats of their power to fight on the surface'.[128]

After the attacks against those four convoys, during which sixteen U-boats had been sunk and others seriously damaged, Dönitz considered that Germany had lost the U-boat battle and ordered those in the North Atlantic on 24 May 1943 to sail with caution to the Azores area.[129]

39. A Coastal Command base in the Azores which was established in October 1943. It was important in the Battle of the Atlantic as on 24 May 1943, Admiral Dönitz ordered his U-boats to that area.

THE BAY OF BISCAY

After Dönitz withdrew his U-boats from the North Atlantic he had to decide whether he should abandon his anti-shipping campaign. He considered that if he did so it would be difficult to reopen that offensive. He was conscious of the other German forces fully engaged in fighting, and opted, therefore, to continue, but with the object of tying down considerable anti-submarine forces of the Allies rather than sinking ships. With the Allies' anti-submarine forces now much stronger, and therefore to increase the chances of U-boats surviving, it was necessary to improve their armament. Against escort vessels, an acoustic homing torpedo, *Zaunkönig*, was provided. With the improved AA armament it was intended that U-boats should be able to remain on the surface and fight it out against aircraft. These tactics, however, gained only a short initial success due to the surprise element.[130]

On 2 August, shortly after a group of U-boats was sunk in the Bay, U-106, an ostensibly well-armed U-boat against attacks by aircraft, was also sunk. As in a previous action, aircraft coordinated their attacks such that quadruple cannon were a disadvantage for a U-boat: the four cannon could only fire in one direction, and fire against a second aircraft was limited to one cannon and machine-guns.[131]

Thereafter, Admiral Dönitz cancelled sailings of U-boats from the Biscay ports. As he conceded, 'It was therefore no longer possible to fight our way through the Bay of Biscay by means of U-boat AA fire.'[132]

Dönitz then expected his U-boats to dive as soon as their receivers detected aircraft. U-boats that had to traverse the Bay sailed along the Spanish coast. By using neutral waters they would not expect to be attacked, and by being near the coastline some shielding against detection by radar would have been given.

The U-boats were given additional cover also by the *Luftwaffe* with flights of Junkers 88s, which resulted in a number of air-to-air combats between a single Coastal Command aircraft against as many as eight German fighters. Such odds came to be accepted by Coastal Command's aircrew despite the additional disadvantage of being out-ranged by the enemy's cannon against machine-guns.

Also, when attacking U-boats, pilots found it desirable to concentrate on the handling of their aircraft rather than using their fixed guns.[133] Sunderlands had a number of air-to-air combats. The one advantage they had was that when one gunner was killed, another crew member could be found to take his place; the specific disadvantage of aircraft such as the Sunderland was the long hydraulic leads that all too often were cut by cannon or machine-gun fire.

By the end of May 1943, Germany was thinking in terms of building more U-boats to compensate for her losses, which in that month had reached a peak of 32.2 per cent of those in operations, having risen sharply from 9.2 per cent average losses.[134] Coastal Command had contributed in no small measure, claiming seventeen U-boats sunk. Seven of those had been sunk in the Bay, and another six seriously damaged in that area. This was before the Command had gained the cooperation of the Navy's hunter-killer groups. The other sinkings by Coastal Command had been one in the north transit area, and the remainder while on convoy escorts.

These successes could be attributed to Air Marshal Slessor pursuing his policy of deploying aircraft where U-boats were most likely to be concentrated, and those areas were the Bay transit area and near convoys. Slessor thought of the Bay as the 'trunk of the tree', where U-boats were bound to be more concentrated. He was therefore prepared to concentrate his forces in an area approximately 300 miles by 120 miles, through which most U-boats (those based in the French ports) had to enter.

In contrast, when once the U-boats entered the Atlantic, they could spread far and wide like the branches of the tree. To answer that challenge, Slessor was fortunate in having a number of bases in southern Britain that were less likely to be closed in by bad weather than those in the north. Thus a programme of sorties laid on had a fair chance of being fulfilled. Other factors were that the enemy was still unaware of the Mark III radar being used by some aircraft, and that more experienced aircrew were then available and dedicated to anti-submarine warfare.

Specifically in the Bay transit area, U-boats were fighting back. By not submerging when an aircraft appeared, they lost the initiative. Aircraft could circle out of range but close enough to prevent the U-boat deciding to submerge, and the aircraft was not limited to the 30 seconds in which to attack. It was able to home in other aircraft for a coordinated attack.

In the following month the enemy effectively increased the anti-aircraft fire of U-boats by sailing in groups of up to five. This was certainly too many for lone aircraft to counter, and Coastal Command's sorties were adjusted accordingly, while the Admiralty organised surface vessels to cooperate with the Command's aircraft. Nevertheless, in June, despite the increased number of Coastal Command's sorties over the Bay, the number of attacks on U-boats dropped to 34 per cent from the previous 53 per cent.[135]

This drop could be accounted for by aircrew being understandably more cautious, and in fact being required to call for assistance. During most of July, the enemy was still prepared to risk U-boats crossing the Bay in groups, and they included their valuable tankers, or 'milch cows'. By then, the Command was gaining support with the Navy's sloops, and the U-boats suffered serious losses.

Accordingly, on 2 August, Dönitz stopped sailings from the Biscay ports, and those that had sailed on 1 August were recalled.[136] In the previous five weeks fifteen U-boats had been lost to Coastal's aircraft and one to the Royal Navy.[137] This fact rather discounts Captain Roskill's chapter, 'The Triumph of the Escorts', where credit tends to be for the surface vessels.[138]

The U-boats that had to traverse the Bay were now required to use the cover of the Spanish coast, and at least one of those was prepared to sail in neutral waters, and also to gain some cover from Spanish fishing vessels.[139]

It was believed by aircrew at that time that Spanish fishermen were in fact covering German U-boats. Operational records of the Leigh-Light Wellington squadrons, which flew at night over the Bay, are indicative of that, albeit with no direct evidence. Apart from those U-boats that were prepared to use the Spanish coast for transit, others were to await new receivers, *Wantzv,* which were able to detect Coastal Command's Mark III radar, which had been available from March. Commander Hessler gives figures that confirm the Allies' success in the Bay of Biscay from April up to the end of August 1943, with 35 per cent lost in the Bay.[140] What came to be known as 'The Battle of the Bay' was considered by Professor Rohwer to be an intermediate phase extending from June to August 1943.[141] Thereafter, Admiral Dönitz deployed his U-boats where there was less opposition. In September he attempted his last offensive in the North Atlantic, pinning his hopes on an acoustic torpedo, *Zaunkönig,* that was to be employed against escort vessels rather than the merchant vessels they were covering.

The outcome was a series of failures against six convoys during September and October.[142] In this final battle by two wolf packs, nine U-boats were lost to aircraft and three to surface vessels. The Allies' success was due to considerable air support, including Liberators and Sunderlands.

Other factors were good intelligence on the part of the Allies, but lack of intelligence for the U-boats. The German historian Hessler attributes success also to 'good cooperation between enemy air and surface escorts keeping U-boats beyond visual range of convoys'.[143]

THE AZORES

Although by May 1943 the Mid-Atlantic Gap had been closed, there still remained another gap in the Atlantic. It was where Dönitz had ordered his U-boats from the North Atlantic – that was, near the Azores.

Following a political agreement with Britain's oldest ally, Portugal, a base for Coastal Command's aircraft was formed at Lagens, on the island of Terceira, and opened in October.[144] It was important, as both Gibraltar and Freetown convoys were able to gain additional air support from that base. For U-boats operating in the Azores area, the enemy had the advantages of Allied convoys being reported by agents, probably in southern Spain, and also by *Luftwaffe* aircraft, which could serve not only for reconnaissance, but also in actual air attacks on convoys. Nevertheless, in the following month three U-boats were sunk by aircraft operating from the Azores, with the successes claimed by a Flying Fortress and Leigh-Light Wellingtons.[145] Those first anti-U-boat successes gained by the Command's aircraft operating from the Azores reflected a complete reversal in respect of U-boats versus convoys.

Convoys MKS30 and SL139, which included sixty-six merchant vessels, had been reported to the enemy, who ordered twenty-three U-boats and twenty-five aircraft against them. Only one merchant vessel was sunk, and one was damaged. As one of the U-boat captains, Lt Cdr Peter Cremer, recorded: 'Only one got near the merchant ships: U-333. All the others were forced away.'[146] This was due to overwhelming support by both escort vessels and Coastal Command. The successful attack on one of the U-boats by a Wellington is notable in demonstrating the training and experience of the pilot (Flg Off D.F. McCrae, DFC).

He had gained an ASV contact at 3 miles to port (indicative of the aircraft having Mark III radar with a scanner); he turned to port and saw by moonlight a surfaced U-boat, and attacked without using his Leigh Light, to achieve complete surprise. Exceptionally, also, he attacked at 90 degrees to the vessel, instead of the more usual 30–35 degrees, or along its track. Thus to achieve a kill he needed to be extremely accurate, to within 19 feet of the hull. Flying at probably 140–60 knots, that was a considerable feat. The reason for attacking on the beam was probably to have the U-boat silhouetted against the moonlight.

This attack was in sharp contrast to a bomber crew employed in anti-submarine warfare. They had a similar aircraft and weapons but lacked the training and experience and were unsuccessful.[147]

Typically, in the early part of the war, convoys would have been lucky to have six surface escorts, and just one aircraft as close escort. These two convoys had up to twenty-eight escort vessels in addition to Coastal Command providing aircraft, not only from the Azores, but also from Britain. For another U-boat captain the attacks on the convoys were a 'complete failure'.[148]

Although the Command was able and prepared to operate many aircraft, including Hudsons, Catalinas, Wellingtons, Beaufighters and Liberators, in support of those two convoys, it 'left only two Liberators available on 22 November'.[149] This deficiency stemmed from the policy of 'Cominch' (Admiral King). The Allies had ostensibly enough aircraft to cover all exigencies, but many Liberators were deployed in the wrong areas.

Two of the sinkings of U-boats by

Wellingtons from the Azores reflected the usefulness of the later type of radar, which was the Mark III with a scanner. On both occasions a trace was made from abeam rather than ahead of the aircraft, and at the very close range of 3–4 miles. Such would not have been possible with Mark II ASV, without beam aerials. Those aircraft then had lethal weapons – 250 lb depth charges.

With both detection and lethal weaponry requirements fulfilled, trained and experienced crews flying a suitable type of aircraft were able to do the job. Yet a further but elusive factor was to have crews of high morale, from a squadron with high morale. In the case of the example given in some detail (Flg Off McCrae, then with No. 179 Squadron), all those aspects prevailed.

SUMMARY –1943

The Battle of the Atlantic against U-boats was won in 1943; the Allies had gained the initiative. This was due to a number of factors: politically there was agreement with both Canada and USA for a North Atlantic convoy system, with cooperation between St John's, Newfoundland, and Liverpool, but with the concurrence of 'Cominch' in the USA, VLR aircraft were to operate from Newfoundland in support of North Atlantic convoys. This resulted in the closing of the Mid-Atlantic Gap south of Cape Farewell. Later in the year, the Azores Gap was closed by Portugal acceding to the Allies having bases in the Azores.

Long-range aircraft, notably the Liberator, became available to the Command, which had begun the year with only half a squadron of those aircraft, but by the end of the year had seven squadrons so equipped. There was increasing availability of aircraft equipped with Leigh Lights, and the Mark III radar (9.1 cm wavelength), which initially could not be detected by U-boats, was coming into service.

While Coastal Command was gaining more and more aircrew with experience in anti-submarine warfare, and with increasingly high morale, Germany was losing its more experienced U-boat commanders, and its crews were being demoralised.

In 1943 Coastal Command had effective weapons, which were lethal to U-boats – the 250 lb Torpex depth charge, fitted with a shallow-depth pistol, the 35 lb rocket projectiles, and the acoustic homing torpedo.

Strategy and tactics had been developed, with the C-in-C Coastal Command opting for the offensive in two areas – the Bay of Biscay against U-boats in transit (Slessor's 'trunk of the tree'), and near convoys that were threatened with attacks. Tactics employed by Coastal Command in the Bay of Biscay were on one or two occasions to 'swamp' a given area with radar transmissions. Tactics that were modified were to opt for a 100 ft spacing of sticks of depth charges, to be released along the track of the U-boat, thereby increasing the prospect of a kill by 35 per cent. Aircrew, on encountering severe anti-aircraft fire, would circle and await assistance from at least one other aircraft, or possibly from surface craft.

The armistice with Italy in 1943 did not reduce the requirements of the Command, rather did it mean that some squadrons, such as Nos 500 and 608, remained in the Middle East area in support of invasion operations. Still lacking in 1943 for Coastal Command were a low-level bombsight and radio altimeters. There was still a need for closer cooperation between the Admiralty and the Command in respect of keeping Coastal Command informed about the movement of convoys and the Navy's vessels, and also to provide hunter/killer groups of such vessels as sloops to operate with aircraft.

A weakness shown in both the German U-boat Command and the Admiralty was the lack of security in transmitting by W/T signals, in the Admiralty's case by giving courses and positions of convoys, albeit in code.

For his period of command, Sir Philip

Joubert gives, in respect of the anti-U-boat campaign, 825 sightings, which resulted in 607 attacks but only twenty-seven U-boats sunk, plus three shared. Additionally, 120 were so damaged that they had to return to base. Against those figures Coastal Command lost 233/4 aircraft, of which 116 were due to hazards such as the weather. Out of the 233 losses, 179 were from No. 19 Group and could be attributed to operating over the Bay of Biscay and encountering many enemy fighters, in addition to heavily armed U-boats.[150]

The comparatively few sinkings in relation to sightings could be attributed to lack of suitable weapons, but also lack of suitable aircraft. To a lesser extent, inexperienced crews were operating in the earlier period of Joubert's tenure. The part played in the defeat of the U-boats in the Battle of the Atlantic by aircraft under Coastal Command's control amounted to ninety U-boats sunk, and fifty-one damaged.

Of the ninety that were sunk, fifty-three had been in the area of convoys; only one ship was sunk in a convoy when an aircraft was in close support. Overall in 1943, Germany lost 258 U-boats due to all causes.[151] As the American Air Force decided after a survey in 1943, 'Attack from the air against the U-boat at sea had been the most effective single factor in reducing the German submarine fleet.'[152]

In 1944 there were three major operations in Western Europe. They were the Allied landings at Anzio in January, Operation Overlord (the Normandy landings in June), and the last German counter-attack during December in the Ardennes. A comparatively minor operation by the Allies was 'Anvil/Dragoon' – landings in southern France in August.[153]

Operation Overlord was to be uppermost in the minds of all Allied services from January onwards. In that month General Eisenhower was appointed Supreme Commander of the Allied Expeditionary Forces, with headquarters in England, whence the Allied invasion of Europe would be launched. This was to have an immediate bearing on Coastal Command, as, although victory in the Battle of the Atlantic had been achieved in 1943, U-boats still posed a threat, particularly against a vast armada of shipping required in taking troops and equipment to the Continent.

Air Chief Marshal Sir Sholto Douglas succeeded Air Marshal Slessor as AOC-in-C Coastal Command in January, and summed up his anti-submarine forces as 430 aircraft, including ten squadrons of Liberators (including three from the USN), and five squadrons of Leigh-Light Wellingtons.

There were also two squadrons each of Halifaxes, Hudsons, Fortresses and Catalinas, and seven squadrons of Sunderlands.[154] Most notable was the improvement in the availability of Liberators, as in 1943 Air Marshal Slessor had begun his tenure with only half a Liberator squadron. There was also an improvement by now, not only in having the 'right type' of aircraft, but also having effective weapons generally available against U-boats, including the 250 lb Torpex depth charges with shallow-depth pistols, and rocket projectiles. The improved radar (Mark III) was also becoming more generally available.

There were still sixty U-boats in the Atlantic well able to pose a serious threat to Allied shipping. U-boats in 1944 were better armed against air attacks, with 37 mm and 20 mm cannon. When on the surface they could use improved detection devices against Coastal Command's radar such as the Mark IIIs. There were an increasing number of U-boats equipped with *Schnorchels*, which comprised two tubes extending above the surface to allow exhaust gases from the diesels to escape, with the second tube taking in fresh air. Dönitz had looked upon the *Schnorchel*-equipped type as the 'one hundred per cent underwater boat',[155] but it was to be proved otherwise.

Although, as Dönitz had hoped, it enabled

U-boats to operate in the English Channel, a great strain was imposed on the U-boat crews due to their remaining submerged for so long in hostile waters.[156] In rough sea conditions the *Schnorchel* was automatically closed, causing at least severe discomfort to the crews. Furthermore, Coastal Command aircrew were able to detect the *Schnorchel* boats with their Mark III radar, and also visually, not infrequently reporting seeing 'white smoke' on the surface of the sea. One such sighting, made from 1,000 ft altitude, included not only mention of the white smoke, but that it was emitted from a grey object 1 ft in diameter, projecting about 2 ft and moving at 12–15 knots. In that specific example the U-boat was sunk with cooperation from a naval escort group.[157] There were, however, two other natural forms of disturbance with which *Schnorchels* might be confused – waterspouts and spouting whales.[158]

The Command's response to *Schnorchel* U-boats was to operate what was coded 'High Tea'. This was to release a pattern of sonobuoys in the area of a suspected submerged U-boat. Sonobuoys could be thought of as the air equivalent of the Navy's Asdic: that was, they could detect sound waves, with signals sent to the aircraft by electromagnetic means. Against such devices, *Schnorchel* U-boats were at a disadvantage, as the noise of their diesels would mask the sonobuoys' signals, but the additional noise from the U-boat would aid detection by the aircraft.

It was the strategy of Dönitz always to deploy his U-boats where they were likely to sink ships with the minimum danger to themselves, and in January thirty-three U-boats were sent to operate against Russian convoys, where in those Arctic waters they could gain the support of the *Luftwaffe* operating from Norway.

Germany had been losing 20 per cent of its U-boats every month, and of 70 per cent that

40. ACHQ Liverpool, May 1993, showing the table where shipping movements were plotted. The telephone on the right coloured red, could be 'scrambled' for security.

returned from operations, some were seriously damaged. While in transit through the Bay of Biscay, U-boats were remaining submerged for as long as twenty to twenty-two hours per day and were taking twelve days in transit. Dönitz had exhorted his crews to accept the harsh conditions as their only option against the Allies' superior forces in both aircraft and escort groups, and as an ex-U-boat captain, Commander Hessler, stated, it was a matter of 'containing the enemy', and 'a more cautious strategy was required'.[159]

In the early months of 1944, although U-boats had ceased making pack attacks on shipping, there was some concentration of U-

41. ACHQ (Area Combined Headquarters) Derby House, Liverpool, c 1942.

boats west of Scotland and Ireland. Furthermore, in the Bay of Biscay, fewer sightings were being made due to the U-boats remaining submerged, and spending a minimum time surfaced to recharge their batteries. Sir Sholto Douglas therefore reduced the density of his patrols in the Bay of Biscay to concentrate his forces off the west coasts of Scotland and Ireland. For this purpose, the operations of his Groups Nos 15, 18, 19 and Iceland were coordinated under No. 15 Group at ACHQ Liverpool. It was a logical decision, as Allied convoys of necessity converged in that area. There was the advantage, also, that his medium-range aircraft such as Hudsons and Wellingtons could effectively operate to a considerable distance into the Atlantic from both Iceland and the north-western bases that by then were available.

The success of this strategy could not be assessed solely on the number of sightings and

'kills' made, however, as just to keep the U-boats submerged could be rated a success. In fact, it resulted in U-boats being dispersed away from the shores of the United Kingdom, 'beyond 15°W where conditions were somewhat better'.[160]

The Command's aircrew came to accept that flying for hours over the Atlantic, now sighting convoys rather than empty lifeboats, was more than justified. The last attack on a North Atlantic convoy was in February. It is notable not just for being the last attack, but for the contrast in points of view by German and British historians. Hessler dismisses it in one short paragraph as the loss of two U-boats in the period 16–19 January. Captain Roskill gives a chart for 29 January to 24 February and states that eleven U-boats were sunk, six by escort groups, against the losses of one straggler and one sloop. Within that period, two U-boats were sunk by Coastal's Wellingtons.[161]

Features of note concerning one of those sinkings were that earlier, on 7 February, one of the Wellingtons had obtained a radar contact at 9 miles that was not lost until the ¹/₄-mile range of the scanner had been reached. This showed what a great improvement in radar had occurred. With the earlier Mark I, a U-boat might well have been missed, or lost in 'sea returns' well before a ?-mile range. The attack on the U-boat that followed did not result in a kill, but later the same Wellington captain was successful. Many operational records indicate that when once a captain has made an actual attack (rather than a practice run), he was likely to be successful in subsequent attacks.[162]

The Wellington successes were notable also in that they used six depth charges spaced at 60 ft rather than what had earlier been advocated – 100 ft spacing. When 100 ft was specified, the Command, perhaps, was thinking in terms of four rather than six depth charges. This success in the final convoy battle demonstrated what had been advocated at the beginning of the war: that was that to combat the U-boat menace a combined effort of both surface vessels and aircraft was required. It had been shown earlier during July 1943 in the Bay of Biscay; but due then to the shortage of escort vessels, the system of combined operations had been discontinued.

At this stage, the German point of view became: 'There was no point in disposing the U-boats primarily for attacks on convoys, and the sole remaining purpose was to discomfort the enemy, while at the same time providing ... sufficient freedom to escape the concentrations of A/S forces.' And the 'Costly convoy attacks were therefore abandoned.'[163] Despite the freedom given to U-boat commanders, their losses 'remained high' and it was 'believed' that most were being lost in an area 700–800 miles south-west of Ireland.[164] This indicated that U-boats could not have made W/T contact with the U-boat Command before being lost, and possibly that they were sunk in a surprise attack by Leigh-Light aircraft, which gave no opportunity for the U-boats to signal their headquarters. Because of such losses, U-boats were ordered on 27 March to avoid that area of the Atlantic.[165]

OPERATION OVERLORD

General Eisenhower, the Allies' Supreme Commander, had for Operation Overlord all the air forces in Britain under his control, but had made an exception of Coastal Command, which he considered 'inescapable'.[166] This decision may have stemmed from his former collaboration with Admiral Sir Andrew Cunningham, at the time of Operation Torch. Certainly when Sir Sholto was considering his own position in respect of 'Overlord' he asked for a directive from the Admiralty by which the Command was ostensibly controlled. The response came from Admiral Cunningham thus: 'You know perfectly well what you've got to do, Sholto, get on with it.'[167] In fact it

was done. Sir Sholto's *Overlord – The Role of Coastal Command* gave an order of battle for each of his groups and headquarters in Iceland, Gibraltar and the Azores. Each squadron was allotted to a specific base and task. It included an appreciation of the enemy's likely moves and the reasons for Sir Sholto's decisions.

Contingencies for which Sholto Douglas was prepared were (i) transits of U-boats between Norway and the Atlantic; (ii) the threat to invasion convoys in the Channel and South Western Approaches; (iii) a possible offensive against Atlantic convoys.[168]

Thus the AOC-in-Chief Coastal Command was effectively given *carte blanche*. His action was then to issue a directive to all his groups and ACHQs on 18 April 1944. It was apparent from Eisenhower's and Cunningham's statements that both had faith in Coastal Command's leadership; and in the case of Admiral Cunningham, that he could trust the Command to counter any offensive by U-boats, as he was later to confirm.

Germany still had about 200 U-boats available for operations, but also twenty to twenty-five destroyers, thirty-five torpedo-boats, 90–100 E-boats, 135 R-boats, and about 150 W-boats (midget submarines). The possibility of a breakout into the Atlantic by heavy warships had also to be considered.[169]

The Allies' plan for Operation Overlord, the invasion of Europe, had been agreed on 8 February,[170] and on 12 April Sir Sholto Douglas had asked his D/SASO to prepare an Order of Battle for Coastal Command's role in Overlord.[171] The D/SASO's directive was issued by Sir Sholto, giving comprehensive details of that role to his group commanders on 18 April.[172] Although the role included other duties, such as anti-shipping operations, the main threat against the Allies' forces was considered to be U-boats, of which it was estimated there were about 200, with many surface craft, such as E-boats.

The U-boats were thought most likely to attack in the South-Western Approaches. To counter this threat, Coastal Command would deploy aircraft from the western limits of the St George's, Bristol and English Channels up to the route of the cross-Channel invasion convoys. Patrols would be so arranged that the whole area would be covered every thirty minutes. Thus that area would effectively be 'flooded', with the object of forcing the U-boats to remain submerged. When they ultimately had to surface to recharge their batteries, they would be attacked by surface forces. This flooding of the Channel area Sir Sholto likened to the cork in a bottle, applied with the pressure eastwards.[173]

Sir Sholto's forces included two dozen squadrons whose prime duties were to be anti-submarine operations in the South-Western Approaches, with aircraft largely Liberators, Wellingtons, Sunderlands and Beaufighters; and seven of the squadrons had Leigh-Light aircraft.

This was a considerable improvement in aircraft and equipment availability compared with just a year previously. Such an improvement itself created a problem; that concerned accommodation both for aircraft and personnel. Not all stations could take aircraft such as Liberators and Fortresses, and Sholto Douglas in 1944 was following the 'horse trading' of bases such as prevailed two years earlier for Sir Philip Joubert.[174]

Such strong forces devoted to a specific area had nonetheless been at the expense of Atlantic sorties, which were 'drastically reduced'.[175] This reduction in Atlantic sorties was, however, offset by the enemy likewise reducing the number of U-boats in the Atlantic to protect his coastline. During this period of preparation for Overlord, Sholto Douglas had to take account of his forces based in Iceland, the Shetlands, Hebrides, Northern Ireland, Britain, Gibraltar and the Azores.

Even maritime squadrons ostensibly outside his control needed to be borne in mind, such as those in the Eastern Mediterranean and West Africa. Some of the squadrons in the Mediterranean outside his jurisdiction, in fact, were subsequently transferred to Coastal Command to alleviate deficiencies. Although the Air Ministry had granted Coastal Command an increased establishment of personnel, Sir Sholto was still short-staffed, and therefore expected both aircrew and ground crews to work much harder to compensate. He specified a requirement of a maximum effort for a month, followed by a second month in which the work would be less intensive. For Sunderland and Liberator aircrew their sorties would be of 13½ hours', and for Wellington aircrew, of 10½ hours' duration.

With possibly a third of each squadron's aircraft operating every twenty-four hours, much was therefore expected of both aircrew and ground staff.[176] Sir Sholto's appreciation of the situation on the German side proved justified, as on 6 June twelve U-boats sailed from Norway *en route* to the Atlantic, and of those in the French ports thirty-five sailed, only to suffer fifty attacks from the air on the first night, with six returning due to damage. From 6 to 30 June twenty-four U-boats were sunk.[177]

In the early stages of the Normandy landings only twelve *Schnorchel*-equipped U-boats were able to act against the seaborne forces, and they were expected to attack 'even at the cost of [the] boat'.[178] Following a breakthrough by the Allies' land forces at Avranches on 4 August, the U-boat bases at Brest, Lorient and St Nazaire were threatened, and the U-boats attempted to transfer to La Pallice and Bordeaux. By 25 August those that were seaworthy left the French ports for Norway, and Dönitz recalled all U-boats operating in the invasion area during 24 and 26 August. This was because of the strong defensive forces that he considered would be progressively increased. By 30 September all had transferred to Norway.[179]

For most people, Operation Overlord, with its maritime counterpart, Operation Neptune, is probably thought of as being confined to the Normandy area. It was not so for Coastal Command. During the month of June one squadron of Cansos (Catalinas) alone sank four U-boats, all north of 62°N, with one captain being awarded a posthumous VC. Another VC was awarded to the captain of a Catalina who sank a U-boat north of the 68th Parallel in July.[180] As Lord Douglas stated: 'The far northern phase of the invasion operations was in its way as hard as the assault on the Norman beaches.'[181]

Sir Sholto Douglas had issued a new directive in September, which gave priority to Coastal Command's operations in the areas of Cape Wrath, Northern Ireland, St George's Channel and the Bristol Channel. This was under No. 15 Group, which was able to draw upon the resources of both Nos 18 and 19 Groups.

This action was in response to U-boats that were then patrolling inshore waters of the United Kingdom.[182] As a result, according to the naval historian Captain Roskill, the north transit area was neglected, allowing U-boats to get through to the Atlantic. One of the reasons for U-boats evading detection at the time was that Dönitz had ordered on 1 June that only *Schnorchel* U-boats should go into the Atlantic.[183]

Nevertheless, as was to be shown, from 6 June to 31 August, twenty *Schnorchel* U-boats were lost out of thirty, and for Admiral Dönitz, it had 'marked the end of the U-boat campaign in the Channel'.[184]

Three illustrations given in the official naval history show clearly the problem that aircrew had to contend with in respect of *Schnorchel* U-boats. Certainly they were able to see the 'white smoke' from *Schnorchel* tubes, but they were all too easy to confuse a water spout for a potential target and thus for a decision to be made in less than twenty-five seconds. Nevertheless, some crews did sink *Schnorchel* U-boats. The deployment of his U-boats by Dönitz in the inshore waters of the United Kingdom represented a tactical advantage, but only in respect of possible attacks by surface craft. The various layers of water of different densities would impede detection by Asdic.

Additionally, Dönitz advised U-boat commanders to do what might not be expected, that was, attack from inshore, and attempt also to escape via inshore, rather than seawards. He rightly gave his U-boat commanders discretion, and W/T silence was maintained, in contrast to their former operations in the Atlantic.[185]

U-boats operating in inshore waters, however, were of advantage to Coastal Command, as those operational areas were all within range of the Command's medium-range aircraft.

By the end of 1944, as Lord Douglas suggests, the second phase of Overlord could be considered over. Of U-boat sightings made by the Command, 47 per cent were attacked, and of those, 20 per cent resulted in the U-boats being sunk. These figures were an improvement on those of the year as a whole, and it was in spite of the increased AA armament of the U-boats, and their preparedness to fight back.[186]

An appreciation of Coastal Command's work in Operation Overlord was given by Admiral of the Fleet Viscount Cunningham thus: 'Our comparative immunity to submarine attack was principally due to the enthusiastic efficiency of Coastal Command.'[187]

THE STRAITS OF GIBRALTAR

In the early part of 1944 there were about fifteen U-boats in the Mediterranean, and there was considerable Allied shipping there, but with limited escort vessels. Sholto Douglas attempted to limit the entry of U-boat enforcements by adopting a system similar to that employed by the former Commanders, Sir Philip Joubert and Air Marshal Slessor.

The procedure was to 'swamp' a given area with aircraft equipped with radar, and in this case, the approach areas to the Straits of Gibraltar. By such means it was hoped to force the U-boats to use their batteries before reaching the Straits, where they would be vulnerable to both surface craft and aircraft. The 'swamp' system was used in other parts of the Mediterranean area, but outside Coastal Command's control, by Wellington aircraft cooperating with the Royal Navy.[188] The conditions in the Straits of Gibraltar lent themselves to the use of a highly specialised system of anti-submarine warfare. That was Magnetic Anomaly Detection (MAD) gear, which was employed in conjunction with retro-rockets. MAD was fitted to the tail of some United States Navy PBYs (Catalinas).

The presence of a U-boat would cause an anomaly in the earth's magnetic field that would be detected by the MAD gear, which was effectively a magnetometer. Retro-rockets would then be fired rearwards, with the speed so adjusted as to counter the aircraft's forward motion. Thus the bomb fired by the rocket would fall vertically onto the detected target. The retro-bombs had the advantage over depth charges of not needing to be set for depth, and the enemy would be unaware of the attack until the bomb struck the U-boat.

Additionally, much less Torpex was required to fill the bomb – only 25 lb. MAD gear was used with some success by VP63 of the United States Navy in the Straits of Gibraltar; it proved less useful in other areas due to topographical conditions.[189] Although the Command's forces had been improved compared with earlier years, they were still stretched, particularly with the need to support Overlord, and Sir Sholto withdrew

some of the forces from the Gibraltar area.

THE BAY OF BISCAY

By early 1944 some U-boats were still crossing the Bay of Biscay on the surface, confident, apparently, that their improved armament of quadruple 20 mm cannon and a 3.7 cm cannon would deter attacks from aircraft, but prepared to 'fight it out'. When a No. 10 Squadron RAAF sighted a U-boat with its conning tower awash, instead of submerging, it surfaced and opened fire at a range of 2 miles.

No. 10 Squadron RAAF was one of the first to install four 0.303 in additional machine-guns in the nose of its Sunderlands, and it opened fire at 1,200 yards. Forward-firing guns were shown to be an important factor in attacks on U-boats because, if used promptly, they could clear the U-boat's anti-aircraft gunners, and in some cases, so many of the U-boat's crew were put out of action that it was required to return to port. The Sunderland, nevertheless, had to make two attempts before sinking U-426 due to the difficulty in deploying its depth charges. This latter aspect was always a matter for Sunderland crews to consider: to run out the depth charges in advance, or wait for a sighting before doing so.[190]

About this time, Sir Sholto Douglas attempted to blockade the Biscay bases within an area from 11°W to 8°W and within latitudes 48°N and 43°N. Because, also, U-boats left their French bases on the surface he hoped to cover that area where the U-boats met or left their surface escorts. This would have been by using Liberators, but with a long-range fighter escort. This plan, however, was rejected by the Chiefs of Staff, as long-range fighters were to be for Bomber Command's offensive.[191] As an alternative measure, a few Mosquito aircraft armed with 6-pounder cannon (Tsetse aircraft) were deployed with limited success in anti-submarine warfare, but were later diverted to anti-shipping sorties for which they were more suited.[192]

Additionally, Sir Sholto deployed, from the end of March, night patrols covering the 100-fathom line from Point du Raz down to the Gironde. The Gironde was an important base for German U-boats, and had been so for Italian submarines, and became increasingly so when the other French bases were captured. The 100-fathom line would have probably coincided with the point where U-boats gained or lost their surface escorts.[193]

They were therefore on the surface and were open to be attacked, despite Coastal Command's aircraft being in turn attacked by enemy fighters in addition to fire from U-boats and surface escorts.

1945

Two major events in January were to have repercussions in the anti-submarine warfare: the beginning of a Russian offensive on 12 January, and the end of the German breakthrough in the Ardennes, with the enemy being forced back.[194] The Russian offensive resulted in German forces progressively retreating westwards such that ultimately they were limited in the area even for U-boat trials.

U-boats at that time were being manufactured in eight sections involving thirty factories, and U-boat equipment and armament required another twelve factories, so production was easily disrupted by the bombing of supply lines and the over-running of factories by advancing Allied forces.

By 15 February Admiral Dönitz still considered that he could exert a considerable U-boat threat, as 237 U-boats were being prepared for operations. That number included 111 of the earlier types, but, significantly, eighty of the greatly improved Mark XXI and forty-two Mark XXIIIs.[195]

It was fortunate indeed for the Allies that the Mark XXI did not become operational until 30 April, as it had an underwater speed of 17½ knots, greater than the corvettes and sloops of the Royal Navy, which were typically 15–16 knots.[196] Eight of the Mark XXIII U-boats of 234 tons were able to prove their worth in Britain's home waters by sinking ships at no loss to themselves. In addition to Schnorchels, they were equipped with echo-ranging gear (S-Gerät) attached to the Schnorchel that could give warning of escort vessels at up to 7,000 m.[197]

Although by January there were ostensibly enough aircraft in the United Kingdom for Coastal Command, in fact there was a shortage of available operational aircraft for all the tasks expected of the Command.

In the case of some Wellingtons, it was due to lack of spares, while for Liberators modifications were required for which skilled personnel were necessary. Some electricians had been transferred from Scottish Aviation, which was involved with the modifications on Liberators, to the Army. It was serious enough for the Ministry of Aircraft Production to request the loan of personnel from Coastal Command, while in turn Sir Sholto Douglas asked the Air Ministry to intervene.[198] There was still a drain on the Command's resources such as Sir Philip Joubert had experienced in 1942, which was crews being trained by the Command but then posted overseas with their aircraft.[199]

In January Coastal Command had thirty-two anti-submarine squadrons, but of those twenty-nine and a half, comprising 420 aircraft, were in the United Kingdom and Iceland. Of those, the First Lord of the Admiralty considered they were 'not enough to patrol transit routes and give continuous air escort to all the many convoys'.[200] The Navy, however, was well equipped against U-boats, with 426 escort vessels, including destroyers and frigates that had a greater speed than most U-boats. The Allies' successes against U-boats about this time reflect those aspects, with forty-three sunk by ships, but only nineteen U-boats sunk by shore-based aircraft during 1945.[201]

Coastal Command's aircraft were, however, becoming better equipped for anti-submarine warfare. There were now a number of marks of radar, ranging from Mark II of 1.5m wavelength to later marks with 3 cm or 9.1 cm wavelength. The increased sensitivity of the short-wavelength radar, however, presented the disadvantage of receiving signals from flotsam. For navigation, at least two squadrons were equipped with GEE, which was geared largely to North Sea sorties and proved accurate enough for a navigator to pinpoint the runway of his base in thick fog.[202] There was a report on a possible new LORAN (Long Range Navigation) chain, but the Americans objected to the equipment being diverted from Bomber Command.[203] Nevertheless, for aircraft operating from eastern England, GEE proved excellent.

It was a feature of Sir Sholto's tenure that much attention was given to the training of aircrew while with their squadrons; this stemmed, no doubt, from the considerable new or modified equipment that was then becoming available. Sir Sholto gave particular attention to the training on radar, but requested a 'submarine sanctuary' for use in No. 15 Group's area for anti-submarine training.[204]

In early 1945 Admiral Dönitz's strategy remained to tie down as many Allied forces as possible. This was achieved by widely dispersing his U-boats as far as the American eastern seaboard in addition to the home waters of the British Isles and eastwards as far as the Scheldt, where Allied ships were to supply the land forces. During the three months February to April, 114 U-boats sailed from Norway, but of that number only thirty reported reaching the Atlantic.[205] In March, Dönitz ordered his U-boats to withdraw from coastal waters seawards. This stemmed from being aware of anti-submarine mines being laid, and also of increasing U-boat losses.[206]

Sir Sholto countered the U-boat offensive in home waters by sorties of Nos 15 and 19 Groups cooperating with the Navy's surface vessels under the C-in-C Western Approaches, but giving priority to the Irish Sea. Patrols were laid on so that the whole of the Irish Sea was completely covered night and day, once every hour. This was because it was believed that the U-boats were sheltering in the shallow waters where they were not easy to detect due to the layers of water of differing density, which affected the use of Asdic, and by *schnorchelling* they reduced also the risk of being detected by aircraft.[207]

There still remained a shortage of aircraft for convoy escorts, and a compromise was to provide an escort only when the convoys were in threatened areas.[208] Additional support was gained for No. 19 Group by the United States Navy providing three anti-submarine squadrons plus a detachment of PBYs equipped with MAD gear. The latter was something of a trial but did gain some success.[209]

While these moves could be considered defensive in response to the enemy's initiative, Sir Sholto took the initiative into the enemy's camp. Anti-submarine aircraft such as Liberators undertook night patrols in the Skagerrak and Kattegat. However, they were vulnerable to air attack in those areas because of fighters based in Norway and Denmark. In April, therefore, the strike wings of Beaufighters and Mosquitoes undertook sweeps against U-boats during the day. This was still a hazardous operation even for fast and heavily armed aircraft, as the Dallachy strike wing experienced in February, because of the still very active German fighters in Norway.[210]

The risks to both the strike aircraft and the Liberators proved justified, as a number of U-boats were sunk by those aircraft in that area, including occasions when rocket projectiles were used by the strike aircraft, although Sir

Sholto still rated the standard weapon against U-boats to be the depth charge, and it could be considered rightly so.[211]

Remarkably, at that late stage in the war, an escort of Mustang fighters was still expected for the squadrons of Beaufighters and Mosquitoes that operated in the Norwegian area, although earlier in the war lone Hudsons just had to take a chance, and suffered accordingly, with 300 aircrew killed over Norway.[212]

Coastal's offensive was extended in the northern area to the Baltic and Bornholm. With the latter becoming the only area available to U-boats for training and working up, there were soon no waters where U-boats could be considered free from air attack.[213]

The last German U-boat claimed by Coastal Command aircraft was U-320. It is notable; not only for being the Command's final kill, but also for showing how far the Command had progressed in respect of equipment and the training of crews since January 1940, when a Sunderland shared the destruction of U-55. Catalina X/210 was airborne at 04.43 hours on 7 May 1945, and while flying at 500 ft altitude gained a radar contact at a range of 2 miles. One minute later a *Schnorchel*, periscope, white smoke and a wake indicating an underwater speed of 7–8 knots was sighted. An attack was made one minute later, within six seconds of the *Schnorchel* disappearing, by releasing four depth charges spaced at 100 ft. A pattern of sonobuoys was then used. Base was signalled for instructions, and it was added that the Catalina had enough fuel for another fifteen hours.

Contact was maintained with the U-boat by sonobuoys for eleven hours before the Catalina returned to base after a sortie of 13 hr 20 min. This episode showed how sensitive radar had become by detecting a *Schnorchel* at two miles, but above all, how remarkably efficient that Catalina crew had become using

a slow, ponderous aircraft designed as a patrol plane in 1928.

Prompt decisions were made by the captain, Flt Lt Murray, and he showed foresight in releasing only four depth charges, when he might well have used eight, so retaining enough for a possible second attack. The Catalina had only two advantages: the sea was calm, which facilitated visual sighting, and in those northern latitudes it experienced only 1 hr 16 min of darkness.[214] The official naval historian, Captain Roskill, gives U-320 as the last of 699 German U-boats claimed by Allied ships and aircraft in the Second World War.[215] From official records, Coastal Command aircraft sank 185 German U-boats in the Second World War and shared the sinking of twenty-three others.[216]

CONCLUSIONS

The first requirement of an air force is to have aircraft, and Coastal Command throughout the war had none that had been designed specifically for anti-submarine warfare. In the U-boat war it was the American-built aircraft such as Hudsons, Catalinas and Liberators that served to a considerable extent and without which the British would have been in dire straits. Notably, the Liberators were able to close the Mid-Atlantic Gap.

Aircrew were trained in their particular aircrew categories, pilot, navigator (observer), wireless operator, etc., and all would have had some training in gunnery. Notably lacking was training in anti-submarine warfare, although some specialist training was later to be given in ASV/radar, either before or when on a squadron. This could be considered a reasonable compromise in view of the constant operational requirements that prevailed right up to and including 8 May 1945. The advent of Coastal Command's Leigh-Light aircraft in 1942 represented a turning point, enabling aircraft to attack U-boats that were on the surface at night, so that at no time throughout the twenty-four hours could the enemy feel free of attacks.

With about forty-two successes against enemy submarines by just the Wellington Leigh-Light aircraft, a major contribution was made by this device, although other types of aircraft were additionally so equipped.

The *Lufwaffe*'s part in the Battle of the Atlantic was threefold: its aircraft attacked ships, served as reconnaissance to the U-boat Command in reporting positions of Allied convoys, and in the Battle of the Bay, endeavoured to protect U-boats in transit from Coastal Command's aircraft. It was not very successful in the latter, notably because Sunderlands were able to defend themselves, and additionally the *Luftwaffe* was reluctant to engage in combat with Beaufighters that were used as a counter-measure.

British strategy was based on having France as an ally, but although the prospect of the French 'holding up their hands' was touched upon, no preparations had been made for that possibility.

In respect of the U-boat campaign, the effect of the collapse of France was twofold: its Biscay ports became the base for both German and Italian submarines, and actions in the French colonies, in both North Africa and the Far East, drained the resources of Coastal Command. The policy of the Allies building ships to keep up with the numbers being sunk may be questioned. No account appears to have been taken of the losses of merchant seamen and the ships' valuable cargoes. The cost of building aircraft to protect the ships should surely have been much less, with lives of many merchant seamen saved thereby.

The Admiralty's belief that the major threat to our trade was from surface warships rather than U-boats was to be proved wrong; as also that Asdic would effectively counter U-boat actions. When ultimately the U-boat threat was acknowledged, tactics for aircraft to attack them were developed. Coastal Command's aircrew demonstrated their

adaptability in this respect with remarkable success. This was despite always lacking both a low-level bombsight and a radio altimeter. It is fairly certain that a number of aircraft and crews were lost through those deficiencies.

Coastal Command modified its ASW tactics with changes in U-boat tactics, and likewise the U-boats adapted to Coastal Command's offensive. Although ASV/radar became available to a squadron in 1940 as a means of detecting vessels on the surface, it was not until 1943 that more efficient radar became available to most squadrons, which initially could not be detected by receivers on German U-boats.

Admiral Dönitz considered radar to be the crucial factor in ASW, but for Professor Jürgen Rohwer the crucial factor was intelligence. Both Germany and the Allies used intelligence extensively through the breaking of codes and ciphers under 'Ultra' and 'Enigma'. It was a mistake on the part of the British Admiralty to disregard the danger of transmitting signals giving positions and courses of Allied convoys, as these were invaluable to the enemy. The practice of Dönitz of directing his U-boats through W/T signals was questionable, but he must have justified it by having control over his 'wolf packs' and being aware of their situation.

Initially, Coastal Command had no weapon lethal to U-boats, and most of its aircraft lacked even suitable armament for defence. For specifically ASW, the most significant improvement in respect of machine-guns was to have more forward fire to counter AA from U-boats during an attack by the aircraft. A crucial factor in air attacks on U-boats was the lethal 250 lb depth charge filled with Torpex and with a pistol for shallow depths. Other weapons that were to be used with some success were rocket projectiles, cannon, retro-bombs and the depth bomb, the latter in conjunction with a medium-altitude bombsight. What was coded the 'Mark 24 Mine'; in fact was an acoustic torpedo, and gained some success with Coastal-controlled aircraft of the United States Navy. It did not, however, displace the 250 lb depth charge, which became the standard primary weapon.

Naval and Coastal Command cooperation was demonstrated from the outset, with Sir Frederick Bowhill transferring his headquarters to be close to the Admiralty. Cooperation between the two services was to become very obvious at Command, group, station, and in convoy escort (that is, crew) level.

This cooperation must represent one of the crucial factors in the anti-submarine war. Coastal Command became the model in ASW, not only for Canada but also for America (which both acknowledge in their histories).

The Command's commanding officers of squadrons led from the front, literally in operations, and this served to promote high morale – one of the conditions for success.

Coastal Command cooperated fully with the other Commands in the RAF, both Fighter and Bomber, which provided additional support in some ASW operations. With both the Dominions and America there was some interchange of both personnel and squadrons, but many nations were represented in Coastal Command, including personnel from Europe.

With their squadrons spread around half the world – USA, Iceland, Gibraltar, North Africa, the Azores and West Africa, the Commanders-in-Chief of Coastal Command had a difficult task.

Both men and machines had to be 'fitted in' into whatever was available at various bases, and to move a squadron involved not just men and aircraft, but certainly about eighty tons of equipment. An important factor was runways: the length had to be considered even for twin-engined aircraft, and HM Treasury limited the funds available.

When Sir Frederick Bowhill was in command in the first stage of the war, his task was largely organising reconnaissance against surface warships; anti-submarine warfare was taking second place. With the resources then available, he could only just hope to hold the line.

The tenure of Sir Philip Joubert, who succeeded him, represented an interim period in changes of policy, in respect of both ASW and anti-shipping operations. His task was not helped by having his trained forces being posted overseas. Nevertheless, this period marked a phase when an offensive was taken against U-boats in Operation Bolero. Despite all their tasks, those two Commanders-in-Chief set the standard that was to prevail in Coastal Command; and when Air Marshal John Slessor succeeded Sir Philip in early 1943, he found that much of the spadework had been accomplished. There was a U-boat crisis in early 1943, with many ships sunk, but Slessor was able to concentrate his attention on ASW, which nevertheless approximated to what Sir Philip had aspired to. He wished the Allies to consider the Atlantic as one battlefield with all forces coordinated, and this was ultimately achieved. For an offshoot of the Atlantic battle – the 'Battle of the Bay' – he considered Biscay as the 'trunk of the tree', through which all U-boats passed to the 'branches' in the Atlantic. Forces should therefore be concentrated in the Biscay transit area, but not at the expense of threatened convoys.

In anti-submarine-warfare, Coastal Command attempted a balance between close convoy escorts, sweeps perhaps ahead of convoys, and patrols in the U-boat transit routes, both in the north from Norway, and along the route from the French Biscay ports, the latter always a serious thorn in the side of the British up to the time that those ports were isolated following Operation Overlord. The Norwegian fjords as cover for U-boats remained a threat right up to and even after 8 May 1945.

In the final stages of the war, some U-boats were fitted with *Schnorchels*, which enabled the U-boats to remain submerged but still using their diesels. They came too late, however, and in too little a number to affect the outcome. Additionally, also, greatly improved designs in U-boat with a high underwater speed came too late. They could well have provided a very serious threat to the Allies' communications.

Overall, one must agree with Professor Rohwer that the prime factor in the Battle of the Atlantic was intelligence, for both Germany and the Allies. The necessity for intelligence was to be demonstrated, not only in the U-boat war, but also for some of the major battles – Midway, Cape Matapan, 'Bismarck', and when Ceylon was saved from attack.

Secondary to intelligence was radar, and to a lesser degree the Allied navies' HF/DF. Of specific importance for Coastal Command were the long-range aircraft and the 250 lb depth charge. From the Command's records a total of 185 German U-boats and four Italian submarines were sunk by aircraft controlled by Coastal Command in the Second World War.

Shared with naval forces were another twenty-three U-boats and one Italian submarine sunk. Additionally another 117 U-boats and four Italian submarines were so damaged by Coastal Command-controlled aircraft that they had to return to port. Against those successes the Command lost a total of 741 aircraft that were engaged on anti-submarine operations. That about six aircraft were lost for every U-boat sunk by its aircraft refutes the belief that flying in Coastal Command was a 'piece of cake'.

The official RAF history acknowledges that Coastal Command's shipping strikes were dangerous; there was also an element of danger in flying over the Atlantic or the Bay of Biscay against U-boats in the Second World War. Some historians tend to single out one Liberator squadron due to its obvious successes in sinking U-boats.

This is unfair to all the other squadrons, including those on loan from Bomber Command. They all served, if only to keep the U-boats submerged and therefore unable to track convoys, as Professor Rohwer acknowledges. The particular Liberator squadron had the advantages of that type of aircraft, with experienced (if not handpicked) crews and the right weapons in abundance, and being in the right place at the right time.

Germany had only fifty-seven U-boats at the beginning of the war, and just one of those, (U-47) sank forty-two ships up to February 1941.

It was fortunate for Britain that of the 1,170 U-boats that Germany produced, most were considerably less successful. A total of 630 were lost at sea, but only 123 in port.

At the Service of Commemoration held in Liverpool Cathedral for the Battle of the Atlantic in May 1993, precedence was given to the British Mercantile Marine; its losses had been catastrophic.

EPILOGUE

In my first tour of operations (500 hours), of the enemy I saw only a guard ship in Trondheim fjord and the periscope of a U-boat north of the Shetlands, and I had air-to-air combat with a *Luftwaffe* fighter over the Mediterranean. I heard later that the U-boat we had reported was sunk by a destroyer. I always wonder about the pilot of the fighter, who, I felt at the time, had no wish to kill me. My home suffered damage due to bombs and a V2, but at no time did I feel bitterness or animosity against either Germans or Italians.

Post war I have had friendly correspondence with a number of enemy submariners, including notably Peter Cremer of U-333 and Wolf Stiebler of U-461. Although there were exceptions on both sides, Coastal Command aircrew were concerned not with killing men but with sinking U-boats. Some risked both their aircraft and their lives in an endeavour to save the enemy, such as the one who dropped his own dinghy to *Korvettenkapitän* Stiebler, and another who landed his Sunderland in open sea to rescue three Italian submariners. Some of the Command's pilots became deeply distressed at the plight of their enemy; in the case of the USN pilot who sank U-388, he 'bottled up' the memory until he related it to me many years later.

The Norwegian who sank U-423 saw the cap of its captain on the sea, and was so affected that he did not join his squadron's celebrations. Some Italian and German submariners have become friends with those who were their former enemies.

Poignant for me were two telephone calls from Peter Cremer asking if there were survivors from the Sunderland that he had shot down. One of his crew had seen two survivors through the flames. 'No', was my reply. As Cremer added, 'I had no choice.' The tone of his voice showed his obvious regret. I had flown in that same aircraft only a short time earlier. There was a human aspect in the U-boat war.

CHAPTER FIVE

Anti-Shipping Operations – Merchant Shipping

PRELUDE

An anti-shipping policy had been agreed by the British with their French allies in April 1939. It stated that the Allies would not initiate air action against any but purely 'military' objectives in the narrowest sense of the word, and would as far as possible confine it to objectives on which attacks would not involve loss of civilian life.[1]

In August 1939 the Admiralty and Air Ministry issued instructions that only enemy warships, troopships and auxiliary vessels in direct attendance on the fleet were aircraft free to attack. In the case of merchant vessels, they were not to be attacked. At best they might be ordered to a port, or for the aircraft to await the arrival of an Allied surface vessel.[2] Coastal Command's role in counter-offensive action was limited to 'in defence of seaborne trade embodying attacks on the enemy fleet, air forces or submarines operating against our trade'.[3] Even against the heavy fleet units, the Command was not allowed to bomb ships in harbour, but only when merchant vessels were not at risk, and with the naval units anchored in more open waters.[4]

Thus Coastal Command was effectively restricted to attacks on the enemy's heavy naval ships when they were at sea, and even then, as a defensive rather than an offensive measure. For that task the Command had only two squadrons of Vildebeest aircraft, outdated biplanes, which were lacking in both speed and range, and thus could not be used for the

task. With Britain inhibited by the 1923 Geneva Convention, and the vacillating French,[5] there was no clear specific anti-shipping policy in September 1939 for Coastal Command. It was to be demonstrated on 13 December, when a No. 220 Squadron Hudson that had shadowed four enemy destroyers needed instructions from base before it could bomb the enemy.

This was the first attack by Coastal Command's aircraft on any enemy shipping. Lack of suitable armament was demonstrated by the attack, made with only two anti-submarine bombs from 2,000 ft.

No success was claimed, but at that time the squadron had hardly completed its conversion to Hudsons, and accuracy from 2,000 ft altitude was limited. Furthermore, the A/S bombs were designed to be dropped onto water. Hudsons, nevertheless, were to claim sixty ships sunk or damaged in the war (including four Japanese merchant vessels in the Far East).[6]

At the outbreak of war the German fleet included two battle-cruisers, the *Scharnhorst* and *Gneisenau*, and the heavy cruiser, the *Admiral Hipper*. Later in the war another heavy cruiser, the *Prinz Eugen* and two modern battleships, the *Bismarck* and the *Tirpitz* came into service. Coastal Command was to become closely involved with all those vessels.

Although the primary task of the Command was specified as reconnaissance to report the outbreak of any surface raiders, it was short of aircraft, and what was to remain a problem throughout the war, a lack of aircraft of sufficient range to undertake reconnaissance of the Kattegat and Skagerrak, the areas through which enemy ships were likely to pass. Aircraft that were becoming progressively available, certainly to operate to the Norwegian coast, were the Lockheed Hudsons, and they were to be followed by Bristol Beauforts and Blenheims. Standing patrols against the possible outbreak of enemy surface raiders began on 23 August 1939 from Scotland to the southern coast of Norway at Stadlandet, albeit when just one squadron, No. 224, of the land-based reconnaissance units, was then fully equipped with Hudsons. The other squadrons were still using Ansons, which lacked the range to operate off Norway.

The Commander-in-Chief Coastal Command, Air Chief Marshal Sir Frederick Bowhill, had anticipated that the *Kriegsmarine* would attempt a breakout of major naval units before war was declared, and thus had laid on patrols on 23 August. Nevertheless, two 'pocket battleships', the *Admiral Graf Spee* and the *Deutschland* had evaded detection, the *Admiral Graf Spee* leaving on 21 August and the *Deutschland* three days later.[7] It was one of their two supply ships, the *Altmark*, that was later to involve the Command.[8]

With emphasis given to countering major fleet units, no specific plans had been made in respect of possible attacks on minor naval units such as destroyers, minesweepers or E-boats. Nevertheless, these smaller vessels were to pose a threat to British shipping, and to require considerable effort on the part of Coastal Command right up to the end of the war in Europe.[9]

Anti-shipping policies for Coastal Command were still being formulated in 1939, and on 12 October there was a directive from the Air Ministry that required Bomber Command to provide three bomber squadrons to cooperate in strikes against German naval units. This bomber force was to be under the direct orders of Coastal Command.[10]

This decision stemmed from a Coastal Command aircraft giving a sighting report of enemy ships that had not been followed up with a strike by Bomber Command against the German naval vessels as was expected. It was indicative of what was to prove one of the weaknesses in anti-shipping operations; which was of a strike force unable to locate the target after a sighting report was transmitted.

Owing to German attacks on Allied shipping, the Chief of Air Staff chaired a meeting on 7 December when the lack of coordination of the British forces in anti-shipping operations was expressed. The outcome from the meeting was that although Naval and Air Staffs would retain executive control of their forces, they would be coordinated by joint Admiralty and Air Ministry staff, with Admiral Holland responsible on behalf of the Admiralty and Air Marshal Sir Philip Joubert representing the Air Staff as 'Advisor on Combined Operations in the North Sea'; this cooperation was with effect from 12 December 1939.[11] During my second tour of operations in 1944/5 I became well aware of the friendly cooperation with the Royal Navy at operational level over the North Sea working with His Majesty's Ships.

At Command level in 1939/40, however, it was found that the advisers had become involved only with forward planning, and in April 1940 Sir Philip Joubert was appointed to a new post, that of Assistant Chief of Air Staff (Radar).

For aircrew there still remained uncertainty concerning the bombing or otherwise of ships, and on 30 December there was a meeting at the Air Ministry with representatives from the Foreign Office and the Admiralty.

This resulted in the Air Ministry issuing instructions on 4 February 1940 that any part of the enemy fleet could be attacked or sunk on sight, but merchant vessels in convoy were excluded.[12]

There remained to be resolved the control of Bomber Command's strike force, and on 22 February it had been agreed that two bomber squadrons should be detached from No. 5 Group, Bomber Command, to be based in Scotland under Coastal's control through the AOC No. 18 Group, but training of the squadrons would rest with No. 5 Group, although advice from Coastal Command would be welcomed.[13] This typically British compromise was representative of what was to prevail for Coastal Command throughout the war; that was, tentative agreements with the other Commands in respect of operational squadrons, as also with the Fleet Air Arm. The agreements also applied, not only for squadrons, but for the use of bases. In respect of Coastal Command's anti-shipping operations, the major event in 1940 was Germany's invasion and occupation of Norway in April.

The ill-conceived Allied Norwegian campaign proved too little and too late to thwart the Germans. From the outset of the Second World War, the Command had laid on patrols to Norway with Hudsons flying the more southerly sorties, while the few Sunderlands available flew the more northerly trips owing to their greater range. The first casualty of that invasion commemorated by the Norwegians was in fact a Coastal Command Sunderland lost on 9 April 1940.[14] The invasion of Norway on 9 April must have served to concentrate the minds of the War Cabinet, as on that day it authorised Coastal Command to attack without warning any ships under way in the Skagerrak.

The directive included notably merchant vessels and those eastwards of 8°E in harbour. It resulted in six attacks in the first ten days, but was limited to those by Hudsons with 250 lb bombs and Blenheims with machine-guns, with the first attack on a merchant vessel in Norwegian waters by a Hudson of No. 224 Squadron on 11 April.[15]

Account now had to be taken of the whole of the vast Norwegian coastline up to North Cape, particularly when, later, Britain was sailing convoys to Russia. This was because Norwegian fjords provided protected bases for Germany's capital ships in addition to bases for the *Luftwaffe*, such as at Stavanger.

The safe anchorages gained additional natural protection by surrounding hills and mountains on which gun emplacements could be located. Such was to be demonstrated in February 1945, when a German destroyer anchored in a fjord near a cliff became an 'impossible' target for a powerful strike force.[16]

What the Admiralty had not realised also was that Norway's *Indreled* (inner leads), the coastal waters with the natural protection of islands, could be negotiated by warships and merchant vessels, and could serve as a route for surface raiders to break out into the Atlantic after leaving the Skagerrak. There was, however, a stretch of open water off southern Norway that ships had to enter, where they were open to attack, and Coastal Command's strike aircraft were to make good use of that fact. Additional protection of the enemy's ships in Norway was given by the *Luftwaffe*'s single-engined and twin-engined fighters, and as late as 1945 the enemy was able to muster as many as forty-five fighters, including some of the latest marks, to protect his ships against Coastal Command's aircraft.

Thus Norway's topography and location provided Germany with excellent bases to protect her own ships, which at the same time could always seriously threaten Allied ships. Germany employed that advantage to the full.

Economically, Germany depended considerably on high-grade iron ore from Sweden and Norway that would have been shipped from the Swedish port of Lulea in the Baltic or Narvik on Norway's northern coastline. The cargoes were received at Emden or Bremen, but after 10 May 1940, when the Low Countries were over-run, the Dutch port of Rotterdam was Germany's preferred route to the industrial Ruhr, with Rotterdam having better port facilities and able to handle a much greater tonnage. By the nature of Norway's topography, the preferred route from Scandinavia was by sea, although there was a railway from Trondheim to Oslo.

In addition to iron ore, Germany required fish and forestry products from Norway. Return trade was such as coal and coke, but with Norway occupied, military traffic was added. Thus, Coastal Command now had the additional tasks of reconnaissance of a greatly extended coastline and an increased likelihood of a breakout by surface raiders, and finally it had to take on an anti-shipping role against merchant vessels sailing between ports such as Narvik and Rotterdam. For all these tasks, it was largely dependent on a converted airliner, the Hudson.

MERCHANT VESSELS

One of the first anti-shipping operations to Norway was against the 12,000-ton *Altmark*, which had been the supply ship for the *Admiral Graf Spee*. It had arrived at Trondheim on 14 February, but on 15 February was reported passing Bergen. The Admiralty, although it had deployed a cruiser and five destroyers, had lost track of the vessel and asked Coastal Command to undertake a search. The *Altmark* was located by a No. 220 Squadron Hudson in Jøssing fjord, then considered 'neutral' waters. Following Winston Churchill's intervention, Captain Vian on HMS *Cossack* entered the fjord, and the Navy's boarding party freed 300 Allied prisoners. The incident gained much publicity for the Navy, and at that time could be considered useful propaganda. Dr Goulter's account of this incident gives emphasis to the intelligence provided through diplomatic channels. I consider it much more likely that there were agents in Norway who would give immediate reports by radio on both ships and aircraft, such as I was to experience in 1942.

Of greater importance than any intelligence reports, in this case, would have been the dedication of the Hudson captain in his search for *Altmark*; it was typical of such men in the early stages of the war that they accepted considerable risks, particularly over Norway.[17]

On 25 April 1940 the Air Ministry signalled groups that aircraft were permitted to attack merchant vessels under way within 10 miles of the Norwegian coast, anywhere east of 6°E and from 61°N to 54°N.

It was thus against coastal traffic from just south of Ålesund down to the north German coast. This decision must have stemmed from the realisation that the enemy was attacking Allied ships while vital enemy supplies were being allowed to sail freely. By that time, however, the *Luftwaffe* had gained bases at Trondheim and Stavanger, and as Coastal's aircrew were to experience, the enemy was prepared to give overwhelming fighter cover to its shipping. Germany had invaded the Low Countries on 10 May 1940, and France capitulated on 21 June with the signing of an armistice. Britain had lost France as an ally but gained the Vichy French as a potential enemy, of which Coastal Command's aircrew were to become acutely aware.

Thus by June 1940 tasks for the Command ranged from the Spanish border up to North Cape, and that vast coastline had to be covered to a lesser or greater degree up to 8 May 1945, and even beyond that date.[18]

On 16 July another Air Ministry directive permitted the Command to 'sink on sight', but in prescribed areas of the North Sea and Skagerrak. In respect of anti-shipping operations, the occupation of Norway, the Low Countries and France resulted in areas to be covered that corresponded generally to three of the Command's Groups: No. 18 for the largely Norwegian sector, No. 16 for the Netherlands, and No. 19 for the French coastline. For anti-shipping, the Norwegian and Dutch coasts remained paramount throughout; for shipping (rather than U-boats), the French ports, after the 'Channel Dash' proved less significant, although there were some destroyer escorts and blockade runners to contend with from time to time.

For anti-shipping operations off Norway, the Command, in 1940, was largely dependent on Hudsons, although some Bristol Blenheims and Beauforts were becoming available. Because of the range, some of the few Sunderlands available were required to undertake the more northerly sorties, along the Norwegian coast, although they could hardly be considered as strike aircraft, and generally would not be so used. For aircraft operating in the northern part of the Norwegian coast there was always the problem that enemy shipping could gain shelter in the leads, particularly from any possible torpedo attack.

The first confirmed anti-shipping success for the Command in the Norwegian area was in fact gained by a Hudson, which damaged a 1,939-ton merchant vessel in Grimstad fjord on 29 April 1940. There was a further directive on 14 June from the Air Ministry, which required all merchant vessels in Norwegian fjords between Trondheim and Kristiansand to be attacked and sunk. This was due to the belief that invasion forces were being prepared in Norway.

The Command's strike force of Beauforts, because of their unreliable engines and limited defensive armament, were considered unsuitable for what was acknowledged to be a dangerous task, and so that was left effectively to the Hudson squadrons. Additionally, however, the Air Ministry required two medium-bomber squadrons to be available primarily against invasion transport, and the sister squadrons, Nos 53 and 59, were transferred from Bomber to Coastal Command.[19] This decision was made at an Air Ministry conference on 26 June, and it was intended that those squadrons should fill the gap left by Coastal Command squadrons

being deployed in the north-west, where there was now an increased need for anti-submarine forces owing to French and Norwegian bases then available to the enemy.

It was a No. 59 Squadron Blenheim that claimed the first sinking of a merchant vessel off the French coast near Cherbourg on 18 September. Off the Dutch coast a Hudson had earlier damaged an auxiliary vessel. A Beaufort from No. 22 Squadron, which had recently rearmed, followed these successes, damaging a merchant vessel off Den Helder. Those examples represented the strike aircraft for Coastal Command up to the end of 1940 – Hudsons, Blenheims and Beauforts – although they were aided by Swordfish from the Fleet Air Arm that came under the Command's control. It was to be late in 1942 before any success against enemy shipping was recorded for Beaufighters and Hampdens.

Meanwhile it was for aircraft such as Hudsons and Blenheims to serve as a strike force and with the low-level tactics employed up to the middle of 1942 to suffer serious losses accordingly.[20] After the Battle of Britain, in September 1940, the German invasion preparations were considered complete, and for Coastal Command emphasis was given to shipping targets rather than anti-invasion reconnaissance. Hitler had planned the invasion, Operation Sealion, for 15 September, but having failed to gain air superiority, postponed it indefinitely on 12 October but did not discontinue it until 9 January 1941.[21]

On 18 September Rover patrols were introduced against enemy shipping off the Dutch coast, but also further south to the areas of Cherbourg and the Channel Islands. This represented the commencement of the Command's change to an anti-shipping offensive.[22] There had, however, been a progression from anti-invasion reconnaissance towards anti-shipping patrols.

Such 'Rover patrols' tended to be referred to as 'armed recces', with aircraft looking for ships and convoys to attack. Former anti-invasion reconnaissance became anti-shipping patrols, with the intention of attacking with bombs and torpedoes.

With the end of the immediate invasion threat, the Prime Minister chaired a meeting of the War Cabinet's Defence Committee on 31 October at which it was agreed that a seaborne invasion threat was reduced during the winter months. Meanwhile Coastal Command would still undertake reconnaissance of potential invasion ports, although offensive patrols were being substituted between Stavanger and Horns Reef, that is, an area where ships would be in open sea and could be more readily attacked.

Four standing patrols were laid on to cover the area from Stadlandet to Horns Reef; and these appeared still in force during the summer of 1942 when I was on sorties to Norway.[23] Generally, it may be said that by December 1940 Coastal Command was undertaking regular sorties covering the enemy-controlled coastline from at least northwards as far as Bergen and southwards down to Lorient.

Thus the three groups at this time, Nos 18, 16 and 15, were involved, with No. 18 responsible for operations to Norway, No. 16 covering the Dutch coast, and No. 15 (later No. 19) concerned with the French coast and the Bay of Biscay.

The year 1940 marked a turning point in the duties to be required of Coastal Command. Its two main roles had become anti-submarine warfare and anti-shipping operations. At this stage in the war, the anti-submarine sorties were still of a defensive nature; but in the anti-shipping role, Coastal Command was on the offensive. Within the year 1940, No. 16 Group's aircraft had sunk or damaged, in the four months September to December, ten ships, while No. 18 Group's aircraft claimed ten ships sunk or damaged in the nine months April to December.

Tactics were being developed in shipping attacks by the squadrons, with low-level bombing, rather than medium- or high-level methods. Low-level attacks resulted in greater accuracy but much greater losses of aircraft and crews. Sir Frederick Bowhill was ever mindful of the welfare of all his personnel; he had taken the view, however, that bombing at low level was safer because of the rapid change in angle of attack. Subsequent records of such as No. 407 (RCAF) and No. 220 Squadrons were to disprove that belief. Coastal Command aircrew again showed that they were prepared to suffer such losses, which the official RAF historians were later to acknowledge.[24]

Sir Frederick Bowhill summed up Coastal Command's shipping offensive for the period 1 June to 31 December 1940 with 141 bombing attacks on merchant vessels at sea, with thirty ships suffering direct hits. Of those, Hudsons scored sixteen, Blenheims thirteen, and Ansons one. Additionally in those 141 attacks, thirty-seven vessels were damaged.[25] That period was a transitional one for the Command's aircraft, with Hudsons replacing Ansons, as the reconnaissance squadrons converted. Ansons were at a disadvantage in shipping strikes by being limited to a 200 lb bomb load, and they lacked also the speed of the Blenheims and Hudsons.

In February 1941, two Blenheim squadrons were temporarily transferred from Bomber Command to Coastal Command; they were No. 107, which went to Leuchars, and No. 114, initially to Thornaby.[26] This was to help maintain Coastal Command's operations in the east in anti-submarine, anti-shipping and anti-invasion patrols.

This stemmed from Coastal Command transferring some forces to the west in anticipation of a spring offensive by Germany's U-boats, and demonstrated how stretched were Coastal Command's forces. There was much rearming of squadrons in Coastal Command during 1941, and the first to become operational with Beaufighters was

No.252.[27] Initially these Beaufighters were intended to protect Allied shipping against the FW200 Kondor aircraft, but later they were to replace the Hudsons, Blenheims and Beauforts in the strike squadrons. It was to be found, however, that better aircraft (as they were in the strike role) did not necessarily result in greater efficiency. Experienced aircrew were also necessary. This period was transitional, not only with the need to gain reinforcements from other Commands, and the rearming of squadrons, but also with changes in tactics. This was most obvious by the change from medium-level to low-level bombing, with some squadrons attacking from literally 'mast height'.

This was to be exemplified later by Plt Off O'Connell of No. 407 (RCAF) Squadron, who left a bomb door on the mast of a ship.[28] These low-level tactics resulted in greater successes against ships, but squadron losses disproved Sir Frederick's belief that low-level attacks were safer.[29]

The need for precise flying if attacking from high levels is shown by the following. A lateral error of 2° in flying the aircraft would result in a ground error of 220 yards, and a fore and aft error of 2° would give a ground error of 250 yards, albeit from 20,000 ft altitude.[30] In this period of attacks on enemy shipping, the weapon most used was the 250 lb general-purpose (GP) bomb, with which 68 per cent of the attacks were made. They represented a balance between high blast and fragmentation, for which a cast-iron case was used. Anti-submarine (A/S) bombs were used in 12 per cent of the attacks, but they were intended to be dropped into water. This was because they provided high blast due to much explosive filling that was contained in a thin casing.

More important for the safety of aircrew and aircraft was the use of an 11-second delay fuse replacing the former instantaneous fuse. This was to enable aircraft to be well clear of the target before the bomb exploded.[31]

Although 7 per cent of the bombs used were 500 lb GPs, they were confined to the Beaufort aircraft, which were able to accept them.

By the end of his tenure as Commander-in-Chief Coastal Command, Sir Frederick Bowhill considered that the Command's anti-shipping operations had developed into a carefully planned and coordinated attack on the enemy's sea communications, against which at that time Germany had no effective countermeasures. He acknowledged Bomber Command's contribution in the development of the low-level attacks that he considered 'most profitable'.[32] Coastal Command still lacked aircraft to undertake a more intensive anti-shipping campaign, as could be said also for anti-U-boat warfare.

When Sir Philip Joubert succeeded Sir Frederick on 14 June, he was aware of no immediate threat of a German invasion and was able to divert more resources to an anti-shipping offensive. This was directed mainly against shipping off the Norwegian coast using Hudsons and Beaufort aircraft. He gave credit largely to the Beauforts,[33] as it was likely that he was pleased that at long last Coastal Command had two squadrons (Nos 22 and 42) of torpedo aircraft, the Beaufort, which had a suitable range and was then operating successfully. However, those two squadrons were posted overseas the following year.[34]

Sir Philip made a change of policy in July by directing squadrons more to an offensive against shipping at sea, rather than to land targets, which had been expected of the Command. Joubert had intended laying on anti-shipping patrols in the Channel and Dover Straits, for which he could have obtained intelligence, not only from photo-reconnaissance, but also from radar or D/F stations in the south-east of England. At a meeting on 15 July, however, it was decided that anti-shipping attacks between Cherbourg and Texel should be the responsibility of Bomber Command.[35] Sir Philip's motives

42. Strike crews of No 404 Squadron RCAF at Davidstow Moor in June 1944. The Beaufighter in the background shows the single machine gun for the navigator.

included the possibility of attracting the fighters that might be used to cover the enemy's ships and thereby lessen the forces against Russia.

These intended shipping operations prompted Sir Philip also to consider tactics against enemy vessels, which he decided should include close cooperation between the Navy's surface vessels and strike aircraft, and a fighter escort for the strike aircraft, which should be provided to engage enemy fighters.

A further requirement was that there should be close liaison by the reconnaissance aircraft with the organisation for the strike force.[36] Sir Philip's appreciation of what was necessary for a successful strike was to be endorsed by aircrew who later formed the strike wings. There were occasions, however, when the system fell short of his requirements:

Reconnaissance aircraft failed to give the essential details of the target's

43. A Hudson of No 320 (Dutch) Squadron. This unit lost twenty-one aircraft while on shipping strikes.

position, time, speed and direction, type of target, and if the enemy was under way. It was important, also, to transmit such intelligence promptly, before the enemy gained cover by, for example, entering Den Helder, which was heavily defended. This question was raised later by the AOC at a conference on 19 September 1941, although he was thinking of the potential targets off Norway gaining cover in the fjords. To counter that he suggested constant patrols covering both reconnaissance and strikes, what in fact were to become 'armed recces'.[37] This appreciation, however, was in the transitional stage of anti-shipping operations, with some crews still untrained in maritime operations and lacking experience. Nevertheless, even reconnaissances that produced no obvious results gave that experience to aircrew, and would have been at least a nuisance to the enemy, and only some of the sorties proved abortive.

Fighter aircraft intended for escort sometimes failed to rendezvous at the right time and position. This was vital for a strike wing with many aircraft so that it could formate in as short a time as possible, due to limited endurance.

Sir Philip, in his appreciation, had stipulated that it was essential that some of the fighter escort should be able to attack the enemy ships in advance of the strike aircraft to neutralise any opposition. In practice, with Beaufighter aircraft forming the main body of the wing, this was to be proved unnecessary. This was because the Beaufighters had such a powerful forward-firing armament. Furthermore, those armed additionally with rocket projectiles were able to harmonise the release of the RPs with their cannon, using the trajectories of the shells as a guide and with positive results.[38]

Fighter Command showed that it was prepared to cooperate with Coastal Command by providing escorts for shipping strikes, and although the C-in-C Bomber Command considered that bombing, whether against ships or other targets, was a task for his Command, he accepted that torpedo attacks should be left to Coastal Command.[39] It was decided that Bomber Command should be responsible for bombing ships between Cherbourg and Texel, with two Blenheim squadrons from No. 2 Group Bomber Command to be based in range of the Dover Straits, with a controller sharing No. 16 Group's headquarters.[40]

This compromise was probably due to Sir Charles Portal, the Chief of Air Staff, who, from Coastal Command's records, demonstrated a remarkably balanced view, although Sir Philip showed that he was always prepared to accept a compromise, after stating his views, in the light of the whole situation. The personality of the C-in-C Fighter Command doesn't 'come through' except as always being prepared to cooperate with Coastal Command if other commitments allowed.

On 2 September 1941 a 'Directive for Coastal Command' was issued following a review by the Air Ministry of the Command's operations. There had been an agreement between the Admiralty and the Air Council that the primary role of Coastal Command was reconnaissance. The Command was still permitted, however, to use bombs, depth charges or torpedoes against naval units and U-boats at sea, and under favourable conditions, torpedo attacks on naval units in harbour.

When there were no naval targets, Coastal Command was permitted to bomb enemy merchant vessels, but not the escort vessels, and the areas were to be outside those allocated to Bomber Command, namely between Texel and Cherbourg.[41]

The Admiralty's reasoning (as it almost certainly was) appears understandable. There were still a number of powerful enemy warships that even singly could wreak havoc should they get within range of an Allied convoy, as was to be shown, for example, by the heavy cruiser *Admiral Hipper*. The Royal Navy would wish to know not only if such a ship had sailed, but its position, its course and speed, and ideally its type and name. Trained and experienced Coastal Command aircrew could best give such details, and such men were coming into service.

With the policy to avoid the escort vessels in bombing attacks on enemy convoys, there was more to be said for attacking the merchant vessels that were likely to carry valuable cargoes, rather than the escorts that were likely to be much more heavily armed, as, for example, the *Sperrbrechers*. Bombing of 'fringe' land targets was permitted, but only when no enemy shipping was sighted.

This was in accord with Sir Philip's policy. Aircrew had from the outset tended to bomb land targets rather than return with a bomb load when no ships were sighted, as, for example, Flt Lt Jim Romanes, who bombed Alderney, albeit at some considerable risk.[42]

On the night of 29 October, nine Hudsons from No. 220 Squadron bombed ships in Ålesund harbour. Smoke and fire was seen from the ship attacked by Wg Cdr Wright, and it was reported sinking. Sergeant Houghton attacked another ship and saw sections of the deck and superstructure blasted into the air. Flg Off Tarrant hit a 2,000-ton merchant vessel with his bombs. Other Hudsons attacked shore installations These details are given from the squadron's record,[43] as three other accounts of the result of the strike all differ.

From the Command's record, one ship of 3,101 tons was sunk and two others of 1,371 tons and 1,108 tons were damaged.[44]

According to the Norwegian historian, Per Skaugstad, with whom I corresponded, another ship, the *Archimede*, was also successfully attacked. Two other Norwegian historians, Jan Flatmark and Harald Grytten, in their book write: '*Resultatet var at D/S Barcelona på 3,100 brt ble senket og Vesla skutt I brann* (The steamship *Barcelona* of 3,100 tons was sunk and *Vesla* set on fire).'[45]

This, I consider, was the most successful strike ever undertaken by Coastal Command, bearing in mind all the factors involved. This is because at least two ships were claimed (if not three or four), and all aircraft returned to base. Only one squadron was used, of Hudsons, which according to Dr Goulter were 'unmanoeuvrable and relatively slow'.[46]

That successful strike may be contrasted with one attempted by the Dallachy Wing on 9 February 1945, when forty-six heavily armed strike aircraft from three squadrons, with an escort of Mustangs, plus an outrider and two ASR Warwicks sank no ships, and one of the three squadrons (No. 404) lost six out of eleven Beaufighters. The reasons for the Hudsons' success I consider were due to their crews, which by then had gained much successful experience; they were a small number, all in one squadron, led by their own Commanding Officer, the raid was in a harbour and they gained surprise. In contrast, the Dallachy Wing had lost surprise and were in a closely confined area in which far too many aircraft had to operate against both ships and enemy fighters.

Sir Philip Joubert, in an analysis of shipping strikes for the period July, August and September 1941, gives eighty-eight vessels being attacked, and of those 62.5 per cent were from altitudes less than 500 ft.[47] From Coastal's record of successes, however, ten merchant vessels were sunk or damaged off Norway by No. 18 Group aircraft, largely by Beauforts, but also Hudsons.

There was just one success by No. 19

Group in the Biscay area.[48] Regular traffic in the Biscay area included ships taking iron ore from Bilbao to Bordeaux or Bayonne. As they sailed at night and close to the Spanish coast, they were difficult to intercept, and the Command had not enough long-range Hudsons for that area.[49]

Sir Philip Joubert considered that the last quarter of 1941 was the most successful since the beginning of Coastal Command's anti-shipping operations, despite shorter days and less favourable weather. He gives fifteen vessels sunk in that time, eighteen severely damaged and thirty-three damaged, all for the loss of nineteen aircraft.[50]

The Command's record, however, gives seventeen sunk and ten damaged.[51] These successes were gained by the three Groups, Nos 16, 18 and 19, covering the three areas of the Dutch, Norwegian and French coasts, but with emphasis on the Norwegian and Dutch coasts.[52]

In the first few years of the war, when Coastal Command was under the command of Sir Frederick Bowhill and then Sir Philip Joubert, the question of dangerous operations undertaken by aircrew was not infrequently raised.

Thus the 'costly patrols' off the Norwegian coast in the Bergen and Stadlandet areas were mentioned, with the suggestion that aircraft should be flown very low at about 50 ft altitude to avoid RDF detection and when there was no cloud cover.[53]

Flying low, however, resulted in some aircraft having their propellers damaged by hitting the sea or rocks. Cloud cover would hardly save them from detection, as, for example, at Ålesund alone, where there were twelve D/F stations coded *Siegfried*, in addition to 'heavy and light flak'.[54] Later in 1941 losses of the Dutch squadron, No. 320, operating off the Netherlands coast, had by early September left it with only six aircraft and five aircrew; and it was considered

necessary to take them off shipping strikes. Normally, a squadron would expect to have sixteen aircraft, with another four in reserve.[55]

There was a notable difference between Coastal Command's operations off Norway and those off the Dutch Coast. In the latter area, certainly for those involved in shipping strikes, intelligence officers would warn crews to beware of the coastal batteries. They were found to be particularly intensive due to the routes used by Bomber Command aircraft. Over Norway, it was acknowledged, and in fact found, that fighter opposition by both single-engined and twin-engined aircraft could be expected.

The strain on all Coastal Command aircrew was raised in connection with the length of their tours of operations. They were so much longer than those for Fighter or Bomber Commands, with the latter having a first tour of 200 hours, and a second of 100 hours. The tour on Hudsons was 500 hours, and on flying-boats 800 hours, although medical officers on squadrons certainly studied their aircrew and responded accordingly.[56]

The major events in 1941 were the German invasion of Russia (Operation Barbarossa) in June and the Japanese attack on the American fleet at Pearl Harbor on 7 December. The effects on Coastal Command because of the invasion of Russia were that *Luftwaffe* forces were drawn away from the west; but more obviously, Sir Philip Joubert's thinking was directed to the prospect of drawing some of those forces back to the west to ease the pressure on Russia, the prospect of escorting convoys to Russia, and ultimately, as was to occur, detachments from his Command to Russia.

Both shipping strike and anti-U-boat squadrons were to become involved in support of Russia. Some of Coastal Command's squadrons already in the Middle East were retained there, and more squadrons were to be posted there, as I was to experience. There remained the need in the Mediterranean to keep open the route to at least Malta. The entry of Japan and America into the war did not reduce the load on Coastal Command, rather was it increased. Squadrons were posted to the Far East, and later, even one to the USA to help the Americans. Some squadrons remaining in the United Kingdom were depleted of their personnel to form new squadrons in the Far East.

By the end of 1941 anti-shipping operations had become a major task for Coastal Command, second only to anti-submarine operations. The other requirements of the Command – photo-reconnaissance, meteorological flights and air-sea rescue (ASR) – were just accepted as part of the Command's routine. Anti-shipping operations had settled into the two main areas, off southern Norway, and the Dutch Coast; occasionally, also, the French coast and the Bay of Biscay.

The battle-cruisers *Scharnhorst* and *Gneisenau* with the heavy cruiser *Prinz Eugen* at Brest were to require considerable effort on the part of both Bomber and Coastal Commands right up to the middle of February 1942. Although the battleship *Bismarck* had been sunk, there remained its sister ship *Tirpitz*.

In respect of anti-shipping operations, at the last meeting for Coastal Command in 1941, it was reported that the Ministry of Aircraft Production (MAP) would be able to supply twenty-four Hampden bombers modified to Coastal Command's requirements for using them as torpedo strike aircraft.[57] The Ministry kept its word, as No. 455 Squadron received them in May 1942, and later I saw the whole squadron circling to land at Sumburgh in the Shetlands, the only occasion when I experienced such a sight.

Despite the requirements to have strike units available, the Command's forces had been depleted by postings of squadrons overseas, and there had also been some serious

losses of aircraft in anti-shipping operations. Losses had been of such magnitude for Bomber Command's No. 2 Group, which had opted to undertake shipping strikes, that it had withdrawn its aircraft from such operations, leaving Coastal Command's Hudsons to accept the risks.[58] The official RAF history gives No. 2 Group Blenheims losing thirty-six aircraft in 297 attacks against enemy merchant vessels during the period 1 April to 30 June 1941, while the Command lost fifty-two aircraft in 143 attacks.

As the official historians stated, 'As a healthy occupation for aircrew in mid-1941, bombing German ships by day had much less to commend it than bombing German towns by night.'[59]

Hampden bombers, modified to Coastal Command's requirements to carry torpedoes, were coming into service in April with the Command's Dominion Squadrons No. 415 (RCAF) and No. 489 (RNZAF). Two more Hampden squadrons, Nos 144 RAF and 455 (RAAF), were transferred from Bomber to Coastal Command. Apart from No. 415, all these units were later to convert to Beaufighters. In 1944/5, during my second tour of operations, I met up with these squadrons when they formed part of the strike wings.[60] The Command's shortage of Hudson aircraft in early 1942 resulted in Sir Philip ceasing to use those machines for anti-shipping operations, and informing the Air Ministry accordingly. The official response was that overseas commitments had caused the shortage, but that further allocations would be made to the Command in the near future.[61] Hudsons were being sent to the Middle East for anti-submarine and anti-shipping operations, and to the Far East for transport, anti-shipping and anti-submarine operations.[62]

Sir Philip reviewed operations against merchant ships during the first six months of 1942 specifically by Hudson aircraft. He contrasted the difference in successes between the months of January and February with those in March and April. Only two ships were sunk in March and April, but five in January and February, although sixteen were damaged in the second two months, and thirteen in January and February. Sir Philip gives no reason for this, although likely causes were increased vigilance on the part of the enemy, and increased numbers of escort vessels, in addition to arming all merchant ships. What is notable, however, is that all the anti-shipping successes claimed by No. 16 Group during the first six months of 1942 were gained by Hudson aircraft. They had sunk eleven ships and damaged five others.[63] These were all off the Dutch coast, and it was a feature of the squadrons involved that they maintained high morale despite their serious losses. They included the Nos 53 and 59 'sister' Squadrons, while the Canadian No. 407 Squadron always cooperated with No. 320 (Dutch) Squadron. The high morale that prevailed in those units, despite losses, must have contributed to their successes.[64]

For the same period, No. 18 Group's successes for operations off the Norwegian coast were eight ships sunk, and of those, Hudsons claimed seven.[65] In those first six months of 1942, the Hudsons were attacking at low level (literally at mast height), and losses were therefore relatively high. Later when one of those squadrons, No. 407 (RCAF) was taken off anti-shipping strikes to operate against U-boats, it was demoralised and wished to return to its more hazardous work.[66]

Although aircrew demonstrated that they were prepared to suffer the risks of low-level attacks on shipping, the Air Officer Commanding No. 16 Group thought otherwise. He sent a memorandum to the C-in-C Coastal Command on 3 June 1942, stating that during May, out of ninety-seven sorties on strikes, the aircraft that returned

reported fifty-four sightings with forty-seven attacks, claiming thirty-four hits but with twelve aircraft lost. In addition to about 20 per cent losses, a further 25 per cent of the aircraft had become unserviceable and required repairs by contractors.

A Hudson captain on No. 407 (RCAF) Squadron gave this account:

No. 407 perfected the science of ship bombing against enemy shipping with a marked degree of success. This required that the attack be pressed home at close range and from zero height, generally lifting over the target ship and flying between the masts. As enemy ships increased their defensive armament our losses mounted and eventually skip bombing was replaced by bombing from heights up to 4,000 feet with limited success.[67]

The same captain gave a terse account in his personal diary that showed that aircrew could not relax after an attack until they had literally reached the end of the runway on their return:

Bright moonlight—good for nightfighters so went in on the deck—found target (a convoy of eight merchantmen with four escorts). Attacked at 0106 hrs scored hits on large MV. Took photographs ... flak hot and heavy. Returned to find Docking under fog ... vis zero down to deck. Diverted to Manston, still zero vis. Diverted to Donna Nook, no vis then Cranwell. Still closed in ... no fuel, flying at 150 ft flashed SOS on downward recognition lights. Searchlights came up and directed me to Hibaldstow. Landed in very low cloud and poor vis. Fuel remaining 10 gallons. Target strike at 5333N 0535E.[68]

Hudsons would typically be using one gallon per minute. As an experienced wing commander remarked to a group of aircrew: 'Gentlemen, remember the bacon and eggs at the end of the runway.'[69]

The AOC No. 16 Group suggested that low-level attacks on convoys were far too costly, and he proposed withdrawing his Hudsons from strike operations for training in high-level attacks. This memorandum was considered by the SASO, who was doubtful 'whether high level attack will be remunerative'. He had reported that for No. 59 Squadron there were only five aircraft operational, with two others 'shot up'.[70]

One of No. 59's Hudsons had come back with a hole in a wing large enough for three of its crew to stand in.[71] At that time also, No. 407 Squadron had only seven Hudsons operational. The SASO therefore considered drafting back No. 53 Squadron to No. 16 Group and 'such few Hudsons as we may be able to pick up', that would 'justify losses which in a short period will mean the non-mobilisation of the main anti-shipping Group'.[72] Sir Philip Joubert agreed to No. 16 Group's proposals, and by July low-level strikes on merchant shipping were discontinued in favour of medium-height attacks. He had rated the strikes in the Hook–Elbe area to be the most important in May, with the four squadrons mentioned using aircraft numbers ranging from two to twenty-nine in a strike.[73]

A naval lieutenant who operated with No. 320 (Dutch) Squadron from Bircham Newton wrote:

Here we started immediately flying operationally making low-level strikes (mast height) at German shipping off the Dutch coast, mostly between Flushing and Den Helder. These strikes were usually at night after a reconnaissance aircraft had reported a convoy. In the meantime crews of 320 and 407 – mostly six crews of each squadron, were standby and took off at once after the report height one had to fly over the convoy, not being able to do any evasive action. During the last stage of the attack run, the observer or second pilot next to the pilot flying the aircraft, calling out speed, height and looking after the bomb doors. The pilot in command dropped the bombs a split second before the attacked ship disappeared under the nose of the aircraft. [sic]

We flew practically every other day and the losses of crews from both squadrons, [320 and 407] in the period April to July 1942 were very high. The Germans split up convoys in two and increased their flak ships. Coastal Command changed tactics and after July we attacked shipping more individually at a height of at least 4,000 feet depending on weather, making a proper bombing run, and using a bomb-sight. Now the Germans didn't use big convoys any more but sent ships in threes or fours, bigger and faster, enabling them to use facilities of Ijmuiden or Den Helder to make harbour.[74]

The procedure described by Lt de Liefde was to be followed to a remarkable degree by the strike wings that formed later. The differences, however, were that after an initial report an outrider would be sent to check the position of the enemy. If at night, a Wellington would be used as a 'pathfinder' to drop flares for the Beaufighter strike aircraft.

Those four squadrons of Hudsons mentioned would not have considered themselves 'élite'; they just became dedicated to their job, and with high morale despite their losses. They became effectively the precursor of the North Coates Strike Wing of Beaufighters. Official records confirm de Liefde's reference to the enemy's reactions. As the SASO at headquarters stated: 'We have forced the Germans to arm their convoys so heavily, even to the extent of every ship, including escort ships, carrying balloons, that I feel the continued low level attack will inevitably mean heavy casualties....'[75] Those strengthened defences that resulted in Coastal Command's losses of over 20 per cent, as Sir Philip stated, 'forced us in July 1942 to discontinue low-level attacks'.[76] The Blenheims from Bomber Command on shipping strikes had suffered even heavier casualties, of 35 per cent.[77]

The positive aspect of these strikes for Britain was that the enemy had needed to employ considerable forces to protect his ships, which, nevertheless, had not only suffered losses but had his supplies between Scandinavia and the German and Netherlands ports seriously disrupted. An estimate of three million tons per annum of iron ore was considered to be shipped to Rotterdam for the industrial Ruhr, with probably two million tons to Emden.[78]

On 19 June 1942 there was a newspaper report from Stockholm, which was repeated in the English press, that Swedish shipowners had protested that Swedish ships were being used to transport iron ore to Rotterdam, while in that traffic only 10 per cent of the ships were German. The Swedes therefore decided that they were no longer prepared to sail to Rotterdam.[79]

Following the decision by Coastal Command to cease low-level attacks on shipping, one of the first medium-height strikes was attempted on 30 July, led by Wg Cdr Brown of No. 407 Squadron, but with No. 59 Squadron and the torpedo unit No. 415. Brown had obviously carefully considered the tactics to be used, and he acted as what was later to be referred to by the strike wings as an 'outrider'. Brown shadowed an enemy convoy and homed in his strike aircraft using his 'SE' or 'IFF'.[80] He released flares to illuminate the target, as also did No. 59

Squadron for the torpedo aircraft to attack. Although this strike was apparently unsuccessful, it exemplified the procedure that was to follow for the strike wings.

One of the first attempts at operating a combined strike force that included surface vessels of the Royal Navy was on 28 August 1942. It was to be based on a sighting report from three Beaufighters. Two of the Beaufighters, however, were shot down by enemy fighters, and the third one returned with a nil report. Coastal Command's squadrons would have included Nos 320 (Dutch), and 407 (RCAF), with Fleet Air Arm aircraft and the Navy's motor torpedo-boats. It had to be cancelled, 'much to everyone's dismay'.[81] This demonstrated once again the need for an initial accurate report on the enemy's position. The two Beaufighters that were shot down probably attempted to 'run for it' and would have been outpaced by the enemy. With a likely attack on their tails, their navigators could have responded to stern attacks with only single machine-guns, out-ranged by the enemy's cannon.

Although the Command's operations off the Norwegian coast were largely concerned with naval units, sixty convoys and independent ships had been sighted in May and June between Trondheim and Kristiansand. Out of thirteen strikes on merchant vessels, ten had been made by Hudsons of Nos 48 and 608 Squadrons.[82]

I had been posted to No. 48 Squadron at the end of May with a number of other aircrew from No. 224 Squadron. It was obvious that this move was to make up for the losses; even the new Commanding Officer lasted only a few months before being seriously wounded in combat with two fighters. My first trip was just one of the standing patrols, Bergen–Haugesund, a flight of only 4 hr 20 min. Sir Philip Joubert stated that No. 18 Group at that time was largely concerned with naval units.

The need to change tactics for attacks on

enemy merchant shipping prompted Sir Philip to consider the formation of a highly specialised strike force, and furthermore, a suitable aircraft had been coming available to Coastal Command as early as March 1941, namely, the Bristol Beaufighter. Although the RAF had bombsights,[83] Sir Philip stated that 'an adequate bombsight was not available'.[84] By 1943 a bombsight for medium heights was available. For daylight attacks against a heavily defended convoy he decided that his strike force should comprise torpedo aircraft of 'good speed and manoeuvrability',[85] and aircraft also of similar speed and endurance, but armed to give covering fire for the torpedo aircraft against anti-aircraft fire. This section of the force was to be trained and briefed together so that their operations were synchronised in attacks.

They would need to fly fast enough to operate with single-seater fighters from Fighter Command that would serve to give 'top cover' against enemy fighters.[86] Such forces did come into being, such as I was to see at RAF Langham, North Coates and Dallachy in the period November 1944 to May 1945.

As torpedoes were very costly, and effectively 'rationed', with priority given to the Navy, one may question their value compared with the rocket projectiles that were to become available. There appeared little advantage in using a torpedo against a ship of low tonnage when it could be more easily sunk with other weapons. Furthermore, torpedo attacks were very much more vulnerable, with the need to fly low, at limited speed and with great accuracy.

As I witnessed some of the outcome of a disastrous strike by the Dallachy Wing, I question the value of the effort involved requiring three strike squadrons plus a squadron of single-engined fighters plus the outrider and ASR aircraft. Perhaps all that effort could be justified against a large convoy off the Dutch coast, but not such as was to apply for strikes in Norwegian fjords, where a

multitude of aircraft might be surrounded by cliffs, anti-aircraft batteries, and modern single-engined fighters in opposition. Such a force, in fact, was used against just one enemy destroyer in February 1945.[87]

Sir Philip appreciated that differences in speed between strike aircraft and those aircraft in support to counter anti-aircraft fire or fighter cover precluded effective use of the strike machines. When, therefore, Hampdens were coming into service in late summer 1942, to serve as torpedo-bombers, and therefore with limited targets, he considered different tactics. They were for only three or four Hampdens to operate at low altitude to avoid detection, either visually or by radar; if in daylight, for cloud cover to be available at say 1,000 ft, because convoys along the Norwegian coast were less well defended that area should be the preferred one for such operations.[88] The results gained by the Hampden squadrons in the last three months of 1942 justified Sir Philip's decision

In that period the Hampdens sank five ships off the Norwegian coast and damaged one other. Four were sunk by the New Zealand squadron, No. 489, and one by No. 144 Squadron.[89] To ensure that the Hampden units did not suffer from low morale through lack of action, they were allocated fringe targets and mine laying. The hardest task for aircrew was always to be just on 'standby'; particularly when there was limited literature to read.

While Nos 18 and 16 Groups contended with anti-shipping operations covering the Norwegian and Netherlands coastlines respectively, No. 19 Group was involved with operations over the Bay of Biscay and the French coastline. In respect of anti-shipping operations this was to prove threefold: the heavy warships that were at Brest up to the middle of February; minor war vessels such as destroyers and E-boats; and the blockade-runners.

During Sir Philip Joubert's tenure as Air

Officer Commanding-in-Chief Coastal Command, two important procedures were adopted. They were a change from low-level bombing attacks on merchant vessels to medium-level bombing.

This had resulted in fewer successes but fewer casualties, or less 'wastage', – loss of aircraft and crews. The second change was the concept of a strike wing with some squadrons devoted to attacks on shipping and operating together.

When Air Marshal John Slessor succeeded Sir Philip in February 1943, his immediate concern was with anti-submarine-warfare in the Battle of the Atlantic. This was because in January and February there had been heavy attacks by U-boats on Allied shipping.[90] Slessor's establishment on 18 February for strike aircraft included five squadrons of Beaufighters, represented by Nos 143 and 236 Squadrons at North Coates, No. 235 at Leuchars, and in the south, No. 404 at Chivenor, and No. 248 Squadron at Predannack. The Australian No. 455 Squadron still had Hampdens at Leuchars but was scheduled to re-equip with Beaufighters.[91] On the enemy's side, by 1943, the German Mercantile Marine had become highly organised, and reached a peak in providing defensive measures against air attacks.

The proportion of escort vessels to merchant ships was greatly increased, such that an enemy convoy might comprise just one merchantman with six escort vessels. Both the merchant vessels and the escorts were heavily armed, and balloons were flown to impede aircraft. Some escorts, known as *Sperrbrechers*, were virtually flak-ships, and the earlier decision by Sir Philip to cease the 'mast-height' attacks was therefore fully justified. It showed, also, that Coastal's offensive was imposing a considerable load on the enemy's resources. For Coastal's aircraft operating off the Dutch coast, there remained the serious hazard of shore batteries. They had been greatly increased on account of Bomber

Command's raids on Germany. At briefings for aircrew operating round the Frisians, intelligence officers would give the warning, 'Don't fly too near the coast.'

The names 'Den Helder' and 'Texel' remain always ominous to me. Although there were also coastal batteries in Norway, such as the '*Siegfried*' installations at Ålesund, there appeared to be a greater prospect of encountering fighter opposition off Norway, as so many aircrew were to suffer. Despite Germany's efficiency in organising its merchant shipping, it depended on Swedish ships for as much as 50 per cent of its transport of iron ore from Norway and Sweden.[92] However, from the Command's record of successes against enemy shipping, few Swedish vessels were sunk.[93]

In January, the Command flew 461 anti-shipping sorties but sank only two ships.[94] These were claimed by the highly experienced Nos 407 and 320 Hudson Squadrons operating off the Dutch coast, and the relatively new No. 455 (RAAF) and 489(RNZAF) Squadrons on a strike off southern Norway. The attacks off the Dutch coast, on 18 January, proved to be the last success out of about fifty-eight claimed by Hudsons in the home theatre since October 1940.

While on shipping strikes, No. 320 of the Royal Netherlands Naval Air Service, but under Coastal Command control, had lost twenty-one Hudsons, which was equivalent to more than a whole squadron, but with no sign of loss of morale. The Dutch had at least one other squadron; many personnel had escaped to Britain, and were able to compensate for casualties.

After the first strike wing operations in November 1942, the wing lost twenty-three aircraft and had been withdrawn from the front line, leaving the work to the Hudsons, and for the Beaufighter crews to undertake further training.[95] The first effective operation by the strike wings was on 18 April, when a well-escorted enemy convoy was attacked off Texel. It had required nine Torbeaus (Beaufighters modified to take torpedoes), covered by six Beaufighter bombers, and six Beaufighters with cannon. They sank one ship and apparently damaged one escort vessel. The merchantman, of only 4,906 tons, received six torpedo hits.

Sir John Slessor, in his account of this episode, gives emphasis to the success of the use of cannon fire by supporting Beaufighters, which cleared the decks of the ships to counter anti-aircraft fire.[96] That the Torbeaus were then able to launch their torpedoes was no mean achievement. That view, of using cannon to counter anti-aircraft fire, was later to be endorsed by some aircrew. Nonetheless, using torpedoes against a non-armoured vessel of low tonnage was a costly way of sinking a ship. The strike with such a strong force did, however, give that wing the opportunity of gaining further experience of operating together and losing no aircraft or aircrew. This first strike by the North Coates Wing in 1943 was against a convoy of nine merchant vessels with six escorts.

The Beaufighters had been provided with a fighter escort of three squadrons from No. 12 Group, as it was considered that 'a very strong single-engined fighter escort was essential to the safety of attacking aircraft'.[97] It was also considered that the minimum economical force was eight Torbeaus, with sixteen Beaufighters, and two squadrons of single-engined fighters as escort.[98] The North Coates Wing followed its initial success eleven days later on 29 April, sinking two merchant vessels and an escort for the loss of one Beaufighter.[99]

In May, the Canadian No. 415 Squadron operated Hampdens off both the Dutch and French coasts, sinking a minesweeper and a naval auxiliary vessel. No. 415 was really the Cinderella squadron within the Cinderella Command, being equipped with whatever aircraft came its way: they included

Hampdens, Albacores and Wellingtons.

Although the new tactics of bombing from medium height rather than mast height still prevailed, torpedoes had to be released from low level, and No. 415's operational records show that altitudes of 60–80 ft were flown for the release of torpedoes against heavily armed ships at a distance as short as 600 yd (which may be compared with the Navy's release of torpedoes during the Channel Dash at 3,000 yd). In 1943, No. 415's Hampdens in No. 16 Group sank four ships, but with serious losses of aircraft and crews.[100]

The record of successes for No. 16 Group during the last six months of 1943 shows a decreasing number of ships sunk, the last one being on 23 November, when a 6,316-ton merchant vessel was attacked off Texel.[101] This apparent lack of success in the number of sinkings in fact represented a success for Coastal Command's offensive off the Dutch coast. It had resulted in the enemy diverting his shipping from Rotterdam to the German ports of Emden and Bremen. This was of considerable importance to the enemy, as Rotterdam was the natural gateway to the industrial Ruhr for notably the iron ore from Scandinavia, and also the exit for the coal and coke required by Sweden. The port facilities at Emden and Bremen were limited compared with those at Rotterdam. Thus an increasing strain was imposed on the enemy's internal transport system.[102]

In giving a brief conclusion to this phase of operations, Captain Roskill states that bad weather and imprecise reconnaissance led to a lack of surprise in making some attacks, and was to result in failures. Operational records of many squadrons confirm the importance of those two factors – bad weather and imprecise reconnaissance; aircrew that had flown on such sorties would likewise endorse that view. Before the Beaufighters were armed with rocket projectiles, they relied on 'four 20 mm cannon and six machine guns ... to strafe enemy ships ahead of the Beaus with their torpedoes as they went in at low altitude to drop their fish'.[103]

By August 1943 rocket projectiles were coming into operation with No. 404 (RCAF) Squadron Beaufighters. As one of their pilots recalls:

They were armed with armour-piercing heads and could pass straight through a ship. They were harmonised so that a pair of rockets arrived with a spread of 20 ft between each pair. When entering the water they levelled out and thereby struck the ship underwater. Aiming was relatively easy; we fired them when we reached a point in our twenty-degree dive from 1,200 ft where our cannon and machine guns harmonised. This could be determined by the splashes in the water. Early in our dive the splashes were all around the ship. As we got closer, the splashes converged until they all met at 700 ft, the point of harmonisation, and when we fired the rockets, they would automatically straddle the ship. Only if our aim of the cannon and machine guns was off or the aircraft was skidding, were we likely to miss. So in our own right we did damage to ships and we still cleared the way for the torpedo-carrying Beaufighters to sneak under. We found that our strafing efforts almost silenced anti-aircraft fire altogether.[104]

The following account of an actual operation in November shows clearly the advantages and disadvantages experienced by strike aircraft on Norwegian operations:

We were five Beaus armed with rockets, a small enough formation to enter a fjord ... we ran into five ships steaming in line ahead into the fjord,

two merchant vessels escorted by two armed trawlers and a destroyer in the rear. I attacked the leading M.V. with cannon and then firing my SAP rockets at 600 yd range. Since I had done a beam attack I now had to turn to port sharply to avoid the steep sides of the fjord and then the second M.V. was dead ahead. I sprayed it with cannon fire and then headed towards the open sea, only to pass over the destroyer to exit the fjord. I was quite low and saw all his guns blazing and wondered how he missed me.[105]

Thus it was advisable under some conditions to have a small strike force, certainly to operate in a fjord, although strike aircrew, even off the Dutch coast, would tend to watch what was happening to other crews, and if in formation, there was the real hazard of collisions in the heat of a battle, and full attention to individual attacks could not be given. The sides of a fjord posed a severe restriction, and if vessels were anchored under the cliffs, beam attacks could not be safely attempted thus, with the prospect of running the gauntlet from both a line of ships and batteries in the fjords.

This same squadron, No. 404 (RCAF), was to become acutely aware of these factors during its disastrous raid in 1945.[106] Aircrew on shipping strikes to Norway favoured the Obrestadt area, where the enemy's ships had to sail in open sea and thus lacked the protection of the many small islands round Norway's irregular coast. The Beaufighter squadrons found that they 'could use RPs as main weapons and this facilitated the use of small formations. A semi-armour-piercing RP could rip as many as three plates out of a ship's hull and the 60 lb high-explosive heads were equivalent to a 6 in shell.'[107]

For the period January to May 1943, 5,151 anti-shipping sorties were flown by the RAF

Commands, resulting in 572 attacks. Twenty-two ships were sunk for the loss of ninety aircraft; thus, four aircraft were lost for every ship sunk.[108] No. 18 Group controlled the aircraft covering the northern areas, which for anti-shipping sorties were largely off the southern coast of Norway. For that purpose, Slessor had intended deploying one squadron of Torbeaus and one anti-flak squadron of Beaufighters at Wick, with a similar force at Leuchars. One Torbeau squadron was to be based at Tain, which was to be considered to be in reserve for either Iceland or Russia against a possible breakout by the *Kriegsmarine*'s heavy warships.

To organise a strike wing for operations off Norway was much more difficult than one for sorties to the Dutch coast. This was because the distances were greater and there were no long-range fighters available in 1943 for Coastal Command to serve as escorts. Owing to the requirements in the Middle East, it had not been possible initially to convert the Hampden squadrons to Beaufighters, and Hampdens were less able to defend themselves against enemy fighters and anti-aircraft fire from ships.

Air Marshal Slessor was therefore unable to form a second strike wing in Scotland as he had intended. For the first five months of 1943, anti-shipping sorties to Norway were therefore flown by Hampdens of Nos 455, 489 and 144 Squadrons. They operated in flights of three to five, such as Sir Philip Joubert had earlier anticipated. They would have expected to operate at night if there was sufficient moonlight, and in the day, when they would have to depend on cloud cover to avoid enemy fighters.

Unfortunately, forecasts giving cloud cover were not always accurate. To avoid detection by R/DF stations or radar, approaches to the Norwegian coast were made at low level; some aircraft did, in fact, skim the waves and rocks.[109]

Near the end of 1943, No. 16 Group had suggested to Headquarters that Wellingtons might be used in conjunction with Beaufighters for shipping strikes off the Dutch coast. It would be for a Wellington aircraft equipped with ASV to locate the enemy, illuminate with flares and release a 4,000 lb bomb in the middle of the convoy to distract the flak gunners during the approach of the torpedo aircraft.

This, however, would need careful timing and might result in damage to Coastal Command's own aircraft. The armament officer advocated a 500 lb GP bomb, rather than 4,000 lb, with a Mark XIV fuse, that is, one that would have detonated in the air at 100 ft altitude. The SASO considered this a 'wildcat scheme' and was at that time thinking of No. 415 (RCAF) Squadron's Wellington Flight that was intended for anti-E-boat operations.[110] In fact, the proposal was to be followed to some extent with Wellingtons being used to provide a rendezvous for strike wings during the day with sea markers, or flares during the night. Although the 4,000 lb, or even the 500 lb, bomb was not used in the manner suggested, 250 lb MC (medium-case) bombs came to be used in 1944 by Wellingtons operating individually but against E-boats.

Sir Sholto Douglas succeeded Sir John Slessor as Air Officer-in-Chief Coastal Command in January 1944. By then, although the German U-boat menace was not over, the Battle of the Atlantic had been won. Sir Sholto, therefore, was able to give more attention to anti-shipping operations, for which he was gaining increasing resources, despite the requirements of forces in the Middle East and Far East. Not only was he receiving more aircraft, notably Beaufighters, but also improved radar, such as the Mark III that had scanners and was more sensitive.

In April, Sir Sholto had to consider and prepare for Operations Neptune and Overlord, the Allied invasion of Europe through the Normandy beaches. For Coastal

Command's role in the invasion of Europe, Sir Sholto issued a directive on 18 April that proved to be a masterly plan in which no possible aspect was overlooked. In particular, all squadrons knew precisely what was expected of them to the smallest detail. Both the Allies and the enemy were in early 1944 using their forces with some reserve in anticipation of an all-out effort that was to follow. Although the Battle of the Atlantic had been won, there were still enough U-boats to pose a serious threat to invasion forces. Coastal Command's role thus comprised two main tasks: they were anti-submarine warfare and anti-shipping operations.[111]

The Command in 1944 demonstrated just how flexible it could be in deploying its squadrons in respect of both task and location. Thus squadrons and wings were moved north and south according to the conditions that prevailed on the Continent, and squadrons that had been on anti-submarine warfare proved their worth in anti-shipping operations. Coastal Command enjoyed close cooperation with both Fighter Command and the Royal Navy; while some of Bomber Command's attacks on enemy-controlled ports aided Coastal Command's anti-shipping operations.

At the beginning of 1944, the Command had to consider the enemy-controlled coastline from the Spanish border up to, typically for shipping strikes, Kristiansund. Following the Allies' invasion of Europe, however, there was a progressive move northwards to operations off Norway and into the Skagerrak, Kattegat and the Baltic Sea, due to the increasing enemy activity in those areas.

These latter operations meant that, yet again, the Command needed aircraft of a suitable type but also with increased range; and additionally, fighter escorts of sufficient range. This was to remain a problem for Sholto Douglas throughout his tenure. Although the strike wings in 1944 were formed largely with Beaufighters, towards the end of the year they were being increasingly displaced by Mosquitoes. Wellingtons were used for operations against E-boats but additionally acted as pathfinders for the strike wings. Some Albacores were used in the Dover Straits also against minor naval units such as the E-boats. Towards the end of 1944 Halifaxes, which had been deployed on anti-submarine operations, were found to be effective in anti-shipping operations in the Kattegat and Skagerrak areas due to their long range and useful bomb load.

There was always the need to provide fighter protection of the strike wings, and Fighter Command showed that it was prepared to cooperate by providing Spitfires on the shorter routes to the Dutch coast, and Mustang escorts for the longer northerly strikes, when its other commitments allowed.

The principle of the strike wings had stemmed from the need to saturate the enemy's defences of his convoys, while attacking aircraft could launch torpedo or rocket projectile attacks. This was achieved by having at least two squadrons, but possibly three or four. One of these would be armed with torpedoes (the Torbeaus), while the other squadrons would be armed with cannon and machine-guns to counter anti-aircraft fire. It was considered that the force should comprise nine to twelve Torbeaus, with fifteen to eighteen Beaufighters with cannon, and a ratio of three cannon aircraft to one in attacks on escort vessels. For the Torbeaus to attack successfully, the target needed to be in open water of suitable depth, and that requirement imposed limits, effectively excluding much of the Norwegian coastline due to the leads, but also off the Dutch coast due to the depth of the water. If daylight attacks were made, a fighter escort was necessary, unless there was suitable cloud cover.[112]

Due to Coastal Command's shipping offensive, the enemy directed his ships from using Rotterdam to Emden and Bremen. There were therefore few targets for the North Coates Wing, although some enemy shipping continued to sail the Ems–Hook of Holland route, and this was used mostly at night.

During the day, enemy convoys sheltered in such ports as Den Helder, which was well protected by anti-aircraft batteries. Thus, at the beginning of 1944 there was a need for the Command to develop a system for night attacks and to obtain fighter cover for strike wing operations over the Ems–Elbe route for enemy shipping. There remained the need to attack enemy shipping in the protected harbours also. For these two latter requirements, Coastal Command looked to Fighter and Bomber Commands respectively for their cooperation, and as was to be demonstrated, not in vain, as both those Commands were prepared to allocate forces for that purpose.[113]

A memo dated 24 February from No. 16 Group to the Senior Air Staff Officer (SASO) at Headquarters suggested that No. 2 Group might attack Den Helder's shipping anchorage.

The specific problem for No. 16 Group at that time was that, when a convoy was sighted off the Dutch coast by the reconnaissance aircraft, the convoy was either stopped or went into Den Helder to avoid strike aircraft, which could not be laid on without a delay of three and a half hours. There was time, therefore, for an enemy convoy in Den Helder either to go north, out of the range of the wing's Spitfire escort, or to sail south in shallow water where torpedoes could not be used. The AOC on No. 16 Group ultimately contacted the AOC No. 2 Group, with the latter readily agreeing to attack Den Helder whenever free.[114]

The close cooperation with Fighter Command stemmed from the SASO, AVM Durston, who had earlier contacted AM Roderick Hill at HQ ADGB, and later had talks with the AOC No. 16 Group, AVM

44. Beaufighter at Davidstow Moor armed with rocket projectiles in addition to cannon. In the foreground is a 'trolly ac' used to start aircraft engines to save using the aircraft's batteries.

45. An attack of the French coast on a *Sperrbrecher* by nos 236 and 404 Squadrons on 12 August 1944. The splashes in the foreground are probably due to cannon fire.

46. An attack on enemy shipping off the French coast by No 404 Squadron in August 1944; rocket projectiles can be seen fired at the ship.

Hopps. Arrangements had been made for twelve fighter pilots from Coltishall to undertake a General Reconnaissance course at Squires Gate, and this was to be followed by two more courses.

Additionally a No. 16 Group intelligence officer had gone to No. 12 Group to brief both controllers and intelligence officers; there were also visits by No. 16 Group intelligence officers to No. 12 Group's fighter bases at Coltishall and Digby.[115]

Arrangements had been made, also, for 45-gallon drop tanks to increase the range of Fighter Command's Spitfires that would be operating in support of Coastal's strike wings.[116]

By 3 February 1944 the North Coates Wing comprised three squadrons, following reinforcement, with No. 143 joining Nos 254 and 236 Squadrons. Indicative of the effort for sinking just one minor naval craft (a 90-ton R-boat) was the use of the whole wing on 21 February using torpedoes and cannon, and losing one Beaufighter in a strike off Texel. Again, on 1 March, the whole wing was involved. The strike force had included three Beaufighters with 25 lb rocket projectiles, nine cannon Beaufighters, three Torbeaus, eighteen anti-flak Beaufighters and a Spitfire escort.

Despite using their considerable armament, they only damaged a 6,415-ton merchant vessel, which was later sunk by a single Wellington from No. 415 Squadron that released three 500 lb bombs from 3,500 ft to gain a direct hit. This was no mean achievement, as the bombing was done by moonlight.[117]

Following the enemy's increasing caution in sailing convoys, there were fewer opportunities for daylight attacks, which resulted in Coastal Command using a night-time procedure, the 'Gilbey' operation. For this a lone Wellington flew on night patrols over the enemy's convoy route using radar. On gaining contact, either with radar or visually, a report would be transmitted to base.

Meanwhile a strike force of Beaufighters armed with torpedoes or rocket projectiles would have been sent to patrol a line to seawards of the Wellington's patrol. Alternatively, the strike force would take off immediately the sighting report was received.

In the former case, the Wellington would release a 'Drem' circle of sea markers ten miles from the convoy at 60 degrees to the enemy's seaward bow, to serve as a rendezvous point for the Beaufighters, which would contact the Wellington as they arrived. When sufficient numbers had reported, the Wellington would close the convoy and illuminate the ships by releasing flares for the Beaufighters to attack.[118]

This was truly a dangerous occupation for the Wellington crew, and meant considerable work under hostile conditions. They nevertheless rated the Beaufighters' task more hazardous, while the Beaufighter crews gave that credit to the Wellingtons.[119] An actual example of this procedure occurred on 3 March when a Wellington of No. 415 Squadron was airborne from North Coates armed with thirty-six flares. On locating an enemy merchant vessel escorted by three minelayers, the Wellington signalled base. When all the aircraft from No. 254 Squadron reported contact, the Wellington released twenty-four flares, despite suffering light and heavy flak. The attack resulted in the sinking of a Swedish vessel of 1,878 tons off Borkum.[120]

On 29 March two German merchant vessels were sunk by No. 16 Group's strike wing off the island of Juist, that is, near the Elbe estuary, in daylight. This was important, as it showed the enemy that Coastal Command threatened his Ems–Elbe route. This strike, however, had only been possible due to fighter cover provided by two squadrons of Mustangs, which had the necessary range but were not always available due to other commitments. Only one Beaufighter was lost.[121]

What should have been a major anti-shipping success on the night of 30/31 March resulted only in damage to a 13,882-ton liner. It was thought to be returning technicians to Germany who had been working on the battleship *Tirpitz*.

Although a considerable strike force was used, it was only partly successful due to the fact that the torpedoes used had been set too deep, and they passed right under the vessel. Of the enemy fighter opposition in that attack, one of the Beaufighter pilots aptly commented: 'We never had time to experience fear, we were too busy.'[122]

The Command must have learnt a lesson from this, as in April one of the strike squadrons involved in this attack, No. 404, was given training in the use of 500 lb medium-case bombs, although, as one of the Beaufighter pilots stated, 'we had no bombsight'.[123] Even if a suitable bombsight had been available for Beaufighters, their navigators were already overloaded with radio and a rear gun, in addition to their essential navigation equipment. Earlier, squadrons such as No. 407 and No. 415 had shown just how effective bombs could be against shipping, even from medium heights, and in November 1944 Bomber Command demonstrated just how effective bombing could be even against a heavily armoured battleship such as the *Tirpitz*, albeit using 12,000 lb bombs.[124]

During Overlord, anti-shipping operations for No. 18 Group had lapsed, but in September they opened again with sweeps between Ålesund and Kristiansand, claiming in that month eight ships sunk and two damaged, all off the Norwegian coast. By then two of the squadrons involved, Nos 235 and 248, had re-equipped with Mosquitoes.[125]

As had occurred in the Dutch operations, so also on the Norwegian coast. The enemy ships sheltered in anchorages during the day, and sailed by night in an attempt to avoid attacks from the air. This meant that the strike squadrons needed to fly the 200 miles from Scottish bases to arrive off the Norwegian coast by first light, before the enemy ships had gained cover.

The tactics that had been developed by No. 16 Group were applied by No. 18 Group using the 'Drem' and 'Gilbey' procedures. Intensive shipping operations had begun on 9 September with strike aircraft on sorties from Banff. This work was obviously considered of considerable importance as the squadrons were visited by the AOC No. 18 Group and the AOC-in-Chief of the Command, Sir Sholto Douglas.

The initial armed reconnaissance from Stavanger southwards to Kristiansand was abandoned due to heavy rain and low cloud; the weather for Coastal Command's aircrew was always the worst enemy. The degree of effort against relatively few ships is questionable. Thus on 14 September forty-three aircraft patrolled from Egero to Kristiansund. Of note was the sighting of a convoy of Swedish ships, which was not attacked, as they were all taken to be wholly neutral.[126] Later, an enemy convoy of three merchant vessels with three escorts was attacked, but only one escort was sunk and one merchantman damaged.[127]

Following a Coastal Command letter dated 16 October, it was suggested by No. 18 Group that Nos 455, 489, 494, 404 and 144 Strike Squadrons should move to Dallachy, with a detachment of four aircraft from No. 524 Squadron. At Banff, there should be Nos 235, 248, 143 and 333 Squadrons. The reason for the latter deployment was that for the Mosquito aircraft, which were constructed of plywood, there was the protection of 'blister' hangars.[128] There were the possible additional advantages of ease of maintenance by having similar aircraft at the same base, and with aircraft of similar performance during take-off for sorties.

The need for increasing the range of the Tsetse Mosquitoes (Mosquitoes armed with 6-pounder cannon) and those armed with rocket projectiles was also raised at a Headquarters conference. The matter was to be taken up with de Havilland, the manufacturers, with factors considered being drop tanks (to increase the range) and the rails for rocket projectiles, which might affect the aircraft's aerodynamics.[129]

One of No. 404's pilots had already mentioned the lack of a bombsight in Beaufighters, and this point was also raised by the AOC No. 18 Group with the suggestion that half a squadron might be withdrawn from operations at a time to train on the Mark XIV bombsight.[130]

With the European war in late 1944 directed increasingly to the northern areas, for anti-shipping operations, there was a need to cover the Kattegat and Skagerrak areas.[131]

The two Halifax squadrons based at Stornoway had the range to reach landfall at Kristiansand at the entrance to the Skagerrak, with still another 350 nautical miles' range available for an anti-shipping patrol.[132] Their first success was claimed by No. 502 Squadron on the night of 12/13 October when a German merchant vessel of 8,000 tons was damaged.[133] From then on until the end of 1944, those Halifax squadrons sank four more ships and damaged five others. The efforts of those Halifax aircraft were more than justified by the results.

They were in sharp contrast to the operations of the strike wings that were using so many aircraft against relatively small targets and with limited success.[134] Although the Scottish bases were within No. 18 Group, and Langham under No. 16 Group's control, the Command was flexible in deploying the anti-shipping forces, as I was to appreciate the following year when sent on detachment to Dallachy from Langham. When there was an awareness of much enemy shipping in the Stadtlandet area, No. 18 Group sent a letter on 9 December to Headquarters suggesting that more attention should be given to the Stadtlandet–Kristiansund section of the Norwegian west coast.

It was added that Sumburgh in the Shetlands would need to be used due to the greater distance to Kristiansund from the mainland. Sumburgh, however, experienced weather that could change very rapidly with strong winds. Nevertheless, a detachment of fifteen to twenty Beaufighters from Dallachy was suggested.

During the latter part of 1944, anti-shipping operations were concentrated in the north under No. 18 Group, due to the enemy depending increasingly on Norway. Sir Sholto's strategy was not only to destroy the enemy's ships, but also to disrupt his supply lines. This was achieved by Sir Sholto extending his operations over as wide an area as possible. Four hundred miles of the Norwegian coastline was in range of the Beaufighters from Kristiansund in the north to Kristiansand in the south.

For the northern section of this coastline, Rover patrols of six or nine Beaufighters with rocket projectiles and six or nine Beaufighters with cannon were laid on. These forces were employed where the enemy's ships could take cover in the leads.

In the more southern section of the coast, where the ships were in open water, the strike wings could be used but preceded by outriders that would report the position of the enemy they had located.[135]

For these northerly operations, the Command was successfully using as many as ten squadrons, including those of the Halifaxes that were covering the Kattegat and Skagerrak areas. The tactics adopted by the Halifax aircraft were to undertake a radar search at 100–200 ft altitudes, but for attacks to climb to 4,000 ft, and using a Mark XIV bombsight release 500 lb medium-case bombs with a short-delay fuse. By operating at night, Halifax casualties were reduced, and losses then were largely due to night-fighters.

Traffic of merchant shipping had been considerably reduced off the Dutch coast, and the two Wellington squadrons based at Langham were largely devoted to anti-E-boat operations, but from time to time providing support for the strike squadrons, at both North Coates and Dallachy.

During the whole of 1944, aircraft controlled by Coastal Command were credited with sinking 170 ships totalling 183,192 tons, and damaging another thirty-nine ships. Most of those sunk were off the Norwegian coast. These successes had been at the cost of 165 aircraft lost.[136] Thus the ratio had been reduced to less than one aircraft lost for one ship sunk.

In the last four to five months of the war in Europe, Coastal Command's anti-shipping operations were directed towards two main areas. They were off the Dutch coast, typically from the Scheldt to the Frisian Islands, and in the north, off the Norwegian coast from Kristiansund down to Kristiansand. The Scheldt was an Allied supply route, while Norway was becoming an escape route for the enemy.

With the Halifax squadrons, and also long-range Mustang fighters becoming available to provide cover for the strike wings, operations in the north were extending more and more eastwards to cover the Kattegat and the Baltic Sea. This latter aspect became increasingly important as the enemy attempted to return troops from Norway to Germany via ships from Oslo to Denmark. In the southern North Sea, the E-boat menace remained, and additionally the enemy's use of midget submarines, *Seehund* and *Biber*.

There were developments in Coastal Command's anti-shipping forces, with more squadrons converting from Beaufighters to Mosquitoes, and improved marks of Halifaxes and Wellingtons going to squadrons. Development and trials of weapons and equipment, including rocket projectiles,

bombs, bombsights and cannon, continued. A limiting factor in this respect was the number of man-hours required to achieve some modifications to aircraft after they had left the factories. Sir Sholto's keenness in endeavouring to equip his squadrons with the latest marks of radar, notably with Mark IIIs or later, was to prove its worth.

This was because with such apparatus it was possible to cooperate with the Navy's surface vessels in giving direct bearings of the enemy to them. Earlier, some anti-submarine squadrons had been taken off that task to undertake anti-shipping operations; near the end of hostilities, there was a need to revert to the task of ASW, certainly towards the *Seehunds*. In the winter of 1944/5 much attention was given by Coastal Command to the anti-shipping operations off Norway and in the Kattegat.[137] Bases being used for Norwegian operations were Dallachy, Banff, Peterhead and Frazerburgh.

There was a strike wing of Beaufighters at Dallachy, one with Mosquitoes at Banff, and at Peterhead and Frazerburgh there were support squadrons of Mustang fighters and air-sea rescue aircraft respectively.

There had been heavy falls of snow along the east coast of both Scotland and England, and at Dallachy 160 officers and men from No. 404 Squadron worked in shifts to clear the runway.

Despite hail, snow and high winds, a strike by twenty-one aircraft on 8 January sank two ships off Norway. On 1 February I was one of a number of aircrew from No. 524 Squadron at Langham sent on detachment to Dallachy to cooperate with the Beaufighter squadrons. On 9 February while on the airfield near our Wellington, I witnessed the return of the strike wing's survivors from attacks on shipping in Førde fjord. About a dozen Beaufighters flopped down like a flock of wounded ducks, and later, in the mess, I saw some of the crews with their battledress battle scarred. It all appeared so much like a Hollywood film, but this was not fiction. One of the survivors gave me this account:

We crossed the coast south of the fjord with orders to await the report of the two outriders. They … reported [wrongly], no targets in the expected anchorages. The basic plan of the strike wing was to commence the attack from the land to seaward, but as the main force proceeded over Førde fjord there was flak from the ships and shore batteries opened fire. This resulted in a change of plans. The main force had to make a large 'S' turn to position for the attack. This prolonged manoeuvre between the steep sides of the fjord, the extra time required to organise into position, gave the German fighters from Bergen sufficient time to join the affray.[138]

47. Førde fjord, 61°29'N 05°39'E on 9 February 1945 when the Dallachy Strike Wing lost a number of aircraft, including six out of eleven from No 404 Squadron. An enemy ship is in the foreground close to the shore.

48. The memorial to aircrew who were lost from the Dallachy Wing which is located at the site of the main gate of the former RAF base. It includes rocks from Australia, Canada, New Zealand and Ireland and was unveiled on 30 July 1992.

The original plan to attack from inland towards the sea would have meant no change in direction after the attack, and they could have escaped directly. The large number of aircraft in the strike was an obvious disadvantage in the confines of a fjord, and invariably, aircrew would be watching not only for the enemy, but also for what was happening to others in their flight, and it was not unknown for friendly aircraft to collide. The desirability of using a small number of aircraft on such occasions was touched upon by Sir Philip Joubert in 1942.[139]

My correspondent, Flt Lt Flynn, who was in this strike, blamed the outriders for failing to report. The official Australian historian blames none, but states that the leader, Milson, cancelled the original plan 'because of the position of larger targets'.[140]

That was the crux of the matter; the 'larger targets', which in this case included a Narvik destroyer anchored near the cliffs of the fjord, thus presented a very difficult target due to that position. The Australian version states that the destroyer and two naval auxiliary vessels were damaged, but they do not appear in Coastal Command's official list of successes.[141] Nine Beaufighters were lost in this strike – six to AA fire, and three to enemy fighters.

No. 404 (RCAF) Squadron lost six out of its eleven aircraft that had been deployed; it was their 'Black Friday'. This episode may be compared with a Bomber Command operation at that time, when out of 1,020 sorties, seventeen aircraft (1.7 per cent) were lost, in contrast to No. 404's loss of 54 per cent.[142]

The disastrous strike on 9 February resulted in repercussions at the Command's headquarters, and on 2 March, the senior Air Staff Officer, AVM Ellwood, wrote to the Air Officer Commanding No. 16 Group, AVM F.L. Hopps, remarking that 'Simpson gave priority to the enemy destroyer', and suggested that tankers were more important. He wrote also to AVM S.P. Simpson at No. 18 Group HQ concerning the 'recent rather expensive Beaufighter strike against the destroyer some 10 days or a fortnight ago'.[143] The Admiralty wrote to Sir Sholto Douglas, giving a revised priority list for shipping strikes, which was modified from what had previously applied.

Surfaced U-boats came first, tankers third, and vessels such as destroyers and other escort vessels sixth.[144] U-boats were a greater threat than destroyers to Allied ships, and without tankers to provide oil they would have been useless. By April 1945, the situation in the north was changing rapidly. Coastal Command's sorties were being extended further eastwards, but at the same time the enemy was able to provide strong cover to his shipping by means of modern single-engined fighters, including Fw190s and Me109s in considerable numbers.

The Command signalled the Air Ministry on 20 April that the enemy's fighters had on two occasions prevented the Command's aircraft from reaching their target areas, and requested that five of the enemy's air bases from Bergen to Kristiansand should be bombed. This request was, however, refused, as the Air Ministry considered that other bases would be used.[145] On 24 April Fighter Command wrote to the DCAS at the Air Ministry, Bomber Command, and Coastal Command, following an Air Ministry proposal to reinforce Mustang fighters at Peterhead.

Fighter Command considered that two squadrons of fighters for Coastal Command was 'definitely below the safe minimum due to deeper strikes into the Skagerrak' and the 'aggressive enemy fighter force in Norway and still in Denmark'. Fighter Command recommended two more Mustang squadrons to support Coastal, leaving twelve squadrons to escort Bomber Command's sorties.[146]

During 1945 No. 18 Group sank sixty-seven ships and damaged thirty-two others; aircraft controlled by No. 16 Group sank thirty-seven vessels, including twenty-three midget submarines, and damaged four more vessels.

It may be said that the additional fighters recommended, and all the total effort at that time, was justified. This was because it was believed that the enemy might well have made a stand in Norway, while further south there was still the need to protect the Allied supply lines to the Continent.

In the first week of May, even the Wellingtons of Nos 524 and 612 Squadrons were operating off the north German coast, at the mouth of the Weser and in Kiel Bay. No. 612 Squadron recorded on 3 May:

> Allied land successes in North-West Europe presage an early end to German resistance. Coastal Command's recces today showed a wholesale evacuation of Nazi forces northwards in the Baltic Sea. In consequence, the squadron tonight assisted in the Command's tremendous offensive against these evacuation ships.[147]

No. 612 Squadron had four Wellingtons operating off the east coast of Denmark, and 'All made attacks and radar operators reported that their screens were covered with contacts.'[148] That Wellingtons, lacking in defensive armament and speed, could operate in an area where earlier even Mosquito fighters were considered to need cover by Mustang fighters, showed how the situation had changed.

The only limiting factor for the Wellingtons at this time would have been the number of bombs carried. In contrast to the Wellington operations of Nos 524 and 612 Squadrons that on 3 and 4 May sank two ships and damaged two others, a strike force on 2 May formed from five squadrons of Beaufighters and Mosquitoes sank only one minesweeper. It was surely questionable whether such large forces were necessary. I was on leave at this time, and when hostilities ceased telephoned No. 524 Squadron's adjutant, asking if I needed to return. 'Yes' was the response. It was thought that the enemy might attempt more hostile action in Norway, and in fact Coastal Command HQ signalled Nos 16 and 18 Groups on 5 May requiring No. 524 Squadron to move from Langham to Wick, with the possibility of cooperating with the Royal Navy's MTBs off the Norwegian coast.[149]

THE BLOCKADE-RUNNERS

The French Biscay ports served Germany not only for its U-boats and surface warships but also for merchant vessels engaged in blockade running. The ships used were of about 6,000 to 10,000 tons, fast, with speeds of about 17 knots, and heavily armed against possible attacks by aircraft. They used the cover of darkness and the Spanish coast and were not easy targets. One route was to and from the Far East, while a comparatively minor second route was from Bilbao along the coast of Spain to Bayonne, taking iron ore. Cargoes from the Far East would include rubber, edible oils and special ores. Return cargoes to the Far East would include machinery and specialised war materials.[150]

Because of the distances involved, about 400 miles, it was difficult for Coastal

Command to devote aircraft specifically to intercept these blockade runners in the Bay of Biscay. It would have been impracticable for the Command to lay on regular patrols to counter them due to the lack of aircraft, and not infrequently it was left for the aircraft on anti-submarine patrols over the Bay to report these ships. During 1942 four of these blockade runners were damaged in attacks by No. 19 Group aircraft, which included a Liberator, a Wellington, a Whitley and Sunderlands.

Because it was only such aircraft as the Sunderland that had the range to reach the Spanish coast, Sir Philip Joubert wrote to the First Sea Lord with the object of obtaining naval cooperation, and on 14 September had a meeting with the Minister of Economic Warfare. Sir Philip suggested that there should be a naval patrol of surface craft or submarines off Finisterre. This was agreed, and submarine patrols were laid on in the area bounded by 44°40'N to the north and the Spanish coast to the south between 05°30'W and 09°00'W.

Coastal Command laid on patrols for reconnaissance rather than strikes, which ought to locate any surface vessel in or approaching the submarine's area during daylight. They were to fulfil Coastal Command Operational Instruction dated 9 October 1942.[151]

When aircraft with insufficient range or endurance were used, an unfair load was placed on the crews. This was exemplified on 1 November 1942 when Hampdens of No. 415 Squadron were required to fly over the Bay of Biscay to attack two enemy merchant vessels that had been reported. On returning to base, one of the Hampdens crashed into a petrol dump and burst into flames.

One of the survivors gave a detailed report stating that it was 'beyond their maximum range deep in the Bay of Biscay' and that the pilot was 'near exhaustion from the strain of flying in formation'.[152] That would have been for many hours at low level and at a low speed to save fuel. This meant that the aircraft controls would be less responsive, making it even more difficult to maintain formation. The survivor's report was enough for the squadron to take seriously, and trials were undertaken to arrive at what could be accepted for that type of aircraft.

Hazards for these lone reconnaissance aircraft were not only the anti-aircraft fire that the blockade runners were able to use, but also the real prospect of being attacked by flights of Ju88s that flew over the Bay to protect the German U-boats. For the aircraft that were used to attempt a reconnaissance of the Spanish coast, they might well have suffered anti-aircraft fire from shore batteries.

At the beginning of 1943 the enemy had a number of destroyers based in French ports, and these were used not only to escort U-boats entering or leaving port, but also in a similar way for blockade runners. In April, despite still being largely concerned with anti-U-boat operations, Air Marshal Slessor wrote to the Vice-Chief of Naval Staff asking for a ruling on the question of priorities. It ultimately resulted in a scheme, 'Sombrero', which required anti-submarine squadrons to be briefed for them to recognise a possible blockade runner.[153]

In my own experience, however, aircrew would invariably report all shipping, and if not escorted by Allied naval vessels, would probably photograph any ship sailing alone. Such a routine procedure, as it was, is evident in many operational records. If there had been intelligence reports of a likely arrival or departure of a blockade runner, crews would have expected to be briefed accordingly.

No. 19 Group covered the Biscay area and the South-Western Approaches, and in 1943 they had available some long-range aircraft, including Halifaxes and Liberators, in addition to those of shorter range,

Wellingtons. Of those aircraft, the Halifaxes had been equipped with medium-altitude bombsights that had been intended for use with a 600 lb 'depth bomb' against U-boats. This bombsight could have been used, however, to attack blockade runners. The Liberators were being armed with both bombs and rocket projectiles, and were effective against ships, in addition to U-boats.[154]

The actual successes achieved by Coastal Command aircraft in 1943 against blockade runners reflect these improvements in the Command's forces. Thus, on 10 April, the 6,240-ton *Himalaya* was damaged by a combined force of Hampdens and Wellingtons; while in August, Halifaxes of No. 502 Squadron sank a German auxiliary in the Bay.

During the summer of 1943 there was a lull in the enemy's blockade running, due no doubt to the lack of night cover. It reopened with the 6,344-ton blockade runner *Pietro Orsedo* being sunk by Nos 248 and 254 Squadrons' Beaufighters on 18 December. A Liberator from No. 311 (Czech) Squadron attacked the 2,729-ton *Alsterufer* on 27 December with rocket projectiles and bombs, setting it on fire.

It had previously been sighted and shadowed by Sunderlands of No. 10 Squadron RAAF, and it was congratulated later by the AOC No. 19 Group, who stated: 'This highly successful operation was largely made possible by consistent accuracy of positions given in sighting reports.'[155]

The combined success of both Coastal Command aircraft and the Navy's ships had resulted not only in the sinking of the blockade runner, but also three enemy destroyers being sunk by HM ships and others damaged. The Admiralty did prove rather lax in this respect, even with regard to giving the positions of the Navy's submarines, seemingly for security reasons, but with potentially serious results, as I was to experience.[156] In the event of an intelligence report of any enemy movements, it was customary to have aircraft on standby, if not a whole squadron, depending on the report given.[157] According to Captain Roskill, it was found 'that interception by surface warships working in close cooperation with the aircraft was the only sure way of bringing the blockade runners finally to book'.[158]

The *Alsterufer* episode, however, had shown that a single aircraft with suitable armament was quite capable of sinking a merchant ship. But certainly there was a bonus at that time for the Navy to engage the enemy destroyers intended as escorts and to sink three of them. The AOC No. 19 Group stressed the essential need for accurate navigation in reporting positions of the enemy, and that credit went to No. 10 Squadron RAAF.

Roskill sums up the three years of Germany's blockade-running in which it lost twenty ships, with fifteen sunk or captured by surface vessels or scuttled, two sunk by its own U-boats, one exploded in harbour, and two sunk by RAF aircraft. That two were sunk by U-boats demonstrated the constant problem at sea, the identification of friend or foe. In the case of the blockade runners, it was even more difficult, as such ships went out of the way to cause confusion, by raising flags of different nationality, altering the name of the ships, and possibly modifying the superstructure.

Twenty-one blockade runners had left France in those three years for the Far East with 69,300 tons of cargo, but only fifteen arrived, with 57,000 tons. From the Far East, thirty-five ships sailed with 257,770 tons of cargo, and sixteen arrived in France with 111,490 tons. Most of Germany's successes in blockade running were achieved before British countermeasures had been properly organised.[159] Here it could be added, 'before Coastal Command had adequate resources'. Roskill continues: 'Only by the use of aircraft and surface ships in close conjunction was it possible to achieve a high proportion of successful interceptions.'[160] For the conditions that prevailed in the Bay of Biscay at that time, and with the forces then available to Coastal Command for that purpose, one must agree with Captain Roskill.

CONCLUSIONS

Coastal Command had no aircraft designed specifically for shipping strikes apart from the Bristol Beaufort, and those were posted to the Middle East. All the others were modified civil aircraft, bombers or fighters.

Armament for attacks was varied in the light of squadron experience, but 250 lb bombs appeared as one of the most useful against merchant shipping, to be followed additionally by rocket projectiles. Torpedoes were seen to be of limited value, particularly within the areas over which Coastal Command was operating.

Tactics were developed at squadron level that commanders at Group or Coastal's Headquarters came to accept. In 1942, however, there was a major change, made at Headquarters, with orders to cease low-level attacks and replace them by attacks at medium level. This was due to serious losses that had been suffered. The result was to reduce losses, but also the successes. Serious losses were nevertheless to be experienced as late as February 1945.

The strike wings that were intended to overwhelm all enemy opposition never achieved that to the full, as the enemy was prepared to use strong air forces to protect his shipping. In addition to sinking ships, the strike wings did, however, tie down much of the enemy's forces. Nevertheless, it is questionable if using four or five squadrons including fighter escorts was justified by the results.

If one accepts the serious losses of aircraft and aircrew, the Command's campaign against enemy-controlled merchant shipping was justified. A total of 876 aircraft were lost on anti-shipping operations of all types, but it is likely that most of those losses were against strongly escorted merchant vessels. If it is reasonable to assume that about three aircrew personnel were casualties for every aircraft lost, this gives casualties of 3,404 aircrew. Bombing Bremen was infinitely safer.

Nevertheless, aircraft under Coastal Command control were credited with sinking 366 enemy vessels, totalling 512,330 tons, and damaging 134 other vessels totalling 513,454 tons.[161] Therefore, not only was over a million tons of shipping put out of action, but other enemy forces, both aircraft and escort vessels, had been required to counter Coastal Command's offensive.

CHAPTER SIX

Anti-Shipping Operations – Warships

HEAVY WARSHIPS

On 4 June 1940 the German battle-cruisers *Scharnhorst* and *Gneisenau* with the heavy cruiser *Admiral Hipper* and four destroyers sailed from Kiel to attack British naval units at Harstad. HMS *Glorious* was sunk, but HMS *Acasta* torpedoed the *Scharnhorst*, which then sailed with *Gneisenau* to Trondheim. This was the prelude to the first major shipping strike by Coastal Command. On 11 June twelve Hudsons from No. 269 Squadron attacked ships in Trondheim harbour and claimed hits on two cruisers. The Hudsons carried only three 250 lb bombs each, and such armament would have been useless against heavily armoured ships such as *Scharnhorst*. They had not only to contend with heavy anti-aircraft fire from the ships but also to suffer attacks by single-engined fighters; it is remarkable that they lost only two aircraft.[1]

That brief description shows how lacking Coastal Command was in both aircraft and armament for an important target. Under the conditions that then prevailed in Trondheim fjord, what should have been used were two squadrons of heavy bombers of high cruising speed, capable of releasing bombs of, say, 4,000 lb rather than 250 lb, and with bombsights to ensure accuracy from medium height or greater; and to counter enemy fighters, two squadrons of long-range fighters such as Mustangs. None of these forces were available to the Command.[2]

49. An artist's impression of the attack on the battle cruiser *Scharnhorst* by Hudsons of Nos 224 and 233 Squadrons on 21 June 1940 off southern Norway. The painting is authentic apart from the enemy fighters being omitted. The attack was led by S/Ldr Feeny who was shot down in flames.

Even towards the end of the war, however, priority was given to other forces for such as the Mustang fighters. The enemy would have been warned by a guard ship at the entrance to the fjord, time enough for their fighters to be ready. The one 'concession' for this strike force was that there was some limited cloud cover.[3]

In June 1940, the Command still had no effective torpedo strike force, but even if such had been available, it is questionable whether it could have made a successful attack after entering a long fjord such as at Trondheim; this was because the key element for such an attack would have been surprise, and that would have been negated by guard ships. They would have lost the advantage of altitude, and would have been 'sitting ducks' for shore batteries.

There were further attacks on *Scharnhorst* by Hudsons from Nos 224, 233 and 269 Squadrons later, when the battle-cruiser was

50. The Catalina of No 209 Squadron which, captained by P/O Dennis Briggs, made the crucial sighting of the battleship *Bismarck* on 26 May 1941.

sailing off Utsire, escorted by destroyers and covered by about fifty enemy fighters. No. 42 Squadron's Beauforts were permitted also to attack, using 500 lb bombs, despite possible trouble with their engines.

Sir Frederick Bowhill accepted these risks, as did the aircrew, because of the importance of the target; it always prevailed in Coastal Command.[4] On 6 April 1941 Flg Off K. Campbell, captain of a Beaufort of No. 22 Squadron, torpedoed the 37,000-ton battle-cruiser *Gneisenau* at Brest. This strike, I submit, was the most important one ever made by Coastal Command aircraft. This was not because the battle-cruiser was put out of action for months, but because the enemy's *Rheinübung*, (Rhine operation) was thwarted to a considerable degree. The *Kriegsmarine* had intended that the *Gneisenau* should sail with the battleship *Bismarck* and the heavy cruiser *Prinz Eugen* on a North Atlantic foray, and that combined force in the Atlantic would have necessitated a very heavy escort for all Allied convoys. On 13 June a combined force of Nos 22 and 42 Squadrons torpedoed the 15,206-ton pocket battleship *Lützow* off south-west Norway, despite heavy anti-aircraft fire and the ship's fighter escort. It was

left to the enemy to acknowledge the courage of the Beaufort crews, who made their attacks with 'superb dash'.[5] The *Lützow* had been damaged by Coastal Command's torpedoes and was out of commission until January 1942.[6] Some officers in Coastal Command may have questioned the desirability of keeping two such squadrons to some extent on standby, waiting for potential targets.

While Germany still had a powerful surface fleet against which the bombs available to Coastal Command were useless, there was surely justification for units specialising in torpedo attacks that could not be learned in a day and that Bomber Command was prepared to accede was a task for Coastal Command.[7]

By November the new battleship *Tirpitz* was at Trondheim, pocket battleships were in the Baltic, while the battle-cruisers *Scharnhorst* and *Gneisenau* with the heavy cruiser *Prinz Eugen* were at Brest.[8]

While the Royal Navy throughout the war had to cover the 'seven seas', the *Kriegsmarine* could devote all its resources against British merchant vessels; its orders were always to concentrate on British trade vessels and if possible avoid major fleet battles.[9] For Coastal Command, not only was it required to provide regular reconnaissance to cover movements of the enemy's warships, but also to have probably at least one squadron on standby in case a strike was required.

Even with the regular reconnaissance squadrons, there was always, in my experience, at least one aircraft with a complete crew on standby, ready to take off at about five minutes' notice, but with nothing positive to do meanwhile, the most unloved task for aircrew.

The aircraft situation for Coastal Command was so stretched at this time that for reconnaissance nine long-range Hudsons were taken from the other squadrons to form a special flight attached to No. 220 Squadron at Wick. By such means they should have been able to cover the Skagerrak and the Norwegian coast as far north as Trondheim, but one would have expected them to operate from Sumburgh in the Shetlands, due to the shorter distance from Norway, or at least to refuel there.

It appears likely that No. 220 was selected for this task, not only because it was at Wick, but because of its experience and obvious aptitude on Norwegian trips. It was to prove to be one of the foremost squadrons in anti-shipping operations.

For a strike force at that time, the situation was no better; after two squadrons had been rearmed with Beaufighters, they were posted overseas. Nevertheless, there was an obvious need for a strike force in the north to cover the Norwegian and Skagerrak areas; similarly in the south, a strike force was required against the three major surface warships at Brest. For the few Beaufort strike aircraft available there was limited ASV. By the end of 1941 Sir Philip had only two Beaufort squadrons up to strength, Nos 42 and 86. I recall meeting some of their aircrew at St Eval at the time of the Channel Dash in February 1942.

Another Beaufort squadron, No. 22, which had proved its worth in the Command, was to be posted overseas.[10] At the beginning of 1942 Coastal Command was required to undertake offensive operations against enemy merchant vessels, the smaller naval units including destroyers and E-boats, and to be prepared to strike against major enemy warships. The latter included the battle-cruisers *Scharnhorst* and *Gneisenau* with the heavy cruiser *Prinz Eugen* at Brest, while at Trondheim was the new battleship *Tirpitz*.[11]

THE CHANNEL DASH

The German battle-cruisers *Scharnhorst* and *Gneisenau* were located by a PRU aircraft at Brest on 28 March 1941, and by June of that year they had been joined by the heavy cruiser *Prinz Eugen*.[12] They posed a serious threat to

Britain's trade routes, and on 29 April 1941 a plan was made by the Admiralty in conjunction with the Air Ministry. It was coded 'Operation Fuller', and the Air Officers-in-Chief of Bomber, Fighter and Coastal Commands were so informed.

The operation was based on the belief that the three warships would sail up the English Channel to German ports, with their departure so timed that they would negotiate the Straits of Dover at night.[13]

No provision was made for the possible alternative of the ships sailing through the Straits in daylight. This aspect was important, as any torpedo attack against such vessels could more safely be attempted under cover of darkness.

The British expected the three warships to be heavily protected by a screen of surface craft, such as destroyers and E-boats, in addition to a fighter aircraft 'umbrella' cover by the *Luftwaffe*. The Admiralty's appreciation was given with remarkable accuracy in this respect.

The only forces that the Admiralty was prepared to deploy against such a powerful fleet, however, were two flotillas of motor torpedo-boats and six destroyers of the 1914–18 era.[14] Bomber Command was expected to provide about 250 aircraft, although ultimately only 100 were to be available.[15]

Fighter Command was required to give cover to torpedo-aircraft of both the Fleet Air Arm and Coastal Command, and to escort Coastal's Hudsons that were to be used to attract the anti-aircraft fire away from the torpedo-bombers. For such cover, Fighter Command had 550 aircraft in the south.[16]

Coastal Command's Hudsons were required also to serve in reconnaissance off the French coast. On 3 February 1942 the Admiralty briefed the Naval staff officers from Bomber, Coastal and Fighter Commands, giving a new appreciation, and the order

'Executive Fuller' was issued to all three Commands. Bomber Command, which had had its aircraft on standby, was by 10 February holding the 100 aircraft at four hours' notice.

Fighter Command was to be responsible for the coordination of fighter cover, effectively under No. 11 Group's control. Coastal Command had only three squadrons of strike aircraft – the torpedo Beauforts of Nos 42, 86 and 217; No. 42 Squadron was, however, at Leuchars to cover against a possible breakout of the battleship *Tirpitz*, which was in Trondheim fjord; No. 86 Squadron was at St Eval, Cornwall, and No. 217 at Thorney Island near Portsmouth. Of Coastal Command's Hudson squadrons the only two to take an active part in Operation Fuller were No. 407 (RCAF) to attract anti-aircraft fire away from torpedo-aircraft and No. 224 to undertake reconnaissance from St Eval.

Sir Philip Joubert, on 8 February, gave his own appreciation to both Bomber and Fighter Commands. He must have based this on the state of the tides, the phases of the moon, and photo-reconnaissance reports. Joubert expected the German fleet to make its dash between 10 and 15 February, and on 11 February photo-reconnaissance showed that *Scharnhorst*, *Gneisenau* and *Prinz Eugen* were out of dock and that there were six destroyers with them.[17]

Patrols by No. 224 Squadron had been laid on to cover the exit of these vessels, but at critical times their radar was obviously jammed, although some official accounts suggest that the radar was faulty. Such might have been the case for one aircraft, but I consider that a powerful jamming signal might well have overloaded the ASV. An air raid on Brest by Bomber Command delayed the German fleet's departure, but the ships sailed at 2245 hrs on 11 February. The Royal Navy's provision to be aware of the breakout of the enemy's ships was to have an agent at Brest to give immediate intelligence by radio.

Additionally, a submarine, HMS *Sealion*, was deployed off Brest. Because of German thoroughness, the agent was unable to pass a sentry to send a radio signal. At a crucial time, also, HMS *Sealion* withdrew to charge its batteries.

Thus the first two lines for intelligence were lost. One might ask, 'Why only one submarine?' Would it not have been prudent to have at least a second one as standby, and bearing in mind the nature of three prime targets for torpedoes from submarines, why not have a line of such craft, such as Germany appeared always ready to deploy? If it was said that it was too dangerous, surely it was no more so than a U-boat entering Scapa Flow? A standby submarine might then have justified the Navy not being prepared to use its own capital ships against a powerful enemy.

Detection of the breakout was now dependent not only on Coastal Command's Hudsons but also on Fighter Command's Spitfires, which made patrols across the Channel, and likewise, the Swordfish sorties of the Fleet Air Arm across the Straits of Dover. Additionally, however, Fighter Command had stations to detect aircraft, and there were shore batteries with radar to detect shipping. Fighter Command did in fact gain plots of the enemy's fighter umbrella at 0845 hrs on 12 February, and its aircraft did sight the enemy's battle-cruisers and heavy cruiser at 1040 hrs. Only belated action was taken, however.

Positive actions were taken by both the Fleet Air Arm and Coastal Command. Lt Cdr Esmonde led six Swordfish torpedo-aircraft with some fighter escort against the ships, but all six Swordfish were shot down; Esmonde was awarded a posthumous VC. Out of Coastal's thirty-six strike aircraft, fourteen were at Leuchars, and they flew south via Coltishall and attempted operations in conjunction with No. 407 Squadron's Hudsons, but owing to very low visibility, given in yards, contact was lost. The Hudsons, led by Sqn Ldr Anderson and Flg Off Cowperthwaite, were well aware that they were on a sacrificial mission, with 250 lb bombs that were completely useless against heavily armoured warships, but nevertheless it was believed that they reached the *Prinz Eugen*. Both were shot down.[18] From No. 217 Squadron Plt Off Carson led Beauforts that attacked the battle-cruisers from as close as 1,000 yards with torpedoes, and they were followed by two more No. 217 Squadron Beauforts, but none of the results were seen.

The weather was given as 8/10ths to 10/10ths cloud, with base as low as 400 ft, and there were rain showers.[19] Therefore flying conditions could hardly have been worse. British coastal batteries had been nullified through the enemy's very effective jamming of radar, such as was suffered by No. 224 Squadron's Hudsons.

Of the Navy's meagre forces that were deployed, four motor torpedo-boats from Dover released torpedoes from outside the enemy's screen, thus at long range and presumably at no recognised target. The motor torpedo-boats from Ramsgate returned to port without making any attack. The six destroyers from Harwich of the 1914–18 era were able to release some torpedoes, but all were avoided by the enemy.[20] The briefing of those destroyers was such that according to the Navy's own intelligence report, they had sailed not knowing what armament they were expected to use.[21]

Bomber Command could not hope to do any damage to heavily armoured ships, because to penetrate the decks with armour-piercing bombs they would need to release them from, say, 7,000 ft or more altitude, and with cloud base as low as 400 ft that was out of the question. Furthermore, they were not trained in attacking a target such as a heavily armed warship travelling at 27 knots and able to manoeuvre. What other forces should one

have expected during the period of the afternoon of 12 February to the morning of 13 February, in the wide area of the northern North Sea? There was surely enough time for the Navy to have at least one capital ship that could outrange the 11 in guns of the German battle-cruisers, as the Royal Navy's battleships had guns of calibre from 14–16 in.[22]

The Navy had been prepared to withdraw cover from convoys to attack *Bismarck*, and had the opportunity well in advance of February 1942 to have at least one battleship available.

The only effective weapons used against the battle-cruisers were mines laid by the RAF. Sir Arthur Harris states that those mines were laid by his Command, but the official history questions that claim.[23]

The Prime Minister, Winston Churchill, was well aware of public opinion, with people shocked that enemy ships could pass British shores unmolested. Furthermore, he needed to be ready to answer questions in Parliament. He therefore ordered, as he stated: 'To allay complaints an official enquiry was held.'[24] This was held by Mr Justice Bucknill, but included service representatives, and I was aware at the time, of aircrew from No. 224 Squadron being required to attend. In respect of Coastal Command's involvement, the enquiry stated that it would have been prudent for an additional reconnaissance following apparent failure of the Command's ASV.

Captain Roskill, in the official naval history, stated: 'The main cause of failure to do more damage to the German ships was that they were at sea for twelve hours, four of them in daylight before they were discovered, and it was undoubtedly the failure of our air patrols, which brought this about.'[25] What of the two naval sources that failed to report the movement of the ships? They should have been the first to inform, namely, the agent at Brest, and HMS *Sealion*. The Navy had made no attempt to fill the gap left by that submarine, as would surely have been 'prudent'. It would not have made the slightest difference if the third line of intelligence, Coastal Command's aircraft, had reported after the other two had failed.

In fact it was an 'air patrol' that gave the first sighting. The naval forces provided to attack the battle-cruisers demonstrated quite obviously that they were incapable of doing any damage, however much time they were allowed. The Admiralty, as Roskill stated, 'realised that a few destroyers, motor torpedo-boats and torpedo-boats were unlikely to do more than inflict some underwater damage'.[26]

Even after passing the Straits of Dover, there would still have been many hours for the Navy to use a battleship against the battle-cruisers, particularly as they had been crippled by mines laid by the RAF. The prime error made by the Admiralty was in its appreciation to make no provision for the enemy's forces traversing the Straits of Dover during daylight, as would have been prudent, in addition to taking for granted that the enemy would use the dark hours. They had thereby nullified the chance of successful torpedo attacks by the meagre light forces in addition to those of the Fleet Air Arm and Coastal Command's torpedo-aircraft.

Dr Goulter states: 'The Command as a whole was acutely embarrassed when it was held primarily responsible for the Channel Dash incident.'[27] She does not, however, give the reason or source for that statement. Goulter states also, that the squadrons at the beginning of 1942 'suffered from low morale'.[28] From 10 February onwards I met aircrew from at least two of the strike squadrons in addition to my own (No. 224); I neither saw nor heard any sign whatever of low morale; rather was it otherwise. Evidence of high, rather than low, morale is to be seen in the operational records.[29]

Sir Arthur Harris acknowledges that the 'weather was too bad for any successful

bombing attack' and that 'minelaying [was] a most effective weapon against the enemy's shipping'.[30] Sir John Slessor acknowledges the enemy's 'operational use of the weather ... under cover of a front of which they must have known the timing and movement to a nicety ...'.[31] Sir Philip Joubert sums up the Channel Dash with:

> It is doubtful whether the forces employed to attack the German squadron were sufficient to cripple the battle-cruisers, even if we had received immediate knowledge of their departure from Brest. A night attack by surface vessels might have been more successful, but the numbers available at that time in the Channel were very small. As it was, on 12 February the attack had to be made by day, when the best prospect of crippling the ships lay with the bombers and torpedo-bombers apart from the possibility of damage by mines. Owing to the very low cloud base the bombers were of very little use and the only effective striking force was the torpedo-bombers.[32]

For successful attacks by torpedo-bombers, however, surprise was essential, and the enemy expected attacks. Furthermore, with very low visibility, they could not have hoped to aim accurately, even should they have been able to break through a powerful screen of E-boats and destroyers, and lacking in cover by other aircraft to counter both AA fire and fighters. For Kim Abbott, one of No. 407 Squadron's pilots, 'The fault lay in questionable planning, lack of preparation, and extremely poor leadership, not sea power.'[33] By 'sea power', he must have thought of the Royal Navy's heavy units that were available.

In referring to 'leadership', Abbott was thinking of the higher command, not his own squadron – far from it. Rather does he rightly refer to those natural leaders, Sqn Ldr

Anderson and Flg Off Cowperthwaite as exceptional, lost as they were, near the *Prinz Eugen*. Their final sorties may be compared with the Navy's VC, Lt Cdr Esmonde, but tactically there were differences, Esmonde had a lethal weapon and had some fighter cover, whereas Anderson and Cowperthwaite had neither. Abbott, in his account, readily acknowledges the valour of Esmonde, but regrets that his own squadron (No. 407), lacked any recognition.[34] Winston Churchill in his war memoirs shows a general reluctance to criticise either personnel or forces, and that policy prevailed in his account of the Channel Dash.[35]

The *Luftwaffe* officer, Adolf Galland, who organised the fighter umbrella to cover the enemy's ships, stated:

> The Vice-Admiral commanding the Dover station had received additional MTBs and Swordfish torpedo carriers. During the previous days British aircraft dropped 1,100 magnetic mines between the Frisian Islands and Brest. It cannot, therefore, be said that the British Command was completely taken by surprise … the British Command showed amazingly little ability to improvise … this operation was accomplished within range of the [British] Home Fleet.[36]

I consider that the Admiralty had no serious intention of stopping the *Scharnhorst*, *Gneisenau* and *Prinz Eugen* from sailing up the Channel, as demonstrated by the meagre forces it deployed. It was apparent that British forces lacked coordination and no satisfactory plan had been made (in sharp contrast to, for example, the Torch operation). The fault lay not with individual forces, but with the Admiralty, whose duty it was, surely, to counter the movement of an enemy fleet. It would have made no difference whatsoever if Coastal Command's reconnaissance had given earlier reports; they did, however, serve as a

scapegoat for the naval historian, Captain Roskill, to justify the Admiralty's indifference.[37]

The enemy had again shown that in moving its heavy warships it was able to choose weather conditions that provided excellent cover and nullified any counter-moves by the British.

As Robertson stated: 'This cleverly executed plan was to be largely responsible for the delays in the British attacks', and 'The Channel Dash remains a monument to muddled leadership.'[38] For the enemy it was a 'tactical victory but a strategic defeat'.[39]

Of the three heavy warships, *Gneisenau* never went to sea again, *Scharnhorst* was sunk in the Battle of North Cape in December 1943, and *Prinz Eugen* was to be attacked again by Coastal Command in 1942, though not effectively.[40]

The advantages that followed from the ships leaving Brest were that for the RAF, Bomber Command had 40 per cent of its effort, which had been devoted to bombing ships in Brest, now able to direct that effort towards Germany. For Coastal Command, its aircraft that had been on regular reconnaissance covering those ships were now free to concentrate on anti-submarine warfare; and so in the case of my own squadron, No. 224, we were posted from St Eval to Limavady to undertake North Atlantic sorties.

The strike squadrons were moved to northern bases such as Wick and Leuchars, as it was still necessary to counter possible movements by the battleship *Tirpitz*, in addition to those by *Prinz Eugen* and *Scharnhorst*. There remained also Coastal Command's requirement to cover the convoys to and from Russia.

For Coastal Command's Air Officer Commanding-in-Chief, Sir Philip Joubert, the Channel Dash episode had demonstrated his shortage of strike aircraft, and his lack of other aircraft to cover the strikes. The *Prinz*

Eugen was located in Trondheim roads with an escort of four destroyers on 16 May. A second potential target, the pocket battleship *Lützow*, also with a four-destroyer escort, was seen in the Kattegat but steaming northwards at 15 knots. Just before midnight on 16 May six Hampdens were sent to mine the Haugesund area, and reconnaissance on 17 May reported enemy warships in positions 59°43'N 05°25'E, 59°40'N 05°35'E, and later at 58°30'N 05°35'E.

From these positions it was estimated that enemy warships would pass Lister Light in southern Norway on 17 May, between 1900 and 2000 hrs. Off Lister Light the ships would be sailing in open waters and so where attacks were possible with both bombs and torpedoes. A total force of twenty-seven Beauforts, six Blenheim fighters, eight Beaufighters and thirteen Hudsons was deployed.

The term 'fighter' for the Blenheims was a misnomer, as they lacked the firepower even of the Hudsons. Nevertheless, they were to attack the enemy fighters that were rightly expected to oppose any attack on shipping. Additionally the Blenheims were expected to make dummy torpedo attacks to confuse the enemy.

The limited number of Beaufighters was to counter anti-aircraft fire and attack the destroyers with cannon. In the first wave of twelve Beauforts, their three leaders were shot down. In a second wave, four more Beauforts were lost. For successful torpedo attacks where the enemy had fighter cover, in this case from Stavanger, surprise was essential, and that had not been achieved. Again, the Admiralty was not prepared to risk units of the Home Fleet off the enemy-controlled coast; thus it was a task for Coastal Command aircrew, with quite inadequate aircraft and armament. A combined Operational Instruction was, however, prepared, which made provision for fighter cover.[41] This was essential for any daylight strikes off the Norwegian coast due to the enemy's strong

fighter forces based there. There remained also the Command's requirement to cover the convoys to and from Russia.

By late summer, major enemy naval units were based at Narvik including the battleship *Tirpitz*, the pocket battleship *Admiral Scheer* and the heavy cruiser *Admiral Hipper*. They therefore posed a threat to British convoys to or from Russia when two were scheduled, namely PQ 18 and QP 14. To give cover against such ships a detachment of Hampden torpedo-bombers from Nos 144 and 455 Squadrons was flown from Sumburgh in the Shetlands.

Twenty-three arrived at Vaenga. Additionally, a detachment of Catalinas from No. 210 Squadron also flew to Russia, where the whole of Coastal Command's forces were under the command of Gp Capt F.L. Hopps, who had earlier served at Wick as Station Commander.

Hitler was not prepared to risk his major fleet units at sea, wishing instead to keep them to protect Norway, and attacks on the convoys were then left to U-boats and the *Luftwaffe*'s aircraft.

The outcome for Coastal Command was that the aircraft were left in Russia for the Russians, including some PRU Spitfires, and the Command's personnel returned to the United Kingdom by sea.[42]

Comments made by aircrew who served in Russia reflect an indifferent attitude in respect of the help given to the Russians, at great cost to the British, particularly of the merchant seamen. Coastal Command's aircrew who served in Russia, however, were awarded Russian decorations after the war.

Leaving aircraft in Russia may have given the impression of Coastal Command being well equipped, but it was not so. Its few squadrons were intended to cover the whole of the enemy-controlled coastline, from possibly Trondheim in Norway down to the Spanish frontier. Because the enemy still had major warships such as the battleship *Tirpitz* in

Norway, it was necessary for the Command to have a strike force based in the north at Leuchars, Wick or Sumburgh to counter any breakout by such potential raiders to the Atlantic or against the Russian convoys. Furthermore, strike aircraft were required to operate over the Bay of Biscay against blockade runners, and also to cover the Spanish coastline from Bilbao to French ports owing to the traffic of iron ore along that route.

As a strike wing was intended to comprise at least three strike squadrons, the forces available were obviously quite inadequate. There remained, also, always the need, from May 1940 onwards, for strike forces to operate against the German E-boats.

My only notable trip to Norway was to seek the battleship *Tirpitz* and the heavy cruiser *Admiral Hipper*, which were thought to be in Trondheim fjord on 6 June 1942. We must have been chosen because we had the best navigator on the squadron, and accurate navigation was paramount for a potential shipping strike.

This sortie must have been rated of some importance as it was the only time that the station commander came into the operations room to check, in addition to the pilot and navigator, that I personally was fully briefed, although I was then only a Sgt Wop/AG (wireless operator/air gunner). Our safety was dependent on cloud cover, but on reaching Trondheim fjord we found none, and in a trip of seven and a quarter hours in that northern latitude, there were only three hours of darkness. We were challenged by the guard ship at the entrance to the fjord, and it must have reported our presence to the *Luftwaffe*, since on return to the operations room the controller asked me if I had seen any enemy aircraft as three fighters were looking for us.

If we had sighted either the battleship or the heavy cruiser, I doubt if we would have escaped. Although we had cut short our trip down the fjord, it was far enough to make an

escape rather difficult.

A single battleship docked in Norway was enough to require considerable effort on the part of Coastal Command because of the possibility of it breaking out into the Atlantic. Furthermore, it meant that convoys to Russia needed naval escorts capable of dealing with a modern battleship that was superior to any single ship of the Royal Navy.

The need for extremely accurate navigation was essential, as also were reliable W/T signals; with at least one strike squadron on standby and armed, they would have had little reserve in fuel to start looking for the target rather than flying direct to its position. This necessity became apparent for the strike wings that came later. The checks made by the station commander at that briefing were typical of that officer (then Gp Capt Hopps). He checked also the records of the link trainer, as all aircrew, and not just pilots, were expected to be able to handle an aircraft, and in fact to stand in for all the other aircrew categories as necessary.[43] All aircrew, likewise, were expected to study intelligence reports in the operations room.

In 1943, when armaments were being considered for the strike squadrons; they were to include torpedoes, bombs and rocket projectiles, in addition to the Beaufighters' cannon. Equipment that was added included ASV aerials, plates for the installation of rocket projectiles and dive brakes. Collectively, these additions could result in the speed of Beaufighters being reduced by as much as 17 knots.[44]

Sir Philip had intended increasing his anti-shipping operations in the stretch of open water south of Stavanger to Lister and including the Skagerrak. That was in October, but the need for reconnaissance against a possible breakout of Germany's major fleet units meant that there were just not enough aircraft for both those tasks.

At the time of Operation Overlord, Germany still had available for operations

90–100 E-boats, 135 R-boats, twenty to twenty-five destroyers, and thirty-five torpedo-boats, in addition to about 200 U-boats and 150 W-boats (midget submarines). The possibility of a breakout into the Atlantic by heavy warships had also to be considered.[45]

Although it was thought that the main threat to the Allies' forces would be from U-boats attempting to enter the Bristol, St George's and English Channels, an enemy offensive was expected using destroyers and other light surface craft against Allied convoys, and Sir Sholto Douglas laid on anti-shipping operations for dusk and dawn and during the night.

These were to be flown largely by Nos 16 and 19 Groups, although the main task for No. 19 Group was considered to be anti-submarine warfare.[46]

For No. 16 Group's prime task of anti-shipping operations, it had strike wings at North Coates and Langham; while a flight of No. 415's Albacores with Fleet Air Arm Swordfish was at Manston. On anti-ship reconnaissance from Leuchars was a flight of No. 333's Mosquitoes. The anti-shipping tactics were those already given. At night the Albacores and Swordfish could be controlled by Nos 10 and 11 Groups with their D/F systems. Wellingtons would undertake reconnaissance sorties and could be used when required by Nos 16 and 19 Groups and in cooperation with light surface forces and/or Beaufighters. The dawn and dusk sorties were against light surface craft when leaving harbour at dusk or returning at dawn, and were to be flown by Beaufighters.

The Home Fleet was responsible for countering any attempt by the enemy's heavy warships to break out. No. 18 Group was to lay on reconnaissance sorties to cover such a possibility.[47] Coastal Command was specific in the armament for its anti-shipping forces in Overlord. Against E- and R-boats cannon were to be used, with bombs being of only secondary use. It was appreciated that if

rocket projectiles were used at night, the first launch of a pair would obscure the target, and therefore it would be better to use either just one pair, or the complete salvo.

Bombs were favoured against ships, but with the first choice being the medium-case (MC) type because of their high charge/weight ratio and with good fragmentation. In fact, this type came to be used against E-boats in the winter of 1944/5. Trials had already shown that MC bombs were the best compromise for attacks on E-boats, as it was found that the fragmentation area for two 500 lb and two 250 lb MC bombs was between 75 and 100 yd diameter.

Against destroyers in Overlord, rocket projectiles and bombs were to be used, but with cannon serving as anti-flak. The most notable decision was that torpedoes were not to be used. This decision, although not so stated, probably stemmed from the likelihood of Allied surface forces being available to use gunfire in support, and perhaps also, the critical nature of releasing torpedoes when friendly vessels were likely to be present.

In the event of Wellingtons on reconnaissance sighting enemy destroyers, they were to transmit so that the Royal Navy's destroyers could home onto the scene. Furthermore, torpedoes were hardly an economic way of attacking small surface craft that were likely to predominate in the hostile areas. As a back-up to the armaments mentioned, depth charges were to be available on all the operational bases, as an alternative to the use of MC bombs.

The Command's directive stated that the armament of E-boats included two 20 mm cannon and two machine-guns, although the E-boats that I was later to see at Felixstowe had just one cannon in the stern, in addition to two torpedo tubes. A flotilla of such craft was, nevertheless, a force to be respected.

The preferred form of attack at the time of Overlord was to release MC bombs from an altitude of at least 1,000 ft, and those tactics were to prevail in the following winter.[48] Against the midget submarines (W-boats), MC bombs could again be used, but if fused to detonate at 25 ft depth with a 14-sec-delay fuse. These craft were to continue operating over the North Sea, long after the Overlord landings, as the operational records of Nos 612 and 524 Squadrons were to show.[49]

A prime need for the Allies in Operation Overlord was to capture a port, although the improvised harbours were to prove their worth. The Americans gained Cherbourg on 26 June and the Canadians captured Antwerp on 4 September. The latter, however, was covered by the enemy on Walcheren Island, and it was 26 November before the first Allied ship reached Antwerp.[50] It was a task throughout for the Command's aircraft to cover the flanks of the Allies' convoy routes to whatever ports were used.

The enemy sank only eleven of the Allies' minor vessels, for, as Dönitz states: 'Since March 1944 our ships had been constantly detected by radar as soon as they left harbour and had found themselves very swiftly exposed to sea and air attack.'[51] Captain Roskill refers to the success of the Wellingtons, and specifically the Beaufighters of Nos 143 and 236 Squadrons, sinking E- and R-boats.[52]

The Command's involvement in operation Overlord had resulted in three new developments during that period. In fact, from 8 to 29 June No. 16 Group's aircraft sank nine small naval vessels, one of 3,500 tons, plus a merchant vessel of 7,900 tons. No. 19 Group's aircraft, in the same period, damaged three of the enemy's destroyers, each of 3,000–4,000 tons, and sank a naval auxiliary vessel.[53]

They were the use of combined wings for strikes on enemy anchorages, the object being for a large force to provide saturating fire power, in contrast to using a small force, which it was considered would result in 'costly failure'.[54] This belief may be questioned, however. It had already been demonstrated

that just one Hudson aircraft, armed with only four 250 lb bombs, could cause devastation and return to base unscathed.[55]

A second development was with Mosquitoes, which had initially been used as long-range fighters from Cornwall, but had proved to be increasingly successful in attacking ships in the Bay of Biscay. Later, Mosquitoes were displacing Beaufighters as squadrons rearmed for operations over Norway.

A third change was for the Halifax squadrons, Nos 58 and 502, which had operated successfully against U-boats, and were now to be used for anti-shipping operations off Norway and in the Kattegat and Skagerrak areas. By August, they were based at Stornoway for that purpose.[56]

The two latter developments indicated what always applied for Coastal Command. That was contending with the 'cast-offs' of Fighter and Bomber Commands, albeit using such aircraft with considerable success. Of all the aircraft being used by Coastal Command against shipping in 1944, none had been designed specifically for that purpose; those machines were Wellingtons and Halifaxes from Bomber Command, and Beaufighters and Mosquitoes intended for Fighter Command. There was, however, a flight of Albacores, intended for the Fleet Air Arm. Even for the Halifaxes and Mosquitoes, there were limitations in their availability, as, earlier in 1944, it was reported that there would be insufficient for Nos 58 and 502 Squadrons to operate Halifaxes much after September. In respect of Mosquitoes, after five had gone to Bircham Newton it was reported 'absolutely the last to be available to Coastal Command'.[57]

E-BOATS

These approximated to the Royal Navy's motor torpedo-boats (MTBs), but with two important advantages over the MTBs: they were powered by diesel engines, and they were much faster. The diesel engines used oil rather than highly inflammable petrol. The speed that my crew estimated, when we first sighted a flotilla of E-boats, was 40–45 knots; this was based on the tremendous wake that E-boats could produce. It was, in fact, their wakes that enabled us to sight them easily in moonlight, rather than the vessels, which were relatively small.

The first recorded attack on E-boats by Coastal Command aircraft was by a battle flight of No. 48 Squadron's Ansons on 20 May 1940 against eight or nine E-boats off the Dutch coast, near Texel. The Ansons used 100 lb bombs and machine guns. A direct hit on an E-boat with a 100 lb bomb would certainly at least have seriously damaged it, and machine-gun fire would have cleared the decks. In that attack, No. 48 Squadron lost one aircraft and another was damaged. The E-boats that I was able to inspect at Felixstowe in 1945 had just one small cannon in the stern, but the German gunners, as I had experienced earlier, were remarkably adept in gunnery.

From May 1940 up to May 1945, the German E-boats operating from the Dutch coast were able to cross the North Sea to attack British shipping using torpedoes (they had two tubes – one to port, one to starboard on the deck); alternatively they were used for minelaying. Because of their speed, manoeuvrability and small size, E-boats were extremely difficult to attack, and sailing as a flotilla their combined anti-aircraft fire was certainly a factor to consider. Coastal Command later developed tactics and weapons to counter this menace.[58] The Command came to use a number of types of aircraft against E-boats, including Ansons, Hudsons, Beaufighters, Albacores, Wellingtons and the Fleet Air Arm's Swordfish.

On 19 February a conference to consider anti-E-boat measures was held at Coastal Command's headquarters. The outcome was

for No. 16 Group to introduce offensive patrols on 1 March. They were to be between 53°10′N and 52°N as cross-over patrols to locate E-boats and report their position, course and speed. It would then be for the reconnaissance aircraft to shadow the E-boats and to await a W/T signal to illuminate the enemy with flares for an attack by other aircraft or naval surface vessels.

As already stated for other strikes, accurate navigation was essential, and at this time, ASV beacons were to aid the reconnaissance aircraft. Later, however, certainly in the winter of 1944/5, GEE became available for Coastal Command's North Sea patrols.[59]

The tactics adopted against E-boats were similar in some ways to what followed with the strike wings of Beaufighters using a pathfinder aircraft, such as a Wellington, that had better facilities for navigation than a Beaufighter. In early 1942, however, anti-E-boat operations were undertaken by the-maid-of-all-work, the Hudson. Hudsons flew the patrols between 10 March and 16 April, operating from North Coates and Bircham Newton, although no enemy contacts were achieved. Some attempt had been made, also,

51. A Wellington of No 612 Squadron. In the later months of the war No 612 was operating against E-boats off the Dutch coast, and additionally was sighting German midget submarines.

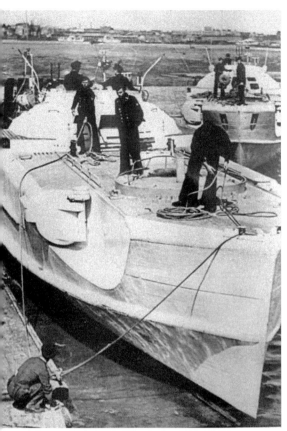

52. German E-boats which operated from the Dutch and also the Norwegian coasts in 1944-45. Nos 415, 524 and 612 Squadrons were directly involved in countering their attacks against British shipping along England's east coast and the English Channel.

to use fighter aircraft armed with cannon in January and February.

Although E-boats could have been sunk by cannon, their speed and manoeuvrability made them difficult targets for such weapons. The fighter operations nevertheless proved enough to stop the E-boats attempting daylight operations.[60]

A feature of the British anti-E-boat operations was the use of shore-based radar stations that could plot the arrival of the enemy. As was the case with U-boats, however, weak spots in the British defences were probed. And so on 7 July E-boats sank six

ships in Lyme Bay, where RDF stations were limited.[61]

In 1942, both the Royal Navy and Coastal Command were increasingly on the offensive against E-boats. The E-boats obviously favoured operations from Dutch ports such as Ijmuiden, although on occasions they were located off Texel, as I was later to appreciate. They also used the French port of Cherbourg.

While the Navy was able to deploy more light surface craft against E-boats in 1942, Coastal Command remained stretched to the limit in respect of both aircrew and aircraft. It was not until 1944 that the Command had suitable numbers of aircraft that could be devoted to anti-E-boat operations with squadrons such as Nos 612, 524 and also No. 415 (RCAF). Meanwhile the light surface forces of the Navy had to contend with an enemy that always posed a difficult target and a serious hazard to Allied shipping.[62] In September 1944, the enemy was withdrawing from north-eastern France and much of Belgium, which resulted in Channel ports being evacuated of merchant vessels and naval auxiliaries, but thirteen E-boats withdrew from Boulogne to Rotterdam and Ijmuiden on 4 September.[63]

I was involved with those E-boats later, on 30 November, as I flew on a cross-over patrol off Ijmuiden looking for E-boats to attack.[64] Those few E-boats based in Dutch ports were reinforced, making the numbers up to twenty, and E-boats and the midget submarines such as the *Seehunds* were to engage two squadrons of No. 16 Group's Wellingtons (Nos 524 and 612), until the end of hostilities.[65]

When posted to No. 524 Squadron at RAF Langham on 14 November 1944, I was asked, 'Have you a car – we have so many here unclaimed?' Another officer with whom I had been posted I met only once subsequently; his time must have been short. Later I became aware of empty bed spaces in the Nissen huts that served as accommodation. No. 524

Squadron was involved mainly in anti-E-boat operations off the Dutch coast, which during the long winter nights were very active. After some practice flights my first operational sortie was a cross-over patrol off Ijmuiden, a port favoured by E-boats. The other requirement of the Wellington squadrons was to cooperate with the strike wings, and on 28 November I was detached to North Coates for practice on a 'Gilbey' operation.

The AOC-in-Chief, Sir Sholto Douglas, was obviously imbued with the need for more training for his anti-shipping squadrons, and my flying with No. 524 Squadron during December included a course on Mark III radar. E-boat successes achieved by the Wellington squadrons are not included in the Command's record due to the decision to omit shipping of very low tonnage. There can be no certainty, therefore, of what they achieved, and aircrew were always reluctant to make claims when there was some doubt.

On 19 January 1945 a conference was held at Chatham to consider ways of improving cooperation between the Navy's surface craft and Coastal Command's aircraft in operations against the enemy's E-boats. The Navy's MTBs were already under the control of a frigate that could communicate with aircraft by VHF/RT, and it was decided to have some MTBs also fitted with VHF/RT.

There were trials undertaken with a Wellington flown by Wg Cdr Knott of No. 524 Squadron on 17 March, which proved successful. It was found that the Wellington, using Mark III radar, that is, with a rotating radar scanner, could detect the relative positions of both the enemy and the Navy's forces up to thirteen miles on the same trace and thus give a direct bearing of the enemy to the Navy.

A new procedure, 'Dictator', which came into effect on 29 March, was adopted along these lines.[66] Sholto Douglas gives the weapons used by Wellington against E-boats, namely, medium-case bombs with air-burst pistols, having only a harassing effect, and they were not decisive. At least three squadrons, however, operating Wellingtons, Nos 415, 612 and 524, were all able to claim successes using bombs, albeit with some serious losses.[67] Sir Sholto considered 20 mm cannon to be the most effective weapon against E-boats, but it could only be used successfully at night under ideal conditions. Only once, in a number of sorties over the North Sea, can I recall the conditions being 'ideal', and Wellingtons were not armed with cannon.[68]

AVM Hopps, the AOC No. 16 Group, reviewed the anti-shipping operations off the Dutch coast in a letter dated 23 January to the SASO, AVM A. Ellwood. Hopps intended extending his sorties further east, using 'Gilbey', as by then he had sufficient Wellingtons for both 'Gilbey' and 'Drem' procedures when nights were down to ten hours. He considered those procedures would be profitable off Borkum and Wangerooge areas to force the enemy to sail before dusk when he could be attacked, or after dawn, when the Drem system would allow a wing to strike. Against E-boats, he considered it important on a clear night for aircraft to fly from Den Helder to the Hook of Holland before darkness to catch any E-boats that started early; and for weapons, cannon and bombs were essential in a general anti-E-boat plan.

Certainly, with good visibility, there was much to be said for using cannon, with more shells available than bombs that could be carried; and cannon could be aimed immediately on making a sighting. Hopps suggested that there should be attacks on anchorages such as Den Helder, but acknowledged that it was 'hazardous' and only justified when suitable targets were there. He did not accept that it was 'too dangerous', given that there was suitable fighter cover. His suggested tactics were for fighters to release bombs against ships a minute before the strike wings arrived, and then to attack the flak positions. These tactics could probably have served, given that complete surprise was achieved, thereby having the raid over before enemy fighters appeared on the scene. There would have been the complication, in any case, of the need for very accurate timing. With the large forces intended, that would not have been easy.

In fact, Den Helder had been attacked on 17 January by thirty Beaufighters, but six were shot down by anti-aircraft fire, for just one small patrol vessel being sunk.[69] During briefings at Langham, I came to expect the warning of not getting too close to either Den Helder or Texel, due to the anti-aircraft batteries; I cannot recall being warned that Ijmuiden had 50 per cent more AA than Den Helder, although Ijmuiden was often the area which Wellingtons were required to patrol.

The friendly cooperation that always appears between Fighter and Coastal Command is apparent in AVM Hopps's letter, as he intended discussing the matter with the AOC No. 12 Group of Fighter Command. In respect of the Dutch coast, AVM Hopps was prepared to 'run recces whenever weather permits, and if there are enough aircraft not to prejudice other Wing activities'.[70] The response from the SASO at Coastal Command's headquarters was that an attack on Den Helder was 'bound to be a costly affair',[71] and the AOC-in-C Coastal Command did not wish to take a decision until he had heard AVM Hopps's views.

In addition to E-boats, the enemy was using a number of midget submarines in 1945. Although there were three types, probably the most important was the *Seehund*, which had a range of 275 nautical miles at 5 knots, and three days' endurance with sixty to seventy hours submerged. They were able to take two torpedoes or mines, and, as was the case with E-boats, posed a threat to shipping off the east coast of England and to Allied convoys sailing to the Scheldt.

One of the other types of midget

submarine, the *Biber*, with its more limited range, was being used to operate off the Scheldt, with its sailings geared to coincide with the tides at high water. In January it had been reported that there were already over 100 midget submarines, in addition to fifty E-boats, and that a continuous reconnaissance was required off the Dutch coast.

It was added that in the face of enemy fighters, it was unwise for Wellingtons to be used.[72] Coastal Command's patrols were therefore laid on to cover the wider area of the *Seehund* and other patrols off the Dutch coast for the *Biber*.[73]

Additional forces were used to counter the midget submarines in April, including Wellingtons from No. 407 (RCAF) Squadron at Langham and the FAA No. 882 Squadron at Manston. In a review of the situation made up to 28 April, it was found that after 17 April day sightings had almost ceased.[74]

No. 612 Squadron, which had been operating against E-boats, with considerable success, reported on 13 April that it was undertaking searches for midget submarines, and that other squadrons operating Mosquitoes, Beaufighters and Swordfish had already sunk a large number.[75]

In the last four to five months of the war, No. 16 Group's aircraft had flown 1,191 sorties against enemy midget submarines, making eighty sightings, and sixty-four attacks. The Navy's forces had made a similar number of sightings and attacks, but with greater success. These efforts could be set against thirty-two Allied ships sunk or damaged.[76]

No. 524 Squadron's flying detail was changed in January, and the crew with whom I would have flown were seen to go down in flames off the Frisian Islands on 13 January. On 29 January I was one of a crew of seven off Texel. It was one of those rare occasions when visibility was good and with moonlight, which not only made the wake of E-boats visible, but also must have clearly silhouetted our

Wellington. We attacked five E-boats with medium-case bombs fused to explode in mid-air. We suffered only one shell-hit, which passed right through the tailplane before exploding. It demonstrated an advantage of fabric covering rather than metal, as almost certainly the enemy's shells were designed to encounter some resistance. It meant that our rear gunner escaped any wounding, and that the aircraft was not seriously damaged.

Base was under fog on return, and the controller demonstrated his concern for aircrew by providing us with a tot of rum. He was a former solicitor; a profession that Sir Philip considered provided good controllers.[77]

Controllers served as a direct link between aircrew on operations and the administration, and an important one in sounding the attitude of aircrew. The controller at Langham had earlier served at Wick, where he always appeared to be on duty.

On the night of 14 March, we were on an anti-E-boat patrol off Ijmuiden, although we were also expected to report the launching of V2 rockets that were being directed towards south-east England. We were involved in only two more attacks on enemy shipping. On 23 March we sighted three minesweepers in position 53°48'N 07°01'E. After instructions from base an attack was made, but the results were not seen. My final involvement in an attack was on 6 April after E-boats were sighted off Ijmuiden. Although there was action in these sorties, they all appeared somewhat mundane, albeit not quite 'routine'; we considered the sorties of the Beaufighters much more hazardous.

There was much to be said for using single aircraft such as Wellingtons and Albacores against the flotillas of E-boats that were severely harassed, if not sunk or damaged. The loss of one aircraft, albeit with perhaps a crew of seven, could be justified on that account, and certainly so if just one ship was saved from mines or torpedoes. Most aircrew adopted a fatalistic and truly philosophical outlook. In action, one would be too busy to be fearful, but still concerned about how others in a crew were coping.

CONCLUSIONS

Anti-shipping operations by Coastal Command had begun in August 1939 with reconnaissance over the North Sea against the likely outbreak of surface raiders. That possibility prevailed certainly up until November 1944, when the battleship *Tirpitz* capsized after bomb hits. The Command had initially been limited in respect of offensive operations due to the wishes of the French.

With the capitulation of France, and the German occupation of Norway, there were progressive modifications in Britain's anti-shipping policy, but with some initial constraints on what, where and when Coastal Command's aircraft might attack. The first acknowledged success was by a Hudson of No. 233 Squadron of No. 18 Group on 29 April 1940; the first for No. 16 Group was also gained by a Hudson, but operating off Terschelling on 3 September 1940. Those two attacks represented what were to remain the two main areas for the Command's anti-shipping offensive, namely the Norwegian and Dutch coasts.

The first success for No. 19 Group proved to be unique. It was on 6 April 1941 when Flg Off Kenneth Campbell of No. 22 Squadron torpedoed the battle-cruiser *Gneisenau* at Brest, putting the ship out of action for months. Flg Off Campbell was awarded a posthumous VC.

Armament used included bombs (typically 250 lb), cannon, rocket projectiles, torpedoes and even depth charges. Throughout the war there were progressive developments in weapons, tactics, strategy and aids such as ASV/radar.

Always lacking, it appears, were effective bombsights, and there was limited availability of radio altimeters, due possibly to labour shortages and priorities. With the capitulation of France, and the German occupation of Norway, there were progressive modifications in Britain's anti-shipping policy, but with still some initial constraints on what, where and when Coastal Command's aircraft might attack.

The only aircraft under Coastal Command's control used in anti-shipping operations, and designed for the purpose, were the Beauforts that were sent to the Middle East, and those of the Fleet Air Arm. All the others were modified airliners, bombers or fighters. A major change in tactics was in the summer of 1942 when 'mast-height' bombing was changed to medium altitude due to the heavy losses, which, for example, for No. 407 Squadron in one strike, was 54 per cent.

A development in strategy was the formation of the strike wings, composed typically of three squadrons, and with another squadron or more of single-engined fighters as cover from Fighter Command. Despite serious losses, morale remained high among the strike squadrons; when, for example, No. 407 was taken off shipping strikes, the aircrew were demoralised! The chain of command from the Air Ministry down to individual aircrew remained remarkably flexible, and this appeared particularly so when Sir Philip Joubert was AOC-in-C Coastal Command, and on occasions briefed or conversed with individual aircrew. Cooperation prevailed with both the Admiralty and Fighter Command, and Bomber Command came to accept the necessity for cooperation.

During the whole of the war, aircraft controlled by Coastal Command sank 366 vessels totalling 512,370 tons, and damaged 134 others totalling 513,454 tons. These successes were against a loss of 876 aircraft, including 101 lost in the few months of 1945. So, despite Coastal Command's apparent superiority in forces in the remaining months of the war, shipping strikes remained always

dangerous.

As Sir Sholto Douglas stated: 'The work done by the strike wings was outstandingly successful; but their casualties in carrying it out were heavier than in any other flying done by the Royal Air Force during the last six months of the war.'[78]

The effect of Coastal Command's shipping offensive in the Norwegian area had resulted in a drop from 8,500,000 tons of cargo in and out of Norway in 1944, to less than 500,000 tons per annum by 28 February 1945. The other effect would have been to tie down many of the enemy's forces in protecting his ever-diminishing shipping against Coastal Command's offensive.[79]

In 1940 Coastal Command lost twenty-seven aircraft for every enemy ship sunk, but in 1945 the ratio was one for one. The efficiency of the shipping offensive had obviously improved. This was due to a number of factors, but there were better trained and experienced crews devoted to that specific task.

Armament had improved with the use of rocket projectiles and cannon, which at one stage were intended to cover for torpedo attacks; nevertheless, in their own right, they were able to sink ships and counter flak at the same time.

Despite the success of a torpedo against the battle-cruiser *Gneisenau*, I question if torpedoes were suitable weapons against most of the shipping encountered by the Command, which was mainly less than 6,000 tons and without armour plating, and therefore vulnerable to rocket projectiles, which were equivalent to a 6 in shell.

The use of bombs against ships was shown to be effective by Coastal Command's Hudsons in low-altitude attacks, by Bomber Command against the *Tirpitz* from essentially high altitude, and most famously by the USN in the Midway battle. Much more attention might have been given to the development of bombing attacks in conjunction with bombsight development.

A part of the Command's anti-shipping offensive was minelaying, which for Coastal Command terminated in 1943. Its usefulness was best demonstrated at the time of the Channel Dash: mines struck by the two battle-cruisers were the only effective weapons.

The many types of aircraft used in shipping strikes with success demonstrated that the type was not a crucial factor.

The 'mast-height' attacks had certainly resulted in serious losses, and yet No. 220 Squadron, which had suffered in that respect, had demonstrated in October 1941 that just one squadron of aircraft, each armed with four 250 lb bombs, could sink and damage ships without loss to themselves and at almost sea level.

There was much to be said for night attacks, and not necessarily with flares to illuminate. What remained important, however, was not so much the type of aircraft, but its range.

I consider that the concept of a strike wing with a close fighter escort was wrong. The fighters were 'tied' to the main force when they might have more effectively devoted their attention to enemy fighter bases near the strike wing's target. A large strike force of typically three squadrons was restricted in manoeuvres just by its own numbers. Both these aspects were touched upon by Sir Philip Joubert and Sir Sholto Douglas.

The latter had asked for attacks on enemy fighter bases, albeit by bombers, but he was refused. Sir Philip had intimated at the time of the conception of strike wings that there were occasions when just three or five aircraft were more suited for some operations. The disastrous strike on 9 February 1945 clearly demonstrated these points.

Coastal Command's shipping offensive from 1940 to 1945 seriously disrupted the enemy's trade with Norway and required the enemy to use considerable resources to counter that offensive. If one accepts the serious losses of aircraft and aircrew that resulted, then that offensive was fully justified by the results.

EPILOGUE

There are now memorials to the aircrew lost in the North Coates Wing at Cleethorpes, and those of the Dallachy Wing at Dallachy. The latter is constructed of rocks from the countries of the various aircrew who became casualties. In Norway, there are memorials to aircrew lost there. Dr Goulter gives the title of her thesis on the Command's anti-shipping campaign as 'A Forgotten Offensive'. I consider that it has never really been known.

CHAPTER SEVEN

'Cinderella' Units

Three additional tasks given to Coastal Command were photo-reconnaissance, meteorological flights and air-sea rescue. The work of the squadrons and flights on such sorties was probably more important for Bomber Command's operations than for Coastal Command's. The photo-reconnaissance aircraft were able to provide intelligence of potential bombing targets, and if required, the results of any bombing. The meteorological flights provided data that enabled weather conditions to be forecast for possible bombing raids. The air-sea rescue service of Coastal Command would expect to rescue the bomber crews that had ditched. Those three services lacked the glamour of Fighter and Bomber Commands, but not the dangers and strain for their aircrew.

AIR-SEA RESCUE

In 1938 there was awareness that in the event of war many of the RAF operations would be over the North Sea and therefore there was the prospect of some crews having to ditch. On 28 February 1939 at an Air Ministry conference it was decided that the organisation of high-speed launches (HSLs) should be under Coastal Command's control. Arrangements were made for a chain of HSLs for rescues to be located round the coasts of Britain from Wick in the north, down the east coast, and along the southern coast to Pembroke Dock.[1]

During the Battle of Britain there were serious losses of aircrew, and on 22 August the Deputy Chief of Air Staff held a meeting at the Air Ministry. The outcome was for a local rescue service to be organised by the Vice-Admiral, Dover, with Fighter Command, using RAF HSLs, naval craft, and Lysander (Army Cooperation) aircraft. While the RAF would be responsible for air searches, the Navy would organise all the surface craft.[2]

Initially, the Battle of Britain pilots had only life-jackets (known as Mae Wests), should they ditch. These could be inflated manually through a tube, or by activating a CO_2 bottle; the latter could cause problems in making one's exit if used prematurely.

A further addition to the Mae West was a fluorescene block to mark the position of the airman when ditched. Individual 'K'-type dinghies were to be provided that could be clipped to parachute harness.

53. An airborne life-boat with its sail raised (although it was provided with Engine power). Airborne life-boats were first designed to be fitted to Hudsons of No 279 Squadron.

54. A Warwick with a life-boat. Such aircraft were used late in the war to support the strike wings on their sorties.

There remained the need to provide additional survival gear after a ditching, and this became a matter for individuals at some stations to improvise with the materials available on stations.

One of those was the 'Thornaby Bag' – a parachute bag containing kapok to keep it afloat, and with tins of food, etc. The Bircham Barrel, devised from cardboard containers that had contained bomb fins, was used to contain distress signals, food, etc. There was a third improvisation, the 'Lindholme Gear', or 'Lindholme Dinghy', which came to be generally accepted. It was devised by Gp Capt Waring at Lindholme, and comprised a string of five containers, one with an eight-man rubber dinghy, the other four with various items such as food, signals, clothing, etc.

There was much to be said for this emergency equipment. Not infrequently, even after an aircraft had ditched safely, the aircraft dinghy might explode due to excess pressure from the CO_2 bottle, or be torn, or drift away, or lack room for all the crew. The Lindholme Gear was officially accepted and was to be produced commercially. From No. 279 Squadron's records, the first of the ASR squadrons, the Lindholme Gear was frequently and successfully used.[3]

A meeting was held on 14 January 1941 to consider the expansion and improvement of the rescue service, and this was to result in the appointment of a Director of Sea Rescue Services with Air rank and with a naval captain as deputy director. They were to have officers at each of the Area Combined Headquarters (ACHQ) of Nos 15, 16, 18 and 19 Groups of Coastal Command. At that time, however, there was a lack of suitable marine craft to cover the increasing needs of the rescue service, and in February representations were made to the Air Ministry.[4]

During the period February to August 1941 only 444 airmen were saved out of about 1,200 who had ditched.[5] In 1943, however, the success rate had still not improved, with 1,684 saved out of 5,466 presumed lost at sea, with percentages of 37 per cent and 31 per cent respectively.[6]

The reasons for so many being lost could be attributed to a number of factors: under very cold conditions, men could die in just a few minutes, and survival could depend on how well the crew had prepared themselves for ditching in respect of making their exits, collecting emergency equipment, etc. Some aircraft were well provided with exits, such as the Hudson, with five for a crew of four, others less so. Paramount would be how well the pilot was able to ditch according to sea conditions, and if the ditching had been reported by whatever means, with ideally the position given.

These aspects were obviously outside the control of the rescue service, although attempts would be made to take bearings from any signals from a distressed aircraft. If reported, it could be taken that every effort would be made to effect a rescue. Some squadrons would immediately undertake their own search.

During a staff meeting at the Command's headquarters on 8 August 1941, it was stated that the Sea Rescue Service was to be 'quite considerably increased' and that all administration would be under Coastal Command.[7] By November it was decided to form four squadrons for air-sea rescue, and for them to be equipped with Hudsons. This was at a time when the Command was being depleted of both aircraft and aircrew due to postings to the Middle East.

To form the first ASR squadron, aircraft were taken from other squadrons, and likewise aircrew were provided by existing squadrons.[8] When a second ASR squadron was being formed, it had to be disbanded as there were only enough aircraft for the first one (No. 279).[9]

The first ASR squadron was formed at Bircham Newton on 16 November 1941. Although it had an establishment of twenty

Hudsons, only seventeen had been received by 1 December. One of the first lectures for its Wop/AGs (wireless operator/air gunners) was not on the subject of ASR but on gunnery. This was to be fully justified, as on rescue missions they had to contend with attacks by enemy fighters, including Ju88s, Me109s and Fw190s. It was significant, also, that they flew with side guns in addition to forward and rear guns.[10]

There was an awareness of the need to provide better survival equipment for those who had ditched far from Britain's shores.

In September 1941, Gp Capt Waring, who had devised the Lindholme Gear, worked in conjunction with a naval officer, Lt Robb, RNVR, and a yachting enthusiast, Uffa Fox. This was to produce an airborne lifeboat that could be dropped using three parachutes. No aircraft was designed to take a lifeboat, but the Hudson was modified. The prototype was dropped on 11 December 1942, but the parachutes failed to open.[11]

The airborne lifeboat was first taken operationally on 17 February 1943. The modifications to the aircraft, however, had made navigation difficult, and heavy fuel consumption resulted in the operation having to be cut short. The all-up weight of the lifeboat, with a maximum of 1,700 lb, meant that the Hudson was overloaded, particularly with the additional armament being taken. The lifeboat, also, would have affected the flying characteristics and made landing difficult due to limited ground clearance and greater weight.

Although not so stated in the squadron's records, crews must have studied the necessary requirements for success, and on 5 May 1943 that was achieved. An airborne lifeboat was released to fall only 30 ft from a ditched crew. They boarded the lifeboat, started the engines, and when out of petrol, hoisted the sail. They were met by an RAF launch.[12] Another drop in July, although less successful, indicated the operating conditions of releasing the lifeboat

from 700 ft and at a speed of 140 knots. The relatively high speed for such a purpose was probably due to the need for a higher cruising speed because of the greater load, and also to ensure more positive control of the aircraft.

The ASR rescue crews needed to be rescued themselves on occasions; this was due to weather conditions and a hostile enemy. The crews did not begin as specialists but became so with service on the squadrons. Their first Commanding Officer, Gp Capt P. Lynham, had in fact earlier served on shipping strikes. In a letter to *The Times*, he quoted from an official account: 'The squadron was directly responsible for the successful rescue of 55 members of aircrew.' Lynham added: 'Not one of those rescued had taken more than three or four minutes to get into his dinghy and most ditchings were at night.'[13]

Gp Capt Lynham also mentioned whistles, which became standard issue to aircrew in 1941. They were worn near the collar of one's battledress, for immediate use to attract attention. Another means of attracting attention was the use of a mirror or any reflector, and at least one crew was located after three and a half days by such means.[14]

By November 1943, two other ASR squadrons, Nos 280 and 281, were using Warwick aircraft These also were adapted to accept an airborne lifeboat, but of greater length than was possible for the Hudson.

As the ASR service was concentrated on the east coast, on 26 January 1944 it was stated that the Air Ministry was prepared to agree to the formation of a fourth squadron for the west. At that time, however, many of the Warwicks being received by Nos 280 and 281 had needed to be returned to the contractors for modifications, while the Command was still expected to provide for overseas services.[15]

Sir Sholto Douglas must have been concerned at the 'Make do and Mend' that was prevailing in the ASR service, as on 14 February he asked staff to contact the Air Ministry for a new directive in respect of ASR.

About that time there was some begging and borrowing of Hudsons and the supply of Warwicks. He must have been conscious, also, of the need to prepare for the intended Operation Overlord.

There was a conference at Coastal Command's headquarters on 29 March, when ASR arrangements were considered. It was chaired by Sir Sholto, but the Air Ministry was represented.[16]

There was an obvious need for ASR arrangements to be made before Overlord, and for the deployment of squadrons and marine craft to be decided by May 1944.[17] The final deployment of the HSLs was for them to range from Plymouth, round the south coast and northwards along the east coast to Felixstowe.[18]

On 30 August, Sir Sholto Douglas held another conference to discuss ASR arrangements.[19] This was due to the changes in the war situation, which was then shifting northwards towards Norway but away from Biscay. The Air Ministry agreed his recommendations on 26 October.[20]

As was the case for other tasks, Coastal Command's ASR service suffered problems of supply and modifications to equipment and to aircraft, as for example, the shortage of Warwick aircraft had held up the re-equipping of No. 279 Squadron.[21] Other aircraft such as Hurricanes and Sea Otters that would have been used for short-range operations were not available.[22] There was a shortage of airborne lifeboats and squadrons were expected to avoid jettisoning them if at all possible.[23]

The Air Ministry proposed on 9 November that the short-range ASR service, that was, up to forty miles from Britain's coasts, should be undertaken by Coastal Command, in place of Fighter Command whose responsibility it had been. Sir Sholto agreed, as for the Channel area enemy fighters were no longer a problem and it was expedient to use aircraft such as the Sea Otter amphibians that were then coming into service. They could serve for both search and rescue, albeit to pick up only a few ditched airmen due to limited space in the aircraft.

The AOC-in-Chief's suggestions were approved on 15 February 1945, and Coastal Command, in conjunction with the Naval C-in-C, became responsible for the coordination of all ASR operations around the British Isles, and also the Command's other areas of Iceland, Gibraltar and the Azores.

The Command was also prepared to assist the Tactical Air Force in its ASR operations from the Continent.[24] Although the Command, in conjunction with the Royal Navy, had set up an ASR organisation; it had been for individuals such as Gp Capt Waring to devise life-saving equipment such as the Lindholme Gear and the airborne lifeboat.

No aircraft were specifically designed for ASR; rather was it a case of modifying existing machines that had been intended for other purposes, such as the Hudson and Warwick. An ASR school was set up, but it was for aircrew on squadrons such as the pioneer unit, No. 279, to learn and adapt by experience. The operational records of such units show that they were just as likely to be attacked by enemy fighters, although their sorties were those of mercy missions.

Crucial factors for aircrew to be saved from the sea were that the pilot should be able to ditch the aircraft without 'nosing in', that the crews could exit quickly, and that they should be able to board a dinghy with the minimum of delay.

Thereafter, it was essential that their position should be known, and that they should be picked up before succumbing to exposure; their one essential intake need was water.

PHOTOGRAPHIC RECONNAISSANCE

In 1938 Sidney Cotton, an Australian aeronautical engineer, was flying an aircraft on behalf of British Intelligence over Germany, ostensibly as a businessman, but with his aircraft equipped with RAF cameras. The RAF had at that time some difficulty in taking a series of photographs from the air because of the high altitudes, and the cameras froze as a result of condensation. Cotton overcame the problems by being prepared to fly at lower altitudes and ensuring that a current of air from the aircraft flowed over the cameras. He began work at Heston on 23 September 1939 after being approached by the Air Ministry, and used a spare hangar for his 'No. 2 Camouflage Unit', as it was known. Cotton used two of his own aircraft, but was allotted Bristol Blenheims to adapt, and two Spitfires. The unit came under the control of the new Photograph Development Unit (PDU) at Heston in October 1939.[25]

Cotton gave first priority to the taking of photographs of high quality, and did not wish his aircraft to be involved in aerial combat. Therefore, to fly over enemy territory with reasonable safety it was essential that the aircraft used could outpace the enemy. The Blenheims in France were too slow and had suffered casualties, and Spitfires were the preferred aircraft. By removing all armament and smoothing the fuselage, the speed of the aircraft was increased. The disadvantage of a one-man fighter aircraft was the difficulty of navigating over long flights in bad weather. Cotton therefore requested Hudsons, which were heated and provided good facilities for the crews, who were therefore able to concentrate on their tasks. His plan was for a Hudson to fly out along the proposed Spitfire route and radio back if the weather was unsatisfactory.

By the end of February 1940, some excellent pictures had been taken, including some of Wilhelmshaven and the battleship *Tirpitz*. Winston Churchill, as then First Lord of the Admiralty, on seeing these photographs, stated that if the Air Ministry did not take over Cotton's unit, then the Admiralty would do so.[26]

On 4 June 1940, Flg Off R.G.M. Walker from No. 224 Squadron, but dressed as a civilian, flew a Lockheed 14, G-AGAR, from Britain, with the intention of being abroad on photo-reconnaissance for three weeks, and accordingly took his own ground crew.

With the capitulation of France, and Italy's entrance into the war, Walker's aircraft became stranded in the Middle East. This was the beginning of what came to be known as No. 2 Photo-Reconnaissance Unit, in the Middle East. The Lockheed 14 received its original RAF serial number, N7364, and together with another Hudson that had flown out with some Hurricanes, became based at Heliopolis to cover the Middle East from Malta to Aden and Greece to Khartoum.

At Heston on 10 February 1940, No. 212 became the first photo-reconnaissance squadron, but on 10 June there was a conference at the Air Ministry. It was then decided that the Photographic Development Unit at Heston and the Photographic Development Interpretation Unit at Wembley were to be under the control of Headquarters, Coastal Command, with effect from 18 June.

They were to be renamed 'Photographic-Reconnaissance-Unit'(PRU), and 'Photographic Interpretation-Unit' (PIU) respectively.[27]

Sir Frederick Bowhill issued an Operational Instruction in July. The PRU was to provide photographs and interpretations as required for the Combined Intelligence Committee of the Air Ministry, Admiralty, War Office and RAF Commands. The PIU was to be administered by the PRU but under the direct control of Headquarters, Coastal Command, and there would be a liaison officer at headquarters to deal with both units. Four operational PRU flights were formed, each equipped with three medium- and one long-range Spitfire, one Hudson and one Tiger Moth. One flight was detached in the south-west at St Eval, and another flight at Wick in the north-east.

When stationed at RAF Wick in 1942, I

saw one of the PRU's Spitfires. It was devoid of armament and camouflaged duck-egg blue. Over Norway, it would have been solely dependent on having greater speed than the enemy's fighters, and yet would have been vulnerable to AA batteries.

For much of the war, it was a case of the *Luftwaffe* and the RAF endeavouring to increase the speed of their fighters, such as the Me109s and the Spitfires, perhaps just a few knots more than the enemy's, for the difference of life or death for one or the other. Without armament, the one advantage the Spitfire had in combat, which was flying in tight circles, would have been nullified.[28] By the nature of PRU operations also, they would have been lacking in cloud cover. At RAF Sumburgh in 1942, I saw in the operations room some of the PRU's work. It included a photograph of the battleship *Tirpitz*, which was so detailed that a line of the crew's washing could be seen on the deck!

By the end of July 1940, the Command had available for photo-reconnaissance: eight medium-range Spitfires, each with an extra 30 gallons, a safe range of 750 miles at 30,000 ft and 300 mph speed; three long-range Spitfires of 1,100 miles' range; and two with 1,300 miles' range.

There were two Spitfires for training purposes, one Blenheim, two Wellingtons, some Hudsons and de Havilland Moths, and a Lockheed XII, the latter probably having been Sidney Cotton's aircraft.[29]

With the enemy's occupation of much of the Continent, many intelligence sources were cut off, and photo-reconnaissance became increasingly important. Initially, the emphasis was on covering enemy-occupied ports, but to be followed by the need to photograph enemy air bases. For that purpose, the Air Ministry, on 20 July 1940, approved an additional flight of six medium-range Spitfires, plus two in reserve.

An increase in the establishment of both the Photo-Reconnaissance Unit and the Photo-Reconnaissance Interpretation Unit was agreed during a conference at the Air Ministry on 2 October 1940. It was also decided that a Deputy Directorate (Photography) should be established at the Air Ministry to look after photographic interests and its future planning. Bomber Command, it was decided, should be responsible for its own interpretation of its bomb damage to targets.

Following this conference at the Air Ministry, Sir Frederick Bowhill held his own staff meeting to consider the future organisation of photo-reconnaissance. He recommended to the Air Ministry that the PRU should move from Heston to Benson. The reasons for this move were the lack of runways and a hangar at Heston, and also the unfavourable weather conditions that prevailed there. Benson was still near London, and the headquarters of both Bomber and Coastal Commands. There was a further conference at the Air Ministry on 18 October 1940, when, although Cranfield was also considered as a possible base for the PRU, it was decided that Benson should be used, with the PRU as a lodger unit at what was then a bomber base. This decision was to take effect from 4 January 1942, and the unit would be under Coastal Command's control.[30]

There was a further development in November at the Air Ministry. It had been proposed that a Central Interpretation Unit (CIU) should be formed. This was due to the increasing demands made by the War Office, Admiralty and the Intelligence staffs of the various Ministries.

It was decided that it should be under the Assistant Chief of Air Staff through the Deputy Director of Photography, but under Coastal Command's control for discipline, accounts, stores and accommodation.

This unit was to move from Wembley to Medmenham in April 1941. In that month, Sir Frederick opposed a decision to centralise the control of the PRU, and the matter was considered by the Chiefs of Staff in May. This resulted in a communication dated 7 June that in accordance with the Defence Committee (Operations), Nos 1 and 3 PRUs were to be amalgamated and to be under the operational and administrative control of Coastal Command with effect from 16 June 1941.

Demands for photo-reconnaissance from Bomber Command, Fighter Command and the Admiralty should go to Coastal Command's headquarters, but requests from other Departments to the Assistant Director of Intelligence (Photography), who would deal also with requests intended for the Central Interpretation Unit.[31]

By this time, photo-reconnaissance had become the prime means for gaining intelligence on the Continent, and in 1941 there were four sorties per day. By January 1942 a new camera was introduced with a magazine for 500 exposures and with a scale of 1 in 10,000 at 30,000 ft altitude.[32]

Sir Frederick had relinquished command in June 1941, to be succeeded by Sir Philip Joubert as AOC-in-Chief. By then most of the 'spade work' of organising an efficient photo-reconnaissance service had been accomplished. It was due to Sir Frederick that Benson was adopted as the main base for PRU operations and that Coastal had operational control over the units.

Much was expected of individual aircrew, and on 10 April 1942, at one of Sir Philip Joubert's staff meetings, a report on the number of crashes in No. 2 PRU was discussed. It was considered that the crashes were due to pilot fatigue, and that the remedy should be for pilots to be 'broken in' to undertake longer and longer flights! It was considered, also, that it would be 'a lever for [the Command] getting its own PRU going quickly'.[33] The Sunderland squadrons had been well aware of this problem, and had alleviated it by endeavouring to provide three pilots for each sortie.[34]

On 19 October 1942, five squadrons were formed at Benson: Nos 540, 541, 542, 543 and 544. No. 540 was equipped with Mosquitoes, Nos 541, 542 and 543 had Spitfires, while No. 544 initially had Ansons and Wellingtons but with a flight of Spitfires at Gibraltar.[35]

The number of personnel (RAF and WAAF) by the end of 1942 exceeded 1,000, and the output for that year included about one and a half million photographs and about five and a half thousand reports.[36]

Sir Philip was succeeded by Air Marshal John Slessor in February 1943, and at the end of that year Slessor outlined the work of the Command in 'Coastal Command Review'. He referred to the five PRU squadrons, by then within No. 106 Wing, which in that year had flown over 3,000 sorties, and of those, 75 per cent had been productive, with operational negatives totalling 470,000. His tribute was:

> The enormous extent to which we rely on this Wing for our knowledge of every aspect of the enemy's activity, is perhaps not generally realised; the science, not only of air photography but of interpretation, has made enormous strides in the last four years and the intelligence staffs would be blind without the courage and skill of the pilots and ground personnel of No. 106 Wing.[37]

He added that photo-reconnaissance was important for the planning of bomber raids, in gaining intelligence of the enemy's shipping movements off the Dutch coast and in the Bay of Biscay, and concluded: 'On no occasion has any Allied Commander always had to go short of information required from visual or photographic reconnaissance.'

Out of the hundreds of staff conferences held by the Air Officers Commanding-in-Chief at Coastal Command's headquarters, only about two dozen give a mention of photo-reconnaissance.[38]

It is apparent that the commanders just found that the system worked efficiently, and so, what appears so often in some operational records, they were considered 'routine', despite enemy activity and often unfavourable weather conditions.

Lord Douglas gives a brief tribute to the five PRU squadrons at Benson, with 'all of them devoting their time to this work which could be, on occasions, as uncomfortable as any other type of flying'.[39]

During the war years, the Press would from time to time publish photographs taken by the Royal Air Force. Perhaps one of the first was of Heligoland taken by a No. 224 Squadron Hudson on 21 September 1939. It gained a headline, 'Heligoland as Seen on a Daring British Flight', but in the *Daily Telegraph and Morning Post* dated 27 January 1940. The newspaper had marked in the gun emplacements and AA batteries, and referred to Heligoland being 'heavily fortified'.[40]

METEOROLOGICAL FLIGHTS

As early as 1925 'weather climbs' were undertaken by the Royal Air Force, but in 1936 Bristol Bulldogs of the Station Flight at Aldergrove were flying high-altitude meteorological sorties. The service began forming meteorological flights and numbers were being assigned to them.

At the outbreak of war, the weather reports from shipping had to be discontinued due to them giving their positions to the enemy in radio transmissions. At that time there was an increasing need for accurate weather reports, which were essential for Bomber Command.

The weather climbs were being undertaken by outdated Gloster Gauntlets and Gladiators; the latter, in fact, were to continue their vertical climbs, typically to 24,000 feet, throughout the war, for which they proved very suitable.[41] Subsequently, Spitfires and Hurricanes were also used for the vertical flights, with the advantage that Spitfires were able to reach the higher altitudes.

In late 1940 Coastal Command authorised the formation of three long-range meteorological flights, Nos 403 at Bircham Newton, No. 404 at St Eval, and No. 405 at Aldergrove. Subsequently, the flights were renumbered in the 14-series.

Initially, Bristol Blenheims were used for the sorties over the Atlantic and North Sea. However, they were obviously unsuited for transmitting weather reports, as the wireless operator was remote from the navigator, and in 1942 the Blenheims were being displaced by Lockheed Hudsons, where the navigator, pilot and wireless operator were in close contact.

Additionally, Lockheed Venturas and Handley-Page Hampdens were used, but Hudsons became one of the preferred aircraft for meteorological flights throughout the war.[42]

At a Coastal Command staff meeting on 9 August 1941 it was decided to revise the administration, and if possible, the status of meteorological flights. Up to that time, the sorties were classified as 'non-operational', which it was acknowledged was 'unfair as their work in this Command is often hazardous'.[43]

It was an important aspect for the aircrew involved, as a tour of operations was normally fixed according to the type of sortie and the aircraft flown. For example, an operational tour on Hudsons became fixed at 500 hours, but on flying-boats, 800 hours. This aspect became reviewed also for the PRU squadrons.

One of the first 'Tannoy' broadcasts I heard at RAF St Eval in February 1942 was: 'All flying scrubbed, except for the Met. Flight.'

55. A Halifax of No 518 Squadron off Tiree in the Inner Hebrides. No 518 was one of the meteorological squadrons that were devoted to such work.

No. 1404 Met. Flight was at St Eval during 1942 and 1943, but with some aircraft detached at Gibraltar. They flew down to the Bay of Biscay at 3,000 ft. At the extremity of the patrol, readings were taken at under 50 ft altitude, and then at regular intervals of 1,000 ft up to 20,000–22,000 ft. The W/T reports were coded by the navigator, and the wireless operator, after obtaining a fix of their position, would be transmitting for about two hours. In addition to weather hazards, there was that of being in range of enemy fighters when about 50 miles from Brest. A wireless operator/air gunner (Wop/AG) gave the following account of one such trip:

> We turned for home but were unable to get a fix due to the atmospheric conditions and had been flying in cloud on met. winds for five hours; we just had to break cloud and get a drift or pin-point for navigation to be checked. We began to feel our way down with everyone straining to spot the sea. We eventually broke cloud at 250 ft into heavy rain, over three flak ships which opened fire with machine guns and pom-poms [cannon]. I saw tracer coming up then we were clear and vanished into the rain. I reported a bullet hole in the tail plane and port engine on fire. We used the extinguisher and the flames died down.
>
> The inner half of the wing was blazing with the flames coming almost to the tail. In the fuselage was a mass of flame with the 'chutes burning; the observer used a fire extinguisher which had no effect.
>
> The bomb bay which contained petrol tanks was on fire and flames were coming up through the bomb inspection covers. We crash-landed on the beach at Cameret in Finisterre.[44]

By 'met. winds' was meant the speed and direction of winds given to the crew when they were briefed. Severe atmospheric conditions prevented the wireless operator from either taking a series of radio bearings from transmitting stations, or calling up a station to give the crew their position after taking bearings from the aircraft's own transmissions.

A Meteorological Observers' Section was set up in September 1942, but it was to be in April 1945 before an 'M' brevet for this aircrew category became available.[45]

An amalgamation of the 1401 and 1403 Flights became No. 1401 Flight at Bircham Newton; at Wick, 1406 amalgamated with 1408 as No. 1406 Flight, and 1402 with 1405 formed No. 1402 Flight at Aldergrove. No. 1404 Flight at St Eval replaced its Blenheims with Hudsons in late 1941, but in 1943 was operating Hampdens.

On 11 August 1943 this flight was reclassified as No. 517 Squadron. It continued to operate in the South-Western Approaches, and in addition to met. flights served also in anti-submarine operations. In 1943 No. 517 and No. 518 Squadrons were converting to Halifax aircraft. These had the advantage for 'horizontal' sorties of greater range, and they were able to fly out 700 miles over the Atlantic, although they became equipped with drop tanks.

From the minutes of the conferences held periodically by the Commanders-in-Chief at Coastal's headquarters, the Halifaxes were not without problems. These were related to the type of engine fitted to the aircraft, the drop tanks, and the addition of depth charges to be used in the event of sighting a U-boat.

Sir Sholto Douglas made a special mention of the Halifax aircraft because of the difficulties that occurred through attempting long flights at the instigation of the Meteorological Section at the Air Ministry. At first the nose of the aircraft had to be modified to accommodate the meteorological observer, and that initially had to be done on the squadrons. It was found, also, that if one engine failed in the first four hours, the Halifax could not maintain height.[46] The number of overload tanks had therefore to be reduced, and this limited the range.

The difficulty had to be overcome partly by using drop tanks. It was finally resolved by having Mark III Halifax aircraft, which were powered by Bristol Hercules engines.

There was also the question of just how to fly the sortie. Thus, at a conference on 4 November 1944, there was a request for a different mark of Merlin engines to be fitted, and the question of the rate of climb and descent to be decided. At a conference on 3 February 1945 it was decided that meteorological aircraft could jettison their depth charges at the end of the outward flight before the ascent commenced. The reason for this was obviously to lighten the load of the aircraft, particularly before it attempted to climb. It would have been logical for the aircraft to traverse the outer route at comparatively low altitude while it still had almost a full load of fuel, but it remained necessary to climb to report conditions in the higher altitudes.

By September 1944 the Meteorological Committee in considering aircraft to replace Hudsons and Halifaxes agreed to Warwicks being used to re-equip the meteorological squadrons, but due to delays in their availability, decided that Halifax Mark IIIs should serve for routine reconnaissance, and for vertical flights Spitfires and Hurricanes would be standardised.[47] Nevertheless, in 1944, No. 520 Squadron came to operate Halifaxes, Hudsons, Gladiators, Spitfires and Hurricanes. No. 521 Squadron, in addition to Hudsons, Venturas and Spitfires, operated Flying Fortresses.

It was customary for Coastal Command squadrons engaged in such activities as anti-submarine operations to give, additionally, a weather report. Those reports, however, would not have been transmitted while the aircraft was on anti-submarine operations, but given at the time of debriefing in the operations room.

Those meteorological units (flights or squadrons), however, which were ostensibly fully engaged in transmitting weather reports, were on occasions sighting U-boats. It was decided, therefore, that the meteorological flights should be armed additionally with depth charges, and out of thirty-six sightings, eleven attacks were made. On occasion they also sighted enemy aircraft, and at least one met. aircraft claimed to have shot down one of the enemy.[48] In addition to the meteorological units in the United Kingdom, some were deployed in Iceland, Gibraltar and the Azores. All came under Coastal Command's jurisdiction.

In 'Coastal Command Review' dated December 1943, Air Marshal Slessor referred to the meteorological squadrons doing 'yeoman service' for all the British and Allied forces operating from the United Kingdom, and of the units being the 'Cinderella of the Air Force' for reasons that included shortage of aircraft.

None of the aircraft used for meteorological work had been specifically designed for the task; rather were they modifications of bombers, fighters and civil aircraft. Slessor mentioned the shortage of aircraft being 'put right' with Halifaxes and Venturas, but there were problems with the Halifaxes, and the Venturas were to prove less satisfactory than their forebears – the Hudsons. He mentioned also the 'veteran Gladiator', which was used as late as 1945 by which time there was a lack of undercarriages for the aircraft.[49]

The post-war tribute of MRAF Lord Douglas was:

It was Coastal Command's job to keep going some fifty aircraft for the

56. Trondheim naval base where the Germans built U-boat pens, in addition to those at French ports.

57. Bordeaux U-boat base. The Gironde provided bases for both German and Italian submarines.

meteorological service which, in their probing for information beyond the friendly home shores, was the sole source of information for all the weather forecasting used for operations by the Royal Air Force, the Royal Navy and the other Services.[50]

Most aircrew in Coastal Command would say that their worst enemy was the weather; it was particularly so for the meteorological units. While those flying east to Germany would expect to be told with some degree of accuracy the state of the weather; those in the meteorological units flew westwards to find out just what weather was coming to Britain, and, as already stated, when flying was 'scrubbed' for other squadrons due to bad weather, those on meteorological sorties were required to find just how bad it was. To fly for ten hours under all conditions up to 700 miles out over the Atlantic was no mean task; as likewise for those pilots in Spitfires who flew up to 40,000 ft for as long as one and a half hours.

The work of the Air-Sea Rescue, Photo-Reconnaissance and Meteorological Units lacked the glamour of fighter and bomber squadrons, but their work was vital for the successes of others. They were the Cinderellas of a Cinderella command.

The aircrew involved in these tasks experienced the same hazards as those on offensive operations – bad weather and a hostile enemy; and by the nature of their work, a great strain was imposed on the crews, and they suffered serious losses. Nevertheless, they remained dedicated to their tasks, as was to be shown by their records.

CHAPTER EIGHT

Coastal Command in Retrospect

When I asked through various service publications for opinions of Coastal Command, I received a number of responses from former Coastal Command aircrew. Most looked upon the work of the Command in the Battle of the Atlantic as Coastal Command's prime contribution to victory.

Gp Capt J.B. FitzGerald, RAAF, who served with No. 500 Squadron, considered the Second World War in three phases – the Battle of Britain, the Battle of the Atlantic and the Bomber Offensive. He added, however, that in Australia, the Battle of Britain and the Bomber Offensive are marked every year, the latter by a number of events; whereas 'the Battle of the Atlantic never gets a mention'. An officer who served after the war in Fighter Command, Air Cdre Mark Tompkins, acknowledges 'Coastal Command's vital part in the Battle of the Atlantic'. The BBC History Unit belatedly recognised, in September 2000, the Battle of the Atlantic as 'the dominating factor all through the war', quoting Churchill, with 'the first comprehensive history of the Battle of the Atlantic on British Television'. The three broadcasts were to include 'men from Coastal Command'.

ACM Sir Derek Hodgkinson considered that Coastal Command was the Cinderella in 'the main battle of the Atlantic' but that 'the air war against Germany had ... to take precedence in the allotment of long-range aircraft'. Flt Lt Bryan Quinlan, RCAF, writes that the Battle of the Atlantic was 'less glamorous when compared to either Bomber

or Fighter Commands and they made for better public relations'.

Most of my correspondents were aware of Coastal Command coming third in order of priority for aircraft, but appeared ready to accept that. As Sir Derek Hodgkinson adds: 'Looking back, I think we did pretty well with what the Air Staff gave us, and do not blame them for their priorities. They had very difficult decisions to make, and on the whole, they did well.'

In an address given at a Coastal Command Association conference in 1992, Flt Lt John Cruickshank, VC, acknowledged the leadership of Coastal Command's 'great Commanders, Bowhill, Joubert de la Ferté, Slessor and Sholto Douglas. Men who could inspire us'. Inspired leadership prevailed at 'grass roots' level also.

As a navigator, Flt Lt Simmons, in No. 143 Squadron, who was on shipping strikes, said: 'I was not unhappy, due to having a good pilot, a good CO [of the squadron] and a good Station CO.' Simmons added, however, 'I survived, but 50 per cent of my original fellow aircrew were lost.'

Others, also, comment on the number of casualties. Of the forty-six students on Wg Cdr Derek Martin's pre-war flying course, 'only two survived the war'. Flt Lt Gron Edwards, who served with No. 233 Squadron Hudsons, was thankful that he was not a torpedo pilot with a 17 per cent survival rate for an operational tour.

The difference between flying in Coastal

Command and either Bomber or Fighter is recollected by such as Flg Off Bob McGill. While Bombers took off as a squadron, for most of Coastal's crews it was in a lone aircraft, 'and probably not seeing another until it landed at base. Coastal Command's enemies were the sea and the weather.' One must add to that statement, however, that a number were involved in serious air-to-air combats. The Australian, Gp Capt FitzGerald, 'found each sortie a challenging assignment, e.g. when we are at PLE on this particular sortie ... I always felt that we were making a worthwhile contribution to the war effort.' That attitude was typical of most captains; they would attempt to fly to the limit of their endurance, particularly when on convoy escort. A Canadian, Flt Lt Bryan Quinlan, appeared no less dedicated: 'We were completely absorbed in our day-to-day operations and existence, wrapped up in our crew members and other friends on the squadron. We were happy to acquire anything that came our way.'

Overall, former Coastal Command men were content with their time in the service, and quite accepted that priority was not given to them. Furthermore, there was no sense of envy towards the other services. Rather were most Coastal Command aircrew mindful of the tasks undertaken by such as Bomber Command, but in particular, the lot of the Mercantile Marine. My own feeling, particularly when leaving a convoy at last light, was that we would probably soon be back at base, while at any moment, after we had left, a ship might well be torpedoed.

A pilot who served with No. 269 Squadron in Iceland, Dr R. Yorston, refers to the mutual respect of Coastal Command and the Mercantile Marine, and quoting a member of the latter: 'When we see your aircraft we go below to rest.' Yorston adds: 'So it had what nowadays would be called "job satisfaction".' Of Coastal Command as the Cinderella, Yorston comments: 'Yes', but look how

Cinderella finished!'

Both Wg Cdr Geoffrey Bartlett and Wg Cdr Derek Martin take a philosophic view. Bartlett expresses 'a general satisfaction with the way Coastal Command dealt with [him] personally, and for a broad and deep reverence for the way "it" conducted the war'. Bartlett quotes John Terraine: 'The end arrived none too soon in the maritime war', and adds that Terraine, rightly, he thinks, believes that 'the Atlantic Victory never got its proper recognition'. Derek Martin also refers to Terraine's view of Coastal Command; post war, Martin was actively involved with an international youth organisation, and of our former enemies he states in retrospect: 'The people we were trying to kill were very similar to ourselves. Similar background, intelligent, technically capable.' One must question, however, that Coastal Command set out to kill people. It was otherwise – to 'kill' U-boats, but not men.

I still receive a number of letters from both war veterans and civilian researchers concerning crashed aircraft, lost aircrew and the restoration or commemoration of former Coastal Command bases such as Carew Cheriton, Thornaby and Silloth. Former aircrew of the North Coates Wing, in addition to a memorial at Cleethorpes, have shared a Dutch memorial at the formerly notorious Den Helder/Texel area. Most exceptional were letters from two eleven-year-old girls at a primary school in Wick. Subsequently I received a copy of their project, which was devoted to RAF Wick, and to those aircrew who operated from there.

A pilot who served with Coastal Command after the war, Gp Capt D. Cook, found that 'the Command was left with few aircraft and modified bombers were pressed into service'. I experienced that briefly in 1950 when on detachment to No. 210 Squadron, which was then flying former bomber aircraft – Lancasters. Gp Capt Cook considered that Coastal Command had been overlooked, and gave lines of verse written by Sqn Ldr Tony Spooner. They begin:

'Fighters or Bombers?' his friends used to ask,

But when he said 'Coastal', they turned half away.

They conclude:

'Fighter or Bomber?' his friends used to ask,
'Coastal' he said, his face a tired mask,
Though not in the spotlight where others may bask,
We've a tough job to do and I'm proud of the task.

It is due to the efforts of such as the late Sqn Ldr Tony Spooner, DSO, DFC, who served with Nos 53 and 221 Squadrons, that at long last a national memorial was unveiled to Coastal Command in Westminster Abbey on 16 March 2004 by HM Queen Elizabeth II.

I agree with the views of all those correspondents, apart from the two provisos made. In what was published during the war about Coastal Command, I was aware at the time of two posters, one depicting No. 220's Hudson raid on Ålesund, and the 'capture' of U-570 by a Hudson from No. 269 Squadron. In contrast, on the back page of some

58. A memorial to the North Coates Strike Wing erected at Cleethorpes on 25 September 1999.

newspapers in small type was: 'From all these operations two Hudsons of Coastal Command failed to return.' Headlines were, however, given to the SS *Kensington Court* rescue.

When at a Coastal Command OTU during the winter of 1941/2, I was very conscious of the effect of good leadership that prevailed there. All the instructors had not only flown on operations, but proved exceptional: three of them later commanded squadrons, two were later knighted, and one became Chief of Air Staff.[1] On posting to No. 224 Squadron, I became aware of the elusive 'squadron spirit' that permeated through all the ranks. This was due to leadership, but also because many squadrons were conscious of their history. Some newly formed units appeared lacking in that spirit.

59. A memorial to No 269 Squadron in Selfoss, Iceland, 1 August 2000. No 269 operated Hudsons from Kaldadarnes, Höfn and Reykjavik for much of the war on anti-submarine operations over the North Atlantic, and also undertook 'ice patrols' to warn shipping. Their work was hazardous and their conditions most grim.

The effect of squadron spirit resulted in high morale, exemplified by No. 48 in early 1943 at Gibraltar, which was acknowledged by the Command. This factor, 'squadron spirit', I put above all other aspects that may lead to success.

It did extend through to the Command upwards, I believe, rather than downwards. Although there could be friendly rivalry, there were also 'sister' squadrons, such as Nos 53 with 59, and 206 with 220. The Command itself became something of a fraternity that extended through all ranks, and after the war was exemplified by the formation of a Coastal Command and Maritime Association.

An aspect of Coastal Command was the lack of direct orders; it was really 'England expects', although, of course, 'Station Routine Orders' and 'Mayflys' (flying details) were always published daily.

I was fortunate in working through the ranks and aircrew grades by beginning as a u/t observer, followed by training as wireless operator and air gunner, but after a tour of operations, re-mustering to pilot/navigator/bomb aimer. While 'on rest' between tours of operations, I was able to appreciate the work of ground staff from blacksmiths, cooks, instrument repairers, etc. in addition to that of the specialist officers. I was lucky in having some brief experience of anti-submarine and anti-shipping operations, as well as reconnaissance. Those operations were over the North Atlantic, the North Sea, the Norwegian Sea and the Mediterranean. Bases used extended from Iceland to North Africa. Overall, it was enough to gain some appreciation of the work of Coastal Command and other services.

Of many recollections, there are those of aircraft coming down in flames, and of crashed aircraft at the end of a runway, and the survivors in the Dallachy Wing 'pancaking' after a raid over Norway. Of other services, FAA Swordfish taking off or landing on their carrier, which was pitching and tossing in half-a-gale. Convoys indicated the vulnerability of merchant vessels, sailing sometimes at only 5 knots, but 'fast' convoys in the Mediterranean at 17 knots. Above all, I best recall the Merchant Navy captain at a convoy conference in April 1942, begging, 'Please may we have more aircraft?' In common with all other veterans of the Second World War, I am conscious of having survived, and of the many friends who did not.

CHAPTER NINE

Conclusions

Coastal Command began the war with one squadron of Hudsons and three squadrons of Sunderland flying-boats. All its other squadrons were equipped with outdated aircraft. It had no effective anti-submarine weapon and its defensive armament was limited to 0.303 in machine-guns. It was therefore in no state to undertake an offensive against either U-boats or enemy shipping. The American Lockheed Hudson provided an invaluable stop-gap for the Command, particularly during the very limited production of Sunderland aircraft.

The German invasion of Norway in April and the capitulation of France in June 1940 opened the way for Coastal to attack enemy shipping. By then, however, the whole of the west European coastline needed to be covered by Coastal, in addition to the western Mediterranean, the South-western Approaches and the North-western Approaches. The entry of Italy into the war meant that some Coastal Command forces had to be deployed in the eastern Mediterranean.

The first successful attacks on enemy merchant shipping were achieved that year by the Command. By then, due to the serious shortage of forces, and its heavy commitments, some bomber squadrons were transferred to Coastal Command.

Although the Command was involved in successful attacks on German U-boats in 1940, it still lacked a lethal weapon, and could only share successes with the Navy's ships. It was to be 1941 before a modified naval depth charge was being carried by both flying-boats and Wellington bomber aircraft that had

transferred from Bomber Command. Outstanding in that year, however, was the 'capture' of U-570 by No. 269 Squadron Hudsons. No less in historical importance was the sighting of the battleship *Bismarck* by a No. 209 Squadron Catalina, and the attack on the battle-cruiser *Gneisenau* by a No. 22 Squadron Beaufort with a torpedo.

The desert campaign in North Africa, and the entry into the war of Japan and America, resulted in Coastal Command being depleted of both aircraft and trained crews to postings in the Middle East and the Far East. Furthermore, due to America's own commitments in the Pacific, it was reluctant to release such valuable aircraft as the Liberator for Coastal Command. Instead, one of the Command's squadrons was deployed off the American Atlantic seaboard to assist in anti-submarine operations.

By 1941, many aircrew had completed their first tour of operations, and it was the Command's policy to use such men as instructors at Coastal Command's own Operational Training Units (OTUs) before flying on a second tour. The German battle-cruisers and heavy cruiser at Brest had 'tied up' considerable forces from both Bomber and Coastal Commands (although little from the Navy). Following the Channel Dash, the Command was able to deploy some of its squadrons to the west to counter both U-boats and *Luftwaffe* aircraft over the Atlantic. This raised an immediate need for bases in the west with runways, and for its limited flying-boats, bases with at least some shelter from wild weather.

The year 1942 marked major turning points for Coastal Command in both its anti-submarine operations and what had become an effective shipping offensive off Norway, the Dutch coast, and to a much lesser degree, in the Bay of Biscay. In anti-submarine warfare, not only were longer-range aircraft such as Fortresses and Liberators becoming available, as they were not required by Bomber Command, but the Leigh-Light Wellingtons were able to overcome the former British weakness, which was the inability to counter night surface attacks by U-boats, against which the Navy's Asdic was useless. In 1942, 250 lb depth charges were available for aircraft such as Hudsons, and in Operation Torch, their effectiveness was clearly demonstrated.

There was a change of policy in the anti-shipping offensive in 1942: that was to cease mast-height attacks, substituting medium-height operations. This was due to the heavy losses that had prevailed in low-level operations. Losses were reduced, but also the number of ships sunk or damaged.

El Alamein was the 'Hinge of Fate' for Churchill in 1942; but for Coastal Command, the turning point was 24 May 1943, when Admiral Dönitz ordered his U-boats away from the North Atlantic to 'safer' areas. This was countered by a base for Coastal Command's aircraft in the Azores. U-boats continued to be a threat, however, up to May 1945, and off the shores of the British Isles. The Mid-Atlantic Gap south of Cape Farewell, where U-boats had operated initially out of range of aircraft, had been closed. This was due to the use of long-range Liberators, but also the whole-hearted cooperation of the Canadians, who, like the Americans, readily adopted Coastal Command's procedures.

In 1943 the Beaufighter strike wings were operating successfully off the Norwegian and Dutch coasts. The intention had been to provide overwhelming forces to attack enemy shipping that were heavily defended by flak ships and fighter aircraft. From the results obtained and the losses suffered, it is questionable whether such considerable forces were justified, particularly in the Norwegian fjords, due to the nature of the terrain and the fighter opposition. The great success of No. 220 Squadron Hudsons in October 1941 had demonstrated an effective alternative.

Strategy and tactics in the U-boat war were varied according to conditions. Air Marshal Slessor considered the Bay of Biscay as the 'trunk of the tree' through which most U-boats passed. There was justification, therefore, in concentrating operations there. Over the Atlantic more surface could be covered by having sweeps by aircraft along the convoy routes rather than by close escort. In practice, all three strategies were used. ASV/radar was used to 'swamp' an area when U-boats had detectors for a specific wavelength, and thus caused U-boats to suffer many alarms. The converse was also applied when U-boats lacked detectors for 10 cm radar, and thus when surprise attacks could be achieved. U-boats at one stage were also prepared to remain surfaced to 'fight it out', but it proved a costly tactic for them, and generally U-boats opted to submerge when aircraft were detected or sighted. The mere presence of an aircraft was therefore a deterrent, and at the critical times of first and last light there was much to be said for close escort of convoys; such was the plea of the Merchant Navy captains.

Radar has been considered by some to be the great innovation in the Second World War. Certainly, even the Mark II in aircraft could detect a surfaced submarine, and there were many such detections. Nevertheless, often U-boats were sighted, as also ships, visually at about the same time as radar detection. The later Mark III radar was a definite improvement, as with a scanner, rather than fixed aerials, and improved sensitivity, accurate bearings could be given, and it was free of 'sea returns'.

Far too little attention was given to the

need for a radio altimeter that would give the height of the aircraft above sea level rather than measuring air pressure. This was because Coastal Command's aircraft operated at low altitudes, and down to 50 ft for attacks on U-boats. Radio altimeters came too late and in too small numbers. There is no doubt that many aircraft were lost due to using an altimeter that had not been corrected for pressure changes.

Initiative was shown by individuals in Coastal Command by the development of such aids as the Leigh Light, and rescue equipment such as the Lindholme dinghy and the airborne lifeboat. Initiative was taken also in improving the forward-firing armament for attacks on U-boats. Many trials were made at squadron level in the development of tactics with cannon, rocket projectiles and torpedoes.

Against ships, the Command gained only limited success with torpedoes, the notable exception being the attack on the *Gneisenau*. Their cost in terms of aircraft, crews and weapons was not justified against merchant vessels. There was limited success with acoustic homing torpedoes against U-boats. The foremost weapon against merchant vessels was the 250 lb bomb, followed by cannon and rocket projectiles. The RPs were also useful against U-boats, but the standard weapon for U-boat attacks was the 250 lb depth charge.

In Operation Overlord, the Command demonstrated that it had developed into a highly efficient force that was able to counter any threat from the enemy's forces at that time. This fact was acknowledged by Admiral Sir Andrew Cunningham.

By 1945, the Command was in conflict with the *Schnorchel*-equipped U-boats, but it was able to counter them to some extent by direct sightings or radar detections, and when they were submerged sonobuoys were used, which in principle were similar to the Navy's Asdic.

For the final wartime Commander, Sir Sholto Douglas, there remained the problem that had prevailed throughout the war for Coastal Command, which was the lack of suitable aircraft with enough range.

From operational records it is apparent that the human factors for aircrew were the space in the aircraft to do their work, space also for the instruments they had to use in sorties of up to eighteen hours and 700 miles out into the Atlantic.

Too little attention was given to the design of aircraft for human beings, the notable exception being the Hudson; the Sunderland had space but lacked effective heating.

Nevertheless, from both operational records and contact with many personnel of all categories, one saw no sign of low morale. In all the squadrons, of those formed from the RFC and the RNAS, there was a 'squadron spirit', and this was obviously so in the Auxiliary squadrons. Coastal's aircrew adopted a fatalistic, philosophical attitude: they just did the job that was expected of them.

My theme has been that Coastal Command was the Cinderella out of three RAF Commands, the two 'sisters' being Fighter and Bomber, which gained precedence; but ultimately Coastal Command achieved much, despite such odds.

Coastal Command's Commanders

No. 10 Group

Apr 1918   Wing Commander A.W. Bigsworth, CMG, DSO, AFC

Air Officers Commanding Coastal Area

Sep 1919   Air Vice-Marshal A.V. Vyvyan, CB, DSO

Sep 1924   Air Vice-Marshal F.R. Scarlett, CB, DSO

May 1928   Air Vice-Marshal C.L. Lambe, CB, CMG, DSO

Oct 1931   Air Vice-Marshal R.H. Clark-Hall, CMG, DSO

Oct 1934   Air Vice-Marshal A.M. Longmore, CB, DSO

Air Officers Commanding-in-Chief Coastal Command

Jul 1936   Air Marshal Sir Arthur M. Longmore, KCB, DSO

Aug 1936   Air Marshal P.B. Joubert de la Ferté, CB, CMG, DSO

Aug 1937   Air Marshal Sir Frederick W. Bowhill, KCB, CMG, DSO

Jun 1941   Air Chief Marshal Sir Philip B. Joubert de la Ferté, KCB,CMG,DSO

Feb 1943   Air Marshal J.C. Slessor, CB, DSO, MC

Jan 1944   Air Chief Marshal Sir Sholto Douglas, KCB, MC, DFC

Jun 1945   Air Marshal Sir Leonard H. Slatter, KBE, CB, DSC, DFC

Nov 1948   Air Marshal J.W. Baker, CB, MC, DFC

Jan 1950   Air Marshal C.R. Steele, CB, DFC

Jun 1951   Air Marshal A.C. Stevens, CB

Nov 1953   Air Marshal Sir John N. Boothman, KBE, CB, DFC, AFC

Apr 1956   Air Marshal Sir Bryan V. Reynolds, KCB, CBE

Summary of Planned Expansion of RAF, 1934–1936

	Home Defence Squadrons	Home Defence Aircraft	Other Home Units, Squadrons	Other Home Units, Aircraft	Overseas Squadrons	Overseas Aircraft	FAA 1st-Line Aircraft	Total 1st-Line Aircraft
Squadron Establishment as at 1 April 1934	42	484	9	75	25	253	150	971
As approved in July 1934	75	884	9	76	27	292	213 (b)	1,465
As approved in May 1935	112	1,386	11	126	27	292	213 (b)	2,017
As approved in February 1936	107(a)	1,568	17	128	37	444	504	2,684

(a) 30 fighter squadrons of 14 aircraft each in place of 12 aircraft
(b) Plus any additional requirements for new construction
[Based on Table No.16 from Grand Strategy Vol. I by N.H. Gibbs]

Coastal Command Order of Battle, 10 September 1939

Group	Base	Squadron	Aircraft
15	Mount Batten	204	Sunderland
	Pembroke Dock	210	Sunderland
	Pembroke Dock	228	Sunderland
	Warmwell	217 (part)	Anson
	Aldergrove	502	Anson
	Carew Cheriton	217 (part)	Anson
16	Bircham Newton	42	Vildebeest
	Bircham Newton	206	Anson
	Thorney Island	22	Vildebeest
	Thorney Island	48 (part)	Anson
	Detling	500	Anson
	Detling	48 (part)	Anson
	Guernsey	48 (part)	Anson
18	Sullom Voe, SS Manela	201	London
	Invergordon	209	Stranraer
	Invergordon	240	London
	Thornaby	220	Anson
	Thornaby	608	Anson
	Leuchars	224	Hudson
	Leuchars	233	Anson
	Montrose	269	Anson
	Dyce	612	Anson

Aircraft in Service with Coastal Command, 10 September 1939

Aircraft	Sqn Estab. IE	Sqn Estab. IR	Economical true speed at 2,000 ft	80% range & endurance in still air	Bomb load with normal tankage	Gun armament (All 0.303s)
Anson	18	6	114 knots 25gal/hr	510 sea miles 4.5 hours	2 x 100 lb	1 x fixed VGO, 1 rear Lewis in manual turret
Vildebeest	12	4	82 knots 26 gal/hr	370 sea miles 4.3 hours	8 x 100 lb or 4 x 250 lb or 2 x 500 lb or 1 x 18" torp.	1 x fixed VGO, 1 rear Lewis on rocking pillar
Hudson	18	6	165 knots 71 gal/hr	990 sea miles 6 hours	10 x 100 lb or 4 x 250 lb	2 fixed fwd Browning, 2 rear in B&P turret
London	6	2	86 knots 55 gal /hr.	450 sea miles 5.2 hours	8 x 250 lb or 4 x 500 lb	1 Lewis in nose, 1 Lewis in centre, 1 rear Lewis, all on ring mounts
Stranraer	6	2	92 knots 55 gal/hr	660 sea miles 7.2 hours	4 x 250 lb or 2 x 500 lb	
Sunderland	6	2	137 knots 130 gal/hr	1,700 sea miles 12.4 hours	8 x 250 lb or 4 x 500 lb	1 front VGO, 2 centre VGOs, 4 Brownings in F-N rear turret

Establishment, Strength and Average Daily Availability During September 1939

Squadrons No. of	Establishment	Reserve	Strength	Average daily availability
6 f.b. sqns	36	12	59	21
13 GR sqns	206	70	239	150
Totals	242	82	298	171

APPENDIX 5

Coastal Command Order of Battle, 1 November 1940

Group	Base	Squadron	Aircraft
No. 15 Plymouth	St Eval	217	Anson/Beaufort
	St Eval	236 (part)	Blenheim fighter
	St Eval	B Flt PRU	Spitfire/Hudson
	Mount Batten	10 RAAF (part)	Sunderland
	Pembroke Dock	209 (part)	Lerwick
	Carew Cheriton	321	Anson
	Aldergrove	502 (part)	Anson/Whitley
	Aldergrove	224 (part)	Hudson
	Aldergrove	48 (part)	Anson
	Aldergrove	236 (part)	Blenheim fighter
	Limavady	502 (part)	Whitley
	Hooton Park	48 (part)	Anson
	Oban	210	Sunderland
	Oban	10 RAAF (part)	Sunderland
	Oban	201 (part)	Sunderland
	Stranraer	240	Stranraer
	Stranraer	209 (part)	Lerwick
	Port Ellen	48 (part)	Anson
No. 16 Chatham	North Coates	22	Beaufort
	North Coates	812 FAA	Swordfish
	Bircham Newton	206 (part)	Hudson
	Bircham Newton	235 (part)	Blenheim fighter
	Bircham Newton	500 (part)	Anson
	Detling	500 (part)	Anson
	Detling	53	Blenheim GR
	Thorney Island	59	Blenheim GR
	Thorney Island	235 (part)	Blenheim fighter
No. 18 Pitreavie Castle	Sullom Voe	201 (part)	Sunderland
	Sullom Voe	204	Sunderland
	Sullom Voe	700 FAA (part)	Walrus
	Sumburgh	248	Blenheim fighter
	Wick	42	Beaufort

Group	Base	Squadron	Aircraft
	Wick	269	Hudson
	Wick	A Flt PRU	Spitfire/Hudson
	Dyce	612 (part)	Anson
	Dyce	254	Blenheim fighter
	Leuchars	233	Hudson
	Leuchars	224 (part)	Hudson
	Leuchars	320	Hudson (training)
	Thornaby	220	Hudson
	Thornaby	608	Anson/Botha
	Stornoway	612 (part)	Anson
Iceland	Kaldadarnes	98	Battle
Gibraltar	Gibraltar harbour	202	London

Additionally, a Photographic Reconnaissance Unit (PRU) was at Heston with Spitfires and Hudsons

Establishment, Strength and Average Daily Availability during November 1940

Squadrons	IE	IR	Serviceable	U/S	Average availability
7 flying-boat sqdns	36	15	33	25	14
22 GR and fighter sqdns	402	14	366	98	197
Totals	438	29	399	123	201
12 FAA sqns	12	-	10	2	9
Totals	450	29	409	125	210

APPENDIX 6

Coastal Command Order of Battle, 15 June 1941

Group	Base	Squadron	Aircraft
No. 15 Liverpool	Aldergrove	254	Blenheim fighter
	Aldergrove	233	Hudson
	Aldergrove	143	Beaufighter
	Limavady	502	Whitley
	Limavady	224	Hudson
	Limavady	221	Wellington
	Nutts Corner	120 (forming)	Liberator
	Lough Erne	209	Catalina
	Lough Erne	240	Catalina
	Hooton Park	48 (part)	Anson
	Oban	210	Catalina
	Port Ellen, Islay	48 (part)	Anson
	Bowmore, Islay	119	C&G flying-boats
Iceland	Kaldadarnes	98	Battle/Hurricane
	Reykjavik	204	Sunderland
	Kaldadarnes	269 (part)	Hudson
	Reykjavik	330 (forming)	Northrop
No. 16 Chatham	North Coates	22	Beaufort
	North Coates	86	Beaufort
	Bircham Newton	206 (part)	Hudson
	Bircham Newton	248	Blenheim fighter
	Bircham Newton	500	Anson/Blenheim F
No. 16 Chatham	Bircham Newton	1403 Met. Flt	Blenheim GR
	Detling	59 (part)	Blenheim GR
	Detling	816 FAA (part)	Swordfish
	Thorney Island	59 (part)	Blenheim GR
	Thorney Island	816 FAA (part)	Swordfish
	Thorney Island	404 and 407(forming)	Blenheim fighters
No. 18 Pitreavie Castle	Sullom Voe	201 (part)	Sunderland
	Wick	269 (part)	Hudson
	Wick	220	Hudson

Group	Base	Squadron	Aircraft
	Wick	612	Whitley
	Wick	1406 Met. Flt	Spitfire
	Wick	C Flight PRU	Spitfire/Blenheim
	Invergordon	201 (part)	Sunderland
	Dyce	235 (part	Blenheim fighter
	Leuchars	42	Beaufort
	Leuchars	320 (Dutch)	Hudson/Anson
	Leuchars	114 BC(on loan)	Blenheim GR
	Thornaby	608	Blenheim GR
	Stornoway	48 (part)	Anson
	Hatston	812 FAA	Swordfish
	Sumburgh	235 (part)	Blenheim fighter
No. 19 Plymouth	St Eval	217	Beaufort
	St Eval	53	Blenheim GR
	St Eval	236 (part)	Blenheim fighter
	St Eval	206 (part)	Hudson
	St Eval	No.1404 Met. Flt	Blenheim GR
	St Eval	B Flt PRU	Spitfire/Blenheim
	Pembroke Dock	10 RAAF	Sunderland
No. 19 Plymouth	Carew Cheriton	236 (part)	Blenheim fighter
No. 200 Gibraltar	Gibraltar	202	London/Catalina
West Africa	Freetown	95	Sunderland
West Africa	Bathurst	200	Hudson
	Benson	No. 1 PRU	Spitfire/Blenheim

Establishment, Strength and Average Daily Availability during June 1941

Squadrons	IE	IR	Serviceable	U/S	Average availability
9 flying-boat sqns	65	7	45	19	17
26 GR and fighter sqns	495	25	408	110	281
Totals	560	32	453	129	298
2 FAA sqns	18	-	16	2	7
Totals	578	32	469	131	305

Three met. flights of total IE 5 + 3 IR and 2 PRU flights of total IE +4 IR

NB No. 120 Liberator, No. 404 Blenheim, No. 407 Hudson, and No. 330 Northrop Squadrons were forming

(Total IE 61 + 8 IR and strength 26 aircraft)

APPENDIX 7

Coastal Command Aircraft Wastage, September 1939 to June 1941

Month	ASW	Convoy escort	Enemy Mvs Strikes/ Recce		Enemy naval units at sea Strikes/ Recce		Air mining	Land targets	Fighter protection	Photo-recce
1939										
Sep.	1	-	-	-	-	9	-	-	-	2
Oct.	4	2	-	-	-	2	-	-	-	-
Nov.	1	-	-	-	-	4	-	-	-	-
Dec.	1	-	-	-	-	4	-	-	-	-
1940										
Jan.	3	1	-	-	-	2	-	-	2	-
Feb.	1	3	-	-	-	1	-	-	-	-
Mar.	1	1	-	-	-	-	-	-	-	-
Apr.	1	-	-	-	2	5	1	3	3	-
May	-	1	-	-	4	19	2	13	1	-
Jun.	-	3	-	-	8	17	3	9	3	1
Jul.	-	2	1	-	2	20	-	9	2	-
Aug.	-	1	2	-	-	18	1	16	2	5
Sep.	-	6	8	-	-	5	1	8	-	2
Oct.	1	4	10	-	1	15	-	2	-	4
Nov.	3	3	5	-	-	2	-	9	5	1
Dec.	2	1	3	4	-	6	2	10	3	2
1941										
Jan.	1	6	2	-	-	5	1	5	1	1
Feb.	1	5	3	2	1	7	2	13	-	2
Mar.	4	5	8	3	-	4	-	2	7	2
Apr.	4	6	13	8	1	7	2	3	6	2
May.	2	5	-	4	-	1	-	4	3	3
Jun.	2	-	5	4	1	9	2	6	4	2
Totals	33	55	60	25	20	162	17	112	42	29

Monthly totals: 12, 8, 5, 5, 8, 5, 2, 15, 40, 44, 36, 45, 30, 37, 28, 33, 22, 36, 35, 52, 22, 35
Grand total for the period September 1939 to June 1941 inclusive: 555 aircraft

APPENDIX 8

Sightings and Attacks on U-boats, September 1939 to June 1941

Month	hrs c/v escort	hrs c/v supt	a/c lost on a/u	sighted	attack	sunk	hrs other tasks	sighted	attack	sunk
1939										
Sep.	1,138	839	1	21	18	-	5,590	6	5	-
Oct.	1,396	685	6	5	4	-	2,090	7	7	-
Nov.	1,038	914	1	2	2	-	2,800	3	3	-
Dec.	1,154	1,314	1	3	3	-	2,600	4	4	-
1940						shared U55				
Jan.	1,025	1,762	4	5	3		2,340	1	1	-
Feb.	1,310	1,762	4	15	11	-	2,080	-	-	-
Mar.	2,800	2,027	2	7	6	-	2,350	-	-	-
Apr.	3,318	1,332	1	9	7	-	3,980	7	5	-
May	4,098	1,719	-	5	4	-	5,310	2	2	-
Jun.	3,990	2,117	1	12	12	-	6,570	1	1	-
Jul.	3,356	1,204	1	2	2	shared U-26	7,340	4	4	-
Aug.	3,437	1,284	2	8	8	-	5,620	6	6	-
Sep.	3,428	965	4	5	5	-	6,000	1	1	-
Oct.	2,337	928	2	4	4	-	4,350	5	4	-
Nov	1,790	869	7	2	2	-	4,670	2	0	-
Dec.	1,443	702	3	3	3	-	4,180	1	0	-
1941										
Jan.	1,445	912	7	1	1	-	2,860	1	1	-
Feb.	1,398	995	6	3	3	-	2,620	1	0	-
Mar	2,079	1,360	9	9	5	-	3,980	-	-	-
Apr.	2,221	1,596	8	4	2	-	5,150	4	3	-
May	2,017	2,362	7	9	5	-	7,650	4	4	-
Jun.	2,063	2,645	1	20	15	-	6,110	6	3	-
Totals	48,281	30,293	78	161	125	2 shared	96,240	66	54	nil

APPENDIX 9

Coastal Command Order of Battle, 15 June 1942

Benson	No. 1 Photographic Reconnaissance Unit	
Gibraltar	No. 202 Squadron	Catalina/Sunderland
	No. 233 Squadron (part)	Hudson
	No. 1 PRU (part)	Spitfire/Mosquito
Iceland		
Kaldadarnes	No. 269 Squadron	Hudson
Reykjavik	No. 612 Squadron	Whitley
	No. 330 Squadron (part)	Northrop/Catalina
	No. 1407 Met. Flight	Hudson

No. 15 Group HQ Liverpool

Aldergrove	No. 206 Squadron	Hudson
	No. 1402 Met. Flight	Hudson/Spitfire
Tiree	No. 224 Squadron	Hudson
Lough Erne	No. 119 Squadron (re-forming)	Catalina
	No. 201 Squadron	Sunderland
	No. 422 (RCAF) Squadron (forming)	Catalina
Nutts Corner	No. 120 Squadron	Liberator
	No. 220 Squadron	Fortress
Oban	No. 228 Squadron	Sunderland
	No. 423 (RCAF) Squadron (forming)	Sunderland
Stornoway	No. 500 Squadron	Hudson

No. 16 Group HQ Chatham

Bircham Newton	No. 235 Squadron	Beaufighter
	No. 407 (RCAF) Squadron	Hudson
	No. 320 (Dutch) Squadron	Hudson
	No. 1401 Met. Flight	Hudson/Mosquito/Spitfire/Gladiator
	No. 279 Squadron	Hudson (Air-Sea Rescue)
North Coates	No. 59 Squadron	Hudson
	No. 415 (RCAF) Squadron	Hampden
Wattisham	No. 236 Squadron	Beaufighter
Thorney Island	No. 233 Squadron (part)	Hudson
	No. 489 (RNZAF) Squadron (forming)	Hampden
	No. 143 Squadron	Blenheim/Beaufighter
Detling	No. 280 Squadron (forming)	Anson (Air-Sea Rescue)

No. 18 Group HQ Pitreavie Castle

Dyce	No. 254 Squadron	Blenheim F.
	No. 404 (RCAF) Squadron	Blenheim F.
Leuchars	No. 144 (Training) Squadron	Hampden
	No. 455 (RAAF) (Training) Squadron	Hampden
	'H' Flight PRU	Mosquito/Spitfire
Sullom Voe	No. 210 Squadron	Catalina
Sumburgh	No. 248 Squadron	Beaufighter
Wick	No. 608 Squadron	Hudson
	No. 48 Squadron	Hudson
	No. 86 Squadron	Beaufort
	No. 1406 Met. Flight	Hudson/Spitfire
	'C' Flight PRU	Mosquito/Spitfire
Woodhaven	No. 330 Squadron (part)	Catalina (PBY5A)

No. 19 Group HQ Plymouth

Mount Batten	No. 10 (RAAF) Squadron	Sunderland
	No. 461(RAAF) Squadron (forming)	Sunderland
St Eval	No. 502 Squadron	Whitley
	No. 53 Squadron	Hudson
	No. 58 Squadron	Whitley
	No. 1404 Met. Flight	Hudson
	'B' Flight PRU	Spitfire/Blenheim
Chivenor	No. 172 Squadron	Wellington (Leigh Light)
	No. 51 Squadron BC (loan)	Whitley
	No. 77 Squadron BC (loan)	Whitley
Talbenny	No. 311 (Czech) Squadron BC (loan)	Wellington
Dale	No. 304 (Polish) Squadron BC (loan)	Wellington

Establishment, Strength and Average Daily Availability, June 1942

Units	Establishment	Reserve	Serviceable	U/S	Av. daily availability
6 Flying-boat Squadrons	48	7	32	22	28
31 GR and Fighter Sqns, inc. those on loan	484	114	356	134	201
Totals	532	121	388	156	229
5 Met. Flights	34	17	21	19	15
No. 1 PRU	58	15	59	12	40
1 ASR Squadron	16	4	12	10	-
4 Flying-boat Squadrons forming	30	6	3	2	non-op
1 Torpedo Squadron forming	16	4	15	4	non-op
1 ASR Squadron forming	16	4	-	-	non-op

APPENDIX 10

Coastal Command Order of Battle, 15 October 1942

Benson	Nos 540, 541, 542, 543, 544 PRU	Mosquito/Spitfire
	Squadrons/Flights detached at Leuchars,	
	St Eval and Gibraltar	Wellington/Anson
West Indies	No. 53 Squadron	Hudson
Gibraltar	No. 202 Squadron	Catalina
	No. 233 Squadron	Hudson
	No. 544 (PRU) Squadron (part)	Spitfire
Iceland		
Kaldadarnes	No. 269 Squadron	Hudson
Reykjavik	No. 330 (Norsk) Squadron (part)	Northrop
	No. 73 VP Squadron USN	Catalina PBY5A
	No. 1407 Met. Flight	Hudson

No. 15 Group HQ Liverpool

Aldergrove	No. 1402 Met. Flight	Spitfire/Hudson/Gladiator
Ballykelly	No. 120 Squadron	Liberator
	No. 220 Squadron	Fortress
Lough Erne	No. 201 Squadron	Sunderland
	No. 422 (RCAF) Squadron (forming)	Sunderland
Benbecula	No. 206 Squadron	Fortress
	No. 279 (ASR) Squadron (part)	Hudson
Oban	No. 228 Squadron	Sunderland
	No. 423 (RCAF) Squadron (forming)	Sunderland
Stornoway	No. 58 Squadron	Whitley

No. 16 Group HQ Chatham

Bircham Newton	No. 320 (Dutch) Squadron	Hudson
	No. 254 Squadron	Beaufighter
	No. 811 FAA Squadron (on loan)	Swordfish

	No. 812 FAA Squadron (on loan)	Swordfish
	No. 521 Met. Squadron	Mosqito/Spitfire
	No. 279 ASR Squadron (part)	Hudson/Albermarle
Langham	No. 280 ASR Squadron	Anson
North Coates	No. 143 Squadron	Blenheim/Beaufighter
	No. 236 Squadron	Beaufighter
Thorney Island	No. 816 FAA Squadron (on loan)	Swordfish
	No. 819 FAA Squadron (on loan)	Swordfish
	No. 59 Squadron (converting)	Liberator
	No. 86 Squadron (converting)	Liberator

No. 18 Group HQ Pitreavie Castle

Dyce	No. 404 (RCAF) Squadron	Beaufighter/Blenheim
Leuchars	No. 144 Squadron	Hampden
	No. 455 (RAAF) Squadron	Hampden
	No. 415 (RCAF) Squadron	Hampden
	No. 540 PRU Squadron (part)	Mosquito
Woodhaven	No. 330 (Norge) Squadron (part)	Catalina III
Sullom Voe	No. 210 Squadron	Catalina
Sumburgh	No. 48 Squadron	Hudson
Wick	No. 489 (RNZAF) Squadron	Hampden
	No. 179 Squadron	Wellington (Leigh Light)
	No. 612 Squadron	Whitley
	No. 1406 Met. Flight	Spitfire/Hudson/Albermarle

No. 19 Group HQ Plymouth

Beaulieu	No. 224 Squadron	Liberator
Mount Batten	No. 10 (RAAF) Squadron	Sunderland
Pembroke Dock	No. 119 Squadron (re-equipping)	Sunderland
Hamworthy	No. 461 (RAAF) Squadron	Sunderland
St.Eval	No. 502 Squadron	Whitley
	No. 407 (RCAF) Squadron	Hudson
	No. 10 OTU BC (on loan)	Whitley
	No. 543 PRU Squadron (part)	Spitfire
	No. 1404 Met. Flight	Hudson/Albermarle
Chivenor	No. 172 Squadron	Wellington (Leigh Leight)
	No. 235 Squadron	Beaufighter
Talbenny	No. 311 (Czech) Squadron	Wellington
	No. 248 Squadron	Beaufighter
Dale	No. 304 (Polish) Squadron	Wellington

Establishment, Strength and Average Daily Availability, October 1942

Units	Establishment	Reserve	Serviceable	U/S	Availability
8 Flying-boat Squadrons, inc. 1 USN	72	21	53	47	44
30 GR and Fighter, inc. 1 BC Sqn	469	111	343	225	180
Totals	541	132	396	272	224
+4 FAA Sqns with 36 a/c on loan					
5 PRU squadrons	67	16	59	23	35
1 Met. sqdn and 4 Flights	38	19	24	28	16
2 ASR squadrons	32	8	28	12	

Non-operational:
4 Flying-boat squadrons forming or converting of totals IE 24 + 12 IR
2 GR squadrons converting to Liberators of totals IE 18 + 6 IR
2 GR squadrons under orders to move to Gibraltar

APPENDIX **11**

Coastal Command Order of Battle, 15 February 1943

Benson	Nos 540, 541, 542, 543, and 544 Squadrons (Flts detached at Leuchars, St Eval and Gibraltar)	Mosquito 15 Spitfire 66, Wellington 2
Gibraltar	No. 202 Squadron	Catalina 1- 12
	No. 210 Squadron detachment	Catalina 1
	No. 48 Squadron	Hudson VI-16+4
	No. 233 Squadron	Hudson III-16+4
	No. 544 PRU Squadron detachment	Spitfires
	No. 179 Squadron	LLWellington VIII-16+4

Iceland

Kaldadarnes	No. 269 Squadron	Hudson III 20+4
Reykjavik	VP 84 USN	Catalina III 12
	No. 120 Squadron detachment	Liberators
	No. 1407 Met. Flight	Hudson III 4+2
	No. 330 (Norge) Squadron detachment	Northrop 6+0

No. 15 Group HQ Liverpool

Aldergrove	No. 1402 Met. Flight	Spit/Hud/Glad 9+5
Ballykelly	No. 120 Squadron	VLR Libs I and III- 16+4
	No. 220 Squadron	Fortress IIA 9+3
	No. 280 ASR Squadron detachment	Anson
Lough Erne	No. 201 Squadron	Sunderland II and III-6+3
	No. 228 Squadron	Sunderland II and III-6+3
	No. 423 (RCAF) Squadron	Sunderland II and III-6+3
Oban	No. 422 (RCAF) Squadron (forming)	Sunderland III-6+3
	No. 330 (Norge) Squadron re-equipping	Sunderland III-6+3
Bowmore	No. 246 Squadron	Sunderland II and III-6+3
Benbecula	No. 206 Squadron	Fortress IIA -9+3

No. 16 Group HQ Chatham

Bircham Newton	No. 320 (Dutch) Squadron	Hudson V and VI 16+4
	No. 407 (RCAF) Squadron	Hudson V and VI 16+4
	No. 521 Metcal Squadron	Spt/Mos/Hud/Glad 15+7

	No. 279 ASR Squadron	Hudson III 16+4
Bircham Newton	No. 280 ASR Squadron	Anson 16-4
Docking	No. 53 Squadron (Hudson) re-equipping	Whitley V
North Coates	No. 143 Squadron	Beaufighter II(F) 16+4
	No. 236 Squadron	Beau.IC and VIC(F) 16+4
	No. 254 Squadron	Beau.VIC(T/F) 16+4
Thorney Island	No. 415 (RCAF) Squadron	Hampden(T/B) 16+4
	No. 833 FAA Squadron (on loan)	Swordfish 9
	No. 836 FAA Squadron (on loan)	Swordfish 9
	No. 86 Squadron partially operational on VLR	Liberator III 16+4

No. 18 Group HQ Pitreavie Castle

Leuchars	No. 144 Squadron	Beaufighter 16+4
	No. 455 (RAAF) Squadron	Hampden T/B 16+4
	No. 235 Squadron	Beaufighter 16+4
	No. 540 PRU Squadron detachment	Mosquito
Woodhaven	No. 1477 (Norge) Flight	Catalina IB 3+0
Sullom Voe	No. 190 Squadron	Catalina IB 6+3
Wick	No. 489 (RNZAF) Squadron	Hampden T/B 16+4
	No. 612 Squadron re-equipping	Whitley/LL Wel. 16+4
	No. 1406 Met. Flight	Spitfire/Hudson 6+3

No. 19 Group HQ Plymouth

Beaulieu	No. 224 Squadron	Liberator II, III and V 9+3
	No. 405 BC Squadron on loan	Halifax 12
Chivenor	No. 172 Squadron	LL Wel.VIII and XII 16+4
	No. 179 Squadron detachment	LL Wellingtons
	No. 547 Squadron	Wellington VIII T/B 6+2
	No. 59 Squadron	Fortress IIA 9+3
	No. 404 (RCAF) Squadron	Beaufighter II (F) 16+4
Talbenny	No. 311 (Czech) Squadron	Wellington IC 16+2
Dale	No. 304 (Polish) Squadron	Wellington IC and X 16+2
St Eval	No. 502 Squadron	Whitley VII 16+4
	No. 10 (B)OTU on loan	Whitley 20
	1st A/S US AAC Squadron	Liberator 12
	2nd A/S US AAC Squadron	Liberator 12
	No. 1404 Met. Flight	Huds/Ven/Albermarle 4+2
	No. 543 PRU Squadron detachment	Spitfires
Predannack	No. 248 Squadron	Beaufighter VIC (F) 16+4
Mountbatten	No. 10 (RAAF) Squadron	Sunderland II and III 6+3
Pembroke Dock	No. 210 Squadron	Catalina I,1B and IIA 6+3
	No. 119 Squadron	Sunderland II and III 6+3
Hamworthy	No. 461 (RAAF) Squadron	Sunderland II and III 6+3
Holmesley South	No. 58 Squadron	Whitley/Halifax 9+3

Establishment, Strength and Average Daily Availability, February 1943

Units	Establishment	Strength	Non-op. U/S	Available
12 2 Flying-boat Sqns inc. one USN Sqn	126	118	69	49
18 ASW GR Sqns. inc. 2 BC and 2 USAAC Sqns	304	293	132	161
13 AS, GR and LR Fighter Squadrons	238	260	115	145
Total: 43 2 Squadrons fully operational	668	671	316	355
5 PRU Squadrons	91	85	31	54
1 Met. Sqn and 4 Flights	68	49	15	34
2 ASR Squadrons	40	34	8	8

To the above must be added 6 squadrons, altogether or partially out of the line:

No. 422 (RCAF) Squadron forming with 6+3 Sunderlands
No. 53 Squadron re-equipping from Hudsons to 16+3 Whitleys
No. 58 Squadron re-equipping from Whitleys to 9+3 Halifaxes
No. 407 (RCAF) Squadron re-equipping from Hudsons to 16+4 LL Wellingtons
No. 502 Squadron re-equipping from Whitleys to 9+3 Halifaxes
No. 547 Squadron with 6+2 Wellingtons on torpedo training

APPENDIX 12

Coastal Command Order of Battle, Establishment, Strength and Availability, 1 March 1943

No. 15 Group	Estab.	Strength	Availability	Remarks
Ballykelly				
No. 120 VLR Lib. I/IIA	16+4	14	11	Det. in Iceland
No. 220 Fortress 1/II	9+3	13	4	
Benbecula				
No. 206 Fortress I/II	9+3	14	5	
Castle Archdale				
No. 201 Sunderland II/III	6+3	11	4	
No. 228 Sunderland II/III	6+3	8	2	
No. 423 Sunderland II/III	6+3	9	3	
Oban				
No. 422 Sunderland III	6+3	9	4	
No. 330 Sunderland III	6+3	5	Nil	Forming
Bowmore				
No. 246 Sunderland II/III	6+3	9	3	
No. 16 Group				
Thorney Island				
No. 86 VLR Lib. IIIA	16+4	17	12	
No. 415 Hampden I torp	16+4	17	12	
No. 833 Swordfish FAA	9	9	7	On loan
No. 836 Swordfish FAA	9	9	6	On loan
Bircham Newton				
No. 320 Hudson V/VI	16+4	13	9	To re-equip Mk XI
No. 53 Whitleys/Libs.	16+4	21	3	Re-equipping
North Coates				
No. 143 Bfter II	16+4	20	9	To re-equip Mk XI
No. 236 Bftr IC/VI	16+4	21	3	Re-equipping
No. 254 Bftr VI torp	16+4	22	14	To re-equip Mk X
No. 18 Group				
Sullom Voe				
No. 190 Catalina IB	6+3	9	4	

	Estab.	Strength	Available	Remarks
Wick				
No. 489 Hampden I	16+4	25	15	
No. 612 Whitley/LL Well.	16+4	18	9	Re-equipping
No. 407 Wellington I/II	16+4	20	9	To re-equip LL
Leuchars				
No. 144 Bftr VIC torp	16+4	20	16	
No. 235 Bftr VIC ftr	16+4	20	14	
No. 455 Hamp. I torp	16+4	20	12	To re-equip
Woodhaven				
No. 1477 Flt. (Norge) Cat. IB	3+0	2	1	Special Duties
No. 19 Group				
Mount Batten				
No. 10 (RAAF) Sund. II/III	6+3	9	4	
Pembroke Dock				
No. 119 Sunderland II/III	6+3	10	5	
No. 210 Catalina IB	6+3	4	3	Half at Gibraltar
Hamworthy				
No. 461 Sunderland II/III	6+3	9	4	
Chivenor				
No. 172 LL Well. VIII/XII	16+4	20	7	
No. 547 Well. VIII torp	6+2	10	Nil	Training at Tain
No. 59 Fortress IIA	9+3	10	7	
No. 404 Beaufighter II ftr	16+4	19	5	To re-equip to Mk XIC
Talbenny				
No. 311 (Czech) Well. IC	16+4	17	12	To re-equip to Mk X
Dale				
No. 304 (Polish) Well. IC	16+4	19	9	To re-equip to Mk X
St Eval				
Nos 1 and 2 USAAF Lib.	24	13	10	On loan-left 5.3.43.
No. 10(B) OTU Whitley	26	20	15	On loan
No. 502 Halifax II	9+3	12	1	Non-op until March
Predannock				
No. 248 Beaufighter VI ftr	16+4	20	14	
Exeter				
No. 834 FAA Swordfish	9	9	6	On loan
Holmsley South				
No. 58 Halifax II	9+3	11	2	Non-op until March
Beaulieu				
No. 224 Liberator II/III/V	9+3	6	2	
ICELAND				
Reykjavik				
No. 120 det.VLR Liberators	-	7	3	
No. 330 det. Northrops	-	9	4	
VP84 USN PBY5As	12	12	8	On loan

	Estab.	Strength	Available	Remarks
Kaldadarnes				
No. 269 Hudson III	20+4	23	16	
GIBRALTAR				
New Camp				
No. 202 Catalina IB	12+0	15	10	
No. 210 Catalina IB	-	7	5	
North Front				
No. 48 Hudson VI	16+4	23	17	
No. 233 Hudson III	16+4	20	12	
Coastal Command Squadrons 42+one Flt	513+145	637	323	
Squadrons on loan 7	89	71	52	

Photo-Reconnaissance	Estab.	Strength	Available	Remarks
Benson				
No. 540 Mosquito Mks var.	18+4	22	10	Det. at Leuchars
No. 541 Spitfires Mks var.	14+4	14	9	
No. 542 Spitfires Mks var.	14+4	22	15	
No. 543 Spitfires Mks var.	14+4	16	10	Det. at St Eval
No. 544 Spitfires, Anson and Wellingtons	7+2	9	6	Det. at Gibraltar

AIR-SEA RESCUE				
Bircham Newton				
No. 279 Hudson III	16+4	12	7	
No. 280 Anson I	16+4	22	17	

METEOROLOGICAL				
Bircham Newton				
No. 521 Mosquito, Hampden, Gladiator, Spitfire	17+8	19	14	Det. at Gibraltar
Aldergrove				
No. 1402 Flt Hampden, Gladiator, Spitfire	9+5	14	8	
St Eval				
No. 1404 Flt Hampden, Hudson	4+2	9	5	
Wick				
No. 1406 Flt Hampden, Spitfire	6+3	9	2	
Iceland				
No. 1407 Flt Hampden, Hudson	4+2	2	1	

APPENDIX 13

Coastal Command Order of Battle, Establishment, Strength and Availability, 1 January 1944

Group	Estab.	Strength	Availability	Remarks
No. 15				
Ballykelly				
No. 86 VLR Liberator V/IIIA	15	18	4	
No. 59 VLR Liberator V	15	14	7	
Castle Archdale				
No. 201 Sunderland III	12	12	4	
No. 422 Sunderland III	12	12	3	
No. 423 Sunderland III	12	11	3	
No. 16				
Bircham Newton				
No. 415 Albacore, Wellington XIII	10, 15	10, 14	5, 8	Albacores on detachment at Manston and Thorney Island
North Coates				
No. 236 Beaufighter X RP	20	18	12	
No. 254 Beaufighter X torp	20	18	12	
Thorney Island				
No. 547 Liberator V	15	12	Nil	Re-equipping
No. 18				
Leuchars				
No. 333 Mosquito VI Flt	6	5	2	
No. 455 Beaufighter X RP	20	16	Nil	Training/re-equipping
No. 489 Beaufighter X torp	20	21	Nil	Training/re-equipping
Wick				
No. 144 Beaufighter X torp	20	21	10	
No. 404 Beaufighter X RP	20	20	4	
No. 618 Mosquito IV Special op.	20	14	Nil	Non-operational
No. 1693 Flt Anson	6	5	2	

	Estab.	Strength	Available	Remarks
Woodhaven				
No. 333 Catalina IB Flt	3	2	1	
Sullom Voe				
No. 190 LL Catalina IB/IV	12	13	2	Withdrawing to re-form as 210
No. 330 Sunderland II/III	12	13	3	
No. 19				
Mount Batten				
No. 10 RAAF Sunderland II/III	12	13	4	
Pembroke Dock				
No. 228 Sunderland III	12	11	5	
No. 461 Sunderland III	12	11	4	
Chivenor				
No. 172 LL Wellington XIV	15	15	1	Det. in Azores
No. 407 LL Wellington XII/XIV	15	15	6	
No. 612 LL Wellington XIV	15	15	4	
St Eval				
No. 224 LL Liberator V	15 1	3	3	1 a/c with RP
Dunkeswell				
No. 103 USN Liberator	12	11	6	On loan
No. 105 USN Liberator	12	12	7	On loan
No. 110 USN Liberator	12	12	7	On loan
St Davids				
No. 58 Halifax II	15	16	6	
No. 502 Halifax II	15	14	4	
Beaulieu				
No. 311 Liberator V	15	12	8	10 a/c with RP
No. 53 VLR LL Liberator V	15	16	7	1 a/c with RP
Predannack				
No. 304 LL Wellington XIV,	15	15	5	
Beaufighter X fighters	20	11	9	Re-equipping to Mos.VI
No. 248 Mosquito XVIII 6-pdr	2	2	1	
Portreath				
No. 143 Beaufighter XIC ftrs	20	18	12	
No. 235 Beaufighter X ftrs and XIC	20	19	7	
ICELAND				
Reykjavik				
No. 120 VLR Liberator I/III/V	15	18	4	All Mk V a/c with LL
GIBRALTAR				
No. 202 LL Catalina IB/IV	12	12	9	
No. 48 Hudson III/IIIA/VI RP	20	20	10	
No. 233 Hudson III/IIIA (RP)	20	17	3	Det. in Azores

No. 179 LL Wellington XIV	15	14	5	

AZORES (No. 247 Group)

Lagens

No. 206 Fortress II/IIA	15	16	4	
No. 220 Fortress II/IIA	15	16	5	
No. 233 Hudson III/IIIA (RP)	-	-	8	Det.from Gibraltar
No. 172 LL Wellington XIV	-	-	2	Det.from Chivenor
Coastal Command Squadrons	630	598	218	
40+1 Flight; Squadrons on loan 3	36	35	20	

AIR-SEA RESCUE

Bircham Newton

No. 279 Hudson III/V/VI	20	16	7	

Thornaby

No. 280 Warwick I	20	21	4	
No. 281 Warwick I	20	16	Nil	

Iceland

No. 269 Hudson III Flight	2	2	2	

METEOROLOGICAL

St Davids

No. 517 Halifax V	23	8	-	Re-equipping

Tiree

No. 518 Halifax V	14	15	2	

Wick

No. 519 Ventura V, Gladiator	17	15	4	

Bircham Newton

No. 521 Ventura V, Gladiator	9	8	2	

Aldergrove

No. 1402 Flt Gladiator, Spitfire	8	7	5	

Iceland

No. 1407 Flt Ventura V	6	-	-	Re-equipping

Gibraltar

No. 520 Halifax V, Gladiator	9	1	-	Re-equipping

PHOTOGRAPHIC RECONNAISSANCE

Benson

No. 540 Mosquito II	20	18	10	Det. at Leuchars
No. 541 Spitfire II/XIII	20	22	16	Det.at St Eval and Gibraltar
No. 542 Spitfire IV/XI/XIII	20	21	13	
No. 544 Mosquito IX	20	17	11	

APPENDIX 14

Distribution Between Anti-U-boat and Anti-Shipping Operations, 1 March 1945

Anti-U-boat					Anti-Shipping			
Group	Squadrons	UE	Strength	Available	Squadrons	UE	Strength	Available
No. 15	59, 120, 304, 201, 202, 423, 172, 815	112	111	53	None	-	-	-
No. 16	810, 822	24	26	19	119, 612, 236, 254, 813, half 524	95	95	60
No. 18	206, 547, 224, 210, 330, 86, 311, half 1693,	105	116	42	143, 235, 248, 144, 404, 455, 489, 58, 502, half 524, half 333	188	173	93
No. 19	14, 36, 407, 228, 10, 422, 461, 179, 103, 105, 107, 110, 112, half 63	187	180	114	None	-		-
Iceland	53, 162	30	35	15	None	-	-	-
Gibraltar	22, 458	35	33	23	None	-	-	-
Azores	220, 144	27	24	11	None	-	-	-
Battle Line	37 squadrons	520	525	277	15 squadrons	283	268	153

APPENDIX 15

Coastal Command Order of Battle, Establishment, Strength and Availability, 1 April 1945

Group, Bases and Squadrons	Estab.	Strength	Available
NO. 15 GROUP			
Ballykelly			
No. 59 VLR Liberator V and VIII	15	15	13
No. 120 LL Liberator VIII	15	15	11
Benbecula			
No. 36 LL Wellington XIV	15	15	10
Castle Archdale			
No. 201 Sunderland III	12	10	5
No. 423 Sunderland III and V	12	13	7
No. 202 LL Catalina IVA	16	16	7
Limavady			
No. 172 LL Wellington XIV	15	13	7
Total in No. 15 Group – 7 RAF Squadrons	*100*	*97*	*60*
NO. 16 GROUP			
Thorney Island (under No. 19 Group control)			
No. 810 FAA Barracuda	12	10	10
No. 822 FAA Barracuda	12	11	10
Langham			
No. 612 Wellington XIV Mk VIA radar	15	15	11
No. 524 Wellington XIV Mk IIIA radar	20	17	9
North Coates			
No. 236 Beaufighter X RP	20	18	14
No. 254 Beaufighter X RP	20	21	11
No. 254 Mos. XVIII Tsetse 6-pounder	4	4	4
Knocke, North Belgium			
No. 119 Swordfish III	15	15	11
Total in No. 16 Group – 5 RAF + 2 FAA Sqns	*118*	*111*	*80*
NO. 18 GROUP			
Banff			
No. 143 Mosquito VI RP	20	18	16
No. 235 Mosquito VI RP	20	20	14

Group, Bases and Squadrons	Estab.	Strength	Available
No. 248 Mosquito VI RP	20	22	18
No. 333 (Norge) Flt Mosquito VI RP	10	9	7
Dallachy			
No. 144 Beaufighter X RP	20	19	12
No. 455 RAAF Beaufighter X RP	20	22	13
No. 489 RNZAF Beaufighter X torp	20	20	11
No. 404 RCAF rearming to Mosquitoes			
Leuchars			
No. 206 LL Liberator VIII	15	15	4
No. 547 LL Liberator VI	15	14	6
Milltown			
No. 224 LL Liberator VIII	15	17	8
Stornoway			
No. 58 Halifax II and III	15	15	6
No. 502 Halifax II and III	15	15	7
Sullom Voe			
No. 210 LL Catalina IVA	12	10	4
No. 330 (Norge) Sunderland III	9	8	2
Tain			
No. 86 LL Liberator VIII	15	15	8
No. 311 Czech LL Liberator VI	15	15	8
Woodhaven			
No. 333 (Norge) Flight Catalina IVA	3	3	-
Sumburgh			
No. 1693 Flight Anson	6	7	5
Total in No.18 Group – 16 RAF Squadrons	*265*	*264*	*149*
NO. 19 GROUP			
Chivenor			
No. 14 LL Wellington XIV	15	16	11
No. 407 RCAF LL Wellington XIV	15	14	10
No. 459 RAAF LL Wellington non-op.	-	-	-
Dunkeswell			
No. 103 USN Liberator	15	15	13
No. 105 USN Liberator	15	14	13
No. 110 USN Liberator	15	15	14
Mount Batten			
No. 10 RAAF Sunderland III	12	15	8
Pembroke Dock			
No. 228 Sunderland III	12	15	9
No. 422 RCAF Sunderland III	12	11	9
No. 461 RAAF Sunderland III and V	12	16	8
St Eval			
No. 179 LL Warwick V	15	12	6
No. 304 LL Wellington XIV	15	15	11

Group, Bases and Squadrons	Estab.	Strength	Available
Upottery			
No. 107 USN Liberator	15	13	11
No. 112 USN Liberator	15	15	14
VP63 USN det, MAD PBY5A	4	4	3
Total in No. 19 Group – 8 RAF+ 5 USN Sqns	*187*	*190*	*140*
ICELAND			
Reykjavik			
No. 53 LL Liberator VIII	15	15	5
No. 162 RCAF Cansos (Catalina III amphibian)	15	13	5
Total in Iceland – 1 RAF + 1 RCAF Squadron	*30*	*28*	*10*
GIBRALTAR			
No. 458 RAAF LL Wellington XIV	15	16	11
No. 22 SAAF Ventura V	20	18	13
Total in Gibraltar – 1 RAF + 1 SAAF	*35*	*34*	*24*
AZORES			
Lagens			
No. 220 LL Liberator VI	15	15	10
No. 114 USN LL Liberator	15	14	11
Total in the Azores- 1 RAF + 1 USN	*30*	*29*	*21*
PHOTOGRAPHIC -RECONNAISSANCE			
Benson			
No. 540 Mosquitoes VI/IX/XVI	20	21	14
No. 541 Spitfires X/XI/XIX; Mustang III	23	19	14
No. 542 Spitfires X, XI and XIX	20	21	19
No. 544 Mosquitoes VI/XVI Det. at Leuchars	20	18	13
Total Photo-Reconnaissance – 4 Squadrons	*83*	*79*	*60*
AIR-SEA RESCUE			
Tiree			
No. 281 Warwick, Sea Otter, Det. at Limavady	18	20	5
Beccles			
No. 278 Walrus,Sea Otter, Det. at Hawkinge	16	14	9
No. 280 Warwick	24	26	10
Banff			
No. 279 Warwick, Hurricane; Det. at Wick, Leuchars and Thornaby	28	35	15
St Eval			
No. 282 Warwick, Sea Otter	18	19	11
Lagens, Azores			
No. 269 Warwick, Martlett, Spitfire, Anson. Combined ASR and Met. Flts	17	17	9
Total ASR – 6 Squadrons	*121*	*131*	*59*

Group, Bases and Squadrons	Estab.	Strength	Available
METEOROLOGICAL FLIGHTS			
Tiree			
No. 518 Halifax V	22	24	7
Ballyhalbert			
No. 1402 Flt Spitfire VII, Hurricane IIC	9	8	6
Langham			
No. 521 Fortress II, Hurriance IIC	9	9	8
Skitten			
No. 519 Fortress II, Spitfire VII	15	14	6
Brawdy			
No. 517 Halifax V	13	15	4
Reykjavik, Iceland			
No. 251 Fortress II, Hudson III	12	14	7
Gibraltar			
No. 520 Halifax V, Hudson, Hurricane	13	11	5
Total Meteorological – 6 Squadrons	*93*	*95*	*43*

Summary of Coastal Command, 1 April 1945

Group	Estab.	Strength	Available	Number of Squadrons
No. 15	100	97	59	7 RAF
No. 16	118	111	80	5 RAF + 2 FAA
No. 18	265	264	149	16 RAF
No. 19	187	185	138	8 RAF + 5 USN
Iceland	30	28	10	2 RAF
Gibraltar	35	34	24	1 RAF + 1 SAAF
Azores	30	29	21	1 RAF + 1 USN
Coastal Command Battle Line	765	748	481	40 RAF + 2 FAA + 1 SAAF + 6 USN
Photo-Reconnaissance	83	79	60	4 Squadrons
Air-Sea Rescue	121	131	9	6 Squadrons
Meteorological	93	95	43	6 Squadrons

APPENDIX 17

Distribution Between Anti-U-boat and Anti-Shipping Operations, 1 April 1945

Anti-U-boat					Anti-Shipping			
Group	Squadrons	UE	Strength	Available	Squadrons	UE	Strength	Available
No. 15	59, 120, 36, 201, 202, 423, 172	100	97	59	None	-	-	-
No. 16	810, 822	24	21	20	119, 612, 236, 254, 524	94	90	60
No. 18	206, 547, 224, 210, 330, 86, 311, half 133, half 1693	105	104	45	143, 235, 248, 58, 502, half 333	160	160	104
No. 19	14, 407, 228, 10, 422, 461, 179, 304, 103, 105, 107, 110, 112, half 63	187	185	138	None	-	-	-
Iceland	53, 162	30	28	10	None	-	-	-
Gibraltar	22, 458	35	34	24	None	-	-	-
Azores	220, 114	30	29	21	None	-	-	-
Battle Line	36 squadrons	511	498	317	13 Squadrons	254	250	164

APPENDIX **18**

U-boats Sunk or Damaged by Coastal-Command-Controlled Aircraft

Group	Number of U-boats Sunk Outright			No.of U-boats sunk shared with Naval Forces	
	By Coastal Command a/c	By US a/c under CC control	By Canadian EAC a/c under CC control	By Coastal Command a/c	By US a/c under CC control
No. 15	31 German	-	-	5 German	-
No. 16	5 German	-	-	-	-
No. 18	39 German	-	-	2 German	-
No. 19	53 German 1 Italian	9 German	-	6 German	1 German
Iceland		9 German	1 German	1 German	-
Gibraltar	13 German 3 Italian	-	-	5 German 1 Italian	2 German
Azores	5 German	-	-	1 German	
Totals	146 German 4 Italian	18 German	1 German	20 German 1 Italian	3 German
Grand Totals	165 German 4 Italian			23 German 1 Italian	

Group	No. of U-boats Damaged by:		
	Coastal Command Aircraft	Bomber or Fighter Command Aircraft under CC Control	American Aircraft under Coastal Command Control
No. 15	16 German	-	-
No. 18	24 German	-	-
No. 19	44 German 4 Italian	7 German	2 German
Iceland	10 German	-	3 German
Azores	1 German	-	
Totals	95 German 4 Italian	7 German	5 German
Command Totals	107 German 4 Italian		

Only U-boats which were so damaged that they had to break off operations or return to port are listed.

APPENDIX **19**

Enemy-Controlled Ships Sunk or Damaged by Coastal-Command-Controlled Aircraft

Year	No. 16 Group		No. 18 Group		No. 19 Group	
	Sunk	Damaged	Sunk	Damaged	Sunk	Damaged
1940	2/2,860	8/32,176	4/2,701	6/15,486	Nil	Nil
1941	9/23,374	3/15,042	16/19,659	15/29,685	3/8,932	2/39,640
1942	13/27,139	5/17,559	8/27,343	6/16,075	5/942	9/48,478
1943	18/41,944	2/19,093	10/33,083	2/1,785	4/9,732	1/6,240
1944	99/80,105	6/15,449	42/68,308	29/98,110	29/34,779	4/13,699
1945	37/14,686	4/24,444	67/116,743	32/120,493	Nil	Nil
Total No. *Ships*	*178*	*28*	*147*	*90*	*41*	*16*
Total Tonnage	190,108	123,763	267,337	281,634	54,385	108,057

Total No. of Ships Sunk by Coastal-Command-Controlled Aircraft		366
	Total Tonnage	512,330
Total No. of Ships Damaged by Coastal-Command-Controlled Aircraft		134
	Total Tonnage	513,454

Mines Laid by Coastal-Command-Controlled Aircraft

Year	No. 15 Group	No. 16 Group	No. 18 Group	No. 19 Group	Yearly Totals
1940	3	396 + 288	13	-	412 + 288
1941	-	110	16	224	350
1942	-	141	6	-	147
1943	-	27	-	-	27
War Totals	*3*	*674 + 288*	*35*	*224*	*936 + 288*

APPENDIX 20

Coastal-Command-Controlled Aircraft Lost During the Second World War

1. On Anti-Shipping Operations

Group	Year							War Total
	1939	1940	1941	1942	1943	1944	1945	
15	4	20	34	24	20	19	3	124
16	3	7	1	-	-	2	2	15
18	2	11	25	19	8	21	10	96
19	-	-	17	117	179	90	9	412
Iceland	-	-	2	12	6	8	1	29
Gibraltar	-	-	4	28	16	7	1	56
Azores	-	-	-	-	4	4	1	9
Yearly Total	9	38	83	200	233	151	27	741

2. On Anti-Shipping Operations

Group	Year							War Total
	1939	1940	1941	1942	1943	1944	1945	
15	-	19	4	-	-	-	-	23
16	10	88	63	79	49	88	20	397
18	9	63	63	59	42	50	81	358
19	-	-	38	26	7	27	-	98
Yearly Total	19	170	168	164	98	165	101	885

3. On Mine-Laying Operations

Group	Year							War Total
	1939	1940	1941	1942	1943	1944	1945	
15	-	1	-	-	-	-	-	1
16	-	9	14	8	4	-	-	35
18	-	-	2	-	-	-	-	2
19	-	-	4	-	-	-	-	4
Yearly Total	-	10	20	8	4	-	-	42

4. Aircraft Lost on Fighter Protection of Ships

Group	Year							War Total
	1939	1940	1941	1942	1943	1944	1945	
15	-	5	8	-	-	-	-	13
16	-	5	6	3	-	-	-	14
18	-	11	8	6	-	-	-	25
19	-	-	15	8	3	-	-	26
Yearly Total	-	21	37	17	3	-	-	78

5. Aircraft Lost During Attacks on Land Targets

Group	Year							War Total
	1939	1940	1941	1942	1943	1944	1945	
15	-	14	14	2	-	-	-	30
16	-	53	17	2	-	-	-	72
18	-	12	2	-	-	-	-	14
19	-	-	10	3	-	-	-	13
Yearly Total	-	79	43	7	-	-	-	129

6. Aircraft Lost on Photo-Reconnaissance

1939	1940	1941	1942	1943	1944	1945	War Total
2	15	31	51	46	40	9	194

Coastal Command's Annual Aircraft Losses

1939	1940	1941	1942	1943	1944	1945	War Total
30	324	382	447	384	356	137	2,060

APPENDIX 21

Coastal Command Casualties, 3 September 1939 to 8 May 1945

	Killed	Missing	Prisoner of War	Wounded
Flying Battle				
Aircrew	5,863	128 (125)	478 (477)	986
Groundcrew	159	3 (3)	5 (5)	49
	6,022	131 (128)	483 (482)	1,035
Flying Accident				
Aircrew	2,261	10 (8)	17 (17)	1,049
Groundcrew	182	-	3 (3)	120
	2,443	10 (8)	20 (20)	1,169
Ground Battle				
Aircrew	18	-	3 (3)	20
Groundcrew	135	-	10 (10)	172
	153	-	13 (13)	192
Ground				
Aircrew	38	-	-	31
Groundcrew	218	-	-	174
Totals				
Aircrew	8,180	138 (133)	498 (497)	2,086
Groundcrew	694	3 (3)	18 (18)	515
Grand Totals	**8,874**	**141 (136)**	**516 (515)**	**2,601**

The above figures are inclusive of Dominion and Allied personnel at RAF posting disposal and include amendments up to 31 May 1947. The figures in brackets represent those included in the adjacent totals, who at the date of amendment had been reported safe. Personnel previously reported missing or prisoner of war and subsequently killed are included as killed.

In addition to the above figures, there were 23 aircrew and 224 ground staff (total 247) who died of natural causes. [From Air 15-162 Table I]

Bibliography

PRIMARY SOURCES

CAB 53/1–11 Imperial Defence Committee; Chiefs-of-Staff Committee, 1923–1939.
CAB 54/1–13 Imperial Defence Committee; Deputy Chiefs-of-Staff Committee, 1932–1939.
CAB 55/1–3 Committee of Imperial Defence; Joint Planning Committee, 1927–1939.

Air 15-

3 War Plans – Tactical Squadron Use, October 1937 to 1938.
4 Role of Coastal Command and Combined Ops. Rooms, 1937–1940.
24 Torpedo Bombing Tactics, 1938–1941.
26 Policy on Air & War Plans, December 1938 to 1941.
46 Aircraft Requirements, July 1939 to June 1943.
51 Coastal Command's Training Policy, 1941–1942.
57 Coastal Command Naval Staff Anti-U-boat File, September 1939 to December 1944.
66 Role of Coastal Command, November 1937 to March 1939.
102 Overlord – Role of Coastal Command.
162 Coastal Command's War Record, 1939–1945.
213 Expansion Programme, July 1940 to June 1942.
214 Re-equipment of Squadrons, July 1942 to September 1943.
279 Analyses of Reports on Anti-Submarine Operations, October 1942 to August 1943.
281 Air Escort for American Convoy Procedure, November 1943 to December 1943.
282 Conferences on Aircraft Situation in Coastal Command, December 1943 to March 1945.
284 Comments on Draft White Paper *The Battle of the Atlantic 1939–1940*.
285 Aircraft Camouflage, January 1942 to November 1943.
286 Coastal Command's Anti-Submarine Committee, May 1942 to March 1943.
287 No. 18 Group's Area Anti-Submarine Operations.
340 Expansion and Re-equipment of Coastal Command, June 1941 to September 1943.
359 AOC-in-Chief's Daily Conferences, July 1941 to April 1942.
360 AOC-in-Chief's Staff Meetings, November 1943 to December 1944.
361 AOC-in-Chief's Staff Meetings, January 1945 to May 1945.
391 Operations Against Ships in the Skagerrak & Kattegat, October 1944 to April 1945.
491 Operations Against Naval, Military and Industrial Targets in Norway & Denmark, October 1944 to April 1945.
530 Mine-laying in Norwegian and Danish Waters, April 1940 to February 1945.
541 No. 16 Group's Attacks on Enemy Ships off the Danish & Dutch Coasts, April 1940 to February 1945.
773 AOC-in-Chiefs' Dispatches, 1939–45.

Air 41-

19 RAF in the Maritime War – The Mediterranean & Red Sea, Vol.VI.
45 RAF in the Maritime War – Atlantic and Home Waters, April 1918 to September 1939.

47 RAF in the Maritime War – Atlantic and Home Waters, July 1941 to February 1943.
48 RAF in the Maritime War – Atlantic and Home Waters, February 1943 to May 1944.
73 RAF in the Maritime War – Atlantic and Home Waters, September 1939 to June 1941.
74 RAF in the Maritime War – Atlantic and Home Waters, June 1944 to May 1945.
79 RAF in the Maritime War – Statistics.
81 SD719 Armament; Vol. I, Bombs and Bomb Equipment.
81 SD737 Armament; Vol. II, Guns, Gunsights, Turrets, Ammunition & Pyrotechnics.

Air 27-Squadron Operational Records:

383/4	No. 36	1928–1947.
399–402	No. 38	1942–1945.
469–72	No. 48	1935–1943.
505	No. 53	1942–1943.
555	No. 59	1941–1943.
1105/6	No. 172	1942–1943.
1126/7	No. 179	1942–1943.
1177/8	No. 201	1914–1943.
1209	No. 204	1940–1943.
1222/3	No. 206	1940–1943.
1294	No. 209	1941–1943.
1298–90	No. 210	1917–1944.
1365/6	No. 220	1939–1943.
1368	No. 221	1940–1943.
1384–8	No. 224	1939–1943.
1412–16	No. 228	1940–1944.
1422/3	No. 230	1918–1945.
1430	No. 233	1939–1943.

Air 27-

1565–7	No. 269	1916–1946.
1609	No. 279	1941–1943.
1668–70	No. 304	1942–1946.
1687/8	No. 311	1942–1943.
1731	No. 333	1943–1944.
1942/3	No. 500	1941–1943.
1997	No. 524	1943–1945.
2098–90	No. 608	1941–1943.
2113–15	No. 612	1941–1945.

Royal Australian Air Force Squadrons' Operational Records:

Roll 84	No. 455	1942–1945.
Roll 88	No. 459	1942–1945.
Roll 90	No. 461	1943.

Air 27-

150–3	No. 10	1943–1944.

Royal Canadian Air Force Squadrons' Operational Records:

C12238	No. 10	1943.
C12259/60	No. 162	1944.
C12269	No. 404	1942–1945.
C12273/4	No. 407	1941–1944.
C12283	No. 413	1941–1942.
C12285	No. 415	1941–1944.
C12295	No. 422	1942–1945.
C12296	No. 423	1942–1945.

United States Navy Squadrons' Operational Records:

NRS-1978-89	VP63	1943.
NRS-256	VP73	1941/1942.
NRS-1977-104	VP84	1942/1943.

Correspondents

Angell, Wg Cdr M., No. 580 Squadron; Bartlett, Wg Cdr G.C.C., AFC, Nos 224 and 59 Squadrons; Baveystock, Flt Lt L., No. 201 Squadron; Bednall, Wg Cdr D., No. 230 Squadron; Bevan-John, Gp Capt D., No. 228 Squadron; Busbridge, Capt D., No. 224 Squadron; Campbell, Flg Off G., DFC, RCAF, No. 162 Squadron; Campbell, Wg Cdr R.I.; Cook, Gp Capt, OBE; Craven, AM Sir Robert, KBE, CB, OBE, DFC, Nos 201, 210, 228 Squadrons; Cremer, K/Kapt P.,U-333; De Liefde, Lt T., RNethNAS; Edwards, Flt Lt G., No. 233 Squadron; Fitzgerald, Gp Capt J.B., RAAF, No. 500 Squadron; Flynn, Flt Lt P., DFC, RCAF, No. 404 Squadron; Giese, O., U-405; Green, Flg Off J., No. 179 Squadron; Goff, F., No. 259 Squadron; Greswell, Air Cdre J., No. 172 Squadron; Hodgkinson, ACM Sir Derek, KCB, CBE, CB, DFC, AFC, No. 220 Squadron; Hodgkinson, Capt V., DFC, RAAF, No. 10 Squadron; Jones, Flt Lt J., RAAF, No. 608 Squadron; Johnson, C., MSc, FRAeS (Lockheed engineer); Lynham, Gp Capt P., DSO, No. 279 Squadron; Marrows, Flt Lt D., DFC, RAAF, No. 461 Squadron; McGill, R.; Martin, Wg Cdr D., OBE, BSc, No. 201 Squadron; Page, Flt Lt C., DFC, RCAF, No. 404 Squadron; Quinlan, B., RCAF; Rackcliff, P., No. 580 Squadron; Romanes, Wg Cdr J., DFC, No. 206 Squadron; Shuleman, Sqn Ldr, DSO, DFC, RCAF, No. 404 Squadron; Simmons, R., No. 143 Squadron; Skaugstad, Per; Smith, Sqn Ldr A., MRAeS, No. 206 Squadron; Spooner, Sqn Ldr T., DSO, DFC, Nos 53 and 221 Squadrons; Stiebler, K/Kapt W., U-461; Symons, Flt Lt J., RCAF, No. 404 Squadron; Taylor, Sqn Ldr C., DFC, RCAF, No. 407 Squadron; Tompkins, Air Cdre M.; Troughton, F., HMS Brocklesby; Warren, L., Nos 459 and 38 Squadrons; Whittaker, D., No. 279 Squadron; Willis, D.; Winfield, E., No. 1404 Flt; Womersley, Wg Cdr L., DFC, No. 224 Squadron; Wood, Capt E., DFC, USN, VP84 USN; Yorston, Dr R., No. 269 Squadron; Zestermann, G., U-533 and U-155.

SECONDARY SOURCES

Abbott, Kim, *Gathering of Demons*, Perth, Ontario, 1987.
Baff, K.C., *Maritime is No. 10*, Netley, South Australia, 1983.
Bednall, D., *Sun on My Wings*, Pembroke Dock, 1989.
Behrens, C.B.A., *Merchant Shipping and the Demands of War*, London, 1955.
Bertini, M. I., *Sommergibili in Mediterraneo*, Vol. I, Rome, 1972.
Bertini, M. I., *Sommergibili in Mediterraneo*, Vol. II, Rome, 1968.
Bolitho, H., *Task for Coastal Command*, London, 1944.
Bowyer, Chaz, *For Valour: the Air VCs*, London, 1992.
Bowyer, Chaz, *Men of Coastal Command*, London,1985.
Bowyer, Chaz, *Coastal Command at War*, Shepperton, 1979.
Churchill, W.S., *The Second World War*, Vols. I–VI, London, 1972–81.
Craven and Cate, *The Army Air Forces in World War II*, Vols. II and III, Toronto, 1976, 1979.
Cremer, Peter, *U-333*, London, 1984.
Crowther and Whiddington, *Science at War*, London, 1947.
Cunningham,Viscount, *A Sailor's Odyssey*, London, 1951.
Deighton, Len, *Blood, Tears and Folly: An Objective Look at WW2*, London, 1995.
Doughty, Martin, *Merchant Shipping and the Demands of War*, London, 1982.
Douglas, Lord, *Years of Command,* London, 1966.
Dönitz, Karl, *Memoirs*, London, 2000.
Eisenhower, Dwight D., *Crusade in Europe*, New York, 1968.
Fioravanzo, G., *Le Azioni Navali in Mediterraneo*, 3rd Edn., Rome, 1976.
Flatmark and Grytten, *Ålesund I Hverdag og Krig*, Vol. I, Ålesund, 1988.
Franks, Norman, *Search, Find and Kill*, London, 1995.
Galland, Adolf, *The First and the Last*, London, 1970.
Gibbs, N., *Grand Strategy*, Vol. I, London, 1976.
Goulter, C.J.M., *A Forgotten Offensive*, London, 1995.
Greenhous, B., Harris, S.J., Johnston, W.C., and Rawling, W.G.P., *The Official History of the R.C.A.F.*, Vol. III, Toronto, 1994.
Halley, James, *The Squadrons of the R.A.F. and Commonwealth 1918–1988*, Tonbridge, 1988
Harris, Sir Arthur, *Bomber Offensive*, London, 1947.
Hendrie, A., *Seek and Strike*, London, 1983.
Hendrie, A., *Flying Cats*, Shrewsbury, 1988.
Hendrie, A., *Short Sunderland in WW2*, Shrewsbury, 1994.
Hendrie, A., *Canadian Squadrons in Coastal Command*, St.Catharine's, Ontario, 1997.
Hendrie, A., *Lockheed Hudson in WW2*, Shrewsbury, 1999.
Herrington, J., *Air War Against Germany and Italy*, Canberra, 1962.
Herrington, J., *Air Power Over Europe 1944-1945*, Canberra, 1963.
Hessler, Günter, *The U-Boat War in the Atlantic 1939–1945*, London, 1992.
Hillmer, Norman, (Ed.), *The Official History of the R.C.A.F.*, Vol. II, Toronto, 1986.
Jane's, *Jane's Fighting Ships of World War II*, London, 1990.
Joubert, ACM Sir Philip, *Birds and Fishes, The Story of Coastal Command*, London, 1960.
Keegan, John, *The Times Atlas of World War II*, London, 1989.
Kostenuk, S., and Griffin, J., *R.C.A.F. Squadrons and Aircraft*, Toronto, 1977.

Longmore, ACM Sir Arthur, *From Sea to Sky 1910-1945*, London, 1946.

Middlebrook, Martin, *Convoy*, London, 1976.

Middlebrook, Martin, *Bomber Command War Diaries 1939–1945*, Harmondsworth, 1987.

Morison, Samuel E., *The Battle of the Atlantic September 1939–May 1943*, Boston, Mass., 1975.

Morison, Samuel E., *The Battle of the Atlantic May 1943–May 1945*, Boston, Mass., 1984

Niestlé, Axel, *German U-boat Losses in WW2*, Annapolis, 1988.

Overy, Richard, *The Air War 1939-1945*, London, 1980.

Overy, Richard, *Why the Allies Won*, London, 1995.

Poolman, Kenneth, *Focke-Wulf Kondor: Scourge of the Atlantic*, London, 1978.

Potter, E.B. (Ed.) *Sea Power – A Naval History*, Annapolis, 1981.

Price, Alfred, *Aircraft Versus Submarine*, London, 1980.

Propert, Henry, *High Commanders of the Royal Air Force*, London, 1991.

Rawlings, John, *Coastal Support and Special Squadrons*, London, 1982.

Rayleigh, Walter, *The War in the Air*, Vol. 1, Oxford, 1922.

Richards, Denis, *Royal Air Force 1939–1945*, Vol. I, London, 1953.

Richards and Saunders, *Royal Air Force 1939–1945*, Vol. II, London, 1954.

Robertson, B., *British Military Aircraft Serials 1911–1979*, Cambridge, 1979.

Robertson, Terence, *Channel Dash*, Bungay, 1958.

Rohwer, Jürgen, *Axis Submarine Successes 1939–1945*, Annapolis, 1983.

Roskill, S.W., *The War at Sea*, Vols. I–III, London, 1954–61.

Russell, James, *United States Naval Aviation 1910–1970*, Washington, DC, 1970.

Saunders, Hilary St.G., *The Royal Air Force 1939–1945*, Vol. III, London, 1954

Saunders, Hilary St.G., *Coastal Command 1939–1942*, London, 1942.

Schull, Joseph, *The Far Distant Ships*, Annapolis, 1987.

Showell, J.P.M. *U-boats Under the Swastika*, Annapolis, 1958.

Slessor, Sir John, *The Central Blue*, London, 1956.

Taylor, A.J.P., *English History 1914–1945*, London, 1970.

Terraine, John, *The Right of the Line*, London, 1985.

Thetford, Owen, *Aircraft of the Royal Air Force Since 1918*, London, 1979.

Ubaldini, U.M. *I Sommergibili Negli Oceani*, Rome, 1976.

Von Müllenheim-Rechberg, Baron, *Battleship Bismarck*, London, 1982.

Wilson, M. and Robinson, A.S.I., *Coastal Command Leads the Invasion*, London, 1944.

Publications that Give Reference to Coastal Command's Operations

OFFICIAL HISTORIES

RAAF

Herrington, J., *Air War Against Germany and Italy 1939–1943*, Canberra, 1962.

Herrington, J., *Air Power Over Europe 1944–1945*, Canberra, 1963.

RAF

Richards, D., *R.A.F. 1939–1945*, Vol.I., London, 1953.

Richards, D., and Saunders, H.St.G. *R.A.F. 1939–1945*, Vol.II, London, 1954.

Saunders, H. St.G., *R.A.F. 1939–1945*, Vol.III, London, 1954.

RCAF

Greenhous, B., Harris, S.J., Johnston, W.C., and Rawling, W.G.P., *The Official History of the R.C.A.F.*, Vol. III, Toronto, 1994.

Kostenuk, S. and Griffin, J., *R.C.A.F. Squadrons and Aircraft 1924–1968*, Toronto, 1977.

Hillmer, N., (Ed.) *The Official History of the R.C.A.F.*, Vol. II, Toronto, 1986.

RCN

Schull, J., *The Far Distant Ships – An Official Account of Canadian Naval Operations in WW2*, Annapolis, 1987.

RN

Roskill, S.W., *The War at Sea*, Vols. I–III, London, 1954–61.

USAAF

Craven, W.F. and Cate, J.L., *The Army Air Forces in World War II*, Vol. I, Chicago, 1975; Vol. II, Chicago, 1976; Vol. VII, Chicago, 1983.

USN

Morison, Samuel E., *The Battle of the Atlantic September 1939–May 1943*, Boston, 1975.

Morison, Samuel E., *The Atlantic Battle Won May 1943–May 1945*, Boston, Mass. 1984.

Italian Navy

Fioravanzo, G., *La Marina Italiana Nella Seconda Guerra Mondiale*, Vol. IV, Rome, 1976.

Ubaldini, U.M., Vol. XII, Rome, 1976.

Bertini, M., Vol. XIII 1, Rome, 1972.

Bertini, M., Vol. XIII 2, Rome, 1968.

OTHER PUBLICATIONS

Abbott, K., *Gathering of Demons*, Perth, Ontario, 1987 (No. 407 RCAF Sqn).

Baff, K., *Maritime is No. 10*, Netley, South Australia, 1983 (No. 10 RAAF Sqn).

Baveystock, L., *Wavetops at my Wingtips*, Shrewsbury, 2001.

Bednall, D., *Sun on my Wings*, Pembroke Dock, 1989.

Bolitho, H., *Task for Coastal Command*, London, 1944.

Bowyer, C., *Coastal Command at War*, Shepperton, 1979.

Bowyer, C., *Men of Coastal Command*, London, 1985.

Bowyer, C., *For Valour- The Air VCs*, London, 1992.

Brooks, R., *Kent's Own – The History of 500 (County of Kent) Squadron*, Rainham, 1982.

Churchill, W.S., *The Second World War*, Vols.1-VI, London, 1972-81.

Creed, R., *PBY – The Catalina Flying-boat*, Annapolis, 1985.

Cremer, P., *U-333*, London, 1984.

Cunningham, Viscount, *A Sailor's Odyssey*, London, 1951.

Deramore, Lord, and Orange, V., Winged Promises, *A History of No. 14 Squadron RAF 1915–1945*, Fairford, 1996.

Deighton, L., *Blood, Tears and Folly*, London, 1995.

Douglas, Lord, *Years of Command*, London, 1966.

Dönitz, K., *Memoirs*, London, 2000.

Eisenhower, D.D., *Crusade in Europe*, New York, 1968.

Flatmark and Grytten, *Ålesund I Hverdag og Krig*, Vol. I, Ålesund, 1988.

Franks, N., *Search, Find and Kill*, London, 1995.

Franks, N., *Conflict Over the Bay*, London, 1986.

Goulter, C. *A Forgotten Offensive*, London, 1995.

Halley, J., *The Squadrons of the RAF and the Commonwealth 1918–1988*, Tonbridge, 1988.

Harris, A., *Bomber Offensive*, London, 1947.

Hendrie, A., *Seek and Strike*, London, 1983.

Hendrie, A., *Flying Cats*, Annapolis, 1988.

Hendrie, A., *Short Sunderland in WW2*, Shrewsbury, 1994.

Hendrie, A., *Canadian Squadrons in Coastal Command*, St Catharine's, Ontario, 1997.

Hendrie, A., *Lockheed Hudson in World War II*, Shrewsbury, 1999.

Hessler, G., *The U-boat War in the Atlantic 1939–1945*, London, 1992.

Jones, G., *The Attacker – The Hudson and its Flyers*, London, 1980.

Joubert, P., *Birds and Fishes: The Story of Coastal Command*, London, 1960.

Longmore, A., *From Sea to Sky 1910–1945*, London, 1946.

Masters, D., *So Few*, London, 1941.

Middlebrook, M., *Convoy – The Battle for Convoys SC122 and HX229*, London, 1976.

Milberry, L., *Sixty Years – The RCAF and CF Air Command 1924–1984*, Toronto, 1984.

Nesbit, R.C., *The Strike Wings: Special Anti-Shipping Squadrons 1942–1945*, London, 1984.

Niestlé, A., *German U-boat Losses in WW2*, Annapolis, 1988.

Price, A., *Aircraft Versus Submarine*, London, 1980.

Propert, H., *High Commanders of the RAF*, London, 1991.

Rawlings, J., *Coastal Support and Special Squadrons*, London, 1982.

Saunders, H.St.G., *Coastal Command 1939–1942*, London, 1942.

Slessor, Sir John, *The Central Blue*, London, 1985.

Southall, I., *Fly West*, Harmondsworth, 1974.

Taylor, A.J.P., *English History 1914–1945*, Harmondsworth, 1970.

Terlinden, L.A., *Mitrailleur dans la RAF*, Brussels, 1985.

Terraine, J., *The Right of the Line*, London, 1985.

Thetford, O., *Aircraft of the R.A.F. Since 1918*, London, 1982.

Van der Vat, D., *The Atlantic Campaign 1939–1945*, London, 1988.

Wilson, M. and Robinson, A.S.I., *Coastal Command Leads the Invasion*, London, 1944.

Notes

INTRODUCTION

[1] Richards D., *RAF 1939–1945*, London, 1953, Vol. I, p. ix.
[2] Butler, J.R.M., Introduction to S. W. Roskill's *The War at Sea*
[3] Roskill, S. W., *The War at Sea*, London, 1954, Vol. I. p. xiv.
[4] Roskill, S. W., *The War at Sea*, London, 1961, Vol. III, p. 397.
[5] Roskill, S. W., Vol III.2, p. 403.
[6] Saunders, H. St.G., *Coastal Command 1939–1942*, London, 1942.
[7] Morison, S. E., *The Battle of the Atlantic Sep. 1939–May 1943*, Boston, 1975, p. 12.
[8] Morison, S. E., *The Atlantic Battle Won May 1943–May 1945*, Boston, 1984, p. 4.
[9] Craven, W. F., and Cate, J. L., *The Army Air Forces in WWII*, Chicago, 1976, Vol. II, p. 244.
[10] Craven, W. F., and Cate, J. L., Vol. II, p. 406.
[11] *La Marina Italiana Nella Seconda Guerra Mondiale*, Rome, 1968–76, Vols I-XXI.
[12] Bertini, M., *Sommergibili in Mediterraneo*, Vol. XIII. 1, Rome, 1972, Vol. XIII.2, Rome, 1968.
[13] Ubaldini, U. M. *I Sommergibili Negli Oceani*, Rome, 1976, Vol. XII.
[14] Bertini, M., *I Sommergibili in Mediterraneo*, Rome, 1972, Vol. XIII.1, p.58.
[15] Cunningham, Viscount, *A Sailor's Odyssey*, London, 1951, p. 299.
[16] Cunningham, Viscount, p. 482.
[17] Cunningham, Viscount, p. 510.
[18] Cunningham, Viscount, p. 604.
[19] Joubert, P., *Birds and Fishes: The Story of Coastal Command*, London, 1960.
[20] Joubert, P., p. 215.
[21] Joubert, P., p. 150.
[22] Slessor, J., *The Central Blue*, London, 1956, p. xiii.
[23] Slessor, J., p. 468.
[24] Douglas S., *Years of Command*, London, 1966, p. 486.
[25] Taylor, A. J. P., *English History 1914–1945*, Harmondsworth, 1970, p. 613.
[26] Goulter, C. J. M., *A Forgotten Offensive: RAF Coastal Command's Anti-Shipping Campaign 1940–1945*, London, 1995, p. xii.
[27] Goulter, C. J. M., p. ix.
[28] Bowyer, C., *Men of Coastal Command*, London, 1985, p. 11.
[29] Bowyer, C., *Coastal Command at War*, Shepperton, 1979, p. 6.
[30] Terraine, J., *Right of the Line: The RAF in the European War 1939–1945*, London, 1985, p. 70, fn. 223, 233
[31] Terraine, J., p. 456.
[32] Terraine, J., p. 456
[33] Franks N., *Search, Find and Kill*, London, 1995, p. viii.
[34] Overy, R., *The Air War 1939–1945*, London, 1980, p. xi.
[35] Overy, R., p. 39.
[36] Overy, R., p. 8.
[37] Harris, A., *Bomber Offensive*, London, 1947, pp. 90, 99, 269. See also: Overy, R., pp. 72, 116.
[38] Hessler, G., *The U-boat War in the Atlantic 1939–1945*, London, 1992.
[39] Waters, D. W., Lt Cdr, RN, to the author.
[40] See Bibliography.
[41] The cost of four part-rolls of microfilm (four 'pieces' or documents) – £1,164.50
[42] Orange, V., and Delamere, R., *Winged Promises: A History of No. 14 Squadron*, Fairford, 1996. Baff, K. C., *Maritime is Number 10: A History of No. 10 Squadron RAAF*, Netley, South Australia, 1983.

CHAPTER 01

[1] Taylor, A.J.P. , *English History 1914–1945*, Harmondsworth, 1970, pp. 619, 613, 628.
[2] Goulter, C.J.M., *A Forgotten Offensive*, London, 1995, p. 76.

[3] Overy, R.J., *The Air War 1939–1945*, London, 1980, pp. 6, 8, 21, 56, 113, 193, 195, 200.

[4] Thetford, O., *Aircraft of the RAF Since 1918*, London, 1979.

[5] Richards, D., *RAF 1939–1945*, London, 1953, Vol. I, p. 57.

[6] Roskill, S.W., *The War at Sea*, London, 1954, Vol. I, pp. 37–8.

[7] Harris, A., *Bomber Offensive*, London, 1947, pp. 99, 104, 265.

[8] Air 15-3 Coastal Command's War Plans Oct.1937–Jun.1939, minute 2.12. 37. Air 15-773 para. 8. Air 15-3 Memo to Air Staff c 8. 10. 37.

[9] Air 15-3 War Plans Oct.1937–Dec.1938, memo to SASO 25.11.37, para. 1.

[10] Air 15-3 Memo 22.12.38. HQCC to Director of Operations & Intelligence.

[11] Air 15-3 War Plans Oct.1937–Dec.1938, résumé 15.12.38.

[12] Air 15-4 Employment of Coastal Command in a Continental War, memo 30.6.39.

[13] Air 15-46 Aircraft Requirements Jul.1939–Jun.1943, memo AM conference 16.4.40.

[14] Air 15-46 Deputy SASO memo 2.4.40.

[15] Air 15-213 Expansion and Re-equipment; Estimated Requirements, Jun.1940, p.118.

[16] Air 15-773 C-in-C's Dispatches Vol. I, para. 10.

[17] Air 15-773 Vol. I, para. 10.

[18] Air 15-3 Coastal Command's War Plan, memo 25.10.38.

[19] Air 15-3 War Plans, 1937–1939, memo to DCAS 25.10.38.

[20] Air 41-73 RAF in the Maritime War, Appendix 7.

[21] Air 15-213 Expansion and Re-equipment, Jun.1940–Jun.1942, p. 137.

[22] Air 15-359 C-in-C's Meetings Jul.1941–Apr.1942, meeting 30.6.41.

[23] Air 15-213 p. 106, Letter 19.6.42. Joubert to AM (Plans).

[24] Air 15-214 p. 67. Expansion and Re-equipment Jul.1942–Sep. 1943. Letter 7.11.42. Joubert to AM.

[25] Air 15-214 p. 90. Letter 9.8.42. Joubert to Sir Dudley Pound.

[26] Air 15-214 p. 100. Letter 27.7.42 Rear Adm E.J.P. Brind to Joubert.

[27] Air 15-214 p. 13. AM letter 18.9.42 to Coastal Command.

[28] Air 15-340 Equipment and Re-equipment, Jun.1941–Sep. 1943, p. 96.

[29] Air 15-340 p. 3. Letter 2.9.43. Slessor to DCAS, AM.

[30] Air 15-340 p. 79. Letter c 26.2.43. Slessor to Admiralty.

[31] Air 15-773 C-in-C's Dispatches Vol. IV, paras 1–4.

[32] Air 15-360 C-in-C's Meetings Nov.1943–Dec.1944, letter 7.2.44 to AM.

[33] Douglas, S., *Years of Command*, London, 1966, p. 246.

[34] Air 15-360 C-in-C's Meetings 12.4.44. 27.4.44.

[35] Air 15-360 Meetings 9.10.44. 6.11.44.

[36] Air 15-361 Meeting 4.5.45.

[37] Air 15-213 Expansion and Re-equipment – Estimated Requirements for Coastal Command, p. 3.

[38] Air 15-284 Govt White Paper, The Battle of the Atlantic, paras 1–3.

[39] Air 15-213 pp. 190–193.

[40] Air 15-46 Coastal's Aircraft Requirements Jul.1939–Jun.1943, memo 11.12.39.

[41] Air 15-46 Letter from the AM (OA) to C-in-C 21.10.39.

[42] Air 15-46 Letter from the AM 21.10.39 to Coastal Command.

[43] Air 41-47 The RAF in the Maritime War, Vol. III, p. 15.

[44] Air 15-46 Coastal's Aircraft Requirements Jul.1939–Jun.1943, memo 5.12.41.

[45] Air 15-46 Memo 6.1.42. By Sep. 1941 U-boats operated up to 35EW, Hessler, G., *The U-boat War in the Atlantic 1939–1945*, London, 1992, para. 136.

[46] Air 15-46 Memo 5.12.41.

[47] Air 15-46 Memo 5.12.41.

[48] Air 15-46 Coastal's Aircraft Requirements. File S/7012/Tactics to ACAS c Feb.1942.

[49] Air 15-3 Coastal's War Plans, CAS memos 31.10.37, 4.1.38, 7.2.38.

[50] Air 15-46 C-in-C's letter to Groups, 7.5.43.

[51] Richards, D., *RAF 1939–1945*, London, 1953, Vol. I, p. 412. Air 15-284, para. 5.

[52] Air 15-213 p. 81. Air Expansion and Re-equipment Estimates. Letter 14.9.41.

[53] Air 15-213 p. 138.

[54] Air 15-213 pp. 66, 148. Air 15-46 letter 7.1.42. to ACAS (T) when 600 miles radius was considered practical.

[55] Air 15-359 C-in-C's 64th meeting 28.10.41. USN VP84 Sqn's ORB NRS-1977-104.

[56] Air 15-213 p. 123, Letter 28.7.41. Air Cdre I.T. Lloyd to Sir Philip Joubert.

[57] Air 15-369 C-in-C's 40th meeting 5.9.41.

[58] Air 15-46 Aircraft Requirements Jul.1939–Jun.1943, letter Jan.1942 Joubert to ACAS.

[59] Air 15-213 p. 152, Letter 12.6.41 Bowhill to U/Sec State AM.

[60] Harper, Flt Lt C., RCAF. Letter to the author. ORB C12238 No. 10 (RCAF) Sqn.. Slessor, J., *The Central Blue*, London, 1956, p. 474. Terraine, J., *Right of the Line: The RAF in the European War 1939–1945*, London, 1985, p. 442.

[61] Joubert, P. , *Birds and Fishes: The Story of Coastal Command*, London, 1960, p. 146.

[62] Air 15-213 C-in-C's Meetings, p. 155.

[63] Air 15-213 C-in-C's meetings, p. 133.

[64] Air 15-360 C-in-C's meetings, 30.11.44. 7.12.44.

[65] Air 15-214 p. 49, letter 14.1.43 from CCHQ to DONC at AM.

[66] Air 15-214 p. 35, letter 6.2.43. AM to C-in-C.

[67] Air 15-360 C-in-C's meetings 2.3.44, 21.4.44, 12.6.44. Richards, D. and Saunders, H., *RAF 1939–1945*, London, 1954, Vol. II, p. 375.

[68] Richards, D. and Saunders, H., Vol. II, pp. 373, 375.

[69] Air 41-47 p. 23. The RAF in the Maritime War, minute 29.3.42.

[70] Air 15-213 p. 39, Letter, AM 7.3.42 to C-in-C.

[71] Air 41-47 p. 20, Statement by the Director-General of Organisation.

[72] Air 15-213 p. 67.

[73] Air 15-213 p. 81 Expansion and Re-equipment Estimates. AM letter 17.9.41 to C-in-C.

[74] Air 15-359 C-in-C's meeting 5.7.41.

[75] Air 15-359 72nd meeting 6.11.41. Air 15-361 C-in-C's Meeting 4.1.45.

[76] The author saw the survivors from a No. 179 Sqn. Wellington that ditched due to engine loss at Gibraltar in 1943.

[77] A Pegasus engine seized on Sunderland W2009 24.8.43. The propeller sheared off, taking a second propeller with it. From the author's log.

[78] Air 15-360 C-in-C's meeting 4.11.44.

[79] Air 15-360 C-in-C's meeting 16.3.44.

[80] Engines cut on Hudson EW930 at 1750 rpm. (No. 48 Sqn. 1942/3).

[81] Winfield E., letter to the author. See also: Saunders, H., *RAF 1939–1945*, Vol. III, pp. 76/7, 103–5.

[82] Coastal Command Review 1943.

[83] Air 27-1422 No. 230 Sqn's ORBs. Sunderland N9029.

[84] Author's experience 1942/3.

[85] CAB 53-7 Imperial Defence Chiefs of Staff Committee 8.2.37. 205th meeting.

[86] Letters to the author from staff of the Lockheed Corporation.

[87] In correspondence with staff of the Lockheed Corporation.

[88] In a letter from Clarence 'Kelly'Johnson to the author.

[89] Harris, A., *Bomber Offensive*, London, 1947, pp. 27/8.

[90] Air 15-359 C-in-C's 15th meeting 24.7.41.

[91] Air 15-359 C-in-C's 23rd meeting 6.8.41.

[92] Air 15-359 C-in-C's 37th meeting 30.8.41.

[93] Air 15-213 p. 94, Letter 9.10.41. MAP to Wg Cdr G. Shaw, CCLS Admiralty.

[94] Air 15-213 pp. 96/7, Letter 13.10.41. MAP to CCLS Admiralty.

[95] Air 15-213 p. 95, Letter 20.10.41. Joubert to Sir Charles Portal.

[96] Air 15-213 p. 88, Letter 6.11.41. Portal to Joubert.

[97] Air 15-213 p. 95, Meeting 13.10.41.

[98] Air 15-359 C-in-C's 27th meeting 11.8.41.

[99] Air 15-359 C-in-C's 28th meeting 14.8.41.

[100] Air 15-359 C-in-C's 32nd meeting 23.8.41.

[101] Air 15-359 C-in-C's 36th meeting 29.8.41.

[102] Air 15-359 C-in-C's 57th and 58th meetings on 8.10.41 and 10.10.41 respectively.

[103] Millar, J.H., letter to the author.

[104] Conan-Doyle, Lady Jean, letter to the author quoting from Bromet's diaries.

[105] Scarborough, W., Capt USN, correspondence with the author.

[106] USN ORBs NRS-1978–89, NRS-1977–104, NRS 256; VP63,VP84,VP73 respectively. C12259/60 No.162 Sqn's ORBs.

[107] Air 15-359 C-in-C's 38th meeting 2.9.41.

[108] Air 15-359 C-in-C's 50th meeting 24.9.41.

[109] Air 41-47 The RAF in the Maritime War, p. 16.

[110] Air 15-359 C-in-C's meetings 116th 29.1.42, 143rd 24.3.42.

[111] Air 15-359 C-in-C's 34th meeting 27.8.41.

[112] Air 15-359 C-in-C's 35th meeting 28.8.41.

[113] Air 41-47 p.20.

[114] Air 15-359 C-in-C's 40th meeting 5.9.41.

[115] Air 15-359 C-in-C's 64th meeting 28.10.41.

[116] Air 15-359 C-in-C's 109th meeting 15.1.42.

[117] Air 15-359 C-in-C's 111th meeting 20.1.42.

[118] Air 15-359 116th, 120th and 124th meetings, 29.1.42. 5.2.42. 11.2.42. respectively.

[119] Air 15-359 130th meeting 25.2.42.

[120] Air 15-359 131st meeting 26.2.42.

[121] Air 15-359 134th meeting 4.3.42.

[122] Air 15-46 Aircraft Requirements, Jul.1939–Jun.1943. Joubert memo to AM c Feb.1942.

[123] Air 15-359 C-in-C's 144th meeting 30.3.42.

[124] Air 15-359 C-in-C's meetings Jul.1941–Apr.1942.

[125] Joubert, P. , Birds and Fishes: The Story of Coastal Command, London, 1960, p. 143.

[126] Slessor, J., The Central Blue, London, 1956, pp. 465/6.

[127] Slessor, J., p. 466.

[128] Air 15-360 C-in-C's meeting 16.12.43.

[129] Air 15-360 C-in-C's meeting 31.12.43.

[130] Air 15-282 Conferences on Coastal's Aircraft Situation, pp. 5–114.

[131] Air 15-360 C-in-C's meetings Nov.1943–Dec.1944.

[132] Air 15-359 C-in-C's meeting 6.11.41. Air 15-360 C-in-C's meeting 5.2.44.

[133] Douglas, S., Years of Command, London, 1966, p. 246.

CHAPTER 02

[1] Air 15-3 Coastal Command's War Plans, AM letter to C-in-C, 29.1.38.

[2] Richards, D., RAF 1939–1945, London, 1953, Vol. I, p. 246. ORBs: Air 27-1384 No. 224 Sqn 1939.
   Air 27-1209 No. 204 Sqn 1940-3. Air 27-1298-99 No. 210 Sqn 1939–43.

[3] Air 15-213 Expansion and Re-equipment, Estimated Requirements, Jun.1940–Jun.1942.
   Letter 29.5.41 C-in-C to SASO.

[4] Battle of the Atlantic symposium, RAF Staff College, Bracknell, 21.10.91. Both were experienced officers.
   See also: Roskill, S.W., The War at Sea, London, 1954, Vol. I, p. 34.

[5] Air 41-81 (AHB/II/117) Armament, Vol. I, Chap. 3, p. 20.

[6] Air 41-81 Vol. I, Chap. I, p. 6.

[7] Air 41-81 Vol. I, Chap. 2, p. 9.

[8] Air 41-81 Vol. I, Chap. 1, p. 35.

[9] Air 15-284 Coastal Command's Part in the U-boat War, 1939–1940, para. 5.

[10] Air 41-81 Vol. I, Chap. 3, p. 20.

[11] Air 41-81 Vol. I, Chap. 3, p. 20.

[12] Air 41-81 Vol. I, Chap. 3, p. 35.

[13] Air 15-57 Coastal Command's Naval Staff Anti-U-boat File, Sep. 1939–Dec.1944, para. 8.
   Richards, D., RAF 1939–1945, London, 1953, Vol. I, p. 61.

[14] From a photograph which the author received from Wg Cdr G.C.C. Bartlett, AFC.

[15] Air 15-57 Coastal Command's Naval Staff Anti-U-boat File, Sep. 1939–Dec.1944, para. 11.

[16] Battle of the Atlantic symposium, RAF Staff College, Bracknell, 21.10.91.

[17] Air 41-81 Vol. I, Chap. 4, p. 62.

[18] Air 27-272 No. 48 Sqn's ORBs, 1943; C12296 No. 423 Sqn's ORBs 1942–5 as examples.
   See also: Roskill, S.W., The War at Sea, London, 1954, Vol. I, p. 135.
   Terraine, J., Right of the Line: The RAF in the European War 1939–1945, London, 1985, p. 233.

[19] Air 27-1368 No. 221 Sqn's. ORBs, 1940-3.

[20] Air 41-81 Vol. I, Chap. 4, p. 58.

[21] Richards, D., RAF 1939–1945, London, 1954, Vol. II, p. 100.

[22] Air 41-81 Vol. I, Chap. 4, p. 62.

[23] Air 15-57 Capt Peyton-Ward, RN, gives the following lethal ranges of anti-submarine weapons:
   450 lb DC – 21 ft; 250 lb DC – 16 ft; 500 lb A/S bomb – 17 ft; 100 lb A/S bomb – 8ft.
   Richards, D., RAF 1939–1945, Vol. I, p. 61, gives 250 lb A/S bomb – 6 ft.
   By 29.11.41.a depth of 26–30 ft was given for Type-13 pistols.

[24] Air 41-81 Vol. I, Chap. 4, letter 31.3.42. Joubert to ACAS(T).

[25] Air 41-81 Vol. I, Chap. 3, p. 38.

[26] Air 15-286 Coastal's ASW Committee. First meeting 8.5.42.
   See also: Hillmer, N.(Ed.), Official History of the RCAF, Toronto, 1980, Vol. II, p. 474.
   Greenhous, B., Harris, S.J., Johnston, W.C., Rawling, W.G.P. , Toronto, 1994, Vol. III, p. 378.

[27] Air 15- 286 8th meeting 16.12.42.

[28] Air 15-57 Naval Staff ASW File, Sep. 1939–Dec.1944, para. 70.

[29] Air 15-284 Government White Paper, Battle of the Atlantic, p. 43.

[30] Air 41-81 Vol. I, Chap. 4, p. 27.

[31] Slessor, J., The Central Blue, London, 1956, p. 466.
   See also: Hillmer, N.(Ed.), The Official History of the RCAF, Toronto, 1980,Vol. II, p. 474.

[32] Air 41-82 Armament Vol. II, Chap. 1, p. 3. See also: Terraine, J., Right of the Line, p. 18.

[33] Air 41-82 Vol. II, Chap. 1, p. 23.

[34] Figures given to the author at No. 1 Air Gunnery School, RAF Pembrey, Oct.1941.

[35] Air 15-286 Anti-U-boat Committee's 6th meeting 21.10.42.

[36] ORBs: Air-27-1223, (1943); 1366, (1943); 1431 (1941-1942), 1566, (1942–1943); 1942, (1942–1943); 2099, (1942); 1299, (1941–1943) 1668, (1942); 1687, (1942); 152, (1943), and RCAF C12259/C12260 (1944). The harmonisation distance of 400 yd would be where the paths of the projectiles would converge; thereafter, the paths would diverge.

[37] Spotswood, MRAF Sir Denis, letter to the author.

[38] USN VP84 ORBs NRS-1977-104.

[39] Air 27-153 ORBs No. 10 (RAAF) Sqn.

[40] Bednall, Wg Cdr D., letter to the author.

[41] Ibid., Chap. 4.

[42] Air 41-82 Vol. II, Chaps. 13–19.

[43] Air 27-149-153; 1178/9, 1830, 1832; ORBs of 10 RAAF; 201 RAF; 422, 423 RCAF 1940-4.

[44] Air 41-82 Vol. II, Chap. 4, p. 25. See also: Saunders, H., vRAF 1939–1945, Vol. III, p. 69. Terraine, J., Right of the Line, pp. 79, 87, 440. Greenhous, B., Harris, S.J., Johnston, W.C., Rawling, W.G.P. , The RCAF Official History, Toronto, 1994, Vol. III, pp. 446/7.

[45] Ibid., Chap. 5. Air 15-162 Coastal Command's War Record 1939–1945, Table B.

[46] Air 41-47 Chap. VI, p. 251. Roskill, S.W., The War at Sea, London, Vol. II, pp. 165, 268. Terraine, J., The Right of the Line, London, 1985, pp. 373, 388.

[47] Air 41-47 The RAF in the Maritime War, Chap. VI, p. 251.

[48] Air 41-47 Chap. VI, p. 251.

[49] Air 15-359 C-in-C's meetings Jul. 1941–Apr. 1942, 30th meeting.

[50] Air 41-47 Chap. VI, p. 251.

[51] Giese, Capt O., (U-405), letter to the author.

[52] Air 15-359 C-in-C's 74th meeting, 11.11.41. See also: Roskill, S.W., Vol. II, p. 84.

[53] Air 15-359 C-in-C's 89th meeting, 11.12.41.

[54] Air 15-286 Coastal's ASW Committee. 8th meeting, 16.12.42.

[55] Battle of the Atlantic symposium, RAF Staff College, 21.10.91. Oulton had sunk U-266 and U-563. See also: Richards, D. and Saunders, H., RAF 1939–1945, London, 1954, Vol. II, p. 155.

[56] Air 15-286 8th meeting 16.12.42.

[57] Edwards, G., Letter to the author. See also: Goulter, C., The Forgotten Offensive, pp. 193/4. Richards, D. and Saunders, H., RAF 1939–1945, Vol. II, p. 155

[58] USN ORBs: VP63 NRS-1978-89; VP84 NRS-1977-104. Niestlé, A., German U-boat Losses During WW2, Annapolis, 1988, p. 284.

[59] Air 15-360 C-in-C's meeting 16.12.43.

[60] USN ORBs: VP63, NRS-1978-89; VP84, NRS-1977-104. Roskill, S.W., The War at Sea, London, 1960, Vol. III.1, p. 22.

[61] ORBs NRS-1978-89; letters from USN officers and from Wg Cdr G.C.C. Bartlett. Two others were sunk using MAD: U-392, U-731. Niestlé, A., pp. 195, 284. Roskill, S.W., Vol. III.1, pp. 246.

[62] Air 41-82 Armament, Turrets and Guns, pp. 170–5. Air 41-47 RAF in the Maritime War, p. 527.

[63] Air 41-82 p. 170.

[64] James, Flg Off, RAAF, letter to the author. Goulter, C., A Forgotten Offensive, London, 1995, pp. 207–9.

[65] James, Flg Off, RAAF, letter to the author. RCAF Vol. III, pp. 447, 453/4. See also: Roskill, S.W., Vol. II, p. 376. Terraine, J., p. 440. Saunders, H., Vol. III, p. 69.

[66] Symons, Flt Lt J. See also: Slessor, J., The Central Blue, London, 1956, p. 547. RCAF Vol. III, p. 455.

[67] Roskill, S.W., The War at Sea, London, 1956. Vol. II, pp. 165, 258.

CHAPTER 03

[1] Roskill, S.W., The War at Sea, Vols. I-III, London, 1954–61.

[2] Morison, S.E., The Battle of the Atlantic, Sep. 1939–May 1943, Boston, Mass. 1975. Morison, S.E., The Atlantic Battle Won, May 1943–May 1945, Boston, Mass. 1984.

[3] Van der Vat, D., The Atlantic Campaign: The Great Struggle at Sea 1939-1945, London, 1988.

[4] Dönitz, K., Memoirs, London, 2000.

[5] Hessler, G., The U-boat War in the Atlantic 1939-1945, London, 1992.

[6] Cremer, P. , U-333 The Story of a U-boat Ace, London, 1984.

[7] Air 41-73 The RAF in the Maritime War, Vol. II, p. 275.

[8] Air 41-73 Vol. II, p. 274.

[9] Churchill, W.S., The Second World War, London, 1979, Vol. III, p. 107.

[10] Rohwer, J., In an afterword to Dönitz's Memoirs, London, 2000, p. 496.

[11] Crowther, J.G., and Whiddington, R., Science at War, London, 1948, p. 94.

[12] Slessor, J., The Central Blue, London, 1956, p. 498.

[13] Slessor, J., The Central Blue, London, 1956, p. 511.

[14] Slessor, J., p. 484.

[15] Joubert, P. , *Birds and Fishes: The Story of Coastal Command*, London, 1960, p. 123. Slessor, J., *The Central Blue*, London, 1956, p. 486.

[16] The theme of my first book: *Wer kennet ihre Namen?*

[17] Air 15-66 *The Role of Coastal Command in War, Nov.1937–Mar.1939*, Memo 1.10.37.

[18] Air 15-66 Memo 1.10.37.

[19] Air 15-66 Memo 23.3.39.

[20] Air 15-66 Memo, Bromet to C-in-C. 1.10.37. para. 4.

[21] CAB 53-11 Meeting 2.8.39.

[22] CAB 53-11 Meeting 2.8.39.

[23] CAB 53-11 Meeting 2.8.39.

[24] CAB 53-10 Meeting 18.1.39.

[25] CAB 53-10 Meeting, 18.1.39.

[26] ORBs: Air 27-1208 No. 204 Sqn. Air 27-1412 No. 228 Sqn. 1939. *London Evening News* 10.6.38.

[27] Roskill, S.W., *The War at Sea*, London, 1954, Vol. I, pp. 194/5, 279–82.

[28] Air 15-57 Coastal Command Naval Staff U-boat file, paras 30, 60. Air 15-773, Vol. II.I, para. 1.

[29] CAB 53-10 264th, 265th and 281st meetings. Air 41-73 RAF in the Maritime War, Vol. II, pp. 3–7.

[30] Battle of the Atlantic Symposium, RAF Staff College, 2.10.91.

[31] CAB 53-10 265th meeting.

[32] CAB 53-10 268th meeting.

[33] Roskill, S.W., *The War at Sea*, London, 1954, Vol. I, p. 34.

[34] Roskill, S.W., Vol. I, p. 34.

[35] Hessler, G., *The U-boat War in the Atlantic*, London, 1992, para. 3.

[36] Air 41-73 Vol. II, pp. 41–4. Hessler, G., para. 54 and Plan 4.

[37] Hessler,G., para. 15.

[38] Air 15-284 Govt White Paper, *Battle of the Atlantic*, paras 1/2.

[39] Air 15-773 C-in-C's Dispatches, Vol. I, para. 10.

[40] Air 41-73 *RAF in the Maritime War, Sep. 1939–Jun.1941*, Vol. II.1, pp. 41–44.

[41] Churchill, W.S., *The Second World War*, London, 1977, Vol. I, pp. 367–9.

[42] Churchill, W.S., Vol. I, pp. 377/8.

[43] Air 15-773 C-in-C's Dispatches, Vol. I, para. 10.

[44] Air 41-73 Vol. II.1, p. 41.

[45] Air 15-57 Coastal Command's Naval Staff ASW File, paras 1–4.

[46] Air 15-57 paras 3–5.

[47] Hessler, G., *The U-boat War in the Atlantic, 1939–1945*, London, 1992, para. 54.

[48] Air 15-73 *RAF in the Maritime War*, Vol. II, p. 2. Hessler, G., para. 15.

[49] Rohwer, J., *Axis Submarine Successes, 1939–1945*, Annapolis, 1983, pp. 1, 4.

[50] Rohwer, J., pp. 1–2.

[51] Air 41-73 Vol. II, p. 16.

[52] Stiebler, W., (Capt of U-461). Letter to the author.

[53] Air 41-73 First Lord of the Admiralty. Air 15-213 pp. 32–8, Sir Dudley Pound's letter.

[54] Churchill, W.S., *The Second World War*, London, 1979, Vol. III, p. 135.

[55] Churchill, W.S., Vol. III, p. 137.

[56] Hessler, G., *The U-Boat War in the Atlantic, 1939–1945*, Plan 2, p. 20.

[57] Air 41-73 Vol. II.1, paras 1/2.

[58] Hessler, G., *The U-boat War in the Atlantic*, London, 1992, para. 333.

[59] Air 15-57 Coastal Command's Naval Staff File, paras 8, 13, 14, 24, 26.

[60] Roskill, S.W., *The War at Sea*, London, 1954, Vol. I, p. 21.

[61] Air 41-73 *The RAF in the Maritime War*, Vol. II, p. 41.

[62] Rohwer, J., at RAF Staff College symposium, 21.10.91.

[63] Air 41-73 Coastal Command's Naval Staff ASW File, Vol. II, p. 42.

[64] Air 41-73 Vol. II, p. 43.
    Hillmer, N., (Ed.) *The Official History of the RCAF*, Toronto, 1985, Vol. II, p. 377.

[65] Air 41-73 Vol. II, p. 42.

[66] Air 41-73 Vol. II, p. 42.

[67] Air 15-57 Coastal Command's Naval Staff ASW File, para. 7.

[68] Joubert, P. , *Birds and Fishes: The Story of Coastal Command*, London, 1960, p. 123.

[69] Slessor, J., *The Central Blue*, London, 1966, p. 486.

[70] Air 27-1384 No. 224 Sqn's ORBs, 25.10.39 and 28.11.39.

[71] Gardner, Lt Cdr W.J.R., at RAF Staff College symposium, 21.10.91.

[72] Rohwer, J., at RAF Staff College symposium, 21.10.91.

[73] Roskill, S.W., Vol. I, pp. 68, 105. Rohwer, J., *Axis Submarine Successes*, Annapolis, 1983, p. 2.

[74] Rohwer, J., *Axis Submarine Successes 1939–1945*, Annapolis, 1983, pp. 1–3.

[75] Roskill, S.W., Vol. I, pp. 68, 105. Rohwer, J., p. 2.

[76] Air 27-1412 No. 228 Sqn's ORB 1939.

[77] Bevan-John, Gp Capt, letter to the author.

[78] Martin, D., *The Web-footed Guinea Pig*, p. 10. (Unpublished).

[79] Hessler, G., p. 1.

[80] Rohwer, J., pp. 1–9. Potter, E.B., (Ed.) *Sea Power*, Annapolis, 1986, p. 258.

[81] Churchill, W.S., *The Second World War*, London, 1977, Vol. II, Chaps. IX and XI.

[82] Air 41-73 Vol. II, p. 2. Rohwer, J., *Axis Submarine Successes*, Annapolis, 1983, pp. 9-12.

[83] Hessler, G., *The U-boat War in the Atlantic 1939–1945*, London, 1992, paras 27, 66.

[84] Air 41-73 Vol. II, p. 2. Rohwer, J., pp. 9–12.

[85] Ibid. Chap. 2.

[86] Air 15-213 Expansion & Re-equipment Estimates, Jun.1940–Jun.1942, p. 193.

[87] Air 15-284 Govt. White Paper, *Battle of the Atlantic*, 1945, Chap. II, p. 11.

[88] Roskill, S.W., Vol. I, p. 129.

[89] Air 15-162 Table B. Air 41-73, Vol. II, p. 2. Air 27-1412 No. 228 Sqn's ORB. Rohwer, J., p. 12.

[90] Air 41-73 Vol. II, p. 45.

[91] Air 41-73 Vol. II.II, p. 45.

[92] Dönitz, K., *Memoirs*, London, 2000, p. 110.

[93] Author's estimate of eight based on J. Rohwer's figures, pp. 18–22.

[94] Air 41-73 Vol. II, p. 55. Hessler, G., para. 88.

[95] From the author's experience.

[96] Air 41-73 Vol. II, p. 54. Hessler, G., para. 87.

[97] Dönitz, K., *Memoirs*, London, 2000, p. 110.

[98] Air 15-284. Govt White Paper, *The Battle of the Atlantic*, Chap. 2, para. 12.

[99] Air 27-1468 No. 221 Sqn's ORB, 1941.

[100] Hessler, G., Chart p. 40.

[101] Air 27-1565 No. 269 Sqd's ORBs, 1940–41. Air 27-1209 No. 204 Sqn's ORBs, 1940–41.

[102] Roskill, S.W., *The War at Sea*, London, 1954, Vol. I, pp. 34, 355.

[103] Ibid. Chap. 4.

[104] Air 41-73 Vol. II, p. 56.

[105] Air 41-73 Vol. II, p. 48 gives 59 ships torpedoed in Sep. 1940. See also: Rohwer, J., pp. 27–31.

[106] Air 15-773 C-in-C's Dispatches, Vol. I, para. 162.

[107] Churchill, W.S., *The Second World War*, London, 1977, Vol. II, p. 529.

[108] Churchill, W.S., Vol. II, p. 537.

[109] Churchill, W.S., Vol. II, p. 537.

[110] Dönitz, K., *Memoirs*, London, 2000, p. 101.

[111] Rohwer, J., at Symposium, RAF Staff College, 21.10.91.

[112] Dönitz, K., p. 101.

[113] Dönitz, K., *Memoirs*, London, 2000, pp. 104/5.

[114] Rohwer, J., Afterword to Dönitz's *Memoirs*, p. 508.

[115] Air 15-773 Vol. III, para. 9.

[116] In the author's experience.

[117] Bertini, M., *I Sommergibili in Mediterraneo*, Rome, 1968, Vol. II, p. 29.

[118] Slessor, J., *The Central Blue*, London, 1956, pp. 512–22.

[119] Air 15-773 Vol. III.2, para. 22.

[120] Craven, AM Sir Robert, to the author.

[121] Morison, S.E., *The Battle of the Atlantic, Sep. 1939–May 1943*, Boston, Mass., 1975, p. 37.

[122] Dönitz, K., *Memoirs*, London, 2000, pp. iv, 104.

[123] Churchill, W.S., *The Second World War*, London, 1979, Vol. III, p. xi.

[124] Morison, S.E., *The Battle of the Atlantic, Sep. 1939–May 1943*, Boston, 1975, Vol. I, p. 45.

[125] Slessor, J., *The Central Blue*, London, 1956, p. 331.

[126] Morison, S.E., Vol. I, p. 37.

[127] Morison, S.E., Vol. I, pp. 37, 46.

[128] Air 15-359 C-in-C's 11th meeting, 17.7.41.

[129] Air 15-51 Coastal Command's Training Policy, memo 9.6.41.

[130] Churchill, W.S., *The Second World War*, London, 1979, Vol. III, p. 99.

[131] Air 41-73 *The RAF in the Maritime War*, Vol. II, p. 297.

[132] Churchill, W.S., Vol. III, pp. 106/7. Air 41-73 Vol. II, p. 298.

[133] Air 15-773 Vol. I. II, para. 124. Air 41-47, pp. 48, 74.

[134] Rohwer, J., *Axis Submarine Successes, 1939–1945*, Annapolis, 1983, pp. 40–5.

[135] Churchill, W.S., Vol. III, p. 107.

[136] Churchill, W.S., Vol. III, pp. 105/6. Air 41-73 p. 298.

[137] Air 41-73 Vol. II, p. 296.

[138] Air 15-340 Equipment and Re-equipment, Jun.1941–Sep. 1943, p. 121.

[139] Air 41-47 *The RAF in the Maritime War, Jul.1941–Feb.1943*, Vol. III, p. 32.

[140] Morison, S.E., *The Battle of the Atlantic, Sep. 1939–May 1943*, Vol. I, p. 80.

[141] Churchill, W.S., Vol. III, p. 385. Air 41-47 p. 32.

[142] Air 41-47 Vol. III, p. 32.

[143] Air 41-47 Vol. III, p. 47.

[144] Slessor, J., *The Central Blue*, London, 1956, p. 491.

[145] ORBs: C12238 No. 10 (RCAF) Sqn; C12240 No. 11 (RCAF) Sqn; NRS-1977-104 VP84 USN.

[146] Air 41-47 Vol. III, p. 30.

[147] Air 41-47 Vol. III, p. 30.

[148] Air 27-761 No. 95 Sqn's ORBs, 1941–3. Air 27-1209 No. 204 Sqn's ORBs, 1940–3.

[149] C12295 No. 422 Sqn's ORB. Pearce, Air Cdre F., letter to the author.

[150] Air 15-51 Coastal Command's Training policy, Jan.1941–Jan.1942, p. 4.

[151] Air 15-340 Expansion & Re-equipment, Jun.1941–Sep. 1943, p. 121.

[152] Author's experience.

[153] Air 15-51 Training Policy, p. 122. C12295 No. 422 Sqn's ORBs 1942–5.

[154] ORBs: IS-1978-89, VP63 Sqn; NRS-1977-104, VP84 Sqn; C12295, No. 422 Sqn.

[155] Air 27-1209 No. 204 Sqn's ORBs 1940–43.

[156] Air 27-1174 No. 200 Sqn's ORB; Air 27-1413. No. 228 Sqn's ORB. Air 15-340 p. 123.

[157] Air 41-73 *RAF in the Maritime War*, p. 293.

[158] ORBs: Air 27-761 No. 95 Sqn's; Air 27-1174 No. 200 Sqn's. Air 15-340 Equipment and Re-equipment Jun.1941–Sep. 1943, p. 123.

[159] Dönitz, K., *Memoirs*, London, 2000, p. 149.

[160] Air 27-761 No. 95 Sqn's ORB 1941.

[161] Air 15-773 C-in-C's Dispatches, Vol. II, para. 2.

[162] Air 15-773 Vol. II, para. 2.

[163] Dönitz, K., *Memoirs*, London, 2000, p. 175.

[164] Air 15-57 Coastal Command's Naval Staff USW file, para. 18.

[165] Dönitz, K., *Memoirs*, London, 2000, p. 149.

[166] U-93 by No. 502 Sqn. 10.2.41. Air 15-162 Coastal Command's War Record 1939–1945, Table B.

[167] Air 15-162 Table B.

[168] *Ibid.*, Chap. 2.

[169] Air 41-47 *The RAF in the Maritime War*, Jul.1941–Feb.1943, Vol. II, p. 52.

[170] Air 27-1668 No. 304 Sqn's ORB 1942.

[171] Giese, O. (ex U-405), in a letter to the author.

[172] Air 41-47 Vol. II, p. 52.

[173] Air 41-47 Vol. II, p. 52.

[174] Air 41-47 Vol. II, p. 54.

[175] Air 41-47 Vol. II, p. 54.

[176] Air 41-47 Vol. II, p. 55.

[177] The author was aware of this modification in No. 48 Sqn. Apr.1943.

[178] Air 27-1565 No. 269 Sqn's ORB.

[179] Roskill, S.W., *The War at Sea*, London, 1954, Vol. I, p. 467.

[180] ORBs: Air 27-1365 No. 220 Sqn's; Air-1566 No. 269 Sqn's. Air 15-773 C-in-C's Dispatches, Vol. II, para. 16.

[181] Air 15-773 Vol. II, para. 5.

[182] Air 15-773 Vol. II, paras 4, 10.

[183] Air 15-773 C-in-C's Dispatches, Vol. II, paras 24–8.

[184] Air 15-773 Vol. II, para. 3.

[185] Air 15-57 Coastal Command's Naval Staff ASW file, para. 18.

[186] Air 15-57 para. 20.

[187] Gregory, R., USN. Letter to the author.

[188] Air 15-773 C-in-C's Dispatches, Vol. II, paras 32/3.

[189] Air 15-162 Table B. Air 27-1227, No. 179 Sqn's ORB. Green, Flg Off J., Letter to the author.

[190] Example: U-177 on 13.6.41.

[191] Examples: U155, U-476 and U-533.

[192] Air 15-773 C-in-C's Dispatches, Vol. II, para. 9.

[193] Air 15-162 Coastal Command's War Record, 1939–1945, Table B.
Air 27-1565 No. 269 Sqn's ORB 1941.

CHAPTER 04

[1] Roskill, S.W., *The War at Sea*, London, 1956, Vol. II, p. 217.

[2] Churchill, W.S., *The Second World War*, London, 1977, *The Battle of the Atlantic, Sept.1939-May 1943.* Vol. IV, pp. 116/7.

[3] Morison, S.E., *The Battle of the Atlantic, Sep. 1939–May 1943*, Boston, Mass. 1975, Vol. I, p. 124.

[4] Air 15-57 Coastal Command's Naval Staff File, Sep. 1939–Dec.1944, paras 34/5.

[5] Dönitz, K., *Memoirs*, London, 2000, p. 195.

[6] Morison, S.E., *The Battle of the Atlantic, Sept 1939-May 1943* Vol. I, p. 127. Dönitz, K., p. 197.

[7] Hessler, G., *The U-boat War in the Atlantic, 1939–1945*, London, 1992, para. 191.

[8] Hessler, G., para. 170.

[9] Morison, S.E., *The Battle of the Atlantic, Sep. 1939–May 1943*, Vol. I, pp. 56/7.

[10] Morison, S.E., Vol. I, p. 254. Hessler, G., para. 188.

[11] Morison, S.E., Vol. I, p. 255.

[12] Leggate, Gp Capt J., letter to the author.

[13] Hillmer, N., (Ed.), *Official History of the RCAF*, Toronto, 1986, Vol. II, pp. 485/6.

[14] Rohwer, J., at a symposium, RAF Bracknell, 21.10.91.

[15] Air 15-359 Coastal Command's Conferences, Jul.1941–Apr.1942.

[16] Dönitz, K., *Memoirs*, London, 2000, pp. 129/30.

[17] Lavenere-Wanderley, N.F., *The Brazilian Air Force in WW2*, Rio de Janeiro, 1976.

[18] Air 15-359 C-in-C's 125th and 127th meetings.

[19] Air 27-1105 No. 172 Sqn's ORBs, 1942–3.

[20] Air 15-773 C-in-C's Dispatches, Vol. II, para. 57.

[21] Air 15-57 Coastal Command's Naval Staff ASW File, para. 45.

[22] Air 27-1105-6 No. 172 Sqn's ORBs, 1942–5.

[23] Hessler, G., *The U-boat War in the Atlantic, 1939-1945*, London, 1992, para. 210.

[24] Hessler, G., para. 211.

[25] Air 27-151/2 No. 10 (RAAF) Sqn's ORBs, 1942–3.

[26] Hessler, G., para. 209.

[27] Air 27-1105 No.172 Sqn's ORBs, 1942–3.

[28] Greswell, Air Cdre J., letter to the author.

[29] Hessler, G., *The U-boat War in the Atlantic, 1939–1945*, London, 1992, para. 235.

[30] Hessler, G., para. 296.

[31] Air 27-1668 No. 304 Sqn's ORB, 19.9.42.

[32] Hessler, G., para. 236.

[33] Air 15-57 Coastal Command's Naval Staff ASW File, para. 44.

[34] Roskill, S.W., Vol. II, p. 108. Dönitz, K., *Memoirs*, London, 2000, p. 245. Hessler, G., para. 236.

[35] Hessler, G., para. 236.

[36] Air 15-773 C-in-C's Dispatches, Vol. II, paras 65/6.

[37] Hessler, G., para. 249.

[38] Hessler, G., para. 238.

[39] Air 27-1178 No. 201 Sqn's ORBs, 1941–3.

[40] Hessler, G., para. 243.

[41] Roskill, S.W., *The War at Sea, 1939–1945*, London, 1954, Vol. 1, p. 492.

[42] Air 15-773 C-in-C's Dispatches, Vol. II, para. 72.

[43] Author's logbook.

[44] Air 27-1830 No. 422 Sqn's ORBs, 1942–5. Letter from Sub Lt H. Hartmann to the author.

[45] Air 15-773 C-in-C's Dispatches, Vol. II, para. 73.

[46] Harris, A., *Bomber Offensive*, London, 1947, p. 121.

[47] ORBs: Air 27-1385 No. 224 Sqn. Air 27-1793 No. 407 Sqn. Air 27-555 No. 59 Sqn.

[48] Overy, R., *The Air War 1939–1945*, London, 1980, p. 71.

[49] Roskill, S.W., *The War at Sea*, London, 1956, Vol. II, p. 353.

[50] Churchill, W.S., *The Second World War*, London, 1977, Vol. IV, pp. 281, 406, 873.

[51] Hendrie, A., *Lockheed Hudson*, Shrewsbury, 1999, pp. 64/5.

[52] Hessler, G., *The U-boat War in the Atlantic, 1939–1945*, London, 1992, para. 268.

[53] Hessler, G., para. 268.

[54] Hessler, G., para. 276.

[55] Eisenhower, D.D., *Crusade in Europe*, New York, 1968, p. 101.

[56] Cunningham, Viscount, *A Sailor's Odyssey*, London, 1951, p. 493.

[57] Eisenhower, D.D., *Crusade in Europe*, New York, 1968, p. 102.

[58] Hessler, G., *The U-Boat War in the Atlantic, 1939–1945*, London, 1992, para. 272.

[59] Air 15-162 Coastal Command's War Record, 1939–1945, Table A.

[60] Herington, J., *Air War Against Germany & Italy*, Canberra, 1962, p. 412.

[61] Andrew, T. and Hoskins, J., letters to the author.

[62] No. 48 Sqn in 1943.

[63] Bertini, Cap. di V., *Sommergibili in Mediterraneo*, Rome, 1968, Vol. I, p. 283.

[64] Dönitz, K., *Memoirs*, London, 2000, pp. 284/5.

[65] Roskill, S.W., *The War at Sea*, London, 1956, Vol. II, p. 340.

[66] Roskill, S.W., Vol. II, p. 205. Air 15-773 Vol. II, para. 110. Hessler, G., *The U-boat War in the Atlantic, 1939–1945*, London, 1992, para. 235.

[67] Air 15-773, C-in-C's Dispatches, Vol. II, paras 110–15.

[68] Hessler, G., *The U-boat War in the Atlantic, 1939–1945*, London, 1992, para. 296.

[69] Air 15-773 Vol. II, para. 116. Roskill, S.W., *The War at Sea*, London, 1956, Vol. II, p. 205.

[70] Air 15-162 Coastal Command's War Record 1939–1945, Table A.

[71] Air 15-773 C-in-C's Dispatches, Vol. II, para. 116.

[72] Air 15-57 Coastal Command's Naval Staff USW File, para. 50.

[73] Rohwer, G., *Axis Submarine Successes, 1939–1945*, Annapolis, 1983, pp. 137–44.

[74] Air 15-57 para. 50.

[75] Slessor, J., *The Central Blue*, London, 1956, p. 670.

[76] Roskill, S.W., Vol. II, map No. 20.

[77] Churchill, W.S., Vol. IV, p. 716.

[78] Saunders, H., *RAF 1939–1945*, London, 1954, Vol. III, p. 38.

[79] Air 15-773 Vol. II, para. 118. Hessler, G., para. 278.

[80] *Ibid.*, Chap. 2.

[81] Hessler, G., *The U-boat War in the Atlantic, 1939–1945*, London, 1992, para. 296.

[82] Air 15-773 C-in-C's Dispatches, Vol. II, para. 126.

[83] Air 15-773 Vol. II, para. 126.

[84] Slessor, J., *The Central Blue*, London, 1956, p. 468.

[85] Hillmer, N., (Ed.), *RCAF Official History*, Toronto, 1986, Vol. II, p. 548.

[86] Hillmer, N., (Ed.), RCAF Vol. II, p. 556.

[87] Hillmer, N., (Ed.), RCAF Vol. II, p. 557.

[88] Air 15-773 C-in-C's Dispatches, Vol. II, para. 9.

[89] Air 15-773 C-in-C's Dispatches, Vol. III.II, para. 10.

[90] Air 15-773 Vol. III.II, para. 10.

[91] Slessor, J., pp. 495/6, 503. Hillmer, N., Vol. II, pp. 548/9. C12238 No. 10 (RCAF) Sqn's ORB, 1943.

[92] ORBs: Air 27-1942 No. 500 Sqn. 1942–3. Air 27-2099 No. 608 Sqn. 1942–3.

[93] Dönitz, K., *Memoirs*, London, 2000, p. 310.

[94] Dönitz, K., *Memoirs*, London, 2000, p. 317. See also Roskill, S.W., Vol. II, p. 217.

[95] Air 15-57 Coastal Command's Naval Staff USW File, para. 17.

[96] Slessor, J., *The Central Blue*, London, 1956, Chaps. XII, XVI.

[97] Churchill, W.S., Vol. IV, p. 708.

[98] Slessor, J., *The Central Blue*, p. 499.

[99] Dönitz, K., p. 341.

[100] Morison, S.E., *The Battle of the Atlantic, Sep. 1939–May 1943*, Boston, 1975, Vol. I, p. 226.

[101] Air 41-47 *The RAF in the Maritime War*, Vol. III, p. 491.

[102] Air 41-47 *The RAF in the Maritime War, Jul.1941–Feb.1943*, para. 487.

[103] Dönitz, K., *Memoirs*, London, 2000, p. 325. Hessler, G., para. 313.

[104] Air 15-773 C-in-C's Dispatches, Vol. II, paras 121/2.

[105] Joubert, P. , *Birds and Fishes*, London, 1960, Chap. 10.

[106] Air 15-773 Vol. II, paras 132–4.

[107] ORBs: Air 27-1668 No. 304 Sqn. Air 27-1105 No. 172 Sqn.

[108] Hessler, G., *The U-boat War in the Atlantic, 1939–1945*, London, 1992, para. 318.

[109] Baveystock, L., letter to the author.

[110] Baveystock, L., letter to the author. Air 15-162 Table A. ORB: Air 27-1179 No. 201 Sqn.

[111] Air 15-773 C-in-C's Dispatches, Vol. III, para. 5.

[112] Stiebler, W. (U-461), letter to the author.

[113] Marrows, Flt Lt D., DFC, RAAF (U/461).

[114] Roskill, S.W., Vol. I, p. 464. Air 15-57 para. 12.

[115] Air 15-361 C-in- C's Meetings, Jan.–May 1945.

[116] Air 15-162 Coastal Command's War Record, 1939–1945, Table A.

[117] Roskill, S.W., Vol. II, p. 364. Hessler, G., para. 311.

[118] Hessler, G., *The U-boat War in the Atlantic, 1939–1945*, London, 1992, para. 366.

[119] Dönitz, K., *Memoirs*, London, 2000, p. 328.

[120] Air 15-162 Table A.

[121] Hillmer, N., (Ed.), *The Official History of the RCAF*, Toronto, 1980, Vol. II, p. 548.

[122] Roskill, S.W., Vol. II, p. 365. Middlebrook, M., *Convoy*, London, 1976.

[123] Air 15-773 C-in-C's Dispatches, Vol. III, para. 14.

[124] Dönitz, K., p. 341. Hessler, G., paras 324/5.

[125] Air 15-162 Table A. Hessler, G., paras 324–31, plans 53–8.

[126] Roskill, S.W., Vol. II, p. 376.

[127] Hessler, G., para. 330.

[128] Dönitz, K., *Memoirs*, p. 341. Air 27-1567/8 No. 269 Sqn's ORBs, 1941–3.

[129] Dönitz, K., p. 341.

[130] Dönitz, K., pp. 406, 418. Hessler, G., para. 369.

[131] Air 27-1415 No. 228 Sqn's ORBs, 1942–3. Dönitz, K., pp. 413/14. Hessler, G., para. 360.

[132] Dönitz, K., p. 415.

[133] Spotswood, D., MRAF, letter to the author. Air 27-152 No. 10 (RAAF) Sqn's ORB, 1944.

[134] Hessler, G., *The U-boat War in the Atlantic, 1939–1945*, London, 1992, plan 59.

[135] Air 15-773 C-in-C's Dispatches, Vol. II, para. 27.

[136] Hessler, G., *The U-boat War in the Atlantic, 1939–1945*, London, 1992, para. 360.

[137] Air 15-773 Vol. III, para. 28.

[138] Roskill, S.W., *The War at Sea*, London, 1956, Vol. II, Chap. XIV.

[139] Cremer, P. , *U-333*, London, 1984, pp. 47/8.

[140] Hessler, G., para. 369.

[141] Rohwer, J., Afterword to Donitz's *Memoirs*, London, 2000, p. 494.

[142] Rohwer, J., at a symposium, RAF Staff College, 21.10.91. Hessler, G., paras 381–3.

[143] Hessler, G., para. 382.

[144] Air 15-773 C-in-C's Dispatches, Vol. II, paras 6, 11.

[145] Air 15-162 Table A.

[146] Cremer, P. , *U-333*, London, 1984, p. 159.

[147] Air 27-1127 No. 179 Sqn's ORB, 1943. Air 27-1667 No. 304 Sqn's ORBs, 1940–1.

[148] Hessler, G., *The U-boat War in the Atlantic, 1939–1945*, para. 393.

[149] Roskill, S.W., *The War at Sea*, London, 1960, Vol. III.1, p. 52.

[150] Air 15-773 C-in-C's Dispatches, Vol. II, para. 141. Air 15-162 Table A.

[151] Niestlé, A., *German U-boat Losses During WW2*, Annapolis, 1998, pp. 193–5.

[152] Craven, W.F., and Cate, J.L., *The Army Air Forces in WW2*, Washington, 1983, Vol. II, p. 254.

[153] Roskill, S.W., *The War at Sea*, London, 1961, Vol. III.2, p. 78.

[154] Air 15-773 Vol. IV, para. 10.

[155] Dönitz, K., *Memoirs*, London, 2000, p. 354.

[156] Dönitz, K., p. 421.

[157] Air 27-1179 No. 201 Sqn's ORBs, 1944–5.

[158] Roskill, S.W., *The War at Sea*, London, 1961, Vol. III.2, p. 182.

[159] Hessler, G., *The U-boat War in the Atlantic, 1939–1945*, London, 1992, paras 408, 414/15.

[160] Air 15-773 C-in-C's Dispatches, Vol. II, para. 15. Hessler, G., para. 414.

[161] Roskill, S.W., *The War at Sea*, London, 1960, Vol. III.1, p. 249.

[162] C1227 No. 407 Sqn's ORBs, 1944–5.

[163] Hessler, G., *The U-boat War in the Atlantic, 1939–1945*, London, 1992, paras 408, 417.

[164] Hessler, G., para. 417.

[165] Hessler, G., para. 417.

[166] Eisenhower, D.D., *Crusade in Europe*, New York, 1968, p. 236.

[167] Douglas, Lord, *Years of Command*, London, 1966, pp. 262, 264.

[168] Air 15–773 Vol. IV, para. 41.

[169] Air 15-102 *Coastal Command's Role in Operation Overlord*. Introduction.

[170] Keegan, J., *The Times Atlas of the Second World War*, London, 1989, p. 24.

[171] Air 15-360 C-in-C's Meetings, Nov.1943–Dec.1944. 12.4.44.

[172] Air 15-102 *Overlord, The Role of Coastal Command*. Order of Battle.

[173] Air 15-102 para. 6.

[174] Air 15-360 Coastal Command's Conferences, Nov.1943–Dec.1944.

[175] Air 15-102 *Overlord, the Role of Coastal Command*, para. 6.

[176] Air 15-102 para. 10.

[177] Niestlé, A., *German U-boat Losses During WW2*, pp. 195/6. Hessler, G., para. 433.

[178] Hessler, G., *The U-boat War in the Atlantic, 1939–1945*, London, 1992, para. 438.

[179] Dönitz, K., *Memoirs*, London, 2000, pp. 422/3.

[180] Air 27-1300 No. 210 Sqn's ORBs 1944. C12260 No. 162 (RCAF) Sqn's ORB, 1944.

[181] Douglas, Lord, *Years of Command*, London, 1966, p. 271.

[182] Air 15-773 Vol. IV, para. 48. Roskill, S.W., *The War at Sea*, London, 1961, Vol. III.2, p. 177.

[183] Dönitz, K., p. 424.

[184] Dönitz, K., *Memoirs*, London, 2000, p. 423.

[185] Dönitz, K., pp. 424/5.

[186] Air 15-773 Vol. IV, paras 56–63.

[187] Cunningham, Viscount, *A Sailor's Odyssey*, London, 1951, p. 404.

[188] Air 27-1368 No. 221 Sqn's ORBs, 1940–3.

[189] USN NRS-1978-89, VP63 Sqn's ORB. See also: Morison, S.E., *United States Naval Operations in WW2*, Boston, 1984, Vol. X, pp. 85–93.

[190] Air 27-153 No. 10 (RAAF) Sqn's ORBs 1944. Roskill, S.W., Vol. III.1, p. 255.

[191] Air 15-773 C-in-C's Dispatches, Vol. IV, paras 30–2.

[192] Air 15-773 Vol. IV, para. 421.

[193] Air 15-773 Vol. IV, para. 37. See also: Morison, S.E., Vol. X, pp. 317–38.

[194] Hessler, G., para. 475. Churchill, W.S., *The Second World War*, London, 1981, Vol. VI, p. 244.

[195] Air 15-773 Vol. IV, paras 62–77. Cremer, P., *U-333*, London, 1984, p. 197.

[196] Hessler, G., para. 472. *Jane's Fighting Ships of WW2, 1944*, London, 1990, pp. 65, 66.

[197] Hessler, G., para. 472.

[198] Air 15-361 C-in-C's Meetings on 22.1.45, 25.1.45, 29.1.45.

[199] Air 15-361 Meeting on 4.1.45.

[200] Roskill, S.W., *The War at Sea*, London, 1961, Vol. III.2, p. 285.

[201] Roskill, S.W., Vol. III.2, p. 285. Niestlé, A., *German U-boat Losses in WW2*, Annapolis, 1998, p. 202.

[202] The author's experience in No. 524 Sqn.

[203] Air 15-361 Meeting on 22.1.45.

[204] Air 15-361 C-in-C's meeting on 3.2.45.

[205] Hessler, G., *The U-boat War in the Atlantic*, London, 1992, paras 478/9.

[206] Dönitz, K., *Memoirs*, p. 427, records six lost in January but twenty-nine in Apr.1945.

[207] Air 15-773 C-in-C's Dispatches, Vol. IV, paras 84–82.

[208] Roskill, S.W., *The War at Sea*, London, 1961, Vol. III.2, p. 281.

[209] Air 15-773 Vol. IV, paras 84–6.

[210] C12269 No. 404 Sqn's ORBs, 1944–5.

[211] Air 15-773 C-in-C's Dispatches, Vol. IV, paras 97–9. Air 15-162 Table A.

[212] Skaugstad, P. , list to the author.

[213] Air 15-773 Vol. IV, para. 94.

[214] Air 27-1300 No. 210 Sqn's ORBs, 1944–5.

[215] Roskill, S.W., *The War at Sea*, London, 1961, Vol. III.2, p. 300.

[216] Air 15-162 *Coastal Command's War Record*, 1939–1945, Table A.

CHAPTER 05

[1] Air 41-73 RAF in the Maritime War, Chap. I.2.iii.

[2] Air 41-73 Chap. I.2.iii.

[3] Air 15-773 C-in-C's Dispatches, Vol. I, para. 8.

[4] Air 15-773 Vol. I, para. 4.

[5] Churchill, W.S., *The Second World War*, London, 1977, Vol. II, Chaps X and XI.

[6] Hendrie, A., *Lockheed Hudson in WW2*, Shrewsbury, 1999, p. 122. Air 27-1223 No. 220 Sqn's ORB.

[7] Roskill, S.W., *The War at Sea*, London, 1954, Vol. I, p. 58.

[8] Air 27-1365 No. 220 Sqn's ORB, 1940.

[9] Air 15-773 C-in-C's Dispatches, Vol. I, para. 51.

[10] Air 41-73 *The RAF in the Maritime War*, Vol. II, Chap. I, p. 14

[11] Air 41-73 Vol. II, Chap. I, p. 14.

[12] Air 41-73 Vol. II, Chap. VI, p. 173.

[13] Air 41-73 Vol. II, Chap. 1, p. 14.

[14] Air 27-1299 No. 210 Sqn's ORB, 1940.

[15] Air 41-73 Vol. II, Chap. VI, p. 174.

[16] Air 41-73 Vol. II, Chap. VI, p. 174.

[17] Goulter, C., *A Forgotten Offensive*, London, 1995, p. 123. Air 27-1365 No. 220 Sqdn's ORB, 1940.

[18] Air 41-73 *The RAF in the Maritime War*, Vol. II, Chap. III, p. 86.

[19] Air 15-773 C-in-C's Dispatches, Vol. I, para. 103.

[20] Richards, D., and Saunders, H., *RAF 1939–1945*, London, 1954, Vol. II, p. 95.

[21] Air 15-162 *Coastal Command's War Record,1939–1945*, Table F.

[22] Air 41-73 *The RAF in the Maritime War*, Vol. II, pp. 156, 161.

[23] Air 41-73 Vol. II, p. 161.

[24] Richards, D., and Saunders, H., *Royal Air Force 1939–1945*, London, 1954, Vol. II, p. 95.

[25] Air 15-773 Vol. I, para. 110.

[26] Air 15-773 Vol. I, para. 116.

[27] Air 15-773 Vol. I, para. 118.

[28] Air 27-1793 No. 407 Sqn's ORB, 1942.

[29] Air 15-773 Vol. I, para. 121.

[30] Student Notes for Aircrew, 1942.

[31] Kydd, Sqn Ldr C., DSO, DFC, to the author. See also: Masters, D., *So Few*, London, 1941.

[32] Air 15-773 C-in-C's Dispatches, Vol. I, para. 121.

[33] Air 15-773 Vol. I, para. 147.

[34] Air 15-359 C-in-C's 134th meeting, 4.3.42.

[35] Air 15-773 Vol. II, para. 155.

[36] Air 15-773 C-in-C's Dispatches, Vol. II, para. 156.

[37] Air 15-359 C-in-C's 48th meeting, 19.9.41.

[38] Air 15-773 Vol. II, para. 156.

[39] Air 15-773 Vol. II, para. 157. Agreed 15.7.41.

[40] Air 15-773 Vol. II, paras 158–62.

[41] Air 15-773 Vol. II, para. 163.

[42] Romanes, J., letter to the author.

[43] Air 27-1365 No. 220 Sqn's ORB, 1940.

[44] Air 15-162 *Coastal Command's War Record, 1939–1945*, Table F.

[45] Flatmark, J.O., and Grytten, H., *Ålesund I Hverdag og Krig*, Ålesund, 1988, p. 168.

[46] Goulter, C., *The Forgotten Offensive*, London, 1995, p. 76. Lockheed's give 208 knots and 291 knots for cruising and maximum speeds. See also: Hendrie, A., *Lockheed Hudson in WW2*, Shrewsbury, 1999.

[47] Air 15-773 C-in-C's Dispatches, Vol. II, para. 166.

[48] Air 15-162 *Coastal Command's War Record, 1939–1945*, Table F.

[49] Air 15-773 Vol. II, para. 168.

[50] Air 15-773 Vol. II, para. 180.

[51] Air 15-162 Table F.

[52] Air 15-162 Table F.

[53] Air 15-359 C-in-C's 24th meeting, 7.8.41.

[54] Air 15-530 *Mining in Norwegian and Danish Waters*, p. 14.

[55] Air 15-359 C-in-C's 38th meeting, 2.9.41. and 74th, 11.11.41.

[56] A medical officer to the author.

[57] Air 15-359 C-in-C's 100th meeting, 27.12.41.

[58] Air 15-773 C-in-C's Dispatches, Vol. II, para. 184.

[59] Richards, D., *RAF 1939–1945*, London, 1953, Vol. I, p. 354.

[60] Air 15-773 C-in-C's Dispatches, Vol. II, para. 185.

[61] Air 15-773 Vol. II, para. 182.

[62] Air 27-471 No. 48 Sqn's ORBs 1941–2. Air -1157 No. 194 Sqn's ORBs 1942–5.

[63] Air 15-162 *Coastal Command's War Record 1939–1945*, Table F.

[64] ORBs: Air 27-504 No. 53 Sqn's; Air 27-555 No.59 Sqn's; Air 27-1793 No.407 Sqn's.

[65] Air 15-162 *Coastal Command's War Record 1939–1945*, Table F.

[66] Air 27-1794 No. 407 Sqn's ORBs.

[67] Taylor, Sqn Ldr C., DFC, in a letter to the author.

[68] Taylor, Sqn Ldr C., DFC, in a letter to the author. See also: Hillmer, N., (Ed.) *The Official History of the RCAF*, Toronto, 1980, Vol. II, p. 607.

[69] At the Aircrew Officers' School, 1944.

[70] Air 15-541 *No. 16 Group's Anti-ship operations Apr.1942–Apr.1945*, p. 4.

[71] Goad, Flt Lt G., letter to the author.

[72] Air 15-541 p. 4.

[73] Air 15-541 p. 4. Air 15-773 C-in-C's Dispatches Vol. II, para. 195.

[74] De Liefde, T., Letter to the author. Richards, D., and Saunders, H., *RAF 1939–1945*, London, 1954, Vol. II, pp. 94–9.

[75] Air 15-541 *No. 16 Groups Anti-shipping Operations Apr.1942–Apr.1945*, p. 4.

[76] Air 15-773 C-in-C's Dispatches, Vol. II, para. 198.

[77] Air 15-773 Vol. II, para. 198.

[78] Air 15-773 Vol. II, para. 190. Greenhous, B., Harris, S.J., Johnston, W.C., and Rawling, W.G.P. , *The Official History of the RCAF*, Toronto, 1994, Vol. III, pp. 447–50.

[79] Hendrie, A., *Canadian Squadrons in Coastal Command*, St Catharine's, Ontario, 1997, p. 39.

[80] Equipment that would serve for both identification of the aircraft and for homing.

[81] C12273 No. 407 Sqn's ORBs 1941–5.

[82] Air 15-773 C-in-C's Dispatches, Vol. II, para. 194.

[83] The author used one at medium heights in Apr.1939.

[84] Air 15-773 C-in-C's Dispatches, Vol. II, para. 206.

[85] Air 15-773 Vol. II, para. 206. See also: Roskill, S.W., *The War at Sea*, London, 1956, Vol. II, pp. 164/5. Richards, D., and Saunders, H., *RAF 1939–1945*, London, 1954, Vol. II, pp. 94–9. Greenhous, B., Harris, S.J., Johnston,W.G, and Rawling, W.G.P. , *The Official History of the RCAF*, Toronto, 1994, Vol. III, p. 419.

[86] Air 15-773 Vol. II, para. 205.

[87] Førde fjord 9.2.45. RCAF Vol. III, pp. 472/3.

[88] Air 15-773 Vol. II, para. 208. See also: Roskill, S.W., *The War at Sea*, London, 1956, Vol. II, pp. 165/6.

[89] Air 15-162 *Coastal Command's War Record 1939–1945*, Table F.

[90] Air 15-773 C-in-C's Dispatches, Vol. III, paras 2–8. RCAF Vol. III, p. 447.

[91] Air 15-46 *Coastal's Aircraft Requirements Jul.1939–Jun.1943*.

[92] Air 15-773 Vol. III, para. 44.

[93] Air 15-162 *Coastal Command's War Record 1939–1945*, Table F.

[94] Air 15-162 Table F. ORBs: Air 27-1713 No. 320 Sqn, C12273 No. 407 Sqn. Roskill, S.W.,*The War at Sea*, London, 1956, Vol. II, p. 387.

[95] Roskill, S.W., Vol. II, pp. 259, 260, 388.

[96] Air 15-162 Table F. Air 15-773 Vol. III, para. 45.

[97] Roskill, S.W., Vol. II, p. 389.

[98] Roskill, S.W., Vol. II, p. 389.

[99] Air 15-162 Table F. Roskill, S.W., Vol. II, p. 389.

[100] C12285 No. 415 Sqn's ORBs. Air 15-162 Table F.

[101] Air 15-162 Table F.

[102] Air 15-773 C-in-C's Dispatches, Vol. III, para. 9. Roskill, S.W.,Vol. II, p. 390.

[103] Page. C., letter to author. See also: RCAF Vol. III, pp. 454/5. Roskill, S.W., Vol. III.1, p. 286.

[104] Symons, J., letter to author. See also: Roskill, S.W., Vol. III.1, p. 286, and Vol. II, pp. 259/60.

[105] Page. C., letter to author. See also: Saunders, H., *RAF 1939–1945*, London, 1954, Vol. III, p. 69.

[106] *Op. cit*. See also: RCAF Vol. III, pp. 472/3.

[107] Page, C., letter to the author. RCAF Vol. III, pp. 455/6.

[108] Roskill, S.W., *The War at Sea*, London, 1960, Vol. II, p. 392.

[109] Air 15-773 C-in-C's Dispatches, Vol. III, para. 47. See also: RCAF Vol. III, p. 452.

[110] Air 15-541 *No. 16 Group's Anti-ship Operations Apr.1942–Apr.1945*, p. 14.

[111] Air 15-102 *Overlord – The Role of Coastal Command*. See also: RCAF Vol. III, p. 464.

[112] Air 15-773 C-in-C's Dispatches, Vol. III, paras 116/17.

[113] Air 15-773 Vol. III, para. 118.

[114] Air 15-541 *No. 16 Group's Anti-shipping Operations*, p. 14.

[115] Air 15-541 p. 78.

[116] Air 15-541 p. 78.

[117] C12285 No. 415 Sqn's ORBs. Air 15-162 Table F.

[118] Air 15-773 C-in-C's Dispatches Vol. III, para. 130. RCAF Vol. III, pp. 461/2.

[119] The author's experience at RAF Langham, 1944–5.

[120] Air 15-162 *Coastal Command's War Record 1939–1945* Table F. C12285 No. 415 Sqn's ORBs.

[121] Air 15-162 Table F. Air 15-773 Vol. III, para. 131.

[122] Symons, J., letter to the author. C12269 No. 404 Sqn's ORBs.

[123] Symons, J., letter to the author. RCAF Vol. III, p. 419.

[124] Roskill, S.W., Vol. III.2, p. 168.

[125] Air 15-162 *Coastal Command's War Record 1939–1945* Table F.

[126] Air 15-773 C-in-C's Dispatches Vol. IV, para. 208.

[127] Air 15-162 Table F, names a number of Swedish ships sunk.

[128] C12269 No. 404 Sqn's ORBs. Air 15-162 Table F.

[129] Air 15-361 C-in-C's meetings 9.11.44, 16.11.44, 7.12.44.

[130] Air 15-391 p. 180. Air 15-361 Meeting 30.11.44. RCAF Vol. III, p. 419.

[131] Air 15-391 *Anti-shipping Operations – Norway and Kattegat*, p. 151.

[132] Air 15-391 p. 2. No. 18 Group's comment on C-in-C's letter dated 16.10.44.

[133] Air 15-162 *Coastal Command's War Record 1939–1945*, Table F.

[134] Air 15-162 Table F. See also: RCAF Vol. III, pp. 470–4.

[135] Air 15-773 C-in-C's Dispatches, Vol. IV, paras 148–51.

[136] Air 15-162 *Coastal Command's War Record 1939–1945*, Tables E and H.

[137] Air 15-391 *Coastal Command's Anti-shipping Operations, Norway and Kattegat*, pp. 61–180.

[138] Flynn, P. , Letter to the author. C12269 No. 404 Sqn's ORBs. RCAF Vol. III, pp. 472/3.

[139] Air 15-773 C-in-C's Dispatches Vol. II, para. 1.

[140] Herrington, J., *Air Power Over Europe 1944-1945*, Canberra, 1963, p. 382.

[141] Air 15-162 *Coastal Command's War Record 1939–1945*, Table F.

[142] Middlebrook, M., *The Bomber Command War Diaries 1939–1945*, Harmondsworth, 1987, p. 662. C12269 No. 404 Sqn's ORBs. RCAF Vol. III, pp. 472/3 Goulter, C.J.M., *A Forgotten Offensive*, London, 1995, pp. 254/5.

[143] Air 15-391 p. 101 *Plans for Anti-shipping Forces, Winter 1944–45, Norway and Kattegat.*

[144] Air 15-391 p. 102 Letter 26.2.45.from HQCC to No. 18 Group.

[145] Air 15-391 p. 60.

[146] Air 15-391 p. 56.

[147] Air 27-2114 No. 612 Sqn's ORBs.

[148] Air 27-2114 No. 612 Sqn's ORBs.

[149] Air 15-391 *Plans for Anti-shipping Operations, Winter 1944–45, Norway and Kattegat*, p. 41.

[150] Air 15-773 C-in-C's Dispatches, Vol. III, para. 41.

[151] Air 15-773 Vol. II, para. 218.

[152] C12285 No. 415 Sqn's ORBs, 1944–5.

[153] Air 15-773 C-in-C's Dispatches, Vol. IV, para. 42.

[154] Air 15-773 Vol. IV, para. 42.

[155] Baff, K., *Maritime is No.10*, Netley, S. Australia, 1983, p. 324. Herington, J., *Air War Against Germany and Italy, 1939–1945*, Canberra, 1962, p. 626.

[156] A No. 48 Squadron Hudson narrowly avoided attacking a Royal Navy submarine in 1943.

[157] Air 15-773 Vol. IV, para. 42; and the author's experience.

[158] Roskill, S.W., *The War at Sea*, London, 1956, Vol. II, p. 410. See also: Goulter, C.J.M., p. 153. Roskill, S.W., *The War at Sea*, London, 1960, Vol. III.1, pp. 73–5.

[159] Roskill, S.W., *The War at Sea*, London, 1960, Vol. III.1, p. 75.

[160] Roskill, S.W., Vol. III.1, p. 75. See also: Saunders, H., *RAF 1939–1945*, London, 1954, Vol. III, pp. 70/1. Slessor, J., *The Central Blue*, London, 1956, pp. 477, 539–56.

[161] Air 15-162 *Coastal Command's War Record 1939–1945*, Table F.

CHAPTER 06

[1] Air 15-773 C-in-C's Dispatches, Vol. II, para. 17.

[2] The first Mustangs reached Britain Oct.1941. Thetford, O. *Aircraft of the RAF Since 1918*, London, 1979, p. 217.

[3] Air 27-1565 No. 269 Sqn's ORBs, 1941–5.

[4] Air 15-773 Vol. 1, paras 20–2.
O'Neill, Gp Capt H., letter to the author.

[5] Roskill, S.W., *The War at Sea*, London, 1956, Vol. II, p. 485.

[6] Air 15-162 *Coastal Command's War Record*, Table F. Roskill, S.W., Vol. II, p. 484.

[7] Air 15-773 Vol. II, para. 151.

[8] Air 15-773 Vol. II, para. 170. Air 51-359 C-in-C's 58th, 60th and 83rd meetings.

[9] M-Rechberg, B. von, *Battleship Bismarck*, London, 1984, p. 51.

[10] Air 15-773 C-in-C's Dispatches, Vol. II, paras 170–5.

[11] Air 15-773 Vol. II, para. 181.

[12] Air 15-773 Vol. II, paras 243–5.

[13] Air 15-773 Vol. II, para. 248.

[14] Robertson, T., *The Channel Dash*, London, 1958, p. 44.

[15] Roskill, S.W., *The War at Sea*, London, 1956, Vol. II, p. 153.

[16] Roskill, S.W., Vol. II, p. 153.

[17] Air-773 C-in-C's Dispatches, Vol. II, paras 251, 253.

[18] Abbott, K., *Gathering of Demons*, Perth, Ontario, 1987, p. 131. C12273 No. 407 Sqn's ORBs.

[19] Abbott, K., p. 131. Richards, D., *RAF 1939–1945*, London, 1953, Vol. I, p. 371.

[20] Roskill, S.W., *The War at Sea*, London, 1960, Vol. II, p. 157.

[21] Seen by the author at RAF Wick, 1942.

[22] Roskill, S.W., *The War at Sea*, London, 1954, Vol. I, p. 577.

[23] Harris, A., *Bomber Offensive*, London, 1947, p. 68. Richards, D., Vol. I, p. 373.

[24] Churchill, W.S., *The Second World War*, London, 1977, Vol. IV, p. 110.

[25] Roskill, S.W., *The War at Sea*, London, 1956, Vol. II, p. 159.

[26] Roskill, S.W., Vol. II, p. 152.

[27] Goulter, C.J.M., *The Forgotten Offensive*, London, 1995, p. 161.

[28] Goulter, C.J.M., p. 161.

[29] ORBs: Air 27-1793 No. 407 Sqn; Air 27-471 No. 48 Sqn; Air 27-1387 No. 224 Sqn; Air 27-1365 No. 220 Sqn.

[30] Harris, A., *Bomber Offensive*, London, 1947, pp. 68/9.

[31] Slessor, J., *The Central Blue*, London, 1956, pp. 379/80.

[32] Air 15-773 C-in-C's Dispatches, Vol. II, para. 281.

[33] Abbott, K., *A Gathering of Demons*, Perth, Ontario, 1987, p. 133.

[34] Abbott, K., *Gathering of Demons*, Perth, Ontario, 1987, p. 131.

[35] Churchill, W.S., *The Second World War*, London, 1977, Vol. IV, p. 102.

[36] Galland, A., *The First and the Last*, London, 1970, pp. 152, 165, 167.

[37] Roskill, S.W., *The War at Sea*, London, 1956, Vol. II, p. 159.

[38] Robertson, T., *The Channel Dash*, London, 1958, pp. 58, 191.

[39] Robertson, T., p. 191, quoting Admiral Raeder.

[40] Roskill, S.W., Vol. II, p. 398.

[41] Air 15-773 C-in-C's Dispatches, Vol. II, para. 183.

[42] Air 15-773 Vol. II, para. 242. Roskill, S.W., *The War at Sea*, London, 1956, Vol. II, p. 278.

[43] Spotswood, MRAF D., letter to the author.

[44] Air 15-46 Aircraft Operational Requirements Policy, Jul.1939–Jun.1943. 12.2.43.

[45] Air 15-102 *Overlord – The Role of Coastal Command*, para. 33.

[46] Air 15-102 *Overlord – The Role of Coastal Command*, paras 8, 14, 15.

[47] Air 15-102 paras 8, 14, 15.

[48] Air 15-102 paras 46–8. Author's experience.

[49] ORBs: Air 27-1997 No. 524 Sqn; Air 27-2114 No. 612 Sqn.

[50] Eisenhower, D.D., *Crusade in Europe*, New York, 1968, p. 278. Cunningham, Viscount, *A Sailor's Odyssey*, London, 1951, p. 609.

[51] Dönitz, K., *Memoirs*, London, 2000, p. 395.

[52] Roskill, S.W., *The War at Sea*, London, 1961, Vol. III.2, p. 58.

[53] Air 15-162 *Coastal Command's War Record, 1939–1945*, Table F.

[54] Air 15-773 C-in-C's Dispatches, Vol. IV, para. 139.

[55] Taylor, C., No. 407 Sqn at Den Helder, 18.9.42.

[56] Air 15-773 Vol. IV, para. 139.

[57] Air 15-282 *Aircraft Situation, Coastal Command Conferences, Dec.1943–Mar.1945*.

[58] Air 15-773 Vol. II, paras 57, 63, 64. Author's experience in No. 524 Squadron.

[59] GEE – similar to radar but using ground station signals in conjunction with a special chart.

[60] Roskill, S.W., Vol. II, p. 162. Air 15-773 Vol. II, paras 299–304.

[61] Roskill, S.W., Vol. II, p. 163. Air 15-773 Vol. II, para. 305.

[62] ORBs: Air 27-2114 No. 612 Sqn; Air 27-1997 No. 524 Sqn; C12285 No. 415 Sqn.

[63] Roskill, S.W., *The War at Sea*, London, 1961, Vol. III.2, p. 138.

[64] The author's logbook.

[65] Roskill, S.W., Vol. III.2, p. 139.

[66] Air 15-773 Vol. IV, paras 218–23. Air 27-1997 No. 524 Sqn's ORB.

[67] ORBs: Air 27-1997 No. 524 Sqn; Air 27-2114 No. 612 Sqn; C12285 No. 415 Sqn.

[68] Air 15-773 Vol. IV, para. 226.

[69] Air 15-541 *No. 16 Group's Anti-shipping Operations, Apr.1942–Feb.1945*, p. 53.

[70] Air 15-541 p. 53.

[71] Air 15-541 p. 53.

[72] Air 15-541 Memo 14.1.45. p. 55.

[73] Air 15-773 C-in-C's Dispatches, Vol. IV, para. 235.

[74] Air 15-773 Vol. IV, paras 242–5.

[75] Air 27-2114 No. 612 Sqn's ORB.

[76] Air 15-773 Vol. IV, para. 249.

[77] Air 15-359 C-in-C's 21st meeting, 1.8.41.

[78] Douglas, Lord, *Years of Command*, London, 1966, pp. 273/4.

[79] Air 15-391 *Anti-shipping Operations, Norway and Kattegat, 1944–5*, p. 30.

CHAPTER 07

[1] Air 15-773 C-in-C's Dispatches, Vol. I, paras 255/6.

[2] Air 15-773 Vol. I, paras 255/6.

[3] Air 27-1609 No. 279 Sqn's ORBs (1941–3).

[4] Air 15-773 C-in-C's Dispatches, Vol. I, para. 276.

[5] Saunders, H., *RAF 1939–1945*, London, 1954, Vol. II, p. 88.

[6] Air 15-773 Vol. IV, para. 256.

[7] Air 15-359 C-in-C's 25th Meeting, 8.8.41.

[8] Air 15-359 68th Meeting, 1.11.41. Air 27-1609 No. 279 Sqn's ORB.

[9] Air 15-359 81st and 100th Meetings, 27.11.41, 27.12.41.

[10] Air 27-1609 No. 279 Sqn's ORB.

[11] Lynham, P., Goff, F., and Whittaker, D. (all ex-No. 279 Sqn), letters to the author.

[12] Air 27-1609 No. 279 Sqn's ORB.

[13] The Times 20.8.97.

[14] Wells, Flg Off D., letter to the author. C12295 No. 422 Sqn's ORB, 1943.

[15] Air 15-360 C-in-C's Meeting, 26.1.44.

[16] Air 15-360 Meetings, 14.2.44, 2.3.44, 20.3.44, 27.3.44.

[17] Air 15-360 Meeting, 27.3.44. Air 15-773 Vol. IV, para. 259.

[18] Air 15-773 C-in-C's Dispatches, Vol. IV, para. 260.

[19] Air 15-773 Vol. IV, para. 268.

[20] Air 15-773 Vol. IV, para. 270.

[21] Air 15-360 Meetings, 5.6.44, 9.10.44, 30.10.44.

[22] Air 15-360 Meeting, 6.11.44.

[23] Air 15-360 Meeting, 20.3.45.

[24] Air 15-773 C-in-C's Dispatches, Vol. IV, paras 274/5.

[25] Air 15-773 Vol. I, para. 205.

[26] Hendrie, A., Lockheed Hudson in WW2, Shrewsbury, 1999, p. 90.

[27] Air 15-773 C-in-C's Dispatches, Vol. I, paras 204, 206, 208.

[28] Spitfire pilots in conversation with the author.

[29] Air 15-773 C-in-C's Dispatches, Vol. I, paras 214–16.

[30] Air 15-773 Vol. I, paras 226–32.

[31] Air 15-773 C-in-C's Dispatches, Vol. I, paras 239–44.

[32] Richards, D., RAF 1939–1945, London, 1954, Vol. II, p. 86.

[33] Air 15-359 C-in-C's 150th Meeting, 10.4.42.

[34] Craven, AM R., to the author.

[35] Rawlings, J.D.R., Coastal Support & Special Squadrons, London, 1982, pp. 231–4.

[36] Richards, D., RAF 1939–1945, London, 1954, Vol. II, p. 87.

[37] Slessor, J., Coastal Command Review, Dec.1943. The Central Blue, London, 1956, pp. 478/9.

[38] Air 15-359 Jul.1941–Apr.1942. Air 15-360 Nov.1943–Dec.1944. Air 15-361 Jan.–May 1945. C-in-C's Meetings.

[39] Douglas, Lord, Years of Command, London, 1966, p. 251.

[40] Womersley, Wg Cdr L., letter to the author.

[41] Saunders, H., RAF 1939–1945, London, 1954, Vol. III, p. 77.

[42] Air 15-361 C-in-C's Meetings, 15.7.44, 29.3.45.

[43] Air 15-359 C-in-C's Meeting, 9.8.41.

[44] Winfield, E. No. 1404 Met. Flt, letter to the author.

[45] Air 15-773 Vol. IV, para. 280.

[46] Air 15-773 C-in-C's Dispatches, Vol. IV, para. 280.

[47] Air 15-773 Vol. IV, para. 282.

[48] Saunders, H., RAF 1939–1945, London, 1954, Vol. III, p. 77.

[49] Slessor, J., The Central Blue, London, 1966, p. 252. Coastal Command Review, Dec.1943.

[50] Douglas, Lord, Years of Command, London, 1966, p. 252.

CHAPTER 08

[1] AM Sir Robert Craven, KBE, CB, OBE, DFC; Wg Cdr A. de V. Leach, DFC; MRAF Sir Denis Spotswood, GCB, CBE, DSO, DFC, FRAeS.

Index

Page numbers in *italics* refer to illustrations.